TRAVELERS' TALES

SPAIN

T R A V E L E R S ' T A L E S

SPAIN

Collected and Edited by

LUCY MCCAULEY

Series Editors
JAMES O'REILLY AND LARRY HABEGGER

TRAVELERS' TALES, INC.
SAN FRANCISCO, CALIFORNIA

Distributed by
O'REILLY AND ASSOCIATES, INC.
101 MORRIS STREET
SEBASTOPOL, CALIFORNIA 95472

Travelers' Tales Spain
Collected and Edited by Lucy McCauley

Copyright © 1995, 1998 Travelers' Tales, Inc. All rights reserved.
Printed in United States of America

Cover and interior design by Judy Anderson
Cover photograph: © 1991 by Chris Vail. During Holy Week (Semana Santa), a penitent
  carries a wooden cross through the cathedral in Sevilla.
Spot illustrations by David White
Section break illustrations by Nina Stewart
Maps by Keith Granger
Page Layout by Cynthia Lamb, using the fonts Bembo and Boulevard

Printing History
November 1995:   First Edition
January 1998:   Second Printing

ISBN: 1-885211-07-4

Palabras y plumas
todas se las lleva el viento.

Words and feathers all
the wind doth bear away.

—CALDERÓN DE LA BARCA

Table of Contents

Part Two
SOME THINGS TO DO

Part Three
GOING YOUR OWN WAY

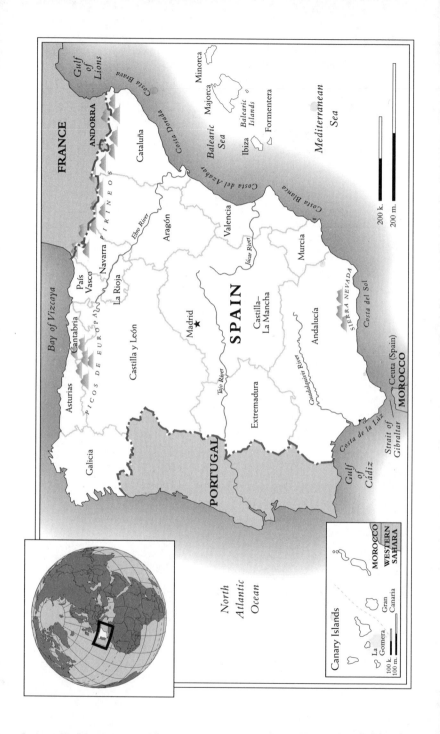

Preface

T R A V E L E R S ' T A L E S

We are all outsiders when we travel. Whether we go abroad or roam about our own city or country, we often enter territory so unfamiliar that our frames of reference become inadequate. We need advice not just to avoid offense and danger, but to make our experiences richer, deeper, and more fun.

Traditionally, travel guides have answered the basic questions: what, when, where, how, and how much. A good guidebook is indispensable for all the practical matters that demand attention. More recently, many guidebooks have added bits of experiential insight to their standard fare, but something important is still missing: guidebooks don't really prepare *you*, the individual with feelings and fears, hopes and dreams, goals.

This kind of preparation is best achieved through travelers' tales, for we get our inner landmarks more from anecdote than information. Nothing can replace listening to the experience of others, to the war stories that come out after a few drinks, to the memories that linger and beguile. For millennia it's been this way: at watering holes and wayside inns, the experienced traveler tells those nearby what lies ahead on the ever-mysterious road. Stories stoke the imagination, inspire, frighten, and teach. In stories we see more clearly the urges that bring us to wander, whether it's hunger for change, adventure, self-knowledge, love, curiosity, sorrow, or even something as prosaic as a job assignment or two weeks off.

But travelers' accounts, while profuse, can be hard to track down. Many are simply doomed in a throwaway publishing world. And few of us have the time anyway to read more than one or two books, or the odd pearl found by chance in the Sunday travel section. Wanderers for years, we've often faced this issue. We've always told ourselves when we got home that we would prepare better for the next trip—read more, study more, talk to more people—but life always seems to interfere and we've rarely managed to do so to our satisfaction. That is one reason for this series. We needed a kind of experiential primer that guidebooks don't offer.

Another path that led us to *Travelers' Tales* has been seeing the enormous changes in travel and communications over the last two decades. It is no longer unusual to have ridden a pony across Mongolia, to have celebrated an auspicious birthday on Mt. Kilimanjaro, or honeymooned on the Loire. The one-world monoculture has risen with daunting swiftness, weaving a new cross-cultural rug: no longer is it surprising to encounter former headhunters watching *All-Star Wrestling* on their satellite feed, no longer is it shocking to find the last guy at the end of the earth wearing a Harvard t-shirt and asking if you know Michael Jordan. The global village exists in a rudimentary fashion, but it is real.

In 1980, Paul Fussell wrote in *Abroad: British Literary Traveling Between the Wars* a cranky but wonderful epitaph for travel as it was once known, in which he concluded that "we are all tourists now, and there is no escape." It has been projected by some analysts that by the year 2000, tourism will be the world's largest industry; others say it already is. In either case, this is a horrifying prospect—hordes of us hunting for places that have not been trod on by the rest of us!

Fussell's words have the painful ring of truth, but this is still our world, and it is worth seeing and will be worth seeing next year, or in 50 years, simply because it will always be worth meeting others who continue to see life in different terms than we do despite the best efforts of telecommunication and advertising talents. No amount of creeping homogeneity can quell the endless variation of humanity, and travel in the end is about people, not places. Places only provide different venues, as it were, for life, in which we are all pilgrims who need to talk to each other.

There are also many places around the world where intercultural friction and outright xenophobia are increasing. And the very fact that travel endangers cultures and pristine places more quickly than it used to calls for extraordinary care on the part of today's traveler, a keener sense of personal responsibility. The world is not our private zoo or theme park; we need to be better prepared before we go, so that we might become honored guests and not vilified intruders.

In *Travelers' Tales,* we collect useful and memorable anecdotes to produce the kind of sampler we've always wanted to read before setting out. These stories will show you some of the spectrum of experiences to be had or avoided in each country. The authors come from many walks of life: some are teachers, some are musicians, some are entrepreneurs, all are wanderers with a tale to tell. Their stories will help you to deepen and enrich your experience as a traveler. Where we've excerpted books, we urge you to go out and read the full work, because no selection can ever do an author justice.

Each *Travelers' Tales* is organized into five simple parts. In the first, we've chosen stories that reflect the ephemeral yet pervasive essence of a country. Part Two contains stories about places and activities that others have found worthwhile. In Part Three, we've chosen stories by people who have made a special connection between their lives and interests and the people and places they visited. Part Four shows some of the struggles and challenges facing a region and its people, and Part Five, "The Last Word," is just that, something of a grace note or harmonic to remind you of the book as a whole.

Our selection of stories in each *Travelers' Tales* is by no means comprehensive, but we are confident it will prime your pump. *Travelers' Tales* are not meant to replace other guides, but to accompany them. No longer will you have to go to dozens of sources to map the personal side of your journey. You'll be able to reach for *Travelers' Tales*, and truly prepare yourself before you go.

—JAMES O'REILLY AND LARRY HABEGGER
Series Editors

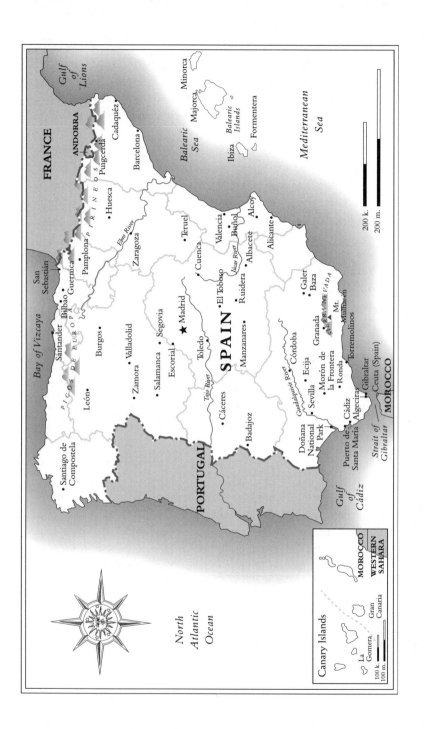

Spain: An Introduction

I first arrived in Spain in 1982, my luggage bouncing behind me over the cobbled streets of Sevilla's Barrio Santa Cruz to a *pensión* embraced by two ancient arms, the streets Vida and Agua. Life and Water. I was just a college student then, but Spain became for me, as it does for so many, a kind of spiritual home where a soul awakening occurred, a place to which I would return for replenishment, for a fix of Vida and Agua.

It is true what they say, that your senses become heightened there. The light is different, hotter; the music stirs the blood. Spain is a banquet of bougainvillea blossoming crimson and orange, and air pungent with sizzling olive oil. It is a land of touch and taste, where the essence of everything seems at its most intense.

Spain also possesses a peculiarly enigmatic character that resonates throughout the country—something the cover photograph captures well: It suggests the flowing movement of both the flamenco dance and the bullfight, a country that understands sensuality and understands death. It evokes a place quintessentially Catholic at its heart, with both the community and ritual that that represents, as well as the dark intolerance of the Inquisition. And it is also the cloaked image of the Moors, a heritage of exotic sensibility bequeathed during their almost 800 years in Spain.

The cover suggests, too, the icon of Don Quixote's windmill—a soulful country of idealistic quests balanced by the earthy practicality of Sancho Panza, the good knight's companion. Don Quixote's presence resonates throughout this book, in fact: each section ends with an excerpt of one writer's travels in the mythical character's footsteps. Surely every traveler is Don Quixote, an individualist who is journeying, one way or another, back to him- or herself.

Similarly, the theme of quest and pilgrimage recurs in the book; people traversing landscapes in search of parts of themselves. There are pilgrims walking the 500-mile road to Santiago de Compostela; a woman moved to learn the "male" art of flamenco guitar; and the story of one man's journey home—the heart's home, which people often seem to find, oddly, in a foreign place.

Spain has always drawn travelers and writers, from Henry James and Simone de Beauvoir to George Orwell and Ernest Hemingway. Travel literature about Spain from bygone centuries fills library bookshelves. Many quotations from those historic travelers accent the book, adding yet another dimension to the contemporary stories. And the contributors here sometimes refer directly to historic visitors from whom they've drawn inspiration to travel—one writer, for example, walks among the Alhambra's courtyards feeling the specter of Washington Irving, a full century and a half after that author lived there.

That is another wonderful thing about Spain: it is in many ways a timeless place, reassuringly unchanging. Its landmarks, its traditions—notably the sociability of the people, their art of conversing over *tapas* or wandering the streets together during *paseo*—have survived centuries and wars and dictatorships. Yet the country has also changed dramatically in recent years, evolving from a dictatorship with close ties to the Church into a Socialist government with a reigning monarch and a free market, a Spain that's an ultra-chic hot spot.

It is the tension between those two contradictory elements, the old-world mores and modern lifestyles bumping up against each other, that this book explores. Several stories therefore reflect back to the Spanish Civil War and the dictatorship of General Francisco Franco, whose era ironically set the stage for today's "New Spain"—a sophisticated society fast reversing the effects of 36 years of oppression.

Anyone who traveled to Spain before Franco's death in 1975 encountered a place that was *in* Europe but hardly "European," an isolated, backward country in many respects. Today Spain has become truly cosmopolitan—more comfortable, more affluent, with transportation systems that are more efficient (and, contrary to the stereotype regarding Spaniards, on time). Barcelona, for example, spent $1.5 billion on buildings and infrastructure for the 1992 Olympic Games, and a high-speed rail and new superhighways link once-remote towns throughout the country. But again the contradiction arises: in the best way, Spain is also un-European. While other countries continue to meld into one great European Union, Spain somehow manages to retain the essence of its rich cultural layers born of conquest and reconquest.

Some years ago, Italo Calvino wrote a wonderful book, *Invisible Cities,* that is in many ways a travel memoir of places imagined, told through the figure of Marco Polo who describes the cities he has known to Kublai Khan, the 13th-century Mongol leader of China. "The city must never be confused with the words that describe it," Marco Polo says. "And yet between the one and the other there is a connection." And later he tells the Khan: "If you saw [the city], standing in its midst, it would be a different city; Irene is a name for a city in the distance, and if you approach, it changes. For those who pass it without entering, the city is one thing; it is another for those who are trapped by it and never leave. There is the city where you arrive for the first time; and there is another city which you leave never to return. Each deserves a different name."

So too is it with the stories in this book. The writers describe places and people, but the way they communicate isn't always with the spoken word. They move within the foreign culture as guests, describing the poetry of the place that was once called Iberia, and communicating with whatever language is closest to their hearts and experiences, be that a guitar chord or a dance step or even— yes—a tomato in the face. And in that sense these stories are descriptions of places of each author's own making. The Sevilla described, for example, the walks through its parks and Moorish gates and narrow *barrio* streets, surely is different from the Sevilla the writer pictured from a distance when planning the trip. And different too from the experience of the place other travelers will have, who will also venture to Sevilla and walk through the gates and narrow streets, and who will take home a tale of a Sevilla that has become theirs.

And yet between the two, between the place that is read about and the place that is experienced, there is a connection. I hope that this book might serve as a bridge.

—Lucy McCauley

A Note on Exchange Rates, Spelling, and Meaning

This is not a typical guidebook, in which prices and accuracy of exchange rates figure prominently. Consequently, I have not tried to convert figures used by authors to current exchange rates as long as they are in a ballpark with admittedly ill-defined borders.

Cities and regions, as well as some festivals, often have both an English name and spelling and a Spanish one, and sometimes a particular regional spelling too. Therefore, one author in this book might refer to "Holy Week in Seville" while another will talk about "Semana Santa in Sevilla"; these are interchangeable, and we have retained each author's own style. Similarly, the Canary Islands in Spanish are the Islas Canarias, Andalusia is Andalucía, Castile is Castilla, Majorca is Mallorca, and the place—and sherry by the same name—is Jerez as well as Xeres. Moreover, the good knight who appears throughout this book is overwhelmingly referred to as Don Quixote, though the Spanish much prefer the spelling Don Quijote.

When it comes to historical dates, writers, including Spaniards themselves, are often vague or contradictory. For example, you might read that Franco was in power 40 years; in fact it was 36 years (40 years would include the Civil War, a period during which Franco was certainly trying to seize power but hadn't actually yet done it). Another confusing issue is how long the Moors were in Spain: was it 700 or 800 years? Variation on this point is understandable; the Moors were on Spanish soil for nearly a full eight centuries, but during their final hundred years they lost considerable power and land to the Christian reconquest. The last of the Moors finally capitulated in 1492—a fateful, star-crossed date for Spain for other reasons, of course, but that is another story.

—LMc

PART ONE

ESSENCE OF SPAIN

ANN AND LARRY WALKER

Crossing into Spain

The border between France and Spain is
even clearer than one might think.

WE HAD BEEN TRAVELING IN BORDEAUX, RESEARCHING SOME wine and food stories for magazines. We had landed in Paris in April with a light snow falling. After that, the weather had gotten bad. In Bordeaux it had alternated between sleet, hail, rain, thunder, and lightning with brief periods of pale sunshine. We had promised ourselves that when our work in France was finished, we would reward ourselves with a few days in Spain.

Not surprisingly, although the almond trees were flowering, it was snowing when we crossed the border at Puigcerdà, after a harrowing drive over the mountain pass in heavy snow in our rented Renault with no chains. Sheer craziness.

The road dropped rapidly beyond the frontier and in a few miles we were in sunshine. We stopped at a truck drivers' café, perhaps ten kilometers into Spain.

At once, we felt at home. The counterman encouraged our rusty Spanish. We drank hearty red wine and ate slices of cured Valencia ham, rough bread, and olives. He made no fuss about accepting our francs (in our rush through the snow, we had neglected to exchange francs for pesetas). You can imagine what the French

3

reaction would have been had we offered pesetas even a few kilometers north.

One of the truck drivers came over to ask if we had driven over the pass. Was it still snowing? He had no chains. Should he wait? Others joined the conversation with advice, concern, a little friendly bantering, which became more friendly when we kept trying out our Spanish.

Very soon, someone bought another bottle of wine. Our benefactor had a cousin who worked in San Francisco. Would we take his cousin's name and address and call him when we returned to California? Perhaps buy this cousin a small brandy? Yes, yes, we could do all that.

It was wonderful. After weeks with the very proper, very correct, but never very friendly Bordelaise, it was like being greeted by a whole pack of warm, friendly puppies.

It was Spain. The wine was cheap and good. The food was abundant and tasty. The sun was shining....

The beach is a circus. A swirling palate of colors, of beautiful horses, beautiful women, and handsome men. Race week at Sanlúcar de Barrameda, the oldest horse race in all of Europe. Beyond the sands of the beach at Sanlúcar, beyond the misty sunset glimmer of the Guadalquivir, the pale green of Doñana National Park hangs in the darkening sky. Watching from one of the bodega boxes erected at the top of the beach, we would like to imagine—and why not—an imperial eagle sweeping out of the Doñana to arrogantly observe the puny markings in the sand below.

It is the last race of the day.

Men in tuxedos with white cummerbunds at their waists dance on the sand with barefoot women in gowns that cost hundreds of thousands of pesetas, pearls like kisses on dark necks.

The steady beat of a rock band from farther down the beach where tall blondes (part of that northern swarm that each August engulfs the beaches of Spain) dance topless. The racing horses flash across the sand, nearing the finish line.

A somber man, dressed all in black, sits on his white horse like an icon just beyond the racing horses. A small girl, no more than three or four, all in white save the red sash at her waist and red ribbons in her hair, sits solemnly on the saddle before him. The beautiful, pale young woman next to us says he is one of the judges.

What does he judge?

She doesn't know. Perhaps riding form, perhaps the winners or losers. Perhaps the dancing that will come later. Somehow, he simply has wandered into the end of the last race of the day.

At the finish, all is confusion. From where we sit it is impossible to tell who has won, nor is there anyone nearby who knows.

At some point, some time, it will matter. Here and now it doesn't. A caterer in black and white does a "hey, presto" routine with a gleaming white cloth on the table set in the sand below us. Plates of shrimp, squid, fried fish, lobster, heaping fruit platters crowd the tabletop; gleaming glasses of chilled *manzanilla* sherry reflect the last light from the sun.

*Q*uien no corre la barraja,
¡Qué mal entiende la flor!

Who treads not the wild,
Little knows he of the flower!

—Guillem de Castro (1569–1631),
El Narciso en su Opinion, Journal II

Someone lights the candles that line the table. The scene repeats itself dozens of times down the beach.

The somber man and the pale young woman join us. Now he is laughing, exchanging toasts with our host. The young girl, his daughter, sits on his lap, smiling shyly, chewing on a huge prawn, red ribbons hanging loose down her neck. He is not a rich man. He has a very small vineyard, but for generations members of his family have been judges in the races at Sanlúcar. If he doesn't have any sons, he expects his daughter to be a judge one day, so she is in training.

No, he doesn't know who won. He must consult with the other judges.

What other judges?

A vague motion down the beach. They are there having dinner at other tables. Somewhere in the dusk or perhaps up on the street, watching the Gypsies from the hill towns to the east—toward Granada and Ronda—dance the *puro* flamenco.

They will get together later.

"You see," says the pale young woman, "if the judges announce the winner now, it will spoil the night for the others. Tomorrow is soon enough for that sorrow."

Yes, we understand.

The judge smiles at us and raises his glass. We raise ours. We drink to the most beautiful women, the finest horses, and the best wine in the world.

Tonight we are all winners.

Ann Walker is a caterer, food educator, and writer. Larry Walker writes about wine for Wine & Spirit International *(London) and other international publications. This excerpt was drawn from their book* A Season in Spain, *which describes their journey through the regions of Spain, sampling the food and wine. The Walkers live in Stinson Beach, California.*

★

Perched in this southern town, one felt intensely the great square weight of Spain stretching away north behind one; felt all there was to leave, from these palm-fringed tropic shores to the misty hills of Bilbao; the plains of La Mancha, *sierras* of pine and snow, the golden villages perched on their gorges, wine smells of noon and sweet wood smoke of evening, the strings of mules crawling through huge brown landscapes, the rarity of grass, the wood ploughs scratching the dusty fields, and the families at evening sitting down to their plates of beans. One heard the silences of the *sierras*, the cracking of sunburnt rocks, the sharp jungle voices of the women, the tavern-murmur of the men, the love songs of the girls rising at dawn, the sobbing of asses and whine of hungry dogs. Spain of cathedrals, palaces, caves and hovels; of blood-stained bull-rings and prison-yards; of weeping Virgins, tortured Christs, acid humour and incomparable song—all this lay anchored between the great troughs of its mountains, locked in its local dialects, bound by its own sad pride.

Spain is but Spain, and belongs nowhere but where it is. It is neither Catholic nor European but a structure of its own, forged from an African-Iberian past which exists in its own austere reality and rejects all short-cuts to a smoother life.

—Laurie Lee, *A Rose for Winter: Travels in Andalusia* (1955)

GABRIEL GARCÍA MÁRQUEZ
TRANSLATED FROM THE SPANISH
BY MARGARET COSTA

Watching the Rain in Galicia

*In his grandmother's childhood home, the celebrated Colombian
author finds a mythical land where the food
seems to grow from the table.*

MY OLD FRIEND, THE PAINTER, POET, AND NOVELIST, HÉCTOR
Rojas Herazo—whom I hadn't seen for a long time—must have
felt a tremor of compassion when he saw me in Madrid in a crush
of photographers and journalists, for he came up to me and whispered: "Remember that from time to time you should be nice to
yourself." In fact, it had been months—perhaps years—since I had
given myself a well-deserved present. So I decided to give myself
what was, in reality, one of my dreams: a visit to Galicia.

No one who enjoys eating can think of Galicia without first
thinking of the pleasures of its cuisine. "Homesickness starts with
food," said Che Guevara, pining perhaps for the vast roasts of his
native Argentina while they, men alone in the night in Sierra
Maestra, spoke of war. For me, too, homesickness for Galicia had
started with food even before I had been there. The fact is that my
grandmother, in the big house at Aracataca, where I got to know
my first ghosts, had the delightful role of baker and she carried on
even when she was already old and nearly blind, until the river
flooded, ruined the oven and no one in the house felt like re-
building it. But my grandmother's vocation was so strong that
when she could no longer make bread, she made hams. Delicious

7

hams, though we children did not like them—children never like the novelties of adults—even though the flavour of that first taste has remained recorded forever on the memory of my palate. I never found it again in any of the many and various hams I ate later in any of my good or my bad years until, by chance, I tasted— 40 years later, in Barcelona—an innocent slice of shoulder of pork. All the joy, all the uncertainties, and all the solitude of childhood suddenly came back to me with that, the unmistakable flavour of the hams my grandmother made.

From that experience grew my interest in tracing the ancestry of this flavour, and, in looking for it, I found my own among the frenetic greens of May, the sea and the fertile rains and eternal winds of the Galician countryside. Only then did I understand where my grandmother had got that credulity which allowed her to live in a supernatural world in which everything was possible and where rational explanations were totally lacking in validity. And I understood from where her passion for preparing food for hypothetical visitors came and her habit of singing all day. "You have to make a meat and a fish dish because you never know what people will want when they come to lunch," she would say, when she heard the train whistle. She died very old and blind and with her sense of reality completely unhinged, to the point where she would talk about her oldest memories as if they were happening at that moment, and she held conversations with the dead she had known alive in her remote youth. I was telling a Galician friend about this last week in Santiago de Compostela and he said: "Then your grandmother must have been Galician, no doubt about it, because she was crazy." In fact all the Galicians I know, and those whom I met without having time to get to know them, seem to have been born under the sign of Pisces.

I don't know where the shame of being a tourist comes from. I've heard many friends in full touristic swing say that they don't want to mix with tourists, not realizing that even though they don't mix with them, they are just as much tourists as the others.

When I visit a place and haven't enough time to get to know it more than superficially, I unashamedly assume my role as tourist. I like to join those lightning tours in which the guides explain everything you see out of the window—"On your right and left, ladies and gentlemen…"—one of the reasons being that then I know once and for all everything I needn't bother to see when I go out later to explore the place on my own.

Anyway, Santiago de Compostela doesn't leave time for such details: the city imposes itself immediately, complete and timeless, as if one had been born there. I had always believed, and continue to believe, really, that there is no more beautiful square in the world than the one in Siena. The only place that made me doubt its authority as the most beautiful square is the one in Santiago de Compostela. Its poise and its youthful air prohibit you from even thinking about its venerable age; instead, it looks as if it had been built the day before by someone who had lost their sense of time. Perhaps this impression does not come from the square itself but from its being—like every corner of the city—steeped to its soul in everyday life. It is a lively city, swept along by a crowd of happy, boisterous students who don't give it a chance to grow old. On the walls that remain intact, plant life makes its way through the cracks in an implacable struggle to outlive oblivion, and at every step, as if it were the most natural thing in the world, one is confronted by the miracle of stones in full bloom.

It rained for three days, not inclemently, but with unseasonable spells of radiant sun. Nevertheless, my Galician friends did not seem to see these golden intervals and apologized for the rain all the time. Perhaps not even they were aware that Galicia without rain would have been a disappointment; because theirs is a mythical country—far more than the Galicians themselves realize—and in mythical lands the sun never comes out. "If you'd come last week you'd have had lovely weather," they told us, shamefaced. "It's very unusual weather for the time of year," they insisted, forgetting about Valle-Inclán, Rosalía de Castro and every Galician poet who ever lived, in whose books it rains from the beginning of creation, and through which an interminable wind blows, perhaps the very same that sows the lunatic seed which makes so many Galicians delightfully different.

It rains in Santiago,
my sweet love.
White camellia of the air,
shadowy shines the sun.

It rains in Santiago
in the dark night.
Grasses of silver and of sleep
cover the empty moon.

See the rain in the street,
lament of stone and crystal.
See in the vanishing wind
shadow and ash of your sea.

Shadow and ash of your sea,
Santiago, far from the sun.
Water of ancient morning
trembles in my heart.

—Federico García Lorca,
"Madrigal to the City of
Santiago" (1935) translated by
Norman di Giovanni, *Federico
García Lorca: The Selected Poems*

It rained in the city, it rained in the vivid fields, it rained in the lacustrine paradise of the Arosa and the Vigo estuaries; and, over the bridge, it rained in the undaunted and almost unreal Plaza de Cambados; and it even rained on the island of La Toja, where there's a hotel from another world and time, which seems to be waiting for the rain to stop, the wind to cease and the sun to shine in order to start living. We walked through this rain as if through a state of grace, eating shellfish galore, the only live shellfish left in this devastated world; eating fish which, on the plate, still looked like fish; and salads that continued to grow on the table. And we knew that all this was by virtue of the rain which never stops falling.

It's now many years since, in a Barcelona restaurant, I heard the writer, Alvaro Cunqueiros, talk about Galician food and his descriptions were so dazzling that I took them for the ravings of a Galician. As far back as I can remember I've heard Galician emigrants talk of Galicia and I always thought their memories were coloured by nostalgic illusions. Today I recall my 72 hours in Galicia and I wonder if they were all true or if I myself have begun to fall victim to the same delirium as my grandmother. Among Galicians—as we all know—you never can tell.

Gabriel García Márquez was born in Aracataca, Colombia, but has lived most of his life in Europe and Mexico, residing now in Mexico City. He began his career as a reporter and film critic in Colombia and went on to produce some of the best-loved works of "magical realism," including the novels One Hundred Years of Solitude, Love in the Time of Cholera, Chronicle of a Death Foretold, The General in His Labyrinth, *and* Of Love and Other Demons. *He won the Nobel Prize for Literature in 1982.*

✳

I think about Galicia and the dance of life and death that I witnessed there, a funny, paradoxical dance where excrement and nutrient become one as pig intestines are turned into sausage casing, as refuse is boiled down to a hearty gruel that in turn fills the animals' hungry bellies. An endless, mysterious cycle that is both comforting and brutal. The rawness of that fecund mother-earth realm, that landscape of infinity, awakened something deep within my ravaged urban spirit and now I long for it like a pining lover. I can see that I am afflicted with "*la morriña de Galicia*," the homesickness for that land that I heard people refer to as though it were a certifiable condition.

I remember evenings around the kitchen fire in that stark, stone dwelling in Laguna de Tablas. The tears streamed down Lola's plump red cheeks as she wheezed with laughter at Manolo's jokes. Jokes poking fun at Franco, Andalusians, priests, wives, provincial Galician thinking. "An old Galician man was making his way down the road," said Manolo, his handlebar mustache dancing up and down and his blue eyes crinkling. "A neighbor with a car drove up and offered him a ride. 'No, I'm in a hurry,' the man said, 'I'll walk.'"

I could not tell whether everyone laughed in gentle mockery of the old man's ignorance—or in knowing appreciation of his wisdom. For the next day, Manolo spoke soberly of the changes invading the old way of life in Galicia these past ten years. Manolo had left his homeland when he was eighteen to earn money at odd jobs in Switzerland. He returned, he said, to find that with modern medicine people were getting sick more easily; that with the movement into the cities, young Galicians were being exposed to drugs and other unsavory influences; that with indoor plumbing and electrical gadgetry in most homes, people were becoming isolated from one another.

I recall the faces around the kitchen table my last night in Laguna de Tablas, faces vacant and slack, mesmerized by the inane game show blaring from the new television set that Jesús had recently bought. I kept waiting for everyone to gather around the fire and start telling jokes again. But at 11 p.m., when they finally clicked the box off, everyone went silently to bed.

The morning I departed, Manolo told me that in days gone by, there was more humor and warmth among the Galician people. I remember the sad look that momentarily shadowed his face and I knew then that Manolo was suffering from *morriña* of the worst kind: *morriña* for a time and place that no one would ever be able to return to again.

—Marguerite Rigoglioso, *"La Morriña de Galicia"*

A Night of *Duende*

*A flamenco evening in the company of
Gypsies uncovers a culture in touch
with the transcendent.*

THEY STOOD IN THE BAR MOST OF THE TIME, CRADLING LARGE shots of brandy in hands heavy with oversized rings, smoking like old-fashioned film stars. One wore a red suit, a poppy-red three-piece, with wide lapels on a jacket fitted tight into the waist and trousers climbing to his rib cage and flaring just enough to break perfectly over the snub-nosed, stack-heeled boots. Beneath the waistcoat his shirt was open, but only a little gold showed. They talked and drank and smoked in groups of three or four, strident, vivid, perfumed huddles apart. Another wore lime green.

They were not bothered about Paco, all that jazz stuff and film scores. Paco's good sure—many say he's technically the best there is—but that's not enough to leave a bar for, not when you know you look as fine as this. The real reason they didn't leave their drinks to listen was because Paco de Lucía isn't one of them, isn't a *gitano*. Camarón is though, Camarón de la Isla is the man from the province of Cádiz, whose voice captures the spirit of these dark men in bright suits. And when he came on they went in, and the whole place watched.

Madrid's large featureless sports palace is not the best place to see flamenco. But a bill that includes Paco de Lucía and Camarón is big business: they are stars. Flamenco has grown immensely popular throughout Spain in recent years. Like most of the folkloric forms which play such a part in the picture-book conception of Spain, its death was prematurely announced in the swinging seventies (things happened later here), when everybody wanted to be the Beatles.

For a while flamenco looked like it was going the sorry way of most Western European folk music. But then in the deep south it was revived through a series of competitions and festivals which were organized to keep the faith alive, and are now as much a part of the Andalusian calendar as the bullfighting *ferias*. Today you can hardly walk across a plaza or through a park without hearing young kids trying to perfect their rapid rhythmic clapping or a drunk trying desperately to warble his way through a sorry song.

What was once the exclusive property of those *gitanos* and somber Andalusian musicologists has spread so that you hear flamenco constantly on popular radio stations. You can hear *cante jondo* deep song, the pure, oriental, and profoundly soulful music of voice and guitar. This is a music of the ages which tells of the loss of many mothers and the ruin of so many sons on the long Gypsy journey from their original home in northern India. It is a difficult, sober music, yet one which people are singing and listening to again.

As with so many aspects of Spanish life, the fading of Francoism was a factor: it took away the

> *Composer Manuel de Falla proposed that the Andalusian song had its roots in Byzantine chant, Moorish music, and the Gypsy tribes who settled in Spain in the 15th century after arriving from India. For [Federico García] Lorca, flamenco was "one of the most gigantic creations of the Spanish people," with the verse form of the* cante jondo *or* copla *characterized by its striking imagery, conciseness, and emotional extremism: "The* cante jondo *sings nearly always at night. It has neither morning nor afternoons, neither mountains nor plains. It only has the night, a night that is wide and profoundly starlit. It doesn't need anything else."*
>
> —Jimmy Burns, *A Literary Companion to Spain*

stigma of nationalism which had attached itself to all the distinctly "Spanish" cultural forms. Young people who would once have been embarrassed to enjoy flamenco or bullfighting because of their conservative, traditionalist overtones could now see them as living parts of their culture. In flamenco there was also a new breed of performers: the young men from the towns and villages of the south who look and live like rock stars, but sing and play a music still drenched in that moving darkness. Of these Camarón is undeniably the king.

That is why there were huge, tank-like Mercedes lined up in the street outside the sports hall on the night when Camarón sang, why the affluent, flashy young *gitanos* had pulled on their best suits. I'd seen Paco de Lucía before and loved his flowing, daring guitar playing. But it was the prospect of catching the wild one, de la Isla, the man of the island, which made me pay way over the odds for a ticket to a shifty Madrileño scalper. It could have been a risky investment though.

Camarón is a man with very bad habits. Unpredictable, often ill, prone to disappearing for long black periods of excess, he loses himself deep in the *gitano* sub-culture of caravans and *chabolas*. And they love him for it. Camarón wears his problems like a badge, and like some latter-day Spanish Billie Holiday, his voice has the cracked, fragile tones that can turn the suffering into something sublime.

Standing on stage that night in a billowing white shirt he sang fierce and soft, sang of all the usual themes, of all the loss. The men from the bar stood in the hall in groups still, shouting their 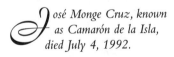 *osé Monge Cruz, known as Camarón de la Isla, died July 4, 1992.*

—LMc

occasional support, letting loose soft and strong *olés* in the trance-like gaps between the sounds. They closed their eyes those men, tapping, occasionally clapping softly to the rhythms, throwing back their heads when Camarón roared. Flamenco music means Gypsy music, and this defiant, self-destructive singer was the essence of flamenco that night. To the strident *hombres* from the bar,

Camarón's very existence is a statement of their outsideness, their difference, a "fuck you" as loud and proud as their suits. To me he was a great singer.

The dance of the *gitanos* was never as endangered as their song. Even in the tacky tourist flamenco tableaux, there is a fair degree of authenticity of step and costume. These tourist shows are usually staffed by girls from the dance academies working to pay their way through school. And in the south at least the movements of flamenco are such a strong and vital part of the popular culture of all Andalusians that it was always danced at *ferias* and weddings. But in the eighties it underwent a huge boom.

Ballet Español, the blend of flamenco with classical ballet which the magnetic Antonio Gades made so famous, was largely responsible for this. His company became hugely popular both at home and abroad through the movies they made with director Carlos Saura: *Blood Wedding* and *Carmen*. By turning two of the most renowned tales of Andalusian pride and passion (*Blood Wedding* is Federico García Lorca's most famous play) into highly stylised and thoroughly modern movies they made flamenco improbably chic.

Going to see flamenco dancers became a society affair, and so too did attempting to do it. *Pija* girls who would never dream of dating a *gitano* got themselves togged up in elaborate flamenco gowns and paid for private tuition. *¡Hola!* was full of pretty, petty aristas who suddenly discovered distant Andalusian ancestry and wore the get-up to prove it.

Throughout the country a rash of more plebeian flamenco classes also appeared. In truth these were a kind of Spanish equivalent of aerobics sessions, where flamenco replaced disco as a medium for losing a few pounds and toning a few thighs. In Barcelona, which is about as far removed from Andalusia as you can get and remain Iberian, every other office girl and shop assistant bought a pair of flamenco shoes and castanets and tried to convince herself that she had Gypsy blood somewhere in her veins. Even my friend Inka, half Catalán and half German, came home one day with a pair of clumpy shoes and castanets, had one lesson, realised just how difficult it is and consigned them to a drawer.

Fans, one of the other potent symbols of fiery southern femininity, started turning up in discos, frequently waved by gay men while doing elaborate mock flamenco dance routines. I wanted to see the authentic stuff first hand.

The outskirts of Barcelona, like those of most large Spanish towns, consist mostly of ugly, neglected estates of dilapidated concrete apartment blocks. Invariably dusty, dreamily depressing places, they are full of ragged-arsed kids and dog shit. Much of the population of these disconsolate suburbs is Andalusian in origin, a legacy of the hungry years when the peasants left the south to live in *chabolas* around the big cities. The shanties have gone from Barcelona now, flattened in a show of civic redevelopment in the seventies, but the flatblocks which have replaced them are not really much of an improvement.

We travelled one night to one of these estates to the northeast of the city, a fairly typical suburb about half an hour's drive out. Although it is not one of the violent, drug-ridden estates which make up the nightmares and inform the prejudices of so many Spaniards, this is not the sort of place that life would normally take me. But on a Friday night Inka and I, accompanied by three friends, crowded into the back of a car and headed that way. One of those friends, Miguel the shameless poet, knew a man named Manolo who ran a bar there and he was expecting us.

Manolo is not a Gypsy, but he is Andalusian and when we arrived at his bar in the main street of this plain, poor community he gave Miguel a huge southern hug. He then did the same with each of us before pouring out five glasses of cold *jerez* for us to drink. With the green and white flag of Andalusia prominently displayed, pictures of matadors and footballers on the walls, and a large number of men playing noisy games of cards, Manolo's bar was clearly a kind of informal Andalusian social club.

But the business of the evening, the reason we'd driven out, was to go to a club of a different kind. A *peña* in Spanish is kind of a fan club. There are *peñas* for bullfighters and *peñas* for football teams, which have a particular bar as their headquarters. And there was the *peña* Fosforito, the club in honor of one of the greatest *gitano* singers of them all. This was a place of flamenco.

On the short walk to the *peña* Fosforito, Manolo went through an intricate sales pitch on a battered 1970s Volvo which he had parked round the corner from his bar. None of us was in the market for a car and we made that clear, but that didn't stop Manolo, a large man with an even larger gut and a pair of trousers at least two sizes too small, from singing the praises of this *magnífico coche* as he called it, insisting that Miguel sit in the driver's seat "to feel how safe it is." We only just escaped having to take it for a test drive. Time was getting on and things were already happening at the *peña*.

Housed in an anonymous-looking bar by a drear, dank apartment block, the *peña* Fosforito has a picture of the great singer on the back wall, a scattering of plastic tables and chairs, and a tiny raised wooden platform which serves as a stage. Manolo led us inside, introducing each of us formally and individually to the owner, and collectively to the 30 or so people who were sitting in the club. He then left to return to his bar, demanding that we all come back to see him soon and reminding us of just how good a car his Volvo was.

There was a certain skepticism in some of the dark eyes, not exactly animosity, but an unconvinced surprise perhaps, that these five young outsiders, clearly well off, were coming to their *peña*. We sat down at a table and ordered some food and some beers, and kept the kind of quiet that the watched keep.

A man with an acoustic guitar had taken up a position sitting on one of the plastic chairs on the small wooden stage. He began playing, softly at first, with a deft touch, but really just doodling, stopping to tune his guitar and to get a bottle of *jerez* which was placed by his chair.

Our food arrived, a selection of strong *tapas* in the southern style, including a wonderful, thick rough *chorizo* oozing oil and taste. As we ate I looked gingerly round. Most of the customers

were adults dressed in a kind of Friday-night best, certainly not the
glamour clothes of the men in the Madrid sports hall—this was a
poor community—but sporting the best they could offer. Despite
the obvious racial differences, they looked to me like the crowds I
knew so well from the rollicking Irish pubs of my native North
London on a Friday night.

And as the music began to flow from the man bent over his guitar, and it became clear that we were there simply to listen, so some
of the same kind of warmth that is generated in those vast gin
palaces off the Edgware Road began to fill that small hall.

The guitar-playing had that hypnotic, rhythmic power which
makes flamenco so compelling, and its circular, propelling dynamic
was already producing positive responses. Then one of the men sitting drinking at a table with his family, a man in his mid-life,
stepped up onto the stage, draped his vivid check jacket over the
back of the chair and sat down.

For a while he sat just cracking the heel of his boot down into
the stage in time to the guitar. Then he took to clapping, his hands
held close by his bowed head, as if he were struggling to hear the
rhythms that his softly colliding palms were producing. His powerful silence was matched by the audience who seemed to be re-
specting some shared, almost religious ritual.

Then, still sitting and with his eyes shut as if searching deep inside himself for something, he let out a soft moan. This swelled into
a lyric, which was dragged and bent into a wail. He was perfectly
in sync with the complex guitar patterns now and between them
they were weaving a magic. There was something both ecstatic and
strangely puritan, introspective and exclamatory, about this deeply
disciplined music with its ululating tones sounding so like the
muezzin who calls the faithful to prayer from the Muslim minarets.

"*Eso es cante moro*"—"That's Moorish singing," proclaimed the
old man sitting at the next table, half to us, half to the man who
was making it. "*Olé,*" sighed another.

The singer was lost in his soul now, his face racked as he expelled demons which came out as song, vibrato, grainy flamenco

song, Gypsy song and the Gypsy audience were all responding to his experience made music.

The word *duende* was used by one of the congregation, a word I knew well, but still do not know how to translate well. In bull-fighting—that other art touched by the Gypsy—certain matadors can create moments which raise those watching to heights of excitement, which can enable you to transcend the bloody spectacle to a point of spirituality. For that transient moment they have *duende*—presence, charisma, that indescribable something which we all know when we are in its presence.

Duende is a vital word in the flamenco canon: it expresses the transcendent, cathartic nature of the music, the way in which the spirit is revealed, sometimes to soar. Camarón de la Isla undoubtedly has *duende*. And this man singing now, who lives his weeks in this grim suburb, perhaps unemployed, surely poor, had left all that on this Friday night in the *peña* Fosforito to rise, so that he had *duende* too. And we all shared it.

When he had finished his song there was applause all round and a hug from a man at the table closest to the stage. The singer picked up his jacket and returned to his family sitting at a plastic table and drank a glass of *jerez*. He sent a smile over to us, and we felt welcome.

The next to climb up was a little older, a skinny man whose features, despite the trenches that life had dug into his face, were so obviously Indian that he could still be living in the sub-continent. Where the last singer had performed a mournful Gypsy blues, this one's aim was to move us in a different way. After communicating with the guitarist in the rapid, nasal accent of Andalusia, where words seem to stick to the palate, the hunched player skipped his fingers across the strings to a faster, more joyous beat, slapping his hands onto the sonorous wood of the soundboard.

The old man, standing cocksure and smiling, sang a tune, uninhibited, lusty, that pulled a woman from another table to the stage. There she danced, her back straight, the tails of her dress, a normal cheap dress of man-made fibre, raised and flicked in a gesture of open sexuality. This woman, as old as the man singing, circled the dais, keeping her eyes theatrically on his, acting out a kind of rhythmic ritual courtship. The place was laughing now, cheering as she grew more expressive, stamping her heels, clicking her fingers as her arms swept in an arc above her head, sweeping back her once dark hair. Finally she kissed the old man before returning to her table with a skip.

Half a dozen of the people in that place sang that night, although none for me came close to the first with his *duende*. Another carried his guitar onto the stage to indulge in an elaborate, racy duet-cum-duel. A couple more danced, including one man who used a walking stick to pound out more sounds than his heels alone could create. The tone of the music varied from the sombre to the gay, though the overriding colour was definitely dark with melancholy; but once revealed in song there was a spirit, a life, even in this suffering, which lighted and lifted us all. So that we felt not brought down but raised up.

It was a good night at the *peña* Fosforito.

> *O* nly the moral embargoes
> of Spanish society, coupled
> with its natural paganism, could
> produce such a volcanic yet exquis-
> itely controlled sexuality as [fla-
> menco]. The man is all voice; the
> woman all pride and hunger.
> While his song climbs into ec-
> stasies of improvisation she coils
> and toils and sobs and throbs
> around him. And always there is
> the invisible guitar, whipping them
> delicately from the dark, feeding
> their secret fevers.
>
> —Laurie Lee, *A Rose for Winter:*
> *Travels in Andalusia* (1955)

Robert Elms, who has lived in both Barcelona and Madrid, now makes his home in London. His work in the travel genre has spanned various media, including as a host of a television series called Travelog *and contributing to the travel pages of* The Times of London. *This piece was excerpted from his book,* Spain: A Portrait after the General.

✳

The general belief today is that all Gypsies were originally from India, and that, after reaching the Bosphorus, some went directly to Europe and others travelled along the southern shores of the Mediterranean, eventually crossing the Strait of Gibraltar. The Spanish and Provençal Gypsies probably chose the latter route, as they are referred to respectively as *gitanos* and *gitans,* which are derivatives of the Spanish and French words for "Egyptian." There is the complication, however, that the Andalusian Gypsies are also often known as *flamencos,* or "Flemings." Were the Gypsies described as such because their colourful costumes were similar to those brought back by Spanish soldiers from Flanders?... Numerous interpretations of the word *flamenco* have been offered, and there is the strong possibility that it has nothing to do with Flanders at all. For instance, it might derive from the Arabic word for a "fugitive peasant" (*Felagmengu*).

—Michael Jacobs, *A Guide to Andalusia*

JACK HITT

⋆ ⋆ ⋆

One Pilgrim's Progress

A traveler confronts dogs, lightning,
and questions of sanity.

AFTER A MONTH OF WALKING THE ANCIENT ROAD TO SANTIAGO, Spain, a pilgrim loses his mind—not in the psychiatric sense, but like an obsolete appliance. Think of an eight-track tape player permanently misplaced in the cellar. It's useless and unnecessary, but should its function ever be needed again, you can always retrieve it. When I walk, I stare at the ground sliding beneath my feet, and I am speechless, lost in a hot pulsing haze. To look me in the eye, you'd see the milky cataracts of an aged ox strapped into his traces, lugging his burden.

I set out one late spring to retrace the medieval pilgrimage route that once bound Europe in a belt of traffic. The old network of roads converges into one just over the Pyrenees; today I am halfway across Spain on the 500-mile path that once accommodated millions and still carries a few thousand each year to Santiago, in that panhandle notched just above Portugal. Like many my age, I had effortlessly cast off the religion of my parents as if stepping out of a pair of old trousers. So I hit the road to Santiago because I had read of its tradition of welcoming those with feeble motives. A 12th-century document at one pilgrims' shelter says: "Its doors are open to all, well and ill, not only to

Catholics, but to pagans, Jews and heretics, the idler and the vagabond and, to put it shortly, the good and the wicked." I believe I can find myself in there somewhere.

On the road today, time is a long silence, and that is why I say a pilgrim begins to lose his mind. I just don't need it. I've spent entire afternoons slogging through a trench cut so deep into a wheat field that I am invisible to all except the birds. Central Spain is nothing but wheat fields, and wheat, it seems, finds me fetching. Mosquitoes inexplicably prefer some people. I've never had a problem with them because apparently I am spoken for by the plant kingdom. I am beloved by wheat. Their stalks bend toward me in the wind, anxious to propel their seed my way. They have mistaken me for rich topsoil (not so surprising after a month of pilgrimage). Wheat burrs assault me from all directions, hitting me in the face, once swiftly—whoa—plugging up a nostril. They gather into harvest decorations in my hair and burrow into the wrinkles of my filthy clothes. After a morning's walk, my legs are dense congregations of future generations of wheat.

When the road occasionally veers out of the wheat fields and overlaps with a highway, I enter a sphere all my own. The cars zoom by so fast, I am but a blur to them, as they are to me. I have left that dimension. My only acquaintances are poor farmers puttering on tractors or families piled onto old hay wagons drawn by mules. These people always greet me kindly. I am one of them.

or centuries there were miracles and apparitions to be seen at every turn of the road to Santiago: you could meet angels, beggars, kings, and status-seekers—the Plantagenet King Edward I on horseback, St. Francis of Assisi walking barefoot, and a certain Flemish wayfarer who is reputed to have carried a mermaid around with him, in a tub.

—Frederic V. Grunfeld,
*Wild Spain: A Traveler's and
Naturalist's Guide*

This morning, as I begin a seventeen-mile leg into the plains of Castile, an old man on a moped stops to talk. He is small and frail with a transparent face and a wheeze like a child's rattle. He smokes constantly as he speaks in the nearly indecipherable, all-vowel nosespeak of a rural man. "You must be careful up ahead," he advises.

"Careful?"

"There is much danger up ahead on the plains of Castile."

"Danger?"

"Yes, and great torments and evil."

In Spanish, the words ring medieval. *"Hay tormentas y mal tiempos."* Great, I am thinking. At last, some action. "What should I do?" I ask.

"You should just be ready. I don't know what pilgrims do. Perhaps you shouldn't walk."

"Are the plains always full of torments and suffering?"

"No, but when it comes, it's bad," says my bony mystic.

"How do you know this?" I ask.

He pauses, a bit sad. "I saw it on television."

I am marveling at this surreal answer, a charming mix of folklore and technology. In my mindless fog, it is a good hour before I open my pocket dictionary and learn that these words mean "rainstorm" and "bad weather." My shaman was quoting the television weatherguy. Every pilgrim claims a saint to serve as a guardian spirit. Saint Groucho of Marx, watch over me.

The only relief from the wheat field is a tiny village named Hornillos. It means "little stoves" and was founded in 1156 to provide my ancient predecessors with a cooked meal before walking into the vast emptiness of the Castilian plains. The stoves are long gone. There is no restaurant here. The only refuge is a tilted shed beside the church so infested with flies that I skip my daily siesta and walk on. Three widows, in elaborate black lace, sit at the end of town in the pose of eternal silence.

I nod my head to acknowledge them.

"Beware of wolves," volunteers one.

"Wolves?"

"On the plains, there are wolves," says another.

"Wolves?"

"Sharpen your stick," she says.

"Wolves?"

"May Santiago protect you," she says.

These words sound eulogistic.

The famous plains of Castile are misnamed. They should be called the plateaus. A few miles outside of Hornillos, the road zigzags up a fierce incline until arriving at a level lip and opens to an infinite vista of…wheat. Wheat and more wheat, as far as the eye can see. Dorothy's poppy fields on the outskirts of Oz hold nothing to this view. I have never seen this much of the planet in one take.

I had frequently been warned about the heat and emptiness of the plains. Not the slightest smudge of shade. Not even a shed. The occasional farmer comes up to plow, but not today. There is no one.

No matter how far I walk, the horizon unwinds like a scroll, laying out more wheat fields. The stalks are sickly thin and translucent up close; no more than eighteen inches high, struggling amid tough clods and rocks the size of fists. The larger rocks and boulders were plucked out centuries ago and gathered into unintended cairns. They are blanched an unnatural white and pitted with hollows by centuries of wind blasts and hot sun, like monuments of skulls.

Pilgrim diaries testify to the terror of the Castilian plains. In April 1670, an Italian pilgrim named Domenico Laffi left Bologna for Santiago. He saw many odd things along the way; on the plains of Castile, he saw a pilgrim attacked and eaten alive by a swarm of grasshoppers.

The narrow channel of dust that scores these wheat fields is so dry that the ground has cracked open in places. Why hadn't I noticed these before? Did these fissures yawn open a few moments ago? These are bad signs. My gaze goes downward, oxen-eyed and cautious.

Hours pass, and the wheat fields unroll. Big clouds bound in— Steven Spielberg props, cottony bales that hang so low I imagine that on tiptoe, I could finger their dark feathery bottoms. Some remnant of childhood superstition keeps my eyes on the ground as if that will keep them from breaking open and soaking me with rain. In the far distance, there's a sound like someone moaning.

About ten feet in front of me, a small brown bird wings its way out of the clouds and falls leadenly on the road in front of me.

Oh, come on.

I am jabbering aimlessly to myself. I sing every song and recite every poem I know. Movies that I have visually memorized, *Diner*, for example, play from beginning to end out here in the whistling expanse of the spacious Castilian Gigantoplex. A few weeks ago, the wind bore only the Doppler squeal of a phantom car. That was then; today it's an hallucinatory open house. I hear singing in the wind, four-part harmonies of Renaissance madrigals, shopping mall renditions of Christmas carols, all the Top 40 hits fried onto my synapses before I left (the opening mandolin riff of REM's "Losing My Religion" perversely floats up every ten minutes like a human rights violation). I hear arguments and complaints—my mother frets again about my quitting my job, a high-school bully apologizes for beating me up, an old girlfriend confesses she can't live without me. It's an auditory Rorschach out here.

The horizon never changes—a thin black line drawn between the brown wheat and darkening clouds ahead. From time to time, the fields betray a slight upward incline. But one mild hump merely leads to another, more wheat, more stones. In the middle of this new field, three dogs scour in the distance. I open my pocketknife and sharpen the point of my stick.

A pilgrim gets to know dogs pretty well. Dogs are everywhere in Spain. Each yard has a savage dog chained to a stake. Every village is overrun with skinny strays. They snake around the corners of buildings and nose up the alleys prowling for scraps. Tailless cats with slack bellies scramble in their wake.

Dogs generally keep their distance. They aren't particularly brave unless there's enough of them. A pilgrim learns to translate the idiom of a dog's bark as fluently as a parent comes to know the meaning of a child's cry.

Barking is a similar language. A healthy throated sound, deep in the bass register, is a statement of territory. A declarative sentence and nothing more. But there are other grammars. Skinny dogs, desperate from hunger, can let rip with a mean scraping sound. In the syntax of the wild, these are the irregular conjugations. Be very afraid.

As I approach their parallel, the dogs send up a few introductory barks. I have no fear because I read them perfectly: territorial claims, nothing more. Suddenly, all three break into a furious sprint, tearing at the air with snapping howls, straight for me.

I can see that they bear the marks of wild Spanish dogs. They all are plagued by mange. The largest one has a dead ear, permanently bent over. The small leader runs a little sidewise, crablike; his backside is rubbed raw, absolutely hairless in bleeding patches. These are seriously ugly dogs.

The three pull up and trot side by side, as one. I walk slowly but deliberately. They circle me, heading out in front on the road. They stop and I inch closer. The lead dog rips with a frightening bark, a fierce shredded blast. I read him clearly.

A strange fear overtakes me, and it's one I have never felt. Of course I'm scared of three dogs attacking me, alone, on this empty plateau. But that's not it. This is a new fear. I am scared because I know that I am prepared to kill them. I have my knife in my left hand and my stick in my right. My breathing is rapid. My pupils must be pinholes. We are locked in direct eye contact. My frontal lobes have shut down and handed off total control to that reptilian stub in the base of the brain. Nerve bundles that haven't been tickled since the Pleistocene epoch have taken over my main features. My mouth is pried open, and my teeth are bared. Sounds gurgle in the back of my throat. I am almost standing on the outside watching when it happens.

On the plains of Castile, I bark. I didn't know humans made a noise the way birds of prey caw, cats caterwaul or coyotes bay. But humans have their noise, and you can't really appreciate the human ululation signifying the will to kill until you've felt it pour out of your very own face. It is a ragged, oscillating sound (Tarzan isn't that far off). Strangely, it's rather high up the register—pubescent, even comical, in its bestial ineptness.

A force sweeps through me and I fly directly at my enemies. My knife is gripped underhanded, and my spear waggles in the air. And then I bark—again and again. It originates somewhere in a sleeping pocket of my solar plexus and screeches through my vocal cords with the force of a childhood vomit. My entire body convulses with explosions: "*La-lu-lalulaluaaaaaa.*" More or less.

The dogs jerk forward, but the force propelling me toward them won't let me flinch. As with any good bluff, you can't let up on your pose, no matter what. My face is squeezed into a Nordic mask of blood-red fury. I lunge and bark. The effect is a threat that roughly translates: I will slice open your bellies, smear your entrails in this dust and perform grand pliés in the viscera.

And without further linguistic exchange, they signal their comprehension of my remarks by bolting in full ignoble retreat, hiding amid wheat.

My hands are shaking. My pulse, which is usually high with all the work of walking, is racing. The succubae who have haunted me all day redescend, and a new, exacerbated spookiness consumes me. I am carrying on a delightfully stupid but vaguely reassuring conversation with myself when a grand blast of thunder rolls across the plains. The clouds are now in full costume dress, big black tumblers wheeling from

It was the first time I had been completely alone since I had started along the Strange Road to Santiago…. Up until that point, I had not been at all frightened; I felt that it would take a lot of imagination to make me fearful of any kind of horrible death. But no matter how long we have lived, when night falls it arouses the hidden fears that have been there in our souls since we were children….

The night was quite dark, and on the horizon I could see the faint lights of the city. I lay down on the ground and looked at the branches of the tree overhead. I began to hear strange sounds, sounds of all kinds. They were the sounds of the nocturnal animals, setting out on the hunt.

Something nearby made a sound. I jumped up immediately.

It was nothing.

—Paulo Coelho,
The Pilgrimage: A Contemporary Quest for Ancient Wisdom

left to right across the Castilian stage. They have dropped in altitude, now brushing my hair with static. A sweet metallic aroma
fills the air. I vacantly ponder its meaning.

Vast sheets of rain explode from the clouds as I frantically pull
out my poncho, logically located at the bottom of my pack. The
wet plastic sticks to my skin and the dripping cowl obstructs my
view. I want to see because I need to count. On the horizon, a
broad streak of light flares as if someone had flashed a spotlight. It's
sheet lightning, well known to be harmless. But I count the seconds—thousand one, thousand two, thousand three, thousand four,
thousand five, thousand six. A peal of thunder sounds. I remember
my father teaching me this trick when I was a little boy. Each second between the blast of light and the sound of thunder represents
a mile. This is part of the lore of storms we learn as children. I am
dredging up a good deal of that lore just now.

A jagged white line—*not* sheet lightning—impales the horizon.
Thousand one, thousand two, thou…

Not a good sign.

Another flash of light momentarily drains all the color from the
landscape. I see this one *hit* the ground—far up the road but inside
the field before me. What was that other bit of lore? Lightning
strikes the tallest object. My eyes sweep the panorama of endless
wheat fields—midget stalks stretching to two feet at best.

I am six foot one. Lore is surfacing unbidden: never stand beneath
a tree.

Lightning is just a gathering of static electricity.

Lightning doesn't come down to earth, but actually moves up…

A bolt explodes directly in front of me, maybe 50 yards away.
This is a network of bolts—a tick-tack-toe grid of light and heat.
Thunder bellows at once. Should I turn around and back away
from the storm? Can I outhike a storm? Should I curl in a little
ball and try to hide like a wild dog in the wheat? Should I stand
still?

I decide to run in a forward direction, and I choose to augment
this plan with a bit of heartfelt shrieking and babbling. Encum-
bered by a pack, this strategy is neither graceful nor effective. I

can't scare away lightning like dogs. This really is some kind of message. The dogs failed, so they wheeled out Zeus's old-standard never-fail legendary *deus ex machina*.

I can't believe that I am going to die out here, struck by lightning. Bolts are now blasting on both sides of me like bombs. I can see them clearly. I can smell them. In my mind, each spot is marked by charred wheat stalks and a modest puff of black smoke. I run for fifteen minutes. Run and scream, to be accurate. Run and scream and hoot and howl and hoo-wee, to be even more accurate.

I am surrounded by illusions. Lightning is exploding at my side. Voices scream in the wet wind. I hear pursuing footsteps. Up ahead, the horizon suddenly telescopes, drawing itself toward me. As it does, the earth cracks open at the edge, and a small black cross erupts from the muddy ground. Following behind it, a small stone pyramid forces the cross higher until it is clear and visible and lovely—an optical illusion that has probably comforted pilgrims for a millennium. Shortly, an entire church pushes its way up out of the earth and into view. Other buildings crowd around its side and rear up. A town in a valley.

Until very recently it has been understood that those who do undertake the pilgrimage to Santiago do so at very little cost. Rooms en route are given out free to pilgrims; simple but nourishing food is offered to them gratis as a gesture likely to win eventual Divine approval for the donor; and there is always a glass of cold water or a restorative vino tinto del país or even a simple pat on the back for a passing traveler, gestures that will doubtless be similarly looked upon kindly when the day of reckoning comes.

—Simon Winchester, "The Long, Sweet Road to Santiago de Compostela," *Smithsonian*

The pilgrim's path suddenly plunges into an alley of stone. I can hear the rumble of cattle and the cackle of fowl. Welcome to Hontanas. The rain gathers and sluices through this street, softening the manure into a sludge of slippery offal and freeing pent-up odors. I appreciate their reassuring aromatic complexity, like a glass of red wine. At the church, I run to its wall to try to get out of the downpour. An open doorway across the street reveals four old women playing cards.

"Pilgrim, would you like a sandwich?" one of them offers in Spanish.

"Yes, yes, please, please, yes."

"I will bring you one."

I call out a thank you from under the slight eaves of the church.

"You were caught in the rain," another says.

"Rain!" I blurt in my awkward Spanish. "Beautiful ladies. Rain! Dogs! Death! Birds! Hell! Fear!"—I am capable only of uttering nouns for the moment—"Rain! Yes, rain, but also"—I can't call forth the word for lightning storm—"How do you say in Spanish when light comes down from the sky?"

"*Tormentas?*" one of the women answers.

"*Tormentas!*" I cry. "Yes, yes, that is the word, isn't it?" A convulsive laughter seizes me. "*Tormentas, sí, sí, tormentas. Tormentas grandes. Muchísimas tormentas.*" I am laughing the laughter of idiots. I can't stop until I am tranquilized by the sight of the old woman carrying food. Half of Spain lies ahead. Another month on foot takes me through the tall meadows of Frómista, across the dead rivers of León, over the craggy hills of Ponferrada, up the alpine mountains of Galicia and then into the comfort of the valley of Santiago. The sandwich is huge—ham and a Spanish omelet on a baguette the size of my arm. I tear into it like a jackal.

Jack Hitt is a contributing editor at Harper's Magazine *and* Lingua Franca, *and writes regularly for* The New York Times Magazine. *A native of Charleston, South Carolina, he had just reached "the Dantean age of 35" when he decided to walk the 500 miles to Santiago. This story was adapted from his book* Off the Road: A Modern-Day Walk Down the Pilgrim's Route into Spain, *and first appeared in* The New York Times Magazine.

*

As I turned to go I noticed something moving in the far distance. I knew what it was: I had seen it in movies. It was the swimming headlights of a train refracted in the warm air and smoke, and it was slowly approaching.

I had no ticket and there was no one else in the station, so I put out my hand to stop it, and slowly it came into the station and drew to a halt. I was so happy I did not even realise that this was cheating. I smiled at the people in the carriage and sat down. It would take us about half an hour to get to Astorga; it would have taken me a day to walk it. I had placed myself in the company of rogue pilgrims of medieval times who surely must have cheated too.

—Colm Tóibín, *The Sign of the Cross: Travels in Catholic Europe*

TED WALKER

Life in Cuenca

*What can be more rich than the human drama
that unfolds daily in a small town?*

THE STREETS WERE QUIET AND THE AIR FELT STRANGELY COLD: so
cold indeed that I thought I'd have a *coñac* somewhere before turning in. An occasional car crossed the intersection. A couple of
Alsatian dogs were nosing a pile of rubbish. Behind balconies
French windows were being slammed tight shut, slatted blinds
were being lowered. There was a sense almost of siege, as in streets
of boarded-up shop windows near British football grounds hours
before the fans arrive. Something bad was on the way.

But the drab and unwontedly lifeless quarter was suddenly
made gorgeous and exuberant as, bursting from a dark alleyway,
sixteen young men in traditional Castilian dress appeared. Most
carried string instruments. They were the *Tuna San Julián* (a *tuna*
being a group of minstrels, usually students). Several times I had
enjoyed listening to them, the hours each side of midnight. But I'd
not seen them: only heard them, a street or two away; and assuming they were in ordinary 20th-century dress, I'd not bothered to
go down in search.

They formed a ring between two lines of parked cars. There
was a short discussion; the music began. Six mandolins in unison
announced the melody, which eight guitars then developed in har-

mony. At the centre of the ring, the tallest member of the *tuna* supplied the beat on a tambourine; outside the ring, the youngest
member twirled a flag and danced. After sixteen bars of instru-
mental introduction, all began to sing. The song was a traditional
May carol. A crowd gathered, as though out of thin air. Shutters
rattled up. Entire families in the apartment blocks came out onto
their balconies to listen and watch.

The musicians' costume was even more sumptuous than their
playing: shoes with silver buckles; black hose and knee breeches;
black and emerald striped doublets with frilly white collars; and
black velvet cloaks festooned with brightly-colored ribbons—lilac,
crimson, apple-green, sapphire,
white—hanging from ruched
rosettes at the shoulder. The
tambourinist wore white gloves.
The flag, attached to a shining
brass standard, was of royal blue
velvet edged with gold. After the
third refrain the song became
louder and more boisterous. The
tambourine player began leaping
high in the air, still keeping perfect time, beating not only
against his free hand but also
against wrist, elbow, shoulder,
thigh and knee. During one
enormous leap he managed to
strike both heels behind him.
The carol shifted to a minor key.
The flag-twirler joined the ring
and sang a verse solo in an un-
certain, immature tenor; a mandolin took over for a short, slow,
bridging passage; there was the briefest pause; then, with all voices
and instruments in unison, the final, surging chorus rang out.

Each side of the street was seven storeys high. Applause erupted,
sounding like thousands of pigeons suddenly released and taking

> *Half drunk, half in love,
> the* tunos—*minstrels
> who comprise each wandering
> group of* la tuna—*bring magic to
> the night, their songs and laughter
> reminding listeners of the
> ephemeral, of youth, and passion.*
> Tunos *are famous for their fleeting
> romances and can be found stand-
> ing beneath balconies of young
> women, crooning songs like
> "Clavelitos" ("I bring you the lit-
> tle carnations of my heart"). The
> colorful ribbons adorning their black
> capes proclaim the number of hearts
> a tuno has won as well as his se-
> niority in the group—or her senior-
> ity, for women have recently begun
> joining the ranks of* tunos *too.*
>
> —Cristina Del Sol, "*La Tuna*"

flight. There were repeated cries of *Bravo, señores.* The singers looked up, beaming; if they saw a pretty girl they waved and shouted compliments.

Each morning I went out for breakfast on the dot of eight, the mellow chimes of Mangana tower playing a tune tantalizingly reminiscent of *Oranges and Lemons* before striking the hour. The traffic policeman, having parked his moped, would be pulling on his white gauntlets ready for confronting the rush-hour from his island (about the size of a tea-tray) at the junction of three roads. Metal shutters would be clatteringly opened; the usual importuning Gipsy in his stubble and anorak would be lounging at the same street corner; familiar office workers would be picking up their paper at the *quiosco* where I got mine.

Having a routine confers a kind of honorary citizenship on the traveller who chooses to put down temporary roots. You know you belong somewhere as soon as you've remained long enough to have a haircut and buy a new cake of soap. You surprise yourself by being able to give simple directions to strangers; you acquire a pot plant for your balcony; you know where to get the best value in a sandwich and a glass of wine. There was a blind lottery ticket seller whose station was the doorway of a shoe shop. He knew me by my footfall, greeting me *"Hola, el Inglés,"* from twenty yards away. I was recognized by the clerks who cashed my traveller's cheques at the Banco de Bilbao, and by waiters setting out chairs and tables on the pavement. I liked that.

Breakfast for me of a weekday was simple and quick: usually a cup of white coffee (*café con leche*) and a couple of little plain cakes, *magdalenas.* Now and again I'd have some other item of *bollería* instead: a *suizo* (rather dry, not very interesting) or an *ocho,* a figure-of-eight flaky pastry. Sometimes I might have a *tostada,* not toast quite as we know it in England, but a square thick slice of bread lavished with margarine on both sides, fried on a hot-plate and eaten with a knife and fork. The *mermelada* served with it wasn't necessarily orange marmalade: more often than not it was peach, apricot or strawberry jam. At the counter in the *cafetería* I liked to watch the *churros* being prepared. Fluted strips of dough round as a finger and long as a hand would be extruded from a glass container into a vat of boiling oil beneath; when they were done, they were drained and piled and sprinkled with sugar. Wonderfully delicious and quite indigestible, crisp, hot and golden they looked. But *churros* were a Sunday treat, not for working days.

It was good, then, to walk in the park for twenty minutes before going back to my room. The Parque San Julián (named after the patron saint of Cuenca) was from the start a favorite place of mine: cool, leafy and delectable. In the middle of town, it was rectangular in shape, with

Early in the morning, crowds of children will be gathered around the churro *maker, buying hoops of the freshly fried treats to take home for the family breakfast—*churros *and chocolate.*

If there was a fiesta the night before, the churro *maker might sleep at the stand because he or she will have been there at the end of the party. At two or three o'clock in the morning it's a marvelous treat to have a small* churro *and a cup of thick chocolate, perhaps with a touch of anise or brandy.*

—Ann and Larry Walker,
A Season in Spain

plenty of benches beside each wide path of sandy gravel. In this part of Spain the climate, winter and summer, is too fierce for close-cropped lawns; instead there were formal rose-beds surrounded by dwarf box hedges, and avenues of tall, graceful trees—planes and acacias—whose crowns intermingled overhead. There was a pretty little bandstand at the centre, and drinking fountains, and at one end a children's play area with climbing frames and swings and such. Soon after eight o'clock every morning a municipal worker was at work with a fireman's brass-nozzled hose, sending a powerful jet of water a good 40 yards among the beds and along the paths, damping down the dust and giving the whole park a delightfully fresh, after-rain scent.

It was the hour when mothers took tots and toddlers to play school, nursery school, primary school. Is there any country in the world where children are so well cared for, so well dressed and groomed? They would be brought to the park for an early-morning session on the swings and slides, beautiful confections from some Impressionist painting when glimpsed momentarily half and half between shadow and dappled sunlight.

There was no school uniform as such (though uniforms still are commonly found elsewhere in Spain, in private schools), and each student I saw made the most of his or her individuality; but in their choice of clothes they conformed to some unwritten code of what was apt. This sense of appropriateness remained with them after school hours. Teenagers you saw early in the day walking in twos and threes through the park with file and textbook under their arms were indeed the same ones you saw during the evening *paseo*, but by then the girls had changed into well-tailored and modish skirts or trousers and light woolen sweaters, the boys into zipper jackets, fashionable casual shirts or summer-weight suits. However, something else—something in addition to their clothes—transformed young people of an evening. They would sit along a wall, chattering and ceaselessly nibbling sunflower seeds like a row of parrots, or foregather in groups of a dozen or so in the squares or in the *cafetería*, and it was not simply the gaiety of release that took over from the serious business of being in the classroom. Underlying the talk and laughter one detected a sense that the social evening hours were a conscious rehearsal for the adult world. The girls, most of them, wore a little discreet jewelry; they stood, sat, held a glass, with elegance and style; and the boys seemed quite without the usual gaucherie of adolescent lads. They didn't jostle you on the street; they were courteous and charming to each other and to their families and to strangers. Often you'd see a girl suddenly break away from her circle of friends and run to greet her parents walking towards her; without self-consciousness or embarrassment she would hug and kiss them and exchange a few words before catching up with her friends and linking arms with them again.

If by comparison with their British and American counterparts, young Spaniards sometimes seemed too good to be true, I felt that this was partly accounted for by the attitude Spanish parents adopt towards sons and daughters from infancy. Children are treated not as a race apart but as small people entitled from the very beginning of their lives to the same respect and consideration required from them. In Spain it's rare to see a father or mother cuffing a child or otherwise humiliating it. On the other hand, it is commonplace to see an entire family—babies in arms to great-grandparents—sitting together in bars. Each member of the family receives equal treatment when it comes to the ordering of drinks. The little ones—the *peques*—are not fobbed off with something they don't want, or sent off to play outside while the adults get on with their chat. If the six-year-old boy feels like it, he will make his way to the bar and ask for—and get—what he fancies. The baby's milk bottle, prepared at home, will stand to warm in a jug of hot water beside the coffee machine.

Language has a big part to play, too, in the Spanish child's early and easy assumption of dignity and good manners. When he learns to talk, he discovers that he must use the formal *usted* to his elders and betters outside the family; while *tú* and *vosotros* betoken affection and familiarity. When he has to be reprimanded, the loving *tú* is temporarily withdrawn from him, to be replaced by the frigid and distant *usted*. Early mornings in the park, I would observe how this was instilled into their tiny siblings during play by even the very youngest nursery school pupils.

Spaniards are among the best turned-out people in Europe: not only during leisure hours but also at work. The man hosing down the park wore a neatly pressed suit; building workers, clerks—even road menders and refuse collectors—dressed smartly. I found within a few days of my arrival in Cuenca that I was shamed by young and old alike into taking more care with my appearance. I checked often that my toe-caps were polished, that my collar and cuffs were clean. When I'd finished my stroll in the park and it was time to go to work, I stepped it out straighter and brisker to my desk. Living in Spain made you conscious of your deportment; also it reminded you of what good manners were really about: on a busy pavement, you stood aside not only for the old lady with her basket of vegetables but also for the three-foot-high *hidalgo* leading his sister to school.

I was often—and not always unwillingly—distracted from the typewriter by sounds from the street. Two or three times a week, about mid-morning, I would hear the pipes of Pan being played exquisitely. Their piercing, poignant notes mingled with the trills and warblings of caged canaries singing fit to bust from the moment the sun was up. I wondered who it was who had this charming hobby; but each time I heard the pipes I was just too late at my balcony to see the player performing. The only person I saw was an old fellow in a beret and a brown suit pushing a power-assisted bicycle. It was a haunting sound, ancient and pagan, from a time before Homer, performed in my imagination by some cloven-hoof satyr cantering up the Calle Ramón y Cajal, invisible to the human eye. But one morning, stuck in midsentence, I happened to be staring down from the balcony as the old man came pushing his bike along. I saw him lift one hand from the handlebars and seem to wipe his nose with the back of his hand. Of course! The pure notes rang out, and the mystery was solved.

I went down to take a closer look at him. He was a knife-grinder, his saddle supporting the grindstone. The pipes of Pan, I learned later, were the customary street-call of his trade all over Spain. He set the bike on its stand, and for fifteen minutes kept up his playing. Nobody brought him so much as a penknife to hone; but from the benign look on his face one might have concluded that he wouldn't have minded if the entire world had gone over to plastic cutlery.

> *Most Spanish towns faced with Cuenca's need to expand in the 18th century would have spread out along the surrounding countryside. But Cuenca, perched on the top of a hill, turned not to the earth but to the sky. Its improbable solution stands all along that part of the town that clings to the side of the hill and that faces the River Huécar: its hanging houses. The flat-fronted dwellings in the Barrio de San Martín, so starkly simple a child could draw them, rise seven or eight teetering stories above a ravine and the River Huécar to the east. It is as if the town were trying to outgrow itself, reaching ever higher in an effort to compensate for the ravine below.*
>
> —Isabel Soto, "Hanging Houses of Cuenca," *The New York Times*

It was time, then, to do my 45 minutes' shopping for lunch. Now, three quarters of an hour may seem like a very long while to pick up one or two items for a modest midday snack; but it must be remembered that in Spain a visit to a food store is no mere matter of entering, choosing, paying and exiting as quickly as possible. No: it is a ritual, an event of the daily social round which cannot be hurried; and this holds true for the modern *supermercado* almost as much as for the traditional grocer's shop. There's something distinctly oriental about the animated, parish-pump exchange of news and views which takes place in every *alimentación*; a throwback, maybe, to many centuries of Moorish occupation. *Tienda* means both "shop" and "tent" in Spanish; when you pass through the tinkling bead curtain it's not difficult to fancy yourself under canvas in some long ago *souk* rather than at the reinforced concrete centre of a 20th-century town.

The other name for a grocer's is *ultramarinos,* a word I like for being so crammed with hints of the exotic. In my local *ultramarinos* I often witnessed an unwitting comic playlet for all the world like an extemporized vignette demonstrating some small aspect of the human condition. To be a minor member of the cast could be stimulating as well as entertaining.

For example, I went in one day, just before closing-time, to find the shop unusually quiet: only the shopkeeper, his wife, their daughter, and one customer—a small boy—apart from myself. The proprietor's face was glowering, for the small boy had just brought in a can of sardines, its lid jaggedly open, which his mother reckoned was off. "Impossible," said

Cuenca

the boss, and he took a large carving-knife, prodded up a bit of fish, tasted it, chewed it, swallowed and grimaced. "I told you not to sell that tin," he bawled at his wife. "Didn't I say it was blown?" At this he looked up and saw me, and his face lit up with pleasure because he hadn't been expecting to make any more sales. "I just want a litre of *tinto*," I said. "Nothing special. Table wine, *corriente*." He told his daughter to go and get a bottle from the crate outside on the pavement and his wife to get rid of the stinking fish. As soon as they had gone out of the shop, he reached up for an un-blown tin of sardines. While his back was turned the boy snaffled a handful of sunflower seeds from an open sack. From where I stood, I could see the daughter of the house trying to get at the wine. She had just lifted a full crate of Mahou beer from the stack by the door and a litre of Tinto Especial from the crate beneath, when the small boy, not waiting to find out whether I would be-tray him, ran out with his stolen seeds and his good tin of sardines. This startled the girl, causing her to drop the wine. Wicked, spiky shards of glass glistened on the pavement. Her father shouted at her for being clumsy. "What do you expect of a woman only eight years old?" yelled her mother, giving me a look that demanded concurrence. "Oh dear," I said, "what a shame."

The girl brought in another bottle, holding it tightly in both hands; and straightway she went back outside to clear up the mess. Her father wrapped up my purchase in a page of *El País* and took my money, sighing. When I left, I saw that the girl was in tears; and without her father seeing, I gave her five *duros* to cheer her up. So: the shopkeeper had won the chance to say "I told you so" to his wife and an extra customer before closing-time, but had lost the profit on a litre of wine; his wife had been able to enlist the moral support of a customer and a foreigner at that, but had had to suf-fer discomfiture over selling the blown tin; his daughter had gained 25 pesetas but had had to endure a harsh reprimand; the boy had profited by a ten-minutes nibbling of sunflower seeds but had in future to keep a wary eye open for a sharp-eyed witness who might report him; and I had something to smile about for the price of a couple of glasses of wine.

✳

In Spain, every day is two days. Twice you get up, twice wash and dress to begin life anew in the cool. If you're used to eight hours sleep, you learn to take them in two unequal periods: five and a half at night and two and a half in the afternoon. If I took my siesta in my room instead of by the river, I darkened it first with shutters and blinds, making no bones about stretching out until the sun stopped raging. Four months of the year, the sun is the enemy in Spain. Indoors, you're grateful for small windows; outdoors, for high walls so there's always shade on the side of the street where you walk. The sun dictates. When it's strongest, you get out of its way; you give it best, the way longshore people give the sea best. It won't let you work or play effectively, so you have no option but to snooze the heat through.

People from northern countries find it hard to get used to this most practical ritual, feeling perhaps a puritanical (or maybe su-perstitious) guilt about losing some daylight time forever from their lives. "Eschew meridional sleep," wrote sententious Francis Bacon several centuries ago. The English in particular have con-served, since the days of the Raj, their deep-rooted suspicion and contempt for the siesta. Noel Coward's song precisely sums them up. They think it a shame and a waste; and so the mad dogs really do mooch about gloomily, sweltering in near-deserted Spanish town centres throughout the afternoon and grumbling because the shops and the public monuments are shut. At night they go to bed at a "sensible" time like eleven o'clock, thus missing some of the best things Spain has to offer. Once back home, they congratulate themselves on their own country's efficient and common-sensical routines, talk piously about Spanish children being kept up late and even maintain, with the wonderful logic of the saloon bar, that it's small wonder Spaniards have to take a nap in the afternoon, given that they're up till all hours at night.

Under my acacia, with a towel and a blanket to protect against the horse flies, I slept within earshot of the ceaseless rushings and turnings of the Júcar. On the opposite bank was a stand of black poplars, *chopos,* favorite shade and plantation trees hereabouts. If there was the slightest breeze I would hear their lacquered leaves rustling deliciously when I awoke. Once, I was awakened by the tonk-tonk-tonking of goat-bells when a flock browsed slowly past, lingering among the dabbled rocks before splashing on towards the upriver water-meadows. Their herdsman, eating an onion the way you'd eat an apple, didn't see me as he passed by. I think he had been having his siesta too, because he yawned wide and made a crucifixion of himself before quickening his pace and whistling up his dog.

Ted Walker is a British writer, editor, radio and television dramatist, and translator who is best known for numerous books of poetry, including Those Other Growths *and* The Lion's Cavalcade. *He is also the author of* You've Never Heard Me Sing *(a collection of his stories published in* The New Yorker *and other magazines), and* In Spain, *from which this excerpt was drawn.*

✳

From my first visit on, simply being in Spain has always occasioned in me a kind of joy, a physical tingle, which comes from a whole crop of elements: its light, its landscape, its language, and most of all its human rhythm, a manner of being that graces the place. It comes, however, not from any such abstract awareness but from intense particularities: bare village cafés loud with argument and dominoes, or else sleepy and empty except for flies; sudden memorable conversations with strangers; the way Spaniards have of imposing human time, so that meals and meetings last as long as they need to. There is a durability about the Spanish people, an acceptance of fate that, paradoxically, gives them a keen sense of the present, a gleeful spontaneity. Their own eccentricities make them tolerant of the oddness of others, which helped them to survive the descent of the tourist hordes. Spain has a sparse, bare, uncluttered look, from its empty landscapes to its stark interiors. Time spent in the village always serves to unencumber me, to a point where the days seem wondrously long, gifts of time, where the weather simplifies existence to a vocabulary of elemental acts, like drawing water or making fire, where a visit to the village store is the only necessity.

—Alastair Reid, *Whereabouts: Notes on Being a Foreigner*

JOEL SIMON

* * *

Yesterday's Paper

A chance encounter on a train interrupts
a quest for Granada.

REBOUNDING OFF THREE WEEKS OF DELICIOUS DECADENCE IN THE
Balearic Islands, I was ready for culture, history, and some serious
tourism. I was anxious to leave the port town of Valencia and was
bound for Granada, home to the Alhambra, the Gypsies of
Sacromonte, and more. Waiting at the station was my ticket west:
a second-class train, green and grimy from years on the rails. I carefully examined the long row of cars and found a second-class com-
partment bearing the stenciled sign: Granada. Near the car's belly,
fossilized paint emerged through an archaeology of oil, in turn
coated by a recent layer of dust. Someone had run an articulate finger along the surface, inscribing the word "*polvo.*" I looked it up in
my Spanish/English dictionary: dust.

I hoisted my backpack and climbed aboard. I was early, but others had come earlier; most seats were occupied. Walking down the
narrow aisle, repeatedly excusing myself, my elbows, my pack, I
noticed an empty seat, occupied by only a disheveled spread of an
old newspaper. It looked as though it was covering something on
the seat unbecoming to even a second-class train. My imagination
took a few ungainly detours.

In the adjoining seat sat a dignified elderly Spanish gentleman. His brown suit was old, but neat. His vest was buttoned snugly up against his paunch. He looked up at me through black-rimmed eyeglasses as thick as vintage headlamps on a Model T. His magnified eyes looked three times their actual size, flatly filling their frames, appearing unnaturally closer to me than the rest of his face. Beneath a trim gray mustache his smile was warm.

"Is this seat available?" I asked.

"Certainly," he replied.

"Are these yours?" I asked, extending an open palm to the papers. Slowly following my hand with his gaze, and with an air of casual indifference, he raised his shoulders slightly, then his eyebrows slightly more.

"No, these were here before me, perhaps long before me," he mused. His mustache elevated, pulled by the hospitality of another smile.

I moved the newspapers onto the floor, where they looked comfortably at home with their counterparts. The seat was clean—well, at least clean enough. I slid my pack snugly into the overhead rack, and sat down.

I asked the gentleman where he was from.

"My name is Ernesto. I am from Granada, but I have family here in Valencia. I travel often between the two cities."

Encouraged by a firsthand source of information about Granada, I began chatting with him as the engine, like an old dog on a leash, pulled us slowly out of the station.

The scenery en route to Granada was dramatic: expansive vistas cut by dry valleys, terraced vineyards, and bluffs. Small towns, dressed in white and capped with red tiles, hung on hillsides, on the edges of cliffs, and nestled in the valleys. The train gently rocked from side to side as it rolled on.

During a lull in the conversation, I became aware that my feet were rocking, in fact, sliding on the newspapers. I bent down to move them underneath the seat. My shoe half covered a front page photo of medieval soldiers on horseback, the smoke of war behind them. Intrigued, I picked up the paper and began to read the caption. Ernesto also took interest, turning his head and bending slightly to bring the page within focus.

"What is this about?" I asked him.

He examined the paper carefully, scrutinizing the print. I watched his magnified eyes move slowly from left to right, in unison with the rhythms of the bouncing train.

"Ah! Alcoy," he said with recognition. "A fiesta to commemorate the war between the Christians and the Moors. I have heard of this. All this week, a grand fiesta."

"Where is Alcoy?" I asked.

"Hmm," he took a moment to think over the question, looking carefully at the precipitous scenery outside the window. "Next stop, I think."

"Next stop?" I echoed.

"Yes, next stop."

"How soon is that do you think?" Before he could respond, the conductor entered our car calling, "Xativa, Alcoy, Ontivent, all out for Xativa, Albaida, Cocentaina, and Alcoy."

I admit there was a moment of hesitation. Granada was in my mind, in my plans, and was printed on my ticket. But just ahead Alcoy was beckoning, a Moorish maiden behind a veil, a prize hidden in a box of Cracker Jack, an unsolicited invitation to a game of chance. Alcoy was on the front page before me. I looked again at the photo held between Ernesto's hands. I didn't have to ask.

"Go," he said simply, as much with his oversized eyes as his soft voice. "I have always wanted to see this myself. You will like it."

As the train slowed, my heart quickened. I stood up, shouldered my pack, and thanked Ernesto, gently shaking his hand. As I turned to go he said, "Here, take these." He gave me the newspapers and a final lingering glance. I stepped off the car, into the unexpected.

Although several people boarded the train at this stop, I was the sole passenger to get off. The train started up again, leaving me alone at the small station beside the empty tracks. Except for the diminishing clackety-clack of the train, all was quiet. Alcoy was nowhere in sight. I poked my head into the station's office. A man in a dark blue uniform was sleeping on a worn wooden chair in the corner, his head slumped comfortably to one side, living out his dreams. Another was talking on the phone. In front of the station, a bruised but polished black-and-yellow taxi was parked by the curb. Leaning against the car, the driver conversed with two men, his hands more audible than his words.

The train runs along the banks of the Henares, close to Guadalajara now. Towards the end it goes fast, almost as if it were in a hurry.

Just before it gets to Guadalajara, the passengers collect their bundles and crowd onto the platforms and into the corridors. The traveler is the last to get off: what he is going to do can be done just as well a quarter of an hour later as sooner. Or he doesn't have to do it at all; nothing will happen.

—Camilo José Cela, *Journey to the Alcarria: Travels through the Spanish Countryside (1948)*

"Excuse me, is Alcoy around here?" I asked. They all smiled, and the driver pointed to the southern hills.

"Of course, just up that road." I saw nothing but barren hills.

"How far?" I asked.

"About 50 kilometers," he replied. "Need a ride? I must go that way anyway."

I needed more than that. "I'm coming to see the fiesta," I said and showed him the front page of the newspaper.

The man looked at the photograph, and then said to his friends, "Look, this is my cousin, here, wearing the turban, on the horse. He is always the leader of the Moors."

"*Bueno,*" I replied. "Take me to your leader!"

The road was stunning, figuratively and literally; a narrow cliff-hanging, twisting, hair-pinned mountain track finally crossing a high stone bridge and ending on the small plateau supporting the town. Here was Alcoy, majestically perched, overlooking deep gorges etched through the millennia by the Barchell, Molinar, and Serpis Rivers. Here was Alcoy, originally a medieval walled fortress, overlooking time itself.

As with many small Spanish towns, the annual festival is the municipal highlight of the year, a temporal exclamation point on the social calendar. Extended families converge, distant relatives arrive, close relatives arrive; grandparents, uncles, cousins, newborn nephews and nieces, and families and friends are reunited. Houses, hotels, and hearts are full; sleepy villages awake with vigor. The annual festival in Alcoy, reenacting fierce 13th-century wars between Christians and Moors, is to live for and to die for. Many did die so others could live during the final battle of 1276, when Al-Azraq once again besieged the citadel after 32 years of liberation. The staunchly resistent citizens of Alcoy—with the assistance of St. George, they say—overcame the invaders, and have celebrated ever since.

In the most traditional commemoration of its kind, black-faced Moorish warriors on horseback, cloaked in embroidered black capes, shoes with upturned six-inch points, and feathered turbans, storm through the cobbled lanes, surrounding a fabricated cardboard castle in the town square. Brandishing scimitars and yelping wildly, they "capture" the fortress. The next day, in march the heroic Christians, horses, and soldiers resplendent in shiny breastplates, velvet tunics, and unbridled enthusiasm. With flashing broadswords and muskets firing clouds of smoke, they emerge victorious from battle, sending the vanquished infidels fleeing from the square. At least until next year. During these days (and nights) Alcoy never sleeps. Dancing and drinking continue well past dawn.

I left Alcoy exhausted, exhilarated, elated at having coincided with such enthusiastic celebration. Eventually, I did reach Granada. Sitting amid the quiet Moorish splendor of the Alhambra, its verdant gardens, the murmur of tranquil fountains, and delicately enscripted walls silently extolling the Koran, I also now heard the echoes of war. I had left Alcoy, but it had not left me.

I sometimes think of Alcoy: the thundering muskets, rampaging warriors with their flamboyant regalia and ornamented steeds, the energetic crowd, and the concluding fireworks shimmering gloriously over the town square. But these recollections always lead me back to Ernesto, with his oversized eyes, and his understated encouragement to look closely and take the unknown road.

Joel Simon's photo assignments have taken him to all seven continents, including the North Pole, the Antarctic, and 95 countries in between. When

not traveling, he's at home in Menlo Park, California, with his wife, Kim,
his cat, Ichiban, and an itinerant possum named Rover. Having learned from
the Spanish how to schedule a day (that "day" actually means "night"), his
light can be seen burning until well past midnight.

★

Qué bonito es no hacer nada, y luego descansar.
How beautiful it is to do nothing, and then rest afterward.

—Spanish proverb

BARBARA KINGSOLVER

Where the Map Stopped

Even Columbus found it hard to leave La Gomera, a Canary Island
where the language is whistled and the weather affected
by camel racing in the Sahara.

THE CANARY ISLANDS WEREN'T NAMED FOR BIRDS, BUT FOR DOGS.
Pliny the Elder wrote of "Canaria, so called from the multitude of
dogs [canes] of great size." In Pliny's day this crooked archipelago,
flung west from the coast of Morocco, was the most westerly place
imaginable; the map of the world ended here. For fourteen centuries navigators used that map to
stop in and visit: Arabs, Portuguese, and eventually the Spanish,
and still it remained Meridian
Zero, the jumping-off place.
When Columbus gathered the
force to head west and enlarge
the map, it was from La Gomera,
in the Canaries, that he sailed.

The other six islands have air-
ports now; Tenerife and Gran
Canaria are reasonable tourist
destinations for Europeans in a
hurry. But the traveler who
wishes to approach or escape La

*Gomera and the other six
Canary Islands (Islas
Canarias)—Tenerife, Palma,
Hierro, Grand Canary (Gran
Canaria), Fuerteventura, and
Lanzarote—make up two Spanish
provinces that lie in the Atlantic
Ocean well southwest of Spain.
They are so far south in fact, just
off the coast of Africa, that few
maps of Spain contain a scale rep-
resentation of their position in rela-
tion to the mainland. (See detail
map on page xviii.)*

—LMc

51

Gomera takes the sea road, as Columbus did. I am such a traveler, taking the ferry in no particular hurry on a bright Saturday. I've been told dolphins like to gambol in the waves in these waters, and that sighting them brings good luck. The sun on the pointed waves is hard as chipped flint but I stare anyway, waiting for a revelation.

The ferry leaves from Tenerife, whose southern coast is a bleached, unimaginative skyline of tourist hotels. For reasons difficult to fathom, the brown hills dropping away behind the port display giant white letters spelling out "HOLLYWOOD." An hour and a half ahead of us lies the tiny island of La Gomera, where the hills don't speak English yet.

Among urban Canarians La Gomera has a reputation for backwardness, and Gomerans are sometimes likened to the people known as Guanches—the tall, blue-eyed, goat-herding aboriginals whom the Spaniards found and extinguished here in the 15th century. Throughout the Canaries the Guanches herded goats, made crude, appealing pottery and followed the life style known as neolithic, living out their days without the benefit of metal. They were primarily farmers, not fishers; anthropologists insist these people had no boats. On La Gomera they used a language that wasn't spoken but *whistled,* to span the distances across steep gorges. I've been told that this language, called *silbo,* still persists in some corners of La Gomera, as do pottery making and farming with the muscle of human and ox. If I see dolphins in the channel, I'll believe the rest of the story.

The blue cliffs of La Gomera seem close enough to Tenerife to reach by means of a strong backstroke. It's hard to imagine living on islands this small, in plain view of other land, and never being stirred to go to sea. Suddenly the dolphins appear, slick and dark, rolling like finned inner tubes in the Atlantic.

San Sebastián de la Gomera is the port from which Columbus set sail for the New World. Fishing boats sit like sleeping gulls in the harbor, rolling in the ferry's wake. A store in port sells t-shirts with the ambiguous message: *"Aqui Partió Colón"*—"Columbus Departed from Here." So did everyone else, apparently. San Sebastián's narrow streets are empty save for the long shadows of fig trees and a few morning shoppers. We drive steeply uphill to the *parador* overlooking the harbor.

Our balcony overlooks the tops of palms and tamarinds leaning perilously over the edge of the cliff, and far below, the harbor. From a rocking chair on the balcony I watch the ferry that brought me here, now chugging back toward the land of white high-rises. The day is bright white and blue. The quiet rattle of wind in the palm fronds invites napping.

In my sleep I hear a conversation of birds. I wake up and still hear it: the birds in the garden are asking each other questions. I look down through the trees. A gardener with bristling white hair thrusts a finger into his mouth and makes a warbling, musical whistle. In a minute, an answer comes back. The *silbo*.

I walk down to investigate. The gardens are as deep and edible as Eden: guavas, figs, avocados, a banana tree bent with its burden of fruit. Another tree bears what looks like a watermelon-sized avocado. I find the gardener I saw from the balcony and ask him about the giant avocado, not so much for information as to nurture my fantasy that he will answer me in *silbo*. He explains (in Spanish, disappointingly) that the tree comes from Cuba, where they use the impressive fruit as a musical instrument. I ask him to tell me its name in *silbo*. His mouth turns down in a squelched smile, and he stands long enough for me to hear dragonflies clicking in the palm trees over our heads. Finally he says, "She doesn't have a name in *silbo*. She's not from here." He walks off toward the guava trees. A parrot in a wrought-iron cage behind me mutters Spanish words in a monotone; I whistle at him but he, too, holds me in his beady glare and clams up.

For ages, gossip and messages have been transmitted across the ravines by the language of El Silbo *(the whistle). This is a real language of regulated tones and rhythms, representing words, whistled with or without the aid of fingers in the mouth, at great volume. Only a small minority of Gomerans keep the language alive. Many younger people may understand it, but they cannot converse in* silbo.

—Ken Bernstein and Paul Murphy, *Berlitz: Discover Spain*

At breakfast there are rosebuds on the tables and a sideboard laden with fresh bread and jars of a sweet something called "*miel de palma*"—palm honey. I'm suspicious. It takes both bees and flowers to make honey, and a palm has nothing that would interest a bee. I mention this to the cook who concedes that it's not honey, but syrup, boiled down from the sap of palms just the way New Englanders make syrup from maple sap. I'm still suspicious: palm trees are something of a botanical oddity, in some ways more closely related to grass than to a maple tree and just about as difficult to tap in the ordinary way. To get the sap, you'd have to decapitate a mature tree. The cook allows that it's true, in the old days *miel de palma* was a delicacy fatal to the trees. North Africans developed a gentler palm-tapping technique and introduced it to La Gomera in this century. He says I should go see the palm groves.

My companion and I are reluctant to leave this elegant paradise, as Columbus surely was—Gomerans maintain that he delayed his voyage for months, having grown comfortable in the arms of the widow of the first Count of La Gomera, Beatriz de Bobadilla. But there are worlds to be discovered. We drive up into the highlands of white-washed villages, vineyards, and deep-cut valleys that ring with the music of wild canaries (ancestors of their yellower, domestic cousins). The whole island is a deeply eroded volcanic rock, just eleven miles across and flat-topped, with six major gorges radiating from the center like the spokes of a wheel. Farms and villages lie within the gorges, and the road does not go anywhere as the crow flies. Often we round a corner to face a stunning view of cliffs and sea and, in the background, the neighboring island of Tenerife. From here it shows off the pointed silhouette of its great volcano, Pico de Teide, snow-clad from November to April, the highest mountain on soil claimed by Spain.

The rugged farm land brings to mind my grandfather's tales of farming the hills of Kentucky: planting potatoes in plots so steep, he said, you could lop off the ends of the rows and let the potatoes roll into a basket. Growing here are mostly grapevines on narrow, stone-banked terraces that rise one after another in steep green stairways from coastline to clouds. Hawks wheel in the air currents rising from the gorges. Birds of prey are a sign of a healthy ecosystem, a good omen for La Gomera, as surely as the dolphins are. For the moment, this island supports a small population, low-intensity agriculture and a relatively low tide of tourism.

At the bottom of the gorge sits the Hotel Tecina, out of sight and unimaginable from here: a microcosm of hibiscus and swim-up bars, tennis lessons, a chrome-and-glass elevator down to the beach. This and the *parador*, the island's two principal hotels, have as much in common as Don Quixote and Madonna. The valley of the Hotel Tecina is an up-and-coming tourist area; in its interest, there is talk of finally carving an airport into La Gomera. The day it happens will be bad luck for the hawks.

The island's green heart is the Garajonay National Park, a central plateau of ancient laurel forest. On an otherwise dry island, the lush vegetation here drinks from a mantle of perpetual fog. At some point between the dinosaur days and the dawn of humankind, forests like this covered the whole Mediterranean basin; now they have receded to a few green dots on the map in the Madeira and Canary islands. An ecologist friend of mine who studies the laurel forest has warned me to watch out for sleek, black rats in the treetops. At certain seasons the trees accumulate in their leaves a powerful toxin the rats crave, against their own and the trees' best interests. The local park ranger confirms this—his advice is to watch for gnawed twigs in the path, then look up to spot the little drug addicts. (The colorful Spanish word for drug addiction is *toxicomania*.) Eventually, he says, the rats get so drunk they fall and lie trembling on their backs.

We hike into the forest, which seems enchanted. The laurels are old twisted things with moss beards on their trunks and ferns at their feet. Green sunlight falls in pools on the forest floor. I feel drugged myself. I watch the path closely, where I see tiny orchids and fallen leaves but no toxicomaniac rats.

When we break out of the cloud layer we're in treeless highlands, on Alto de Garajonay. The peak is named for the legendary lovers Gara and Jonay, Guanche equivalents of Romeo and Juliet, who supposedly killed themselves on this mountain top. The wind whistles over the peak's stone lid, and in the brightness we can see the islands of Hierro and La Palma to the west, Tenerife nearby and dominant to the east, and behind it, hazily, Gran Canaria; beyond that lies a long bank of clouds signifying the coast of West Africa. We are that close. The easternmost Canary Island is only 65 miles from the Saharan sands of mainland Africa. Canary Islanders are citizens of Spain, but geography asserts itself from time to time, as a reminder that this land will always be Africa's: the trade winds get interrupted by strong gusts from the east that bring hot dust and sometimes even torpid, wind-buffeted locusts. Canarians call this dismal weather the Kalima. They like to suggest that its meteorological cause is camel racing in the Sahara.

Today, above the clouds, the air is as clear as glass. We descend from the peak and drive west to a clearing in the forest called La Laguna Grande. In a country restaurant we're served watercress soup and the country staple, "wrinkled potatoes," served with a spicy cilantro sauce. The soup is thickened with *gofio*, the ubiquitous, strong-tasting roasted flour that Canarian housewives buy in ten-kilo bags. The local wine has personality. So does the waiter. I tell him we've heard rumors of a village where they make pottery the way the Guanches did. "Go to Chipude," he says. "That's not where they make it. The town where they make it doesn't have a name, but you can see it from Chipude."

We follow his advice, and at Chipude they wave us down the road to a place marked on few maps, but whose residents insist *does* have a name: El Cercado. I spot a group of white-aproned women sitting in an open doorway, surrounded by red clay vessels. One woman wears a beaten straw hat and holds a sphere of clay against herself, carving it with a knife. She is not making coils or, technically speaking, building the pot; she is sculpting it, Guanche fashion. When she tilts up her straw hat, her gold earring glints, and I see that her eyes are Guanche blue. I ask her where the clay comes from, and she points with her knife, "that *barranco*"—the gorge at the end of the village. Another woman paints a dried pot with reddish clay slip; mud from that other *barranco*, she points. After it dries again, she rubs its surface smooth with a beach rock. Finally, an old woman with the demeanor of a laurel tree polishes the finished pot to the deep, shiny luster of cherry wood. Her polishing stick is the worn-down plastic handle of a toothbrush. "What did the Guanches use?" I ask, and she gives me a silent smile like the gardener's and the parrot's.

The youngest of the women, a teenager named Yaiza, carries a load of finished pots to the kiln. We walk together through the village, past two girls sitting on the roadside stringing red chilies, down a precarious goat path into the grassy gorge. The kiln is a mud hut with a tin roof and a fire inside. Yaiza adjusts pots on the scorching tin roof, explaining that each one must spend half a day there upside down, half a day right side up, and then it's ready to go into the fire, where it stays another day. If the weather is right, it comes out without breaking. After this amount of art and labor, each pot sells for about US$13. I tell Yaiza she could charge ten times that much. She laughs. I ask her if she has ever left La Gomera, and she laughs again, as if the idea were ludicrous. I ask her if a lot of people know how to make this pottery, and she replies, "Oh sure. Fourteen or fifteen." All belong to two or three families, all in this village. We return to the pottery house, and I buy a pair of clay bowls. I pack them into my car with care, feeling that they belong on an endangered species list.

We leave the forest for the dry, windy side of the island, a terrain with the feeling of North Africa. Date palms wave like bouquets of feathers. These are the trees tapped for *miel de palma*, and I can see that it doesn't kill the tree but it doesn't do it any good, either. The leaves that spring up after tapping are dwarfed and out of kilter. In the gorge below we look down on groves of palms with bad haircuts.

The Playa de la Alojera, at the base of the gorge, is a deserted beach on the island's western margin. If this is not the end of the map, you can surely see it from here. The shoreline is windy, rocky and wild. In tide pools, fish and crabs scuttle in their claustrophobic soup, waiting to be rescued by the next high tide. On the black sand beach I find shells so beautiful I pocket them with the feeling I've stolen something, but there are no witnesses. In this village of maybe two dozen white houses and half a dozen streets, nothing moves, not even a cat, and I feel spooked. We creep tentatively into one of the empty houses and sit on its terrace to watch the sun go huge and round, then drown itself, leaving a mournful red streak on the face of the sea.

We aren't alone, it turns out; back at our car, a brightly dressed pair of German hippies ask for a ride to the nearest food. They've rented an apartment here, from a proprietor who promised peace and quiet but neglected to say how much peace and quiet. These two seem unfazed, and it occurs to me that people pay fortunes to find this much emptiness. At length we come to a village with lights burning in the windows, where we leave the Germans, and make our slow way back through the cloud forest. Winding into the fog, it's impossible to keep the word "ghost" out of mind: long fingers of mist reach down to touch the windshield, looking exactly like special effects.

In the morning, the air is changed. The garden of the *parador* is quiet, and the sky is stifled with pale haze: they're racing camels in the Sahara.

The Kalima deepens its hold as we board the ferry and head back toward an invisible destination. The white-block hotels of southern Tenerife and even the giant cone of Pico de Teide are mirages in white. As we leave the port of San Sebastián the haze closes down behind us, suspending our ship on a blank sea between lost worlds. If there are dolphins here now, they are only someone's dream of good luck.

Barbara Kingsolver lived in the Canaries while researching a novel. Her books include The Bean Trees, Animal Dreams, Pigs in Heaven, *and* Another America. *She grew up in eastern Kentucky and now lives in Tucson, Arizona, with her husband and daughter.*

*

Driving into the forest of the Parque Nacional de Garajonay, the cloud cover became thicker, the road more winding, until I became slightly disoriented: no sun, no sound, no view further than six metres (twenty feet) ahead, below or above. The cloud layer that rests almost permanently on the shoulders of Gomera streams downwards through the trees, catching and blowing free like fleece on bushes. Again I was completely lost, this time for more than an hour, and was eventually relieved to see an ordinary black chicken cross the rutted track.

—Frederic V. Grunfeld, *Wild Spain: A Traveler's and Naturalist's Guide*

COLM TÓIBÍN

✦ ✦ ✦

The Legacy of War

The Spanish Civil War, often romanticized by outsiders,
seems to be something most Catalans
would rather forget.

IN THE ENGLISH-SPEAKING WORLD THE SPANISH CIVIL WAR HAS developed certain connotations. Books about it in English have titles like *The Last Great Cause, A Poet's War, A Writer in Arms, Volunteer in Spain.* It is still much talked about on the Left. It is seen as a time when writers and intellectuals believed in a cause enough to go and fight for it, or at least visit the ruined villages and cities and send home reports and poems. Hemingway, Orwell, Auden, Spender and MacNeice were all inspired by the conflict.

MacNeice wrote that the anti-aircraft defense in Barcelona was "beautiful both to see and hear—balls of cottonwool floating high in the blue day, or white flashes at night. The searchlights also are beautiful, and the red tracer bullets floating in chains gently, almost ineptly, like decorations at a fair." Auden wrote a poem called "Spain" in which he talked about "the necessary murder." (Orwell replied: "Personally, I would not speak lightly of murder. To me, murder is something to be avoided." Orwell, unlike Auden, had been to the Front.) In the English-speaking world the Spanish Civil War is like a folk-tale in which youth and courage and conviction and imagination are crushed by a dark, cruel, evil force.

"The police dissected/The tongues of peasants/To cut out the words/The poet had made pleasant," wrote Stephen Spender.

Among the Catalans it is different. In Barcelona, no one talks about the war: it is not romantic or heroic; it is a trauma that everybody went through, everybody fears, and nobody wants to go through again. In Barcelona, most people will tell you that it was never discussed at home, or even mentioned; most people who live in the city have no interest in the war, or their interest is so bound up with pain and fear that they don't want to talk about it.

The idea that the past is intriguing, or that Louis MacNeice thought that the anti-aircraft defense was "beautiful both to see and hear" or that the Café Moka, at which George Orwell pointed his rifle for three days in May 1937, is still called the Café Moka, doesn't interest Catalans now. It is as though there were two Civil Wars, one for the outsiders, recorded by Orwell, by *For Whom the Bell Tolls* and by *The Penguin Book of Spanish Civil War Verse*; the other for those who live in the country which tore itself apart and have suffered the consequences all their lives.

The hesitant and wounded tone in the writings of the three Goytisolo brothers catches, perhaps more than any other writing, the inward-looking, guilt-ridden feeling which people in Spain have about the Civil War. José Agustín Goytisolo became a poet, Juan and Luis novelists. Their mother, Julia Gay, was killed in the bombing of Barcelona in March 1938.

When you are taking part in events like these you are, I suppose, in a small way, making history, and you ought by rights to feel like an historical character. But you never do, because at such times the physical details always outweigh everything else. Throughout the fighting I never made the correct "analysis" of the situation that was so glibly made by journalists hundreds of miles away. What I was chiefly thinking about was not the rights and wrongs of this miserable internecine scrap, but simply the discomfort and boredom of sitting day and night on that intolerable roof.

—George Orwell,
Homage to Catalonia (1938)

Juan Goytisolo, author of *Signs of Identity*, the classic novel of the long exile in France after Franco's victory, wrote about their mother in his book *Coto Vedado* (translated into English as *Forbidden Territory*).

> On the morning of 17 March 1938 my mother set out as usual. She left the house at the break of dawn, and even though I know the tricks which memory plays...I have a vivid memory of having leaned out of the window of my room while she...walked with coat and hat on and her bag towards a final absence: extinction, emptiness, nothingness. It seems without doubt suspicious that I would have woken precisely on that day and, alerted to my mother's departure by her steps or the noise of the door, I would have got out of bed to follow her with my eyes. Nevertheless, the image is real and for some time it filled me full of bitter remorse; not having shouted after her, not having stopped her leaving. Probably it was the result of a subsequent guilt mechanism: an indirect way of blaming myself for my inertia, not having realised the imminent danger, not having made the gesture which, in my imagination, could have saved her.

In October 1988 a statue of David and Goliath was unveiled in the outskirts of the city to commemorate the International Brigades who fought on the Republican side in the Civil War, on the 50th anniversary of their departure from Spain. Men who had fought in the war came back to the city from all over the world; others came as well, who had been too young to fight in the war but also wanted to commemorate the International Brigades.

The commemoration was being organised from a tiny, cramped office at the top of a building on Portal de l'Angel. The organisers, themselves veterans of the war, complained about the lack of official interest in the event. The town hall and the Catalán government had agreed to receive the veterans only under great pressure, only when it was explained that some of the old soldiers held important positions in their own countries. The mayor of Barcelona agreed to unveil the statue.

But the newspapers had no interest in the event, nor did the television or radio stations want to interview any of the old men.

A few posters were put up, but otherwise there was nothing. Instead there were flags all over the city to commemorate the Great Exhibition of 1888, with the words *La Nostra Energia* (Our Energy) printed on them.

On the morning of the unveiling the old men gathered in the square where the statue stood. The four Irishmen who had come back after 50 years stood together and had their photographs taken. But the journalists and the photographers were from Ireland, or England, or the United States; there were no Catalans taking photographs or interviewing veterans about what it was like to leave your own country and join in the fight against fascism.

The mayor of Barcelona, Pasqual Maragall, stood on the platform and held a replica of the statue aloft as though it were a trophy. He spoke in Catalán and French and then in English. He spoke of the need for reconciliation in his country, the need not to humiliate the other side. "They too had their ideals," he said in English. There was a stunned silence. One old man shouted up at Maragall, but others did nothing. Quickly, Maragall changed the subject. A

A long history of struggle between Spain's working class and aristocracy—peppered by Basque and Catalán quests for independence from Madrid—created the climate for war. In 1931, that climate ripened with the election of Socialist and Anarchist leaders, who proclaimed the Second Republic and drafted a new constitution. The state ceased subsidizing the Catholic Church, the monarchy was renounced, and the government initiated agrarian reform and granted Catalonia semi-autonomy. In 1933, however, the rightist Falange party won a small plurality.

As in any conflict, the atrocities committed before and during the Civil War were not one-sided. When the Left won a majority in 1936, a daily spate of assassinations erupted on both sides. By July 1936, Nationalist rebels led by General Francisco Franco's army commenced the Civil War to overthrow the elected government.

The Nationalists presented a united front in contrast to Republicans who, though they shared an opposition to fascism, were divided by infighting. With Franco's capture of Madrid in April 1939, the war was over, leaving one million Spaniards dead and beginning 36 years of a totalitarian regime.

—LMc

Socialist, he now worked closely with Juan Antonio Samaranch, the president of the International Olympic Committee, who was responsible for the running of Barcelona during Franco's regime. In the Catalán government, a new minister had been appointed who had also served under Franco. The Civil War was over; its politics and its legacy were now buried.

The veterans of the International Brigades stood up at the end of the ceremony and they sang *L'Internationale*. They had fire in their eyes that morning in Barcelona, 50 years after their defeat, despite the indifference. All the old men and women of the Left, who had kept the faith so long, raised their right arms and in all the languages of Europe they sang their hymn.

Colm Tóibín is a novelist and one of Ireland's best-known journalists, a regular contributor to Dublin's The Sunday Independent. *His books include* The Heather Blazing, The Sign of the Cross: Travels in Catholic Europe, *and* Homage to Barcelona, *from which this piece was excerpted. He is a winner of the E. M. Forster Award from the American Academy of Arts and Letters.*

★

One of the major obstacles in the way of human progress, of human understanding, is cynicism. The cynicism that states that people only act in their own self-interest. And you can listen to this for a while and maybe agree up to a point, but then you say, "What about the guys in the Lincoln Brigade?"

They won't go away, those guys who shipped out [from America] for Spain to fight for other people's freedom: they stand up in history like the one tree on a battlefield not levelled by the bombing, stand up and make you ask, "How did that happen?" They won't go away. If you talk to them or read their accounts what you hear again and again is that they went to Spain because of a belief in what people could be, in how people could live together, and they put their lives on the line for that belief and a lot of them died.

> —John Sayles, "But What About the Guys in the Lincoln Brigade?"
> *¡No Pasarán! The 50th Anniversary of the Abraham Lincoln Brigade,*
> edited by Abe Osheroff and Bill Susman

Agreeing to Forget

The author searches for remnants
of an era not-so-long gone.

DESPITE ALL THE EVIDENCE TO THE CONTRARY I HAVE NEVER BEEN able to eradicate the notion that Spain is at heart a Catholic, censorious country. Even when you know things have changed it is difficult to accept sometimes that they have changed quite as much as they have. So I spent much of my time in Madrid walking on the shady side of the street and looking for proof that the past is still present. It is certainly easier to see signs that the old days have been put away.

Just around the corner from my friend Carlos' apartment in an adjunct to the famed Prado, known as the Casón del Buen Retiro, a one-time Royal ballroom and a suitably bombastic building for the kings of Madrid to twirl in, stands the most potent public symbol of the end of yesterday. For next to a room of nondescript 19th-century paintings, in a gallery all its own, stands the most famous Spanish painting of the 20th century, and the most notorious image of the last bloody bout of internecine strife, Picasso's *Guernica*.

The day that *Guernica* arrived in its new Madrid home from the New York Museum of Modern Art late in 1981 was a wildly symbolic one. Before his death Picasso had decreed that this epic depiction of the bombing by Hitler's airmen (they were on loan to the nationalist forces at the time and practicing the skills they would later use on London) of the sacred Basque town of

Picasso's Guernica *has since been moved to the national museum for contemporary art, the Reina Sofía Art Center.*

—LMc

Guernica could not return to Spain until liberty had also come home. So after five years of democracy it was decided that the time had come to bring back the picture.

Today it stands behind a fat sheet of bullet-proof glass, lest some necrophiliac fanatic should decide to take a pop at this famed anti-authoritarian tirade. Seeing the real thing for the first time I found it hard to imagine any of the mix of Americans and out-of-towners who filed past it alongside me getting so wound up. Picasso's *Guernica* is a little like the New York City skyline, one of those famous sights which we have all seen vicariously so many times before we ever actually set eyes on the real thing. Unlike the powerful profile of the cubic city though *Guernica* failed to fill me with awe.

It has been reproduced so many times, used so often as a piece of propaganda or just as a convenient form of historical shorthand, that its ability to shock or even move has largely gone. But perhaps conversely its power as a painting has increased. Picasso's *Guernica* has been turned into a *Mona Lisa*, into an icon of the everyday which sits in its place so that tourists can add another tick to their scorecard of travellers' collectibles. It is perhaps fitting that this work, overburdened as it has been with its origins, can now be allowed to become a painting again in the same way that Spain is becoming a normal country.

If *Guernica* has come back then the eagle has definitely gone. The stern and strident-looking black eagle who nested in the middle of the Spanish flag during the dictatorship has disappeared from almost every standard now. Like so many of the relics of the General's rule they have just been allowed to fade away, as quickly and discreetly as possible. Street names throughout Spain were changed after the War: the Diagonal in Barcelona became the

Avenida Generalísimo Franco; and streets and squares named after Falangist heroes like Calvo Sotelo and Primo de Rivera sprung up everywhere.

Since the return of the democracy though they have largely reverted to their former names. No one I spoke to can remember any renaming ceremony, people just started using the old names (in some cases they always had) again, and the street signs mysteriously switched. It was almost as if they had never been altered in the first place, as if you were remembering it wrong. That feeling that maybe the Civil War never happened after all was beginning to worry me.

I asked some of my newfound Madrileño mates about this apparent collective amnesia and in mock-conspiratorial tones they let me in on the *pacto de olvido*. This, they explained, is basically a tacit national agreement to forget the past, to stop harking on about the old days and, for the sake of Spain, to go forward with the new democracy no matter which side you were or are on.

"To understand this country, you must always remember what the Civil War did to people," Daniel told me. "Families were destroyed. Brothers fought on different sides." A transition without retribution was also a practical matter. Franco's chosen successor, King Juan Carlos, had been a Francoist, naturally, and so had Adolfo Suárez, the first post-dictatorship prime minister. "If we had started looking under the bedsheets of everyone in power, we would have created the largest possible political party—Those Who Were Afraid—at a time when there were no parties yet," Xavier Robert de Ventós, a Catalán Socialist and classics scholar, told me. Spain's task, de Ventós said, was to break the cycle of vengeance. He drew a lesson from the Greek philosophers. "Aristotle was right," he said. "Whoever wants to organize a polis must organize the amnesia of the people."

—William Finnegan, "Our Far-Flung Correspondent: Catalonia," *The New Yorker*

The fact that the *pacto de olvido* has been so well observed in such a divided nation is a testament to the fundamental, collective desire for it to work. The fact that my friends had let me in on the pact was a testament to their collective desire to get me to shut up about the Franco days and stop asking them stupid questions. I agreed not to bug them so much, but I still went off looking for some memories which were intact. I did though wonder whether they had a pact to forget because they hadn't quite come to terms, whether this self-willed amnesia was actually a substitute for a genuine reconciliation. Most Spaniards I believe have real trouble accepting the recent past and so they would rather dismiss it from their minds. But there is no doubt that it has worked.

I was determined though to search out the remains of that past and in a crusty, dense, little shop by the Plaza Mayor I found a place where the recollections are still alive. The old part of Madrid contains numerous purveyors of relics. There are shops flogging religious regalia, another with iron-age corsets, a third with artificial limbs and yet another which sells Guardia Civil outfits, Falangist badges, flags with eagles, and ceramic busts of Franco staring sternly, or riding a white horse in his El Cid crusader gear. Rifling through this silly paraphernalia reminded me of nothing more than the claustrophobic, pedantic hours I spent as a youth in my brief but devout period as a stamp-collector. The shopkeeper was an old, quiet man who would not have looked out of place in a library, and the only browser seemed to suit the anorak he was wearing. I certainly couldn't find the militant spirit of the old Spain here, in anything other than a pickle jar.

Another possible contender proved fairly fruitless. Opposite a porno-cinema in a run-down eastern sector of Madrid are the offices of the CNT, the Anarchist trade union. I entered the building full of romance and left it with a certain sadness. I wanted heroic visions and there were certainly a few murals of square-jawed revolutionists waving black-and-red flags. But there was also an air of decrepitude and bygones as a few old comrades mingled with a couple of young anarcho-punks in an unlikely coalition of rebellion. There was an ageing dandy with a surrealist mustache who sold me a copy of their paper, but there was also a smell of cat's piss and distant dreams. I sipped a beer opposite in a bar full of workers and wondered.

I did stop in my tracks one day while searching the streets for echoes of the old conflicts. On a huge roadside billboard I saw the legend, writ large, *No Pasa Nada*. Was this the famous old Communist slogan of defiance, "They Shall Not Pass"? But that of course is *No Pasarán;* this was "Nothing Passes" and as I looked closer I realized it was a slogan advertising sanitary towels, not La Pasionaria and the heroic resistance of the staunchly Republican people of Madrid. Time, I realised, to go to the museum.

About two hundred yards from Carlos' flat is a museum which I walked past almost every day without giving it a second glance. Carlos though was adamant that I should go inside. "It's great, you get the place completely to yourself, nobody ever goes there." Exactly what everybody is missing is the shiny detritus of hundreds of years of Spanish military history as it is stored in the Army Museum. Those memories I was searching for were all in here.

Real guns and toy soldiers, endless standards and medals, muskets and mortars. Objects of death through the ages sit in glass cases in an oddly unstructured paean to the wonders of the Spanish army. There is much talk of fatherland and honour, numerous references to God and glory and a kind of polished pomposity which seems almost camp. Also there was at the time of my visit almost nobody there save a few soldier boys with savage crops standing with their backs unnaturally straight, a handful of what I would guess were ex-servicemen and their wives and a couple of the anoraked philatelists I had seen in the shop in the Plaza Mayor. The one thing that the Army Museum did provide me with though was a real sense in which the last Civil War was just one chapter in a grisly national flirtation with blood-letting. A flirtation which truly and finally and thankfully seems to be over.

The Ultras though like to let it be known that they like to let some blood occasionally. The kind of hooliganism which British youths regularly unleash on the *costas* has never caught on with the Spanish. But like so much of mainland Europe, Spain has recently taken to the very British tradition of fighting at football. They certainly haven't adopted football hooliganism with the rigour or vigour of the Dutch and Germans, but the larger teams now have crews which very occasionally clash, and the crew which follows Real Madrid is the Ultras. And the Ultras are naturally out on the right wing.

"Patriotism, Justice and Revolution" is the most common piece of rightist sloganeering seen in Spain today. It is the slogan of the FFJ, the Falangist youth, just one of the myriad groups which exist on the now splintered far Right. Occasionally in Madrid that will be accompanied by the name of the Ultras and the slogan "White Power" (in English) which refers both to the famous white strip of Real as well as to the more obvious racist meaning.

Searching still for this elusive ghost of mine I spent a small part of an evening in a lugubrious bar in the southern suburbs of Madrid talking to a pair of sorry Ultras. Pablo and Paquito are both in their early twenties, both supporters of Real and both self-professed fascists. That choice of word is actually very informative, for the Falange, for all their evils, were never Nazis. After a few minutes talking to these two young men I realised that I knew them and knew them well.

I had met the pair of them near the Plaza Mayor, and approached them because Pablo had the close-cropped hair and the MAI flying-jacket uniform of the new Nazis. I asked if they were Ultras, they said yes and agreed to talk to this odd English journalist, seemingly pleased by the attention. Once I arrived at their barrio though I realised that this was a futile journey; I wanted to know about the Falangist heritage, and the authoritarian Right in an age of pluralism; they wanted to cadge some beers and natter about the British "Oi" group Screwdriver and the exploits of Leeds United's away firm.

The reason I knew them so well is that these boys were not Spanish exotica, but carbon-copy white euro-trash. Pablo and Paquito are indicative of the kind of juvenile malcontent who is now commonplace throughout the continent. Unemployed, ill-educated and aware that their traditional working-class culture is disappearing, they have looked towards Britain's disaffected bovver boys for a role model. They even poured out some fairly standard venom against blacks, learned I guess by rote, because Spain is a country with a minuscule (although rising) black population. After a short and thoroughly depressing time I made my excuses and left.

Obviously Pablo and Paquito are not entirely typical of every young right-wing Spaniard. There is still a bourgeois, Catholic, traditionalist movement, but it is tiny. When the media runs a scare story about the rise of the new Right it is the likes of the Ultras, of those two kids who could have come from Dresden or Bruges or Barnsley, that they talk about. The fact that its fanatics are now the same as everyone else's is perhaps another perverse sign that Spain has become part of the European consensus.

Still though there are enough who care, enough to mount a march every year to the Pharaoh's tomb.

Each November, on the anniversary of the death of Francisco Franco there is a march to honour his memory, which ends up with a wreath-laying ceremony at his tomb in the Valley of the Fallen. I had first seen this peculiarly chilling but compulsive spectacle on TV back in Barcelona and my friend Inka told me then how in 1976, one

"In Franco's time, there was more respect," he said. "Nowadays, no one cares about the family."

Despite my being in a strange country, where it is never advisable to talk politics, I could not let this pass without a response. I said that Franco had been a dictator and that nothing during his time could have been better than now.

The vendor's face turned red.

"Who do you think you are, talking like that?"

"I know this country's history, I know the war the people fought for their freedom. I have read about the crimes of the Franco forces during the Spanish Civil War."

"Well, I fought in that war. Whatever stories you have read don't interest me. I fought against Franco, but when he won the war, life was better for me. I'm not a beggar, and I have my little popcorn stand. It wasn't this Socialist government we have now that helped me. I'm worse off now than I was before."

I remembered what Petrus had said about people being content with very little, I decided not to press my point of view, and I moved to another bench.

—Paulo Coelho,
The Pilgrimage: A Contemporary Quest for Ancient Wisdom

year after his demise, there were nearly two million people marching, two million people from all over Spain who would gladly have
welcomed back their master. The numbers decreased rapidly,
though, until now where it is down to a few thousand old die-
hards and young hot-heads.

The Ultras are there, as are the more disciplined Falangist youth
with their neat haircuts, Sam Browne belts and blue shirts. There
are also veterans of the struggle, old nationalist soldiers who
haven't completely faded away yet. Then there is the oddest group
of all, the nice, middle-class families in their suits and pleated skirts
who would look more at home at a flower show or a school sports
day. On that day in November all of Spain is reminded that the
wounds have not entirely been healed, that they may have agreed
to forget, but they do not all agree. The rest of the time you
wouldn't really notice. The rest of the time the Valley of the Fallen
is a theme-park.

Carlos agreed to drive me out to the great monument on a
dreamily steaming Madrid Sunday. It lies about 40 kilometers out
of town, a little past the famed Escorial. El Escorial is the vast,
gaunt, pointless monument to the devout vanity of Philip II, which
is part palace, part monastery and a complete monstrosity of giant
proportions. This testament to the excesses of Inquisitorial
Catholicism is the most famous piece of architectural extremism in
Spain. Franco's folly a few kilometers up the motorway is its main
competitor.

Although nominally a monument to all those who died in the
Civil War, the fact that the church and its giant cross were constructed by Republican prisoners, many of whom gave their lives
blasting it out of the rock, is indicative of exactly which side is celebrated here. It consists of a vast cave-like basilica excavated out of
a granite mountain and an impossibly tall stone cross (490 feet, in
fact) on top. The cross is said to be the largest in the world and the
overgrown, freakish edifice dom-inates the bleak, grey valley in
which it sits.

That it is impressive is without doubt. The scale of the whole sorry, silly endeavor is such that when you first see it from afar you are rocked back in your seat. As a monument to death it is unsurpassed in the sheer immensity of its proportions and its inflated imagery. At the base of the cross souped-up lions and eagles sit, trying desperately to be imperial. Beneath the towering crucifix there is a monastery, dwarfed by the scale of everything around it, which houses the monks whose sole job is to attend the graves of the two famous men buried in the cavernous church. José Antonio Primo de Rivera, the founder of the Falangist movement, who was killed early in the Civil War, and Franco himself.

Comparisons with the great pyramids of Egypt are almost inevitable and the place is known by Madrileños as the Pharaoh's tomb. And in the same way that the Valley of the Kings has become a tourist attraction, so the Valley of the Fallen is now on the coach party and picnic itinerary.

During the drive to the tomb Carlos explained how there had been a raging debate about whether the whole thing should be dynamited because of the offense it caused to so many people. Obviously those on the Right, especially the widows of men

I'm sure there are some advantages to a dictatorship, otherwise they wouldn't happen with such regularity. But I remember the fear of living under Franco in the small things. I remember my professor going to the classroom door and searching the halls before whispering about politics. Not seditious things mind you but innocent opinions about his country's state of affairs. I remember letting go of my girlfriend's hand as we walked the streets at night, simply because the Guardia Civil might not approve of her going out with a foreigner. (Of course she was a commander's daughter, so maybe I was being stupid. The first time I went to visit her, I was surrounded by scowling men with submachine guns and frogmarched to the family's quarters.) I remember the bowel-liquefying fear of being picked up by the police in a place where habeus corpus *is a joke: a friend of mine who was giving me a ride cheerily informed me, upon noticing that a car full of police were giving us the eye, that he was carrying marijuana and amphetamines in his van. These things didn't necessarily make a liberal of me, but they further deepened my suspicion of humorless men who are overly fond of uniforms and eagles and flags.*

—James O'Reilly, "In Salamanca"

who had fallen for Franco, wanted the monument retained. More surprisingly though many on the Left argued that it should be left to stand as a terrible testament to the horrors which occurred, a massive reminder of where dictatorships lead. It is such an ugly and repulsive edifice that they were undoubtedly right. Perhaps they also knew that it was bound to become such a trivial behemoth.

Complete with a funicular to carry you to the top of the cross, a snack bar with video games and a souvenir shop, the place now has an almost festive feel. Try as it may to be a grave grave, it has become a kind of Disneyland of death where American tourists play Frisbee in the square and sunbathe on the lions. Inside the supposedly sombre temple, the last resting place of the Generalísimo and the spiritual home of the souls of all those who perished fighting "For God and Fatherland," I heard a fat *yanqui* in shorts say to his wife, "It's kinda nice here." Death by tourism is surely a more fitting end than any explosion.

It is still said though that some of the tourists standing gawping at the stone slab which bears the name of the dictator are actually plain-clothes policemen hovering to catch anybody spitting on or attempting to deface the graves. There are always fresh flowers on Franco's tomb and when I was there, there were a couple of those Nationalist widows wearing black re-membering their men. But the real

*Valley of the Fallen
(Valle de los Caídos)*

sign of how Spain now deals with its most recent skeleton is to be found in the souvenir shop.

There are plenty of picture postcards and ashtrays of the monument, key-rings bearing the face of Juan Carlos and various members of his family. You can purchase a holy virgin, an eagleless flag and a valueless coin. But there is not a single trace, not a mention or murmur, about the man who commissioned the thing to act as his eternal mausoleum. In a re-write of Stalinist proportions, Franco has been edited out of the story, expunged from history and expelled even from his own bloated memorial. The whole thing has been stripped of all meaning and left to the ravages of scantily clad visitors.

When I asked the ageing superintendent of the souvenir shop why there is no Franco memorabilia on sale he simply shrugged and said it had been taken out a long time ago. Then sensing that maybe I was a fellow believer he leaned forward and whispered conspiratorially but with some pride, "There is a little shop near the Plaza Mayor."

Robert Elms also contributed "A Night of Duende*" in Part One. Both stories were excerpted from his book* Spain: A Portrait after the General.

✳

Whatever Franco thought his legacy to Spain would be, he cannot have imagined that it would be a kind of deliberate oblivion. Spain's reaction to the Franco years has been to remove them abruptly to a remote past, to see them overall as a limbo.

The older ones are still wondering to themselves how they could have let him last so long. The younger generations feel as though they had been released from prison after a false arrest. The living present has obliterated that past in the manner of a windshield wiper.

—Alastair Reid, *Whereabouts: Notes on Being a Foreigner*

A Noble Apology

*Centuries after the Jews were expelled,
a descendant tries to go home again.*

ON A SCORCHING JUNE DAY, 504 YEARS AFTER MY ANCESTORS were booted out of town by the Inquisition, I drove back to the little Spanish city of Baza from which my family takes its name.

I had schemed my return for some time. I'd crammed Spanish, pored over guidebooks, even faxed the mayor to tell him I was coming. Since my family hadn't left town under the happiest of circumstances, I was beginning to feel a little nervous as I drove into town with my wife and kids. I parked the car and we got out.

The town square was deserted. All sane beings, ourselves excluded, were hiding from the sun. A church and half-a-dozen whitewashed buildings huddled around a dormant fountain. In a nearby portico a fat dog snoozed in the shade of an old black cannon. While our children went to pet the dog, my wife and I went to pet the cannon. A sign (which I did my best to decipher) announced that the cannon had served Ferdinand and Isabella when they took Baza by siege in 1489. I rubbed its muzzle. I wanted it to know that although 500 years had passed, I at least had not forgotten.

We tried the door of the old church, but it was locked. I was looking around for Torquemada when the church clock struck high noon in Baza. The Jews were back in town. So where was the mayor? Where was the welcoming committee? I pumped myself up by telling myself that I owed something to my ancestors, that they had sent me here on purpose. It was time to inform the authorities that we were back. Leaving my family astride the cannon, I walked across the plaza to the town hall. My heart was pounding.

Moments later, I charged into the mayor's office and informed a young man in an Izod sport shirt that my family had lived here centuries ago. They had been driven out of town, I said. I had sent a fax. So why had no one answered? The mayor's man stared at me, and I stared back. He stood up—and held out his hand. Yes, he said, now he remembered. His Honor had left word that I was to be given a private tour of the museum, archives and the ancient Jewish baths. Could I possibly wait until after lunch? He—Xavier, the mayor's secretary—would be happy to conduct the tour. I knew my ancestors would be pleased.

Tomás de Torquemada was the Inquisitor General for Isabella and Ferdinand. It was he who ultimately persuaded the monarchs to issue an edict in 1492 expelling the Jews, causing 100,000 to 200,000 Jews to flee Spain that year. Today Spain's population of about 39 million includes only 15,000 Jews.

—LMc

So we waited for Xavier in a busy café down a narrow street. My family and I had splendid *tapas* of fried sardines, squid, ripe tomatoes and sweet onions in olive oil—and those fresh green olives which alone were consolation for the centuries of exile. It occurred to me that this sense of exile had been part of my family lore for as long as I could remember—I'd breathed it in along with the smell of potted chicken and baked farfel in my grandmother's kitchen. By the time it had come down to me, the story of my family's exodus from Spain had acquired a few romantic, if spurious, details—including a secretly Jewish Bishop of Córdoba supposedly responsible for rescuing his relatives from the hands of the Inquisition.

I guess my pilgrimage to Baza began with these stories, since they nourished a curiosity about the etymology of my name. At the turn of the 20th century, when my grandfather moved from Cracow to New York, he changed the "z" in his last name into an "s." He did this, I am told, because he wanted to melt into the melting pot—and leave the past behind. Because my own impulse has always been to restore old relics, I took the lost "z" back. Nonetheless, the meaning of the old word remained a puzzle. But every scholar I consulted confirmed the family tradition that it was Spanish.

After lunch, not far from a remnant of the town walls still known as Solomon's Gate, Xavier led us down a narrow street to a dilapidated building. There an old man opened a door—and took us downstairs into a cool cellar with arches striped like barber poles and windows in the ceiling shaped like stars of David. I was standing in the Jewish baths. While our guide described the workings of the steambath (pointing out where the bathers had undressed, steamed, scrubbed themselves and been massaged with fragrant oils) I was struck by the fact that this old place and my own last name were among the few vestiges of a community which had vanished. If the past had any secrets to tell, they were here in the *mikveh*. But the walls of the old steambath were disappointingly reticent.

So it was with a feeling of tantalized incompleteness that we next visited the city museum and archives, where the census books from 1943 kept company with King Ferdinand's banner. Since now the tour was over, the mayor's secretary said goodbye and, suggesting that we get a guidebook, recommended a nearby bookstore. In the Cervantes bookstore, I struck up a conversation with the aging man behind the counter who showed me a history of Baza and the Baza newspaper, which he printed. I offered to pay for them, but he refused my money. "José," he said, and pointed at himself.

I told José my last name, handing him my card—and when he saw the similarity to the name of his city, he flinched. I told him that in 1489 my ancestors had been driven out of Baza, abandoning their splendid steambath but taking their last name to remind them of home, and that after five centuries I'd finally come back.

"Come here," José said, and motioned for me to follow him.

I found myself standing in a decrepit courtyard. The lintel beams were held up with crutches. The whitewashed plaster, in its extreme old age, was crumbling off the walls. Everywhere, in pots and coffee cans, green plants were growing in riotous profusion.

"What is this place?" I asked.

José pointed at the broken remains of an ancient coat-of-arms. Right here, he said, on the prime real estate next to the church, one of Ferdinand and Isabella's captains had built himself a noble house. This old courtyard was all that had survived. With a wave of his hand, he asked me to admire the rotting timbers. He wanted me to enjoy the downfall of the conqueror.

"What a very foolish thing," he said quietly, "to send away the Jews. How colossally stupid. I am sorry."

There was a courtly melancholy in the way he said it. It was an apology for my family's inconvenience—for the damage to our old steambath, for the Inquisition and for five centuries of exile. Maybe it was for this that I had come.

On the 500th anniversary of the expulsion of the Jews from Spain, King Juan Carlos and Israel's President Chaim Herzog prayed together in Madrid's synagogue. In a speech to commemorate the day, the king pledged, "Never again will hate and intolerance provoke desolation and exile."

—LMc

Terry Richard Bazes is the author of Goldsmith's Return, *a comic novel about a Jewish surrealist painter from New Jersey whose life is overshadowed by a family curse dating back to Napoleonic France. His essays have appeared in* The Washington Post Book World, Newsday, Hadassah, Columbia, *and other national publications.*

✳

Now 65, Victor Papo arrived in Barcelona after fleeing Paris with his parents and siblings in 1941. The effects of the Civil War were still greatly in evidence. Everyone was poor, Gentile and Jew alike. Much of the city was in rubble, food was scarce, and jobs were scarcer.

Papo's grandfather had lived in Turkey, descended from Sefarad who fled to the Ottoman Empire when expelled by Isabella and Ferdinand. His father had moved to France, where he took advantage of the law passed by Primo de Rivera's government in 1924 to obtain Spanish passports for his family, although he had no intention of ever leaving Paris. It saved his family's life. Because they were under the protection of the Spanish consul, they were able to continue living in Paris for almost two years after the Nazi occupation.

Barcelona was not only poor, it was under the control of a government friendly toward the Nazis, and a rigorous, anti-Semitic Catholicism was the state religion. Nevertheless, to be out from under the direct daily observation of the Nazis was a big relief.

"Just to be on equal footing with everyone else in the streets was wonderful," said Papo, his gaze direct under a furrowed brow, a fringe of grey hair. "There wasn't much food, and work was hard to find, but with our passports we were treated like Spaniards, and had the same opportunities they did. We did not tell anyone we were Jewish, and they didn't ask."

—Richard Schweid, *Barcelona: Jews, Transvestites, and an Olympic Season*

T. D. ALLMAN

The King Who Saved His Country

A courageous political maneuver by Juan Carlos
may well have ensured Spain's future.

"YES IT'S TRUE," KING JUAN CARLOS ANSWERS, "THE STORY ABOUT the hitchhiker, the motorcycle, and me."

The way the King of Spain tells it, he had no intention of creating a legend that day—he just felt like taking a spin on his motorbike. So the king put on his helmet, pulled down the visor, and raced down the three-mile driveway of his Zarzuela Palace, burning rubber out onto the freeway.

"Then what happened, sir?" I ask. We're standing under an immense crystal chandelier in an ornate salon. White-coated majordomos are passing watercress sandwiches, smoked-salmon canapés, and silver salvers laden with flutes of champagne and glasses of orange juice. The king grabs some orange juice and tosses it down in one gulp, as if he's really thirsty, not just sipping something to be polite.

"I saw the hitchhiker," says the king, "so I slammed on the brakes. He hopped on behind me and I said to him, 'Where to?'

"'I've run out of gas,' he told me. 'I've been stranded here for hours.' So I took him to a gas station.

"Actually," the king explains, "I didn't want to take off my helmet when we got there. But he kept saying he wanted to thank me, and asking my name. So I took off my helmet, said 'My name is Juan Carlos,' and shook his hand. He was really quite surprised."

"And then what happened?"

"Nothing," the king answers. "I got back on my bike and continued on my way." Another waiter passes, bearing a tray of the superb *jamón serrano*, the air-cured ham Spaniards traditionally eat with their fingers. The king's hand darts out and he grabs what, were he not a reigning monarch, might be described as a fistful. This too he wolfs down.

That night at dinner, no one would think of touching food with his hands. A legendarily wealthy and cultivated American lady is hosting a dinner at the Jockey restaurant in Madrid. There are more grandees, marquesses, and other titled eminences than you can shake a stick at, yet it soon becomes evident why the lady has seated me next to her.

"These stories about the Princess of Wales and the King of Spain," she inquires, "are they true?"

Recently, a New York newspaper more notable for its circulation than its accuracy had run the banner headline THE KING & DI. The sweaty innuendo: the King of Spain and future Queen of England are an item.

Since my hostess is as renowned for her moral probity as for her graciousness, I dutifully set the record straight. Princess Diana, as well as Prince Charles, I explain, is a friend of King Juan Carlos and his wife, Queen Sofía, and visits them often. But that's all they are: friends.

My hostess listens attentively. Then she says, "So you are telling me that there is no truth whatsoever in the allegations the king and the princess are having an affair?"

"None whatsoever," I reply.

"You are absolutely certain?"

"Absolutely."

"Poor Diana," she sighs. "Poor, poor Diana. How terribly unfortunate for her." And then, her Waspy blue eyes flashing like a flamenco dancer's, she adds. "What a man!"

King Juan Carlos is one of those men who men as well as women instantly love: he eats with his fingers, he looks you straight in the eye. He's a motorcyclist, an avid skier, an Olympic-class sailor. With him, there's no regal reserve. And women? When Juan Carlos looks them in the eye, their pupils dilate and their hearts go pitter-patter. They think thoughts that would have made Anaïs Nin blush. Days later, they're still whispering, "What a man!"

The king's charm partly accounts for his immense popularity in Spain, a country with a fierce anti-monarchical tradition. But the royal charisma also obscures the main reason that, in Spain, even Marxists and Republicans respect him so deeply: Juan Carlos isn't simply a charming man who happens to be king; he's also one of the great heroic figures of modern Spanish history, the person who, more than any other, has made it possible for the 40 million people of his country to lead decent, free, and increasingly prosperous lives.

Simply put, if it weren't for Juan Carlos, the country might not be "the California of Western Europe," as the Spanish proudly call it, but the Yugoslavia of the West. There might have been another Spanish Civil War, just a decade ago, had King Juan Carlos not sped to the rescue of Spain's infant democracy the same way he came to the aid of that stranded motorist on the freeway.

A generation ago Spain had a lower average per capita income than Cuba; by many standards it was a Third World country. Today Spain has the seventh or eighth largest GNP in the world and the Spanish peseta has become one of Europe's hardest currencies. "The Spanish have done in 10 years what it took the rest of us Europeans 30 years," a French economist says. "They've created a modern democratic technological society."

By 1995, economic growth in Spain was curbed by steep interest rates, and unemployment was the highest in the EU. Such problems, however, don't detract from the astounding rebirth and exponential growth of the country, in terms of world influence, since General Franco's death. Indeed, Spain, along with France and Germany, has led the movement toward European integration.

—LMc

The Spain of *Carmen* and Ernest Hemingway is still here, but the siesta is a thing of the past. In fact, the only thing more astonishing than the prices (Spaniards now vacation in Switzerland because things are so much less expensive there) is that no one ever seems to sleep. Work starts at nine a.m. and, following a long break for a business lunch, continues until eight, nine, or ten at night. Then comes dinner in Spain. One night in Seville, a crowd including the Duke and Duchess of Segorbe and Henry Kissinger did not sit down to eat until after midnight. When I finally dragged myself off at two, the streets were still full of people, as though it were early evening.

"When I want to sleep," says Xavier Corberó, the famed Catalán sculptor, "I go to New York."

After the death of Generalísimo Francisco Franco—the dictator who, along with Mussolini and Hitler, incarnated fascism in Europe—it's as though Spain had never suffered through a dictatorship at all. For nearly 40 years Franco dominated Spain, the bleeding abscess of a nation whose suffering impelled George Orwell to compose *Homage to Catalonia* and Picasso to paint *Guernica*. Many doubted Spain would ever escape his repressive imprint. Yet almost overnight, historically speaking, Spain has become a buzzing democracy of faxes and traffic jams.

"It seems like a century ago that Franco died," says Narcís Serra, Spain's deputy prime minister. "Most days even I find it hard to believe Spain was once so poor and desperate, and afraid."

A journalist who works in Madrid describes Spain's remarkable transition in another way: "When I first got here, Spain was on the crime pages. Now it's in the business section." She adds, "When *Time* and *The New York Times* close their bureaus in a country, you've got to admit things are going right."

That things would go so right, so fast in Spain was something no one imagined possible as recently as 1975, when an enfeebled, 82-year-old Franco was still clinging to life and power. The prince the dictator had chosen to succeed him as Spain's chief of state had the looks and the manner of a bit player in a Viennese operetta, which was only appropriate. For, until Franco died, that was all Juan Carlos was, a student prince. Few doubted he would wind up exiled in a villa in Portugal like his father, Don Juan de Borbón, or living in diminished circumstances in London, as his brother-in-law ex-king Constantine of Greece later would. The politicians in Madrid had already chosen a title for the king-in-waiting: he would be "Juan Carlos the Brief," a hapless transitional figure who would reign only until monarchy, Franco's Falangism, and all the other vestiges of Spain's violent, bad, and backward past were swept away.

Instead, Juan Carlos became the most powerful man in Spain after Franco's belated death in 1975. And he used that power more astutely—and to greater good—than perhaps any other reigning monarch since his distant cousin King Louis XVI was beheaded during the French Revolution.

> *he policeman who directed me to the Crystal Palace, an airy greenhouse built in the last century and used now for art exhibitions, could not have been more accommodating. I thought of my last encounter with Spanish authority, in 1964. I was saying good night to some American friends at their car, which was parked on a dark street, when we were suddenly bathed in light from a police vehicle. Several uniformed men, guns at the ready, demanded to know who we were and what we were up to. From such small gatherings, they perhaps felt, revolutions grow.*
>
> —Gordon Cotler, "Morning in Madrid," *Travel Holiday*

"The king orchestrated the transition from dictatorship to constitutional monarchy so adroitly," Javier Tusell, a Madrid university professor, told me, "that people tend to forget just how masterful a performance it was. When Franco died, the king inherited his absolute powers. He could have done anything. Yet he used his absolute powers systematically to strip himself of power—to create a democratic system."

In Madrid, I asked Prime Minister Felipe González to assess the king's role in the establishment of Spanish democracy. "He was absolutely indispensable," González answered quickly. "He still is," he added, citing such delicate matters as Spain's military relations with the United States, and the current controversy over unemployment benefits.

Once a man on the cutting edge of history, Juan Carlos now prefers to play the role of model constitutional monarch, painstakingly referring even the most minor matters to his government for approval. "When the king gives a dinner party in New York," I was told, "he submits the guest list to the Spanish Embassy in Washington. He wishes to be seen as a king who reigns but does not rule."

In a typical twelve-hour workday, the king probably spends three-quarters of his time on ceremonial functions. But these are much more likely to take him to a factory or a rural village than a gilded salon. He and the queen have neither the time nor the inclination for traditional court protocol. And they have no interest at all in hobnobbing with Spain's traditional aristocracy.

"The king spends virtually all of his time with three sorts of people," one titled Spaniard told me rather regretfully. "First, with his family, because when you are king what does status matter? The only thing that really counts is your blood relations. Second, with politicians. Third, the king spends an enormous amount of time with bankers. After all, they are the real grandees these days."

In fact, of all his titles, the one Juan Carlos seems to enjoy most is "Spain's Number-One Salesman." A Spanish industrialist told me, "I have seen him charm foreign investors time after time. Businessmen all over Spain know that if they really need it to clinch a big deal they can call the palace and the king will come."

The emphasis on the king's ceremonial role does not change the fact that he still wields considerable influence over affairs of state. Recently, a friend of mine was visiting Zarzuela Palace when he ran into Felipe González coming out. "He had a bundle of documents under his arm. He clearly had run over to the Zarzuela to get the king's advice on some pressing matter," he told me. "I was surprised to see him, but he was a lot more surprised to see me, because this isn't how the system is supposed to work at all. The prime minister is supposed to advise the king, not the other way

around. But the fact is that the king is so well connected and respected that people want to use his advice all the time."

The king's populist manner and González's socialist principles
have made for a productive marriage. "They like each other," said
an associate of the prime minister. "They work well together. But
I certainly wouldn't describe them as friends. By instinct, the king
is much more free-market-oriented than Felipe. The king likes the
idea of lots of people making money, whereas with Felipe's socialist background this is still something of a necessary evil."

"Also there can't help being an element of rivalry," a González
associate told me. "Underneath, in his heart of hearts, I think
Felipe would also like to play the ceremonial role, as well as run
the government—and, of course, that he can't be. That's what the
king does."

Meanwhile, a friend of the king told me, "The king keeps getting more democratic, while the prime minister keeps getting
more regal. You have two lives which, while they have intersected
fruitfully for many years, keep moving in opposite directions. The
prince has grown up to be a commoner, and the commoner a
prince. Twenty years from now, I wouldn't be surprised to find
Juan Carlos puttering around a marina, scraping barnacles off the
bottom of his boat and making himself a sandwich, while Felipe
González arrives for a gourmet meal in a chauffeur-driven
limousine."

The king's populist principles and his desire to place himself
under the law extend to the smallest details. Like all Spanish
citizens he carries a laminated identity card with his photo on it,
even though it's inconceivable he would not be recognized wherever he goes. Spanish IDs state the bearer's profession, and on his
card, Juan Carlos's profession is listed as *funcionario del estado,* "em-
ployee of the state."

The Spain of the 1992 Olympics, of Expo and Europe and
construction cranes, was born on the night of February 23, 1981,
though no one at the time realized it. On the contrary, most citizens feared the country was about to slip back into catastrophe that
night—back into the dictatorship they had escaped six years be-

fore, into anarchy, or worse, a replay of the Spanish Civil War, when one million people were killed.

At 6:20 that evening, soldiers wearing the funny black cocked hats of the Spanish Guardia Civil, and carrying leaded subma-chine guns, burst into the 350-member Cortes, the Spanish par-liament, while it was voting on a new prime minister. When a government minister ordered the armed invaders to desist, they pistol-whipped him back to his seat. The outgoing prime minis-ter, Adolfo Suárez, stood up to protest, and a soldier shouted, "Sit down, pig!"

The invaders fired into the rococo ceiling of the chamber. As plaster rained down on everyone, members of the Cabinet braced themselves in their seats, ready to die for Spain's new democracy. The rest of the parliament was forced at gun point to lie face down on the floor.

The leader of the attack, a mustachioed Franco fanatic named Lieutenant Colonel Antonio Tejero Molina, mounted the podium. Brandishing a pistol, he announced that the Cortes was henceforth abolished, that "a competent military authority" was taking control.

The gunshots; the falling plaster; the hostage legislators; Tejero's banana-republic braggadocio; and all this melodrama unfolding in such an ornate chamber: it was a scene so surreally dark with men-ace Goya might have painted it. As one report put it, "Never in postwar memory had the democratically elected parliament of any Western nation been subjected to such an outrage."

There was the terrible sense that history was repeating itself— and no one could stop it. The three-year Spanish Civil War had begun in 1936 with a military attack on a civilian government. And now it seemed to be happening all over again. "I was con-vinced that we would be moved from parliament to a concentra-tion camp," one member of the Cortes said later.

"The worst thing was the lack of information," recalls José María de Areilza, the Count of Motrico and one of the key figures in the post-Franco transition. "The soldiers took all our transistor radios, and cut the telephone lines. We were completely isolated, prisoners. So far as we in the Cortes knew, Spain had become a military dictatorship again."

The *coup d'état* had been expertly timed. Since a change of government was occurring, the country's entire political leadership was in the Cortes. So all of Spain's democratic leaders were now prisoners—except one, the king himself. But the plotters were convinced Juan Carlos was not really a democrat. He had only been pretending to be a constitutional monarch and, they believed, would surely side with the forces of repression if the military gave him the chance.

The plotters had historical precedent on their side: back in 1923, Juan Carlos's grandfather King Alfonso XIII had supported a military coup against Spain's civilian government. The ensuing dictatorship was only the beginning of Spain's, and the royal family's, woes. By 1931 the nation was so violently divided that King Alfonso and his family fled the country lest his continuing presence provoke Civil War, which nonetheless broke out five years later. Decades of bitter exile followed: Alfonso died in a Rome hotel suite in 1941; his son and heir, Don Juan

By the early 1990s, the tricornio—the shiny black hat worn by the Guardia Civil since its founding in 1834—was replaced by a round, brimmed cap. Though the tricornio had long been a powerful emblem of law and order, for many Spaniards it was also a symbol of repression and a reminder of Franco's dictatorship.

Lt. Col. Tejero's 1981 coup attempt, broadcast by Spanish television and seen around the world, brought additional negative exposure to the already-known emblem. It's no wonder, then, that the government decided to give the Guardia Civil a new hat with a more modern and less-threatening look, perhaps providing its members with something lighter to wear as well. Nostalgic Spaniards and tourists needn't worry, though. The Guardia Civil still wears the tricornio for military parades and religious processions.

—Ricardo Maldonado,
"El Sombrero de Tres Picos"

tricornio hat

de Borbón, bided his time in Estoril, Portugal, vainly hoping to reclaim his father's throne. Juan Carlos, raised in Switzerland and Portugal, would not set foot in Spain until he was ten.

It's often been said of the Bourbon family—which has given both Spain and France some of the most inept kings and queens in history—that they remember everything, while learning nothing. That certainly was what the coup plotters were counting on.

But when the plotters contacted the palace, they received from Juan Carlos de Borbón y Borbón quite a different response from the one they had expected: "Over my dead body."

That, at the time, was widely said to have been the king's answer. "Actually, it was slightly different," someone who was with the king that night told me.

I remember the day I met King Alfonso XIII. I was standing at my window at the Residencia, my hair slicked back fashionably with brilliantine under my boater. Suddenly the royal carriage, complete with two drivers and someone young and female, pulled up to the curb directly below me; the king himself got out of the car to ask directions. Speechless at first (I was theoretically an anarchist at that moment), I somehow replied with perfectly shameful politeness, addressing him correctly as "Majestad." Only when the carriage pulled away did I realize that I hadn't removed my hat. The relief was overwhelming: my honor was still intact.

—Luis Buñuel, *My Last Sigh,* translated by Abigail Israel

"There was a report Tejero would put one bullet in the body of every member of the Cortes who stood in his way. At which point the king said, "In that case, they will have to put two bullets in me."

"The intellectual key to crushing the coup," another of the king's confidants told me, "which the king grasped very quickly, was arriving at the understanding that the seizure of the Cortes was not the essence of the conspiracy." In fact, Tejero's attack was only the cat's-paw of a larger conspiracy, involving military officers who ranked much higher. "The essence of the conspiracy was to implicate the king in the overthrow of Spanish democracy," he went on, "to use the king to legitimize the seizure of power."

Some people told me it was Queen Sofía who first deduced that the mastermind of the coup was the king's own former military tutor, General Alfonso Armada Comín. Others credited the current head of the king's household, Sabino Fernández Campo, with understanding the full dimensions of the plot. But most told me the king himself had figured it out.

The conspirators' plan: while Tejero held parliament hostage, General Armada would take control—or at least seem to take control—of the palace. Then, with both parliament and king under wraps, the commanders of Spain's eleven military regions would proclaim martial law all over the country.

"Once His Majesty understood the exact nature of the conspiracy," said one person, "everything fell into place. He knew what he had to do and he did it. The first thing was to prevent Armada from getting anywhere near the palace. Then, once he was neutralized, to rally the rest of the Spanish armed forces to the cause of democracy."

Before doing anything, however, the king called his father, Don Juan, who was still living in his villa in Estoril, Portugal. The king's father had gone to the movies. Someone rushed to the movie theater, found Don Juan, and drove him home.

"Stay in the palace," Don Juan advised his son. "Hold your ground, whatever the cost. Do not leave under any circumstances—whatever they promise, whatever they threaten. If you give up one inch, all will be lost." (The Spaniard who recounted this saw I was very affected by what he said, and asked why. I answered, "A couple of years ago in Manila, Cory Aquino told me the same thing, when she explained how she puts down *coups d'état*.")

General Jaime Milans del Bosch, another principal conspirator, had declared martial law in the Valencia region and put tanks in the streets half an hour before Tejero actually seized parliament. Of the remaining ten Spanish regional commanders, only two spontaneously rallied to the defense of Spain's legitimate government—one of them in the faraway Canary Islands. "The generals were sitting on the fence," one person told me. "Had the king wavered for a moment, all would have been lost."

While the reaction of the generals caused anguish, the reaction of Spain's two most important democratic allies, as one person put it, "made the king mad as hell." U.S. Secretary of State Alexander Haig dismissed the coup attempt as an "internal affair," as though it were of no concern to the United States if democracy was extinguished in Spain. President Valéry Giscard d'Estaing of France made matters worse, I was told, by offering to send a plane to fly the king and his family out of the country.

"The king was born in exile," one person in the palace that night said. "He is determined to die in Spain. He was ready to die that night, defending his government. He was absolutely resolved never to leave the country, the way his grandfather did."

The king spent hour after hour on the telephone, calling every regional commander directly. In some cases, the sound of the king's voice was sufficient to ensure loyalty. In others, I was told, "very considerable persuasion had to be applied." But within four and a half hours of the attack on the Cortes, the coup had been broken.

There remained, however, the delicate matter of extracting the parliament members from the Cortes alive. Tejero and his soldiers still held Spain's entire elected government hostage.

It was time for the king to turn to his next great task: going on TV to prove to the nation that history was not repeating itself, that democracy and the monarchy, united, had faced a great test and prevailed. But supporters of the coup had seized the Madrid television station. "So we waited," one royal friend remembers. "And we waited."

Finally, loyal troops managed to retake the TV station and escort a crew to Zarzuela Palace. It was nearly one a.m.—though, this being Spain, the whole nation was still wide-awake—when the face of King Juan Carlos flashed on the screen.

Every Spaniard who saw the king that night would never forget it. "It was like the Kennedy assassination," a Spanish historian told me, "only in reverse—an unforgettable moment of absolute confidence and joy that remains with you the rest of your life. It was the moment," he said, "when every Spaniard realized: we have a future. Spain is not going to be a failure anymore."

At the height of the drama, the king had called his father. Now, as it ended, he called for his son, the thirteen-year-old *infante* Felipe. It was past three a.m., I was told, "when Juan Carlos put his arm around his son's shoulder and said, 'Felipe, I want you to remember this moment.' Then the king took the boy, step by step, through everything that had happened. He explained about elections, and how an elected parliament was the representation of the people's will. He explained how the military was the defender of the people—and therefore the greatest treason the military could commit was to turn against the elected representatives of the people.

"Then he explained about the monarchy. He told his son that, while the first duty of a king was to serve the people, a king's ultimate duty was to be the people's last defense.

"It was nearly four by the time the king finished," this person continued. "Things had started to calm down. Besides the king, the queen, and Prince Felipe," he said, "there were only a few other people still there. You know," he said, "we all felt terribly privileged, to have been at the king's side that night."

But historians may never know in minute-by-minute detail what happened that night. "The king wants silence," explains a palace insider who was there. "He wants his heroism to be forgotten. When he dies and his son succeeds him, he wants to be remembered as this nice old man who never did much of anything. Because that is what constitutional monarchs are supposed to do."

"Everyone looks around and still can't quite believe we've all come so far, so fast," a ranking Spanish politician told me. "Intellectually I know there will never be another *coup d'état*. But emotionally? Way back inside me is the feeling: the men with machine guns could come after us again."

By January 1938, when Juan Carlos was born in Italy, the Bourbon family, like Spain itself, seemed to have reached the point of historical bankruptcy. No longer a reigning sovereign, the exiled Alfonso XIII and his family had become ornaments of fascist society in Mussolini's Rome. Il Duce himself took an interest in the infant Spanish prince; he reputedly was the first to suggest to his fellow fascist dictator Francisco Franco that he take Juan Carlos's education in hand.

The family lived in Rome, Switzerland, and later Portugal with little or no money. "Hotel managers grew anxious when the royal family checked in," I was told. They depended on handouts from Spanish nobles and others with a stake in the eventual restoration of the monarchy.

While the parents of the infant Juan Carlos were worrying about money, the parents of other Spanish children were watching their sons die in one of the most gruesome civil wars of the 20th century. In 1936, Francisco Franco launched a military mutiny against the Republican government which had prompted Alfonso XIII to leave the country. One of Franco's many contradictory promises was to restore the monarchy.

"Sure, he planned to restore the monarchy," an elderly Spanish monarchist told me, with bitterness still evident more than 50 years later, "but only after he was dead."

When his forces won the war in 1939, Franco made himself Spain's uncrowned king. Even on Spain's coins he was "*Caudillo* of Spain, by the grace of God." Actually it was by the grace of mass murder and, ultimately, by force of inertia that Franco remained Spain's ruler for the next 36 years.

Franco's rule created an exceedingly strange relationship between him and the Spanish royal family. If he had not overthrown the republic, they would have had no chance at all of regaining the throne. But, having won, Franco became the great obstacle to their dream of return. They played a cat-and-mouse game, decade after decade, for Spain's future. And from the beginning, there was no doubt that the Spanish royal family were the mice.

Juan Carlos's grandfather Alfonso XIII at first was certain he would eventually regain the throne. When he died in 1941, at age 54, everyone considered his only healthy male heir, Don Juan, the next King of Spain. A dashing young prince, Don Juan had volunteered to fight on Franco's side during the Civil War. But the last thing Franco wanted was a young, royal war hero whose popularity might complicate his own plans for the future. The offer was refused. Don Juan sat out the Spanish Civil War, as well as World War II, in exile.

By history, heritage, and expediency, the Spanish Bourbons were natural allies of the Axis powers. Living in Rome, the royal family owed its precarious existence to Mussolini and its precarious hopes of regaining the throne to Franco. But after his father died, Don Juan removed himself and his young family from the fascist orbit—going first to neutral Switzerland, and then, after the Allied victory, to Portugal.

"He foresaw everything," a man who once worked closely with Don Juan told me, "the whole next 50 years: the defeat of Nazism, the triumph of democracy, the emergence of a united Europe, of which Spain must be a part. He understood 50 years ago that the next King of Spain had to be king of all the people. Whether Communists or workers, or professionals or rightists, the king had to be the friend of all, the enemy of none."

There was one thing Don Juan did not foresee: Franco's staying power. Don Juan intended to be Spain's first "king of all the people." But this would never happen. "Franco frustrated him at every step," this person told me, "except one. Don Juan defeated Franco in the battle for the heart and soul of the boy"—"the boy" being Juan Carlos.

"You know," he added, "it's a terribly sad thing to be the son of a king, and the father of a king, but never to be a king yourself."

In March 1945, from Switzerland, [Don Juan] denounced Franco's "totalitarian concept of the state," and called for the establishment of a democratic system, based on "the inherent rights of the human being," and guaranteeing all the "corresponding political rights," including not only freedom of expression but also a just distribution of wealth.

In his "Lausanne Manifesto," as it subsequently was called, Don Juan went on to say that Franco's repressive system was "in flagrant and dangerous opposition to all the political and economic trends of our time." Then, even more remarkably, Don Juan "solemnly" called on Generalísimo Franco to "abandon power" and let an orderly transition to democracy begin.

"The Lausanne Manifesto was a remarkable document—in many ways the first-draft charter of Spain's present democracy," according to the Count of Sert, a Barcelona-based writer and analyst of the monarchy. "Intellectually it was decades ahead of its time, especially in its emphasis on human rights. Even into the '80s, Spanish political discourse was dominated by fascists and Marxists. But that far back Don Juan knew both were wrong."

In August 1948 the dictator and the royal democrat met at sea off San Sebastián, the resort city near the French border. It was a location full of bizarre historical resonances. Here, 80 years earlier, Queen Isabella II—escorted by both her minstrel lover and her king consort—had abandoned Spain. Also on the Spanish-French border, in 1940, Franco and Hitler had met at the moment when the triumph of fascism seemed irreversible.

The encounter between Don Juan and Franco was equally surreal. Don Juan, a direct descendant of Louis XIV, exemplar of the divine right of kings, was now the advocate of popular democracy. Francisco Franco, the son of a naval paymaster, was the tyrannical defender of the absolutist principle.

In 1940, Franco had kept Hitler waiting half an hour so he could complete his siesta. So unyielding was Franco that the *Führer* later remarked he would prefer to have four teeth pulled than undergo such an ordeal again. But this time it was Franco's turn to be discomfited. As the dictator's large ship and Don Juan's little yacht rendezvoused in the choppy Atlantic, Franco got seasick. Don Juan, an experienced sailor, was in perfect form.

The fact that they were meeting in international waters indicated how deeply these two rivals mistrusted each other. For the exiled Don Juan to have set foot in Franco's Spain—and for Franco to have permitted it—would have implied a mutual acceptance that neither was willing to make.

They were meeting to discuss the future of a ten-year-old boy. Both agreed that, one way or another, young Juan Carlos someday would be King of Spain. Both also agreed that Spain's future king should not grow up a foreigner. Therefore, the boy must go to school in Spain.

By getting Franco to welcome his son and heir into the country, Don Juan had gotten the dictator, more practically than ever before, to commit himself to the restoration of the monarchy. But for Franco this was also an opening gambit worthy of the grand master he was. His strategy: to deny Don Juan the throne by turning his son into the usurper; to make sure Francoism lived even after he himself died by turning Juan Carlos into Franco's own ideological heir.

The following November—all scrubbed and tidy—Juan Carlos boarded the *Lusitania Express* in Lisbon, accompanied by his younger brother, Alfonso. The next morning he arrived in Madrid to start school, and enter history. The fates of two jealous men and the future of a country he had never seen before depended on this child.

After World War II, Franco had raised the royal family's hopes by formally proclaiming Spain a kingdom, as well as allowing Don Juan's sons to be educated in Spain. But in 1947, Franco's rubber-stamp parliament enacted a Law of Succession, which gave Franco the right to name the next King of Spain—but only if he wanted to.

Franco now had the power, if not the right, to bypass Don Juan and his family entirely and bestow the crown on some rival branch of the Bourbon family. He was also free to leave the throne vacant, in which case he would have been succeeded by a regency, a committee of func-

It is true Franco was lucky. Untimely deaths removed his two principal rivals in the 1930s and so made him master of Spain when the Nationalists won. He knew he was lucky. That was why he played the football pools once a week, even when he was dictator, and he won twice. He reinforced his luck by appropriating a key religious relic, the hand of St. Teresa of Avila, which had been stolen from a convent and fell to Franco as the spoils of battle at Málaga. He refused to give it back to the nuns and kept it by his side in its reliquary, even on his travels, until his death.

—Paul Johnson, "There is Nothing Else to Be Done. Shoot Them," a review of *Franco: A Biography* by Paul Preston, *The New York Times Book Review*

tionaries dedicated to perpetuating the Generalísimo's fascist state.

What if Franco had decided to deny Don Juan's family the throne in perpetuity? "Nothing and no one could have stopped him," said a man who, at various times, was very close to both Franco and Don Juan. "There were many sleepless nights in Estoril."

Franco's power to fulfill or crush their hopes hung over the Spanish royal family like a Sword of Damocles. In this atmosphere of masterfully contrived uncertainty, Prince Juan Carlos had to tread very cautiously around the dictator and his deputies. One misstep could have cost him and his family everything.

Ostensibly, Juan Carlos was learning to be king. But Franco gave him no chance to observe, let alone participate in, the way Spain was ruled. His only real "job" was serving time at various government ministries, the same way he'd earlier studied at the different military academies. This he did with bonhomie and enthusiasm. But Juan Carlos's friendly and open manner aroused only irritation and suspicion within Franco's authoritarian, closed bureaucracy. "In the ministries," I was told, "he was regarded as a pest."

Don Juan, still living in Portugal, was observing the movements inside Spain closely. More than twenty years younger than Franco, he believed he had time on his side. But now he feared that the dictator, having usurped his throne, had stolen his son. Franco was holding out a most tantalizing and divisive possibility: a restoration of the monarchy with the young Juan Carlos, not his middle-aged father, as king.

"There was a family pact," José María de Areilza, Count of Motrico, told me. "Don Juan would do everything he could and Juan Carlos would do everything he could. Whichever of them actually got to become king would have the other's support.

"They still talked together for hours almost every night," he added. "No one can spend that much time screaming over the telephone."

Whatever the provisions of the agreement between father and son, the emotional tensions became enormous. Kingship raises the normal intergenerational conflict to an affair of state; it makes the clash of paternal pride and youthful ambition into the stuff of which, since time immemorial, historical catastrophe has been made.

There is not the slightest doubt that—much more assiduously than his father ever intended—Juan Carlos kept his side of the bargain. He did do everything he could to become king. And "everything" in those years included toadying up to Franco, and, worse, toadying up to his fascist beliefs.

Juan Carlos's activities thus raised the specter of double betrayal: betrayal of his father's life ambition as well as his deepest conviction, that the next king must be a democratic "king of all the people."

In 1969, Franco made his move: he offered to name Juan Carlos his successor. Juan Carlos, without consulting his father, accepted instantly.

In order to make his nomination formal, Juan Carlos was required to swear loyalty to the principles of Falangism, Franco's brand of fascism. This he solemnly, publicly did with no sign of doubt, hesitation, or regret. However, in the course of his investiture, he did murmur to Franco, "I wonder what my father will think?"

Franco—in what he supposed was his moment of greatest triumph, the moment when he ensured that fascism would govern Spain in perpetuity, thanks to his puppet prince—was human consideration itself. "Do not worry, Your Highness," Franco replied gently. "Everything will turn out for the best."

As indeed it did, because, having betrayed his father to become king, Juan Carlos would go on to betray Franco—in order to fulfill his father's ideals of what the kingship, in a new Spain, should be. Don Juan lost the throne, but in the end his principles triumphed, thanks to his son.

Today, Spaniards tell you that the king is loved, the queen is revered—but that Don Juan may be the most deeply respected member of the royal family. "His life is a parable of democratic stoicism," one historian told me. "Don Juan triumphed by subordinating his own ambitions to his principles. For a new democracy, that is an all-important object lesson."

Quite by chance I met Don Juan while I was in Spain. The Spanish Institute, a New York-based organization which promotes cultural and other links between the United States and Spain, was presenting King Juan Carlos with its Gold Medal. The king and his father arrived together. As they reached the door, the king motioned to his father to go in before him. But Don Juan refused. He made his son enter first, as if to say: No, you are the king.

All eyes were on Juan Carlos. Most foreigners there had no idea who this large old man was. Yet though now almost 80, Don Juan was instantly recognizable from the photos, taken 30 or 50 years ago, I'd seen in history books.

I walked over, and the old man immediately extended his right arm. He shook my hand firmly. He understands English perfectly, though he has been unable to speak since his larynx was removed in a recent operation.

"Sir," I said, "I do not know your country well, but I have been reading a lot of Spanish history lately. I would like you to know I deeply respect the sacrifices you have made for your country."

on Juan de Borbón died April 1, 1993.

—LMc

At the mention of the word "sacrifices," Don Juan reached out again, encircling my upper left arm with his hand and squeezing it tightly. His voiceless lips formed the words "Thank you."

For Juan Carlos, the years after Franco named him his successor were like *Night of the Living Dead*. Every time it seemed that Franco, finally, would loosen his grip on power and life for good, he came staggering back. "Worst of all," one of Juan Carlos's intimates during those years told me, "was living a lie everyday."

One of his only weapons was his charm. "His Majesty's charm is genuine," explained someone who knows him well, "not an act. But he also uses his charm coldly, as a political tool. He knows it is very useful that people believe he is less intelligent, and less calculating, than he really is.

"He certainly fooled Franco," this person added. "But then, he's fooled lots of people."

I asked for examples.

"His father. His wife. Me. Many others. But only with the best of intentions!" he added. "And only with the most honorable results."

Some people still claim, however, that Juan Carlos never lived a lie, because he was a simple opportunist—that there was no conflict between his principles and his public pledge to preserve and defend Falangism.

This harsh criticism is refuted not only by the king's later actions on behalf of democracy but also by specific actions during those years. Three years before Franco's death, Henry Ford II visited Spain. The American auto magnate wanted to set up a massive new factory but worried about the taint of dictatorship and the threat of political turmoil after Franco died.

"Juan Carlos spent most of an afternoon with Mr. Ford," I was told. "He explained in great detail exactly what he was going to do after Franco died—how he was going to pilot the country into a new era of democratic stability and economic growth. Ford was so impressed he invested one billion dollars in Spain. That was an enormous amount in those days, a decisive opening for the Spanish economy."

It was also a courageous move by Juan Carlos, who knew Franco's security police were always watching him.

On November 20, 1975, Franco finally died. Two days later, Juan Carlos was crowned king. Not even fellow royalty was much impressed by the accession of "Juan Carlos the Brief." Among all the world's reigning sovereigns, only Prince Rainier of Monaco and King Hussein of Jordan took the trouble to come to Madrid. They were joined by General Augusto Pinochet [of Chile]. The guests seemed to sum up the world's assumptions: the new king would turn out to be a café-society monarch or a pawn of the generals—if he wasn't simply overthrown first.

Six years later, when Juan Carlos rode to the rescue of the infant democracy, Spain was a motorbike monarchy. "Today," as one Spaniard remarked to me, "we have a Mercedes monarchy."

It's commonplace now to say that these are Spain's best days since "the Golden Century," but that misses the point. Under Juan Carlos, the Spanish people have found a new kind of greatness by escaping, finally, the false notion of greatness that tortured Spain for nearly 500 years.

"I have caused great calamities. I have depopulated provinces and kingdoms. But I did it for the love of Christ and his Holy Mother," Queen Isabella wrote just about the time the conquistadors were beginning their conquest of America. In that quote you have all that was wrong with Spain from Isabella through Franco: the conviction that violence can solve problems, and that doctrines can save nations, let alone souls. King Juan Carlos's achievements are entirely different—as different as today's Spain is from the Spain of the past.

"What a weird thing it is to be king!" a Spanish friend exclaimed at a farewell dinner just before I left the country. "Why do people need them? Why do people agree to be them?"

He went on to answer his own question: "Kings show that all human relationships are based on emotion, not logic. If they're good kings, kings show us that there's more to life than politics or economics or nationhood. They demonstrate that, in some fundamental way, we're all family."

That no doubt will be how Juan Carlos, when the time finally comes, will be remembered in Spain: he took a country riven by war, and traumatized by history, and made it family again.

And his larger place in history?

When the grand accounts of the democratic revolution which swept the world at the end of the 20th century are written, there will be long chapters on Russia, Eastern Europe, and the fall of the Berlin Wall. History will relate how common people, of the humblest origins, shaped the future with their own hands. But the chapter on Spain will also show that even a direct descendant of Louis XIV can change the world for the better.

T. D. Allman is foreign correspondent for Vanity Fair, *where his iconoclastic coverage of political events has included interviews with Yasser Arafat, Corazon Aquino, and Manuel Noriega. His work has appeared in publica-*

tions such as Harper's, The New York Times, The New Republic, *and* Le Monde; *his books include* Unmanifest Destiny *and* Miami: City of the Future. *He lives in Paris and Brooklyn.*

✳

Who among us, among the writers gathered in Valencia a half century ago, would have been able to predict the kind of constitutional regime Spain would have in 1987, much less the political complexion of the government? Such blindness should not surprise us; the future is impenetrable to men. But in every age there are farsighted people. I was privileged to know one such.

After World War II, I lived for some time in Paris. There, in 1946, I met the Spanish Socialist leader Indalecio Prieto....

For two hours—he was rather long-winded and liked to spin out his ideas in detail—he explained to me that the only viable and civilized regime for Spain was a constitutional monarchy with a Socialist prime minister. The other solutions would issue either in civil chaos or in the prolongation of a reactionary dictatorship. His solution, on the other hand, would not merely assure a transition to a stable democracy, but would also open the doors to national reconciliation.

—Octavio Paz, "Who Won the Spanish Civil War? The Barricades and Beyond,"
The New Republic

BRUCE SCHOENFELD

Man and Beast

*An aficionado contemplates the meaning
of the bullfight.*

AT A SINGLE GRAVESITE IN A CEMETERY ON THE NORTHERN FRINGE
of Sevilla lie the mortal remains of three of the most successful
bullfighters of this century. Another monument is being constructed to a fourth. And the tomb of Juan Belmonte is a short
distance away.

The cemetery is in the Macarena district, about a fifteen-
minute drive from downtown. It's easy to spot the entrance once
you get near because the row of waiting taxis stretches through the
iron gateway and into the street. They're for visitors who came by
foot or by bus but are too tired or stricken or distracted to return
that way.

Atop the gravesite of the three bullfighters is a statue of a procession bearing an open casket. This is Joselito El Gallo, who died
of trauma eight days after his 25th birthday, gored by a Viuda de
Ortega bull in Talavera de la Reina, which is on the road from
Badajoz to Madrid. The date, set in a metal plaque, was May 16,
1920.

Joselito was the last great bullfighter to use a simple style without ornamentation and his seven years of concurrent majesty with
Juan Belmonte were a true golden age. There are many Spaniards

who consider Joselito the greatest bullfighter who ever lived. A young matador named José Arroyo has recently emerged using the same nickname and to some it is tantamount to blasphemy. Just about every Spanish man, woman, and child knows about the original Joselito, and the majority could tell you details of his life. Of course, true bullfight aficionados know everything about him and especially about the tragedy: the name of the bull that killed him, the time of day, the intricate series of passes he performed just prior to his death.

His genius manifested itself in technical proficiency. Killing bulls came easy to Joselito, or at least appeared to. Rarely was his effort evident. His death was a terrible surprise to all of Spain, which had considered him invulnerable and had feared instead for the life of Belmonte.

I have collected some numbers to reinforce my appreciation of Joselito. For instance: in seven full years as a matador, Joselito fought and killed all six bulls in a *corrida* 22 times, rather than alternating with two other matadors as is nearly always the case. On 257 occasions he appeared with Belmonte. He fought 81 times in Madrid, 64 in Barcelona, 58 in Sevilla and 49 in Valencia, and those statistics are notable because succeeding in the big cities is the truest test of a bullfighter.

Some one with English blood has written: "Life is real; life is earnest, and the grave is not its goal." And where did they bury him? And what became of the reality and the earnestness? The people of Castille have great common sense. They could not produce a poet who would write a line like that. They know death is the inescapable reality, the one thing any man may be sure of; the only security.... They think a great deal about death and when they have a religion they have one which believes that life is much shorter than death. Having this feeling they take an intelligent interest in death and when they can see it being given, avoided, refused and accepted in the afternoon for a nominal price of admission they pay their money and go to the bull ring.

—Ernest Hemingway,
Death in the Afternoon (1932)

He understood bulls and the geometry of bullfighting and was able to do whatever he wanted with almost any bull—and yet he was killed in the ring. That lesson is learned early by every bullfighter.

To Joselito's right is the gravestone of Ignacio Sánchez Mejías. He was born June 4, 1891, and he died August 23, 1934. Sánchez Mejías had little natural grace, and limited ability as a bullfighter, but he brought such pluck and valor to the *corrida* that he became the favorite matador of Andalusia, of which Sevilla is the capital.

He started his career as Belmonte's *banderillero,* what is called a peon or subaltern, but against all advice went out on his own as a matador. He retired with health and fortune intact but was persuaded to make a comeback—a fatal mistake. He was a great friend of the poet Federico García Lorca, and after Sánchez Mejías died of a goring García Lorca wrote *Llanto por Ignacio Sánchez Mejías* which is arguably the most famous poem composed in Spanish in this century. Its haunting refrain, "...at five in the afternoon," *a las cinco de la tarde*, denotes the hour of Sánchez Mejías's death.

A few steps down the path I see a vast hole in the earth with concrete girders protruding and cream-colored bricks piled to either side. A small sign has been hand-lettered in pencil and leans against the brick. Don't ask, it says. This is for Paquirri.

His is a sad story, and stunningly modern. It's easy to think of the death of Joselito happening in some sepia-toned time of poor sanitary conditions and general confusion, but there is no sloughing off Paquirri's death. It happened in the middle of the Reagan era, days after the Los Angeles Olympics: a recent event.

Francisco Rivera, called Paquirri, as handsome as a movie star and married to a popular singer, was tossed and wounded in Pozoblanco on September 26, 1984. Medical help was delayed because the local hospital was under construction and the nearest city, Córdoba, was 80 kilometers away on rough road. Paquirri survived the ambulance ride but died on arrival. He was 36.

Early in his career he had married Carmina Ordóñez, the daughter of the matador Antonio Ordóñez. He discarded Carmina in a scandalous divorce because he had fallen in love with a willowy black-haired entertainer named Isabel Pantoja. The strength of his bullfighting was always in his daring and the force of his will but after he married La Pantoja there were whispers that he was no longer willing to take the same risks because now life was going too well for him. It is said two things can make cowards out of brave bullfighters: a serious goring and a contented marriage.

There had been talk of retirement all that season and the *corrida* in Pozoblanco would likely have been his last. He had been married to La Pantoja a year when he died, and she has never recovered from the loss. She's still a tremendously popular entertainer, probably more popular than before because of the profundity of the tragedy, and you can see her now performing as far away as Miami, singing songs about Paquirri and crying onstage.

In 1959, Ernest Hemingway followed the matadors Antonio Ordóñez and Luis Miguel Dominguín through Spain to watch them fight bulls, documenting their rivalry for a Life *magazine three-part series, which later became the book,* The Dangerous Summer. *Ordóñez, who was engaged at the time to (and later married) his rival's sister, was Hemingway's clear favorite.*

—LMc

It's a short walk from Paquirri's monument to the grave of Belmonte. The tomb is a modernesque sculpture of many-faceted black marble resting on a thick white stone base. It looks like no other gravesite I've seen and says simply 1892-1962 Juan Belmonte. Three bunches of carnations, one red, one pink, and one white, have been placed on its shiny black surface.

Juan Belmonte was the transcendent figure in the history of bullfighting. He changed everything. His style was absolutely the opposite of Joselito's and in opposition to all the rules of classical *toreo*. In his 1953 book *What Is Torear?* bullfight critic Gregorio Corrochano wrote: "The *toreo* of Joselito astonished with its mastery, its extension, its dominion...its facility solving whatever problems were presented by the bull in the plaza. The *toreo* of Belmonte surprised us with just the opposite, by the unexplainable: he bothered us with the impossible; it hurt to see him *torear.*"

In the end it was Joselito, the invulnerable one, who was caught and killed by a bull. Belmonte lived on in an apartment overlooking the Guadalquivir River in the center of Sevilla, five blocks from La Maestranza [bullring] and in a massive country home outside the city with its own bullring and bulls he used to cape at night.

And then, when he was 70 years old and the most renowned citizen in Sevilla and, save Franco, perhaps all of Spain, Belmonte put a gun to his head and killed himself, just as his friend Ernest Hemingway had done the year before.

When I first came to Sevilla in 1986, to learn about bullfighting, I searched for and found the American matador John Fulton, whose relentless love for the bullfight is as consuming as any Spaniard's. Fulton has essentially wagered his life on success in this most intransigent of arenas, and he has endured. After three decades, even his detractors admire his tenacity.

This hardly satisfies him, for he had set his sights on what you might call immortality, an acknowledged greatness, a place beside Joselito, Belmonte, Rafael El Gallo and the rest, refusing to admit that for him such a thing was impossible. He ran up against a fundamental truth: that he who would be considered a great bullfighter had best be Spanish born....

And one who arrives in the world in Philadelphia, USA, of Hungarian and Italian parentage, and decides at age nineteen to become a bullfighter because he is infatuated with an old Tyrone Power movie that represents the life as glamorous and exotic and rewarding, and comes to Spain with no money and no connections to seek knowledge and respect and fame and maybe fortune, that man is attempting to buck such long odds and overcome such obtrusive and variegated difficulties that the nicest thing anyone could call him is foolish.

John Fulton came anyway and essentially beat the odds—but in the end he didn't. Because even though he was the first American to graduate from *novillero* to full matador in Spain, a ceremonial advancement known as the *alternativa,* and although he had several indisputable triumphs such as cutting an ear with a Miura [bull] in Sevilla, the wall of prejudice eventually proved unassailable and his noble character is today speckled with bitterness.

He is 57 years old and tall—some say too tall for a matador—with a handsome, wide-open face and a receding hairline and protuberant ears, and he lives in a spacious house in the southern part of Sevilla not far from the rich section. He supports himself as a painter and sculptor. Some of the painting is done in bull's blood.

Fulton has not officially retired as a matador and still hopes to fight again but he hasn't appeared in a full *corrida* in Spain in a decade and now a comeback is all but impossible. He continues to train often with a mechanical bull, however. It is instructive to note that he has been working on his autobiography for some time and plans to publish it with the title *John Quixote.* The comparison is apt, except that the windmills he tilted at tilted back.

The studio where his work is displayed is on the Plaza de la Alianza in the oldest and most beautiful quarter of town, the Barrio de Santa Cruz. His adopted Gypsy son, Federico, works there and prospective matadors looking for a break are often around. Through both his kindness and his karma, Fulton seems to attract the luckless.

Those who have read *Iberia,* James Michener's magnificent nonfiction volume on Spain, have already found John Fulton. There he is on page 69 of the Fawcett paperback edition dancing in an attic during the *feria,* and later Michener praises him for his generosity and describes his struggles during his early days as a bullfighter, "stone broke and trying to make his way in one of the toughest professions in the world...."

"How Fulton supported himself during those bleak and wonderful years I do not know," Michener writes. "Most of us who trespassed on his hospitality managed in some way or other to leave behind donations: one brought the wine, another anchovies, another the cheese. Hemingway made his contribution by check; a delightful woman from Cleveland made hers by throwing memorable flamenco parties at which she gave John a fee for his professional help; I made mine by commissioning Fulton to paint me a picture, for I judged that he had more chance to succeed as an artist than as a matador. I was right."

Those words were published in 1968 and on Christmas Day of that year, an unorthodox date for a *corrida*, Fulton triumphed with the Miura in Sevilla. He was 36 years old.

"Now, if I had been some Spaniard, any Spaniard, that would have assured me of a fight in the April *feria*," Fulton says. "But I have never been able to get any kind of fight in Sevilla since then."

He tells me that a friend has sent him a clipping of an interview with a Spanish painter, a fool of the most parochial stamp, who believes that in order to paint bulls one must be Spanish.

"Then you go out and prove that not only can you paint them, you can fight them," Fulton says. "And they say, God, what are we going to do now? I mean, let's face it, the Miuras are the killer bulls, man. Some snot-nosed kid from Philadelphia goes out there and swings his ass off with them and that means either one of two things. Either John Fulton really is a good bullfighter or the Miura bulls are a piece of shit."

I tell him neither of those things could be true, the way the Spaniards think.

"Right," he says. "So they ignore it. And that's the frustrating part."

The Christmas *corrida* was many years ago but the frustration has festered. John Fulton, respected by his peers as a man and as an artist, has become the spiritual leader of a cadre of English-speaking aficionados, professional men, men of some wealth and substance, who revere him because he has done what they haven't dared dream of. He is also an accomplished painter and loving father and grandfather, with a winsome California blonde for a companion and a multitude of friends and well-wishers.

In April 1994, at the age of 62, John Fulton retired from bullfighting after his last fight in San Miguel de Allende, Mexico, where he had also fought his very first corrida. *At the end of his final performance he was awarded two bull's ears, and his son Federico ceremoniously cut the bullfighter's pigtail from the back of his father's neck.*

Fulton continues to paint and operate a gallery in Sevilla, and since June 1994 has been training Spain's first Japanese matador, Atsuhiro Shimoyama, known as The Rising Sun Kid.

—LMc

All of this is important to him, but not of the ultimate importance. "Only when I am bullfighting," Fulton says, "do I feel truly full."

I have a discussion with some American students about the merits of bullfighting. Several who have never seen a bullfight disparage anyone who has.

This is at the Mesón Serranito, which is just off the Plaza del Museo on Calle Alfonso XII, a brief walk from my apartment....

There is a vast photo of La Maestranza on the wall up front and elsewhere in the bar a full suit of lights in a frame with a set of real *banderillas.* A stuffed bull's head is mounted beside that, not as big as the one in Tres Reyes but big enough to make me pause before offering criticism of any matador.

The discussion starts when someone mentions visiting John Fulton's studio in the Plaza de la Alianza and seeing paintings done in bull's blood. Swiftly we divide into pro- and anti-bullfighting camps. The argument is long and debilitating and nobody's mind is changed. One girl from Texas insists on shouting. She says her distaste of the *corrida* is too strong for her to talk in a normal voice. "Y'all are butchers," she says, then plugs her ears with her fingers when we try to argue.

Any aficionado from outside the Spanish culture knows he must always have a defense for bullfighting handy, something to counter the inevitable opposition. It almost always comes from people who have never seen a bullfight, or have seen one but knew nothing about it. There are two ways in which people react when they hear you

> *Beside me sat a blooming matron, in a white lace mantilla, with three very juvenile daughters; and if these ladies sometimes yawned they never shuddered. For myself, I confess that if I sometimes shuddered I never yawned. Yet I thought the bull, in any case, a finer fellow than any of his tormentors, and I thought his tormentors finer fellows than the spectators. In truth, we were all, for the time, rather sorry fellows together. A bullfight will, to a certain extent, bear looking at, but it will not bear thinking of.*
>
> —Henry James, *Collected Travel Writings: The Continent* (1876)

enjoy bullfighting, have made a study of it and travel to Spain often simply to watch it: with fascination or with disgust. Nobody I've met has reacted with boredom.

At lunch the next day I ask Pleas Campbell about his own taurine defenses. He's a good person to ask because he has few bullfighting pretensions and no interest in any of its academic justifications. There are books linking the intricacies of bullfighting to various tribal rites in Iberian prehistory, books detailing the sociological value bullfighting holds in modern-day Spanish culture, books with every kind of theory you can imagine. Pleas disdains them. He attends bullfights because he enjoys them; he appreciates the nobility inherent in both man and beast. Bullfighting gives him a kick, he says. And that's the best defense of all.

He tells a story about the local preacher in his hometown of Hickory, North Carolina, stopping by the family house to pay a condolence call following the death of Pleas's father. This was just a year or so ago. The preacher was there to see the mother because Pleas had moved out of Hickory as a teenager and has hardly been back since. He's lived in Barcelona and on the Costa del Sol and all over, and now he has a house in Miami, in Coconut Grove, and spends about four months of every year in Spain. But at that time Pleas was home for the funeral and met the preacher, and eventually the preacher asked what he did with his summers.

"I told him, Well, I go and see the bullfights," Pleas relates. The preacher reacted with horror, so Pleas trotted out his best defense. He has been using it for almost four decades now, since he first came to Spain in 1951 as an enlisted man in the Navy, although he has probably had relatively few such encounters with men of the cloth.

"I said, Whoa now, wait a minute," Pleas says. "I said, Don't judge lest you be judged. And then I started telling him a little something about bullfighting. I told him that it's not a sport, and there are rules to the game, and it only lasts about ten minutes because after that the bull starts feeling pain. And I told him to think about the meat he eats every day, and how the animal dies. Maybe they clubbed it to death, maybe they put it in the back of a van to suffocate it.

"Now, the bulls out there in a bullfight, I told him, they've had a hell of a life, they're tranquil. They've been out on the pasture doin' nothing. Nobody's bothered them with anything. Then the bull comes in and he gets his moment of glory. He dies, but sometimes he takes his tormentors with him. I think if I were an animal, by God, I'd like to be a fighting bull. At least my name might go down in history, and at the very least I know I'm going to end up on somebody's table just like some old cow."

The preacher started to argue that the bull is being tortured in the ring, but Pleas interrupted. He told him that the bull is so distracted by the task of getting

I believe it to be impossible for anyone of northern blood to sit through a corrida with an easy conscience, or without moments of acute embarrassment and distress. Nevertheless, the thrill and the beauty can seduce; more than that, can be remembered with longing. Bravery, grace and self-control; the cunning of cape and sword against incalculable force; sunlight and the hovering of death; comedies and tragedies of character; tinny music timing an old and tricky ritual; crazy courage and sickening failure and the serenity of great matadors curving in peril along the monstrous horn. There is no defense. Either it gets you, or you're sick.

—Kate O'Brien,
Farewell Spain (1937)

to the waving material in front of him that it barely feels anything. "Think about a time maybe you were in a fight, and you hit somebody and you got hit." Pleas told him. "Or you were having so much fun and you scraped your leg, but you didn't realize it until the next day. Wait a minute, you say, how did I get that bruise? You don't even remember. Now, what if the bull is fighting and he doesn't feel anything? See, it's all in hot blood!"

The arguments against the bullfight are multiple, and they vary enormously in logic and coherence. Those who call themselves animal lovers often decry the inhumanity of the spectacle. Yet I know few people as keenly attuned to animals as those involved in bullfighting. A bullfighter or bull breeder or even a true bullfight aficionado understands the characteristics of the *toro bravo* in the same way that a racetrack trainer has an affinity for thoroughbred horses.

The traditional North American cowboy, who lives on a ranch surrounded by animals and depends on them for his living, has that same special attunement to the animal world, although he raises livestock for the marketplace. Because he relies on animals to survive, he's likely to have a far more accurate sense of their—and our—proper place in the universe than many animal lovers, who enjoy eating meat but are philosophically opposed to the slaughter. Some of them would prefer to wait until every animal died of natural causes, or was hit by a bus.

Some who would ban the bullfight say it is a misuse of prime agricultural land, and that is an argument more difficult to dispute. But on equal footing is the idea that the *toro bravo*, which has been on the earth thousands of years and according to cave drawings was interacting with man before the time of Christ, would cease to exist without the ranches. If a Spanish government ever came to power determined to stop bullfighting forever, it would be easy: strip the land from the *ganaderías*. Once the existing strains of these precisely bred animals die out it will be impossible to create others, and the wonderfully noble wild bull will go the way of the carrier pigeon.

There are also those who argue that the bullfight takes advantage of the underclass of Spanish society, dangling the alluring prospect of riches and fame before the poorest males as an incentive for them to risk their lives by providing entertainment for the wealthy. I agree, and I know that for every El Cordobés who gains financial security there are tens of thousands of aspirants who never see the inside of a bullring. Nobody keeps statistics on how many of these are seriously injured or even killed in some informal neighborhood bullfight, trying to cape some one-eyed six-year-old bull that has been fought a dozen times before, the local streets blocked off by makeshift barricades and everybody taking a turn with a single, torn *capote*—for that is often the only way a would-be torero with no money can afford to practice. It is horribly dangerous, something no established bullfighter would ever dare to do, and yet it happens all the time around the country. To hear the stories tears at the heart.

But is bullfighting so different as a means of escaping poverty from elective military service? Or professional boxing? Tossing off the shackles of a life of extreme poverty, in Spain or anywhere else, requires more than a dedicated work ethic. The economic inequality of generations isn't often overcome by scrubbing floors for eighteen hours a day. Risks must be taken, and those risks can take many forms, from dangerous sports to a life of violent crime, or even revolution. Outlawing the bullfight won't make the lives of those underfed urchins any better. All they would lose is an avenue of possible escape.

Among Spaniards, banning the bullfight has for years been the goal of a tiny number of activists, although in the years since Franco's death they have become increasingly zealous. And the ongoing European flux is currently polarizing opinion, pro- and anti-taurine. There are those who sincerely believe bullfighting to be a throwback to the entertainments of the Roman Colosseum, a barbaric remnant in the modern age, and they don't want Spain to be considered the embarrassment of a united Europe....

[Bullfighting supporters contend that] that which is essentially Spanish must be cherished, not banned. Flamenco must be saved, and the afternoon siesta, and the *paseo* around the town plaza at night. And the bullfight—for nothing is more uniquely Spanish than that.

I have heard this from several Spaniards who themselves do not care for bullfighting. They are not arguing out of self-interest, but for their grandchildren. And their culture.

Bruce Schoenfeld lives in Boulder, Colorado, and is the author of The Last Serious Thing: A Season at the Bullfights, *from which this story was excerpted. He has written for the* Wall Street Journal, *the* Los Angeles Times, Details, Saveur, *and* The New York Times Magazine, *among other publications.*

✳

At five in the afternoon
It was exactly five in the afternoon,
A boy brought the white sheet
at five in the afternoon.
A frail of lime ready prepared
at five in the afternoon.
The rest was death, and death alone
at five in the afternoon....
A coffin on wheels is his bed
at five in the afternoon.
Bones and flutes resound in his ears
at five in the afternoon.
Now the bull was bellowing through his forehead
at five in the afternoon.
The room was iridescent with agony
at five in the afternoon.
In the distance the gangrene now comes
at five in the afternoon.
Horn of the lily through green groins
at five in the afternoon.
The wounds were burning like suns
at five in the afternoon.
and the crowd was breaking the windows
at five in the afternoon.
At five in the afternoon.
Ah, that fatal five in the afternoon!
It was five by all the clocks!
It was five in the shade of the afternoon!...

It will be a long time, if ever, before there is born
an Andalusian so true, so rich in adventure.
I sing of his elegance with words that groan,
and I remember a sad breeze through the olive trees.

—Federico García Lorca, "Lament for Ignacio Sánchez Mejías" (1935),
translated by Stephen Spender and J. L. Gili,
Federico García Lorca: The Selected Poems

RICARDO MALDONADO

How to Get There

Some roads can take you farther
than others.

SUNLIGHT GLINTS OFF THE WHITE LINES ON THE PAVEMENT—
straight, clear lines that seem to have been painted with a ruler. I
have seen only a few cars in the last hour and passed even fewer
trucks. I saw some horses a few kilometers back, on far hillsides,
and some small white towns in the distance. But now, looking
ahead, there is no sign of life to interrupt this flat, deserted extension of land and asphalt, this bright, new highway in Spain.

My childhood memories of Spain are full of roads. Roads, not
highways. Not so long ago, the back country roads of today were
the only roads we had in Spain. For 40 years my father worked as
a civil engineer building all kinds of Spanish roads. Now, when my
wife and I return for our yearly visit, I can't help thinking of those
old roads while driving on the modern highways. I wonder how
my father feels. He, more than anyone, knows just how much has
changed.

I remember boyhood trips with my father to visit his work sites.
Sometimes we would stop where a road was being fixed, the air
filled with a pungent, not unpleasant scent of tar: these were the
chocolateras at work—machines that throw hot tar on the pavement
and black smoke and steam into the air. Though they received

their friendly nickname from the chocolate-making machines they resembled, they looked like frightening creatures to me. I watched impressed as the men worked so close to them while I stood many feet away, at my father's insistence. A group of men would walk behind the machine, spreading tar and sand, followed by another heavy dinosaur, *la apisonadora,* which used its enormous cylinder to flatten the road and anything that happened to be in its path.

On other occasions I would help my father and the workers survey the distances where they were building a new road or needed to eliminate a dangerous curve. Those curves in the road, so rare in the mainly flat province of Salamanca where we lived, always took inexperienced or distracted drivers by surprise and caused innumerable accidents. Most of the curves were adorned with not only traffic signals asking drivers to slow down, but also small wooden or stone crosses for those who, having overlooked or ignored the signs, had lost their lives there.

My invaluable help to my father and his coworkers consisted of holding sticks painted with wide red and white stripes that apparently would help them determine the exact distance and position of the spot where I stood in relation to them. It wasn't easy. I was supposed to stand completely still while they looked through their optical instruments and took what seemed to me like endless notes.

It was during one of those trips, on the road connecting Salamanca to the town of Alba de Tormes, that my father pointed out what looked like a rocky terrain on the side of the road. This was in fact part of the old Roman road; the "modern" road had been built over it, he said. We were driving over the very same road that the Romans had used two thousand years before, and the Visigoths after them, and then the Moors, and possibly Napoleon's troops invading Spain, and so many others throughout the centuries.

The Romans were experts in public works. Those paved-over parts of ancient road, which can be found throughout Spain, seem more solid and require less maintenance than the newer ones. Indeed, the often precarious and weak roads of today, fashioned too quickly, pale in comparison with the stability and strength of the Roman public works—austere and functional, but built to last centuries.

You can see this workmanship especially in the bridges. The Roman bridge in Salamanca that crosses the River Tormes—and offers a beautiful view of the city—has a clean, simple structure. Back when the city had only two bridges (it now has three), the heaviest trucks were diverted to the Roman bridge and only lighter traffic could enjoy the *puente nuevo*. On weekends and special occasions the Roman bridge was illuminated at night, adding more beauty to the already magical view of the city and its cathedral from across the river. Only those heavy trucks, lumbering across the only bridge that could support them, would dispel the magic.

The Romans built at least twelve thousand miles of highways in Spain. The roads were built first for military use, but they later served well for traders. Many modern highways follow the old Roman roads, and in some cases (notably the Roman bridges at Mérida in Extremadura) are still in use.

—Ann and Larry Walker,
A Season in Spain

Driving along this pristine new highway, I think too about the trees that used to line the old roads of the Castilian plains. Before cars existed, the trees provided shade for people and animals traveling along them. Later, as cars replaced carriages, the tree trunks were painted white so that drivers could avoid hitting them. Cars got faster, however, and these trees became a deadly hazard even with their white trunks. Since there was no need to provide shade for cars that sped by, a government order decreed that they be cut down, and many disappeared. But some small communities defied the order. They kept their trees, especially along the roads near villages, so today you can still spot some very old ones.

The roads of my youth were designed to connect towns, not avoid them. The road always led right through the main street (often the only street) of small towns that happened to be in the way.

Though I lament that from this highway I can't see even the dimmest light from a distant town, it is true that the highways make small towns much safer than they once were. This is especially true for children, who can play with more abandon near roads that aren't main travel routes. The chickens, too, are fortunate now that their main cause of "natural" death is no longer linked to the asphalt. And some would say that the new highways protect the towns from destructive hordes of tourists.

But a lot has been lost. The highways have left many villages in near isolation, with too little contact with the outside world. Moreover, the big, expansive freeways have become obstacles for townspeople who have to somehow cross them to reach their wheat fields, olive trees, or pastures. Not long ago, my father told me he'd had to add a small underpass to a large highway design to enable a shepherd to move his animals to pastures on the other side.

A friend—I'll call her Carmen—happened to know a small boy whose father was caretaker of the cathedral. One fine autumn night he unlocked a door to the tower and we three climbed silently, carrying lit candles, to the rooftop. There we stood in awe, as the moon and racing clouds sketched fantastic forms on the roof and town below.

—James O'Reilly, "In Salamanca"

Perhaps what I miss most of those old routes through towns is watching the rituals of human life. Driving through the villages, we could sense the daily lives of the people we passed. We could smell *tapas* being cooked in olive oil, *churros* frying, wood burning in a fireplace, or horse manure, depending on the village and the time of the day. Or listen to conversations wafting out the open doors of taverns. And we could see people's faces. The smaller the village, the more inclined people were to wave to passing travelers. In some towns, the houses were so close to the road that we could see deep inside them, through the windows, gleaning snapshot images of people's lives.

If you passed through town on a weekend evening, you'd be sure to observe the *paseo* along the main street, and with it the courting ritual, a poignant manifestation of the tenacity and perseverance of young Spaniards. It usually begins with brief, subtle eye contact initiated by boys as they pass girls walking in the opposite direction. This preliminary phase takes several weekends and normally is followed by the exchange of almost undetectable smiles. After many weekends of corresponding smiles, the process might culminate with the boy's courageous approach to the girl after Sunday morning Mass. Official couples then gain the right to walk the road together, most likely accompanied by distracted chaperons watching all the other people parading through town. I think how Spain's new highways seem much less conducive to bringing couples together this way.

The glare off the highway from the setting sun has made my eyes tired. I haven't stopped or even slowed down for more than two hours. Up ahead, I see the exit for the town of Palma del Río. My foot lifts off the gas pedal and begins to tap gently on the brake.

It is Sunday evening. If I slow down enough on my way through town, maybe I'll glimpse a bit of the drama of human exchange, a *tapa* shared between friends at a bar, a wink given and returned across an open road. This may not be the fastest way to reach my destination tonight, but perhaps it will take me where I most want to go.

Ricardo Maldonado was born and raised in Salamanca, Spain, and moved to the United States in the early 1980s. He now lives in Cambridge, Massachusetts, with his wife, Lynn Shirey, and their young son, Daniel, whom he someday hopes to show the Spain of his youth.

✳

So I remember only the personal things: my father fishing off the pier at Arenys de Mar, wearing his black beret, his white skin reddened and freckled by the sun and his crumpled linen jacket looking like some remnant of his colonial past; my mother turning up her face and hands towards the blazing sun in near ecstasy, or stooping from her great height to converse in fluent Catalán with Pedro, the one-armed car-park attendant, waving her hands and seeming like a stranger to me. And, of course, I remember the place itself.

Only now, over this past year or two, looking at the poems I write, have I realized that places co-exist with people in my emotions. Perhaps it was another, more significant, move to a new house that made this clear; perhaps it was a more general shift away from dependence on people. In any case, I have finally admitted my love of places, an emotional stance I certainly learned from my mother. Though she never articulated it directly, her eloquent use of the Spanish language in our British home and her defiant sun worship in our suburban back garden clearly demonstrated her enduring relationship to that place.

—Judith Barrington, *Lifesaving: Towing Myself to Shore*

PETER FEIBLEMAN

A Sacramental Return

*What effect do years and memory have
on a place like Seville?*

"WHEN I FIRST WENT TO SEVILLE I WAS BLINDED: I WALKED INTO a street and stopped in the wheeling brightness. The light was harsh and shattered. There is no way to define or wholly describe the sun-swollen air filled with the smells of olives, horse dung, violent jasmine, fish frying in oil, tomatoes, bitter-orange and bitter-lemon groves, black tobacco, cinnamon, cloves, rotting river odors and the raw smells of sea animals mixed with the tar of boats and the open, burnt smell of the earth itself. I sat at a dusty outdoor bar in the shade near the river under a trellis of bougainvillea topped with honeysuckle like a surf of flowers. It was June and the heat shone in the city: Seville was like a huge balloon of dust with the sun in it. The place is a river port on the Guadalquivir, and for most of the year something in the air seems to sharpen the senses—the thing that seduced the Moors from the deserts of Africa and kept them here for eight centuries—you can feel the ripening of your own body. I remember sitting under the froth of flowers and hearing in the heat bubble the muted sound of a child's castanets that floated out of a distant courtyard like the spilling of shells under the sea...."

I wrote that 22 years ago, about a summer's day 18 years before that. It's 40 years now since the morning I first went to live in Seville.

This year I went back for a look, uncomfortable about the effect of the place on memory—the effect of memory upon me. What had seemed lyrical at 18, sensual at 36, might have dried up and disintegrated with time, disappearing along with my youth into a pretentious heap of mush-mouth nonsense. Which is, I suppose, a fancy way of saying that I was afraid.

It was a cool morning in late April when I drove into town, and it was Holy Week. For several days, processions of church floats had been roaming the streets. This had started on Palm Sunday and would end on Easter Sunday, but from Thursday on were the best-known figures—La Virgen de la Esperanza de Triana, La Virgen de la Macarena and El Cristo del Gran Poder. In Seville these three are legion, but every church in Spain, no matter how small, contains a carved image of Jesus and another of the Virgin Mary. During Holy Week the two are lifted onto individual floats and carried by hand through each city or town, where people worship the Virgin of their choice—forsaking all others, forgetting that they represent the same Holy Mother. The pagan origins of certain rites still show, though all religion has long since been taken over by the Catholic Church.

"*No me fío de la Esperanza*," an old Sevillan friend said, sitting at an outdoor café after lunch the first day, "I don't trust the Esperanza, but the Macarena—now *she* works miracles…." Isabel is my age, tall for an Andalusian, with dense graying hair that has gleams of black in it. She is often given to talking about her past, her head thrown back and her mouth open as if she were laughing at the sky.

Next to the café where we sat, a wisteria vine bloomed, pulsating here and there like a delicate blue vein in the brilliant light. Now and then clouds scudded across the sun and the light dimmed. The walls of the city shone at this hour, deep and glowing, a color unlike that in any other city of the world: you can't paint Seville because Seville itself is a painting. A few kilometers away, in a village named Alcalá de Guadaira, is a sand unique in color as well as availability, since it doesn't exist anywhere else. Called *albero*, it reflects a kind of golden ochre that heightens in sunlight. Mixed with paint on countless walls around the city, it appears pale yellow at dawn, copper at noon, gold in the afternoon and flesh-colored at night. Mingled with the myriad tints of old roofing tiles, the terra-cotta look of other walls, the dried-blood effect of well-worn brick, the ancient gray stones and the red earth of Seville itself, it produces a richness that is unthinkable: the color of time.

"She's a beauty, my city." Isabel was following my gaze around the facades. "I remember when you first saw her."

So did I: on an afternoon 40 years ago, Isabel had walked me around Seville, careful never to touch or hold hands because, in those days, it would have been considered too intimate. The rules of social conduct were strict and I remember reaching out to take her arm when we crossed the street and seeing her cringe away. "You don't understand," she had said that day, "you aren't my *novio*, my fiancé, you don't understand.... People would call me a *puta*, a whore, if I let you touch me in public."

Now she laughed and pointed at a scantily dressed young couple crossing the street with their arms around each other, the girl's head resting on the boy's shoulder. "The world has changed—all of it. You know the only thing that hasn't?"

I didn't.

"Seville," she said. "Down under. We have tall buildings across the river in Triana, where the Gypsies used to live, and two department stores in town, and new

If a stranger could inspect but one city in Spain and if he wished to acquire therefrom a reasonable comprehension of what the nation as a whole was like, I think he would be well advised to spend his time in Sevilla, for this city, even though it is too individualistic to be called a microcosm of the whole, is nevertheless a good introduction to classical Spanish life. I was familiar with the rest of Spain before I saw Sevilla, but nothing I had learned elsewhere taught me so much about Spanish behavior. Others have reported a similar experience, for Sevilla does not have ambiente; *it* is *ambiente.*

—James A. Michener, *Iberia: Spanish Travels and Reflections*

condominiums and hotels and restaurants. The city's a little dangerous—in Madrid they call us the drug capital of Spain, *tienen
muy mala lengua, los Madrileños* [always bad-mouthing something,
those Madrileños]. But in the end, Seville's always Seville. After a
certain age it's only the surface of a city that alters. Like a person.
I'll show you."

We got up and walked down a street and Isabel stopped to point
at a balcony a block away. At first I didn't recall and then I did: late
one night I'd seen a man eighteen or nineteen, my age then, come
around the corner with a guitar and place himself below the balcony; he went on playing a long time after the shadow of a girl's
face appeared at the window above, and I'd laughed because it
seemed so like a film cliché—as if he were an actor, the street a set
in some Hollywood back lot. "Oh, stop trying to sound superior,
you're lucky to be seeing this," Isabel had said, "it's not done any
more...it's old-fashioned."

"Imagine my thinking it was old-fashioned *then*," she said
laughing, "look at us now...we're old-fashioned."

A procession was moving somewhere in the distance; you could
hear the familiar band music, the silence and drums, then the short,
dissonant melody of Holy Week. Isabel led me by the hand to a
corner near the cathedral where a crowd had gathered to watch.
La cofradía, the brotherhood, came first, dressed in the costumes of
the Inquisition, with pointed hats and masked faces, purple robes
swaying as they marched. Each statue of the Virgin has her own
cofradía, costumed in her color, the men who protect and contribute to the cost of her train and her float each year. The brotherhood walked in silence, some with banners, a few with incense,
more with candles at the top of long poles. From time to time a
child darted out of the crowd with a ball of soft wax, and the men
with the candles tilted them so that the melted part at the top
dripped down and the child could catch it and add to the growing ball. The Virgin's *paso*, float, followed, encrusted with gold and
surrounded by flowers and silver candelabras—the Christ soon
after—each *paso* carried by 20 or 30 men who show their devotion by supporting the enormous weight for several hours.

Farther along, on a cross street, were tiers of wooden chairs placed for out-of-towners who come to see Holy Week each year; almost any hotel concierge has access to the seats and sells tickets. But I like standing as we were, with a bunch of locals on a side street, watching as the men beneath the float moved on, rocking the Virgin gently from side to side.

"You used to like it better in *la madrugada*," Isabel said, "early in the morning, when it's dark. Me too...we'll come back. I know people with a balcony...."

Beginning Thursday were two long series of processions four hours apart, the first from three in the afternoon to midnight—the second from about four in the morning till noon the next day. As a rule, after the first one, people went home for dinner and a nap until it was time for the second, the most famous procession of all.

Isabel left me, and we met again a little before two a.m. in the bar of my hotel, after I'd eaten, slept, showered and changed clothes. She had her mother with her, and two of her children, both grown and married now, with babies of their own. There was a curious tension,

In almost all the shop windows of the city I saw tiny robed figures with tall, pointed hoods that gave me a creepy feeling, for these objects reminded me of the Ku Klux Klan of the old American South....

White-hooded and masked penitents, members of church organizations known as brotherhoods, came, each carrying a huge candle.... The huge candles rested upon the hips of the penitents and the flickering flames danced above their heads, the molten wax streaming and sparkling in the bright sun, spattering in translucent spots on the dark cobblestones—flying white drops that were like semen spraying, jutting from the penises of sexually aroused bulls....

Tired, I went home. I sat on the edge of my bed and attempted to sort out what I had seen. Those hooded penitents had been protecting the Virgin, and in the old American South hooded Ku Kluxers had been protecting "the purity of white womanhood."
Even if the white South in America had copied their tactics and costumes from here, it did not explain why men loved to march in defense of what they felt was female purity.

—Richard Wright,
Pagan Spain (1957)

something unspoken, and we all walked together under street lamps through the clotting crowds to an old, dingy-looking building, where Isabel led the way up three flights of stairs to an apartment belonging to a friend. The little apartment was dark, lit only by candles, and a table had been laid with a fine linen cloth used once a year, covered with dishes of food. There were two kinds of sausage and an earthenware casserole of baked partridge and another of veal kidneys cooked in sherry. Down at the end was a spread of pastries and other sweets, all of them decorated in filigrees of sugar or honey, cobwebbed and intricate, relentlessly geometric, a reminder that the Koran forbids the representation of human figures. The eight centuries of Muslim rule that ended the year Columbus found America have left their mark all over the city from which he set sail.

There were other guests in the shadowy apartment, people who'd come with bottles of sweet anisette and *aguardiente*, homemade moonshine, along with the pastries; Isabel went to the table with her straw bag and took out a potato omelet and two bottles of wine. Above the table on the wall were four family pictures, and beside them an old photograph of the Virgin of the Macarena— head and shoulders draped in a heavy black cloth. I pointed to her.

"*De luto*," Isabel said, "the only time the Macarena ever wore mourning. In the '40s it was, they dressed her like that for Joselito El Gallo, the bullfighter, the day he was gored—he was the head brother of her *cofradía*." I asked whether our hostess was a relative of Joselito El Gallo. "No," Isabel said, "of the Macarena. She thinks so, anyway. She thinks of the Macarena as family, lots of people do."

We drank some wine with the other guests and had some food, then more wine and *aguardiente* or anisette. I was a little drunk by the time the processions began to pass and we all went out onto the balconies. Branches of wild rosemary had been strewn over the cobblestones beneath us, and the men carrying the floats walked on them, crushing the leaves with their feet. The scent, fused with incense and candle smoke, rose in a cloud, and my eyes watered: the street was narrow and the glow on the floats made everything hazy. The third float was the Macarena. There was a hush when she turned the corner and headed our way. "That face wasn't made by any sculptor," a man beside me said quickly, "that face was made by the angels."

Tiers of flickering candles on her float caused light to caress her as she came, translucent in appearance, oddly lifelike, her embroidered train stretching down and out behind her. The wide float almost filled the street; when the Macarena came near, our hostess stepped forward to the edge of the balcony, and the men below recognized her and stopped to put the float down. She began to sing *saetas*, "arrows" of praise, a hymn to the Virgin—her voice agonized-sounding, raw and harsh—guttural as it must be in all *cante jondo*. "Deep song," this kind of singing, is as dark as it is sensual. It is the essence, the secret, the pith, of true flamenco. When you know it and you hear it sung the right way, it makes an electric wave down your back, and there's no other singing quite like it. An impossible mixture of Iberian and Oriental, Moorish and Jewish—sex and Christianity—it carries with it somehow the meaning of Spain.

When she had finished, the men lifted the Virgin and began to rock her with great tenderness. For a moment or two the float became her cradle, and the

I was surprised, as I turned the corner, to come face to face with a life-sized Virgin, bethroned in her glittering brocade gown. The large wooden platform beneath her was draped in heavy cloth falling in folds to the ground. Holy Week would begin in a few days, I knew; this must have been a dress rehearsal for a procession. At the sudden shatter of drumtaps, the Virgin trembled and rose before my eyes. Beneath the swinging drapes, pairs of trousers and athletic shoes appeared, anonymous float-bearers inching the Virgin forward.

"Pssst! Pssst!" A persistent hissing shook me from my bemused trance. "Pssssst!" and then, "¡Rubia!" (something like "Hey, Blondie!"). I looked around. The drummers were ahead of me, and the Virgin seemed to have other things on her mind. That left only the presumably pious and straining wearers of the trousers below. But how could they see?

—Lynn Shirey,
"Miracle in Córdoba"

people in the balconies all along the street began to applaud; then the *paso* moved on. After a while came the Christ, following the

Virgin in his *paso*, his face furrowed and fantastic, wild in the candlelight—the two figures seeming identical in age, more like a married couple than mother and son.

There were seven days between Holy Week and the April Fair, a latter-day version of the rites of spring. During the transition, the city held its breath, recuperating from the religious ecstasy of one and preparing for the hedonism of the other. While I waited, Isabel kept me company, walking through the streets and visiting other places we'd known together.

There's so much to see in Seville that I have the same problem I get in certain museums: my eye gluts. After a while I want to lie down and look at nothing for a day. The first morning after Holy Week I slept late and went jogging in María Luisa Park, trying not to look at the white doves or the red earth or the green trees or the spring flowers or the swans or the pedestals or the statues. It wasn't easy.

Toward noon I jogged around a corner without thinking and ran straight into the Plaza de España. If there's a way of not looking at that, I'd like to know it: designed by Aníbal González, it took years to build, a gigantic semicircle girdled by a stream, with brickwork and ceramics that mingle in a perimeter of arcades, each dedicated to a Spanish province. The doves I'd avoided looking at in the park had all come here to wait for me and were roosting smugly in the facade, and there were several attractive young people dancing *sevillanas* together on the bridge. I felt like a man who'd eaten a dozen heavy chocolate éclairs at dinner, dragged himself out of

The symbol of Sevilla is the rubric NO-8-DO, in which what looks to be an eight is really a skein (madeja), so that the whole reads: "No madejado" (She has not abandoned me), referring to a time when a king in trouble appealed to Sevilla for help.

—James A. Michener, *Iberia: Spanish Travels and Reflections*

Insignia of Sevilla

bed in the morning, gone for a run to burn them off and tripped over a lollipop.

Isabel met me at a shop near the hotel and we went for a stroll before lunch. "Stop trying not to sightsee, *idiota*," she said. "You know Seville—see what you like best."

What I liked best was the Barrio de Santa Cruz, the old Jewish ghetto; I'd always liked it. In the past, Muslims and Jews got along well in Spain where both were persecuted by the Inquisition before their final expulsion in 1492. Neither religion permits the eating of pork or shellfish, so Spaniards who wanted to prove they were Christians began to add one or both to every dish; in the 15th century, if you were seen eating pork or shellfish in public, you were a member of the True Faith, not an infidel. Today, in the Santa Cruz quarter, you can stop at a bar for a glass of wine or beer and a *tapa*, an appetizer of shrimp or clams, alongside a small slice of pork, either garlic sausage or *jamón de jabugo*, the deep red, cured ham from the mountains in the neighboring province of Huelva. The best dishes in the world were invented for the worst reasons, and the fusion of tastes is superb.

Isabel and I had a beer and wandered through the streets listening to the fountains, the familiar trickle of water ubiquitous in any land that has been inhabited by the Moors. From the Calle de Mateos Gago, once a shoemakers' street, we went looking at bookstores and antique shops and an old convent in cool Gothic shadow, past clumps of orange trees heavy with fruit. We came out at the Plaza Virgen de los Reyes.

Standing there we could see Seville at the hour when the sun was at its zenith, and for a moment the city seemed to be showing off. The flagrant succession of epochs and styles fanned out, raucous and gorgeous, with the hard pride of a brothel that was once a nunnery, in a teeming array of times. Unlike the static beauty of a city like Florence where sameness is all, Seville reflects her centuries in stupendous contradiction—a dazzling, chance-taking, multilayered outrage of a place. To our right was the crenellated wall whose door opens onto the Patio de los Naranjos, bordering the leftover Almohade mosque that was begun in 1172; the slim

minaret called the Giralda appeared to be growing gracefully up
through space-time toward a belfry added in the 16th century. Left
of us was the great gaping Gothic cathedral, built on the site of the
mosque, the fourth largest in Christendom—to the left of that, the
soft Renaissance curve of the *capilla real*, the royal chapel—then on
and on. The effect as a whole had magic and so the Andalusians
say that Seville has *duende*, an untranslatable word meaning a kind
of dark spirit, not an external muse or an angel but the spirit inside, the thing that gives you electric chills when *cante jondo* is
sung. "Everything that has a black sound has *duende*," said the great
Spanish composer Manuel de Falla. Because of it, visiting musicians and writers who came here often tried to cast their own
spells: Carmen, Don Juan, the Barber of Seville, all are imaginary
citizens of the place.

Today the best way to sense it for yourself is to stop at the local
tourist office and ask for a copy of a pamphlet called "Sevilla,
Capital of the New World." Never mind its title; the pamphlet is
short, well laid out and very much to the point. It's a fast guide to
the enchantment of the city and if you follow its walking directions, you will either love Seville or leave town.

That afternoon we had lunch in Sol y Sombra, a *tapas* bar across
the river in Triana that serves the best appetizers anywhere around.
As a rule, food in Seville is less than wonderful—in no way com-
parable to the great Catalán cuisine of Barcelona or even the
somewhat eclectic fare of Madrid. With one or two exceptions,
local restaurants are so-so, and given the choice, I'd rather stand up
for a sequence of *tapas* than sit down to a formal meal. Sol y
Sombra is a dark little place whose walls are plastered with antique
bullfight posters, and the menu changes at least daily, often twice
or three times a day. We had frogs' legs cooked with beans, aspara-
gus with eggs, grilled swordfish, and *caña de lomo*, sliced smoked
pork—all of them good, with crusts of fresh hot bread and ice-cold
beer. There was sawdust on the floor to catch the drippings and a
maze of *jabugo* hams hanging from the ceiling that added to the
deep mixed odors.

Lunch in most of Andalusia is eaten around three o'clock, dinner between ten and eleven, a mystery to most Americans, who want to know how Spaniards can go to sleep at night on a full stomach—just as Spaniards always ask why Americans, who eat dinner at seven, don't get hungry again at ten. Spaniards tend to laugh at our health fads and tend to live longer than we do, largely because they shun the use of butter and consume fresh farm produce, never having seen the mass-produced, plastic-wrapped, pesticide-tinged foods in our markets, let alone the fatty chickens or injected beef. Beef itself is seldom eaten in Spain, where all edible animals are killed young, before fat forms on the body. Food from the sea abounds on all the coasts and fills the markets in most cities: Seville is no exception, and if it can be said that there's a specialty here, it's fresh fried fish, which has a delicacy and lightness that is hard to find anywhere else. Then, too, there is the wine called sherry, the name of which is an anglicized corruption of "Jerez"— a world-famous town about an hour's drive south. If you happen to be as addicted to good sherry as I am, you'll drive into Jerez just to try the different varieties. Or you'll do as we did that afternoon and drive an hour more to a town called Sanlúcar de Barrameda, where the Guadalquivir River meets the open sea.

Between Holy Week and the April Fair, it's nice to get out of the city for a day or so, and our purpose in going was to visit an old friend, Luisa Isabel Alvarez de Toledo, duchess of Medina Sidonia, who lives in the Ducal Palace at the top of Sanlúcar. The palace was built in the 11th century under Muslim rule, and Columbus, a friend of the second duke, left from here for his second voyage. Recently, the duchess, 21st grandee in her line, who now bears the oldest noble title in Spain, has opened three rooms and a suite adjoining the palace as a bed-and-breakfast inn, one of the most charming in this part of the world.

We sat late into the night with Luisa and some of her friends in a garden of fruit trees that topped the view below: lime-white houses cascading down into the muddy Guadalquivir water where it foamed into the green of the sea. A scent of jasmine filled the air as night came and we laughed and talked of the past: I once lived and worked in the palace during the mid-sixties, a time when the duchess became a kind of local folk heroine because, unlike most Spanish nobility, she spoke out against the fascist regime of Franco and was jailed for her forthright behavior. Since then she's been busy in the palace collating the Medina Sidonia family archive, which dates back to the 12th century, writing about its contents.

Till dark we sat in the cool of the garden, chatting and sipping *manzanilla*, my favorite sherry of all. Bottled in Sanlúcar, it cannot be taken halfway to Madrid without losing its flavor: something about the sea air is said to be responsible for *manzanilla's* extraordinary bouquet, which disappears in direct proportion to the distance between the bottle and the next town.

The next day, before going back to Seville, we drove with Luisa and two of her friends along the coast for a couple of hours, past the ancient town of Cádiz, to a little village called Bolonia where she goes once or twice a year to get a special honey for her own breakfast and for the B&B. Driving two hours for a bucket of wildflower honey is nothing to a duchess who has never seen a supermarket in her life, and Bolonia by itself was worth the trip. A tiny village nestled at the foot of an archeological site whose layered treasures, constantly unearthed, go back to Phoenician days, Bolonia is almost as far south as you can go on land in all of Europe. When you look out to sea, the shadow of Africa looms on the horizon.

Once there, we drove up into the hills above the town, over a dirt road that ended suddenly; we stopped and walked half a mile to a stark little dwelling inhabited by two people. A man in his 80s nodded to us, then turned his back and went on drinking a cup of coffee into which he was dunking a crust of bread. He meant no rudeness—here in the country, you do not interrupt a man who is eating—and while we waited for him to finish we chatted with his mother, who was, she said, as far as she knew, 104 years old. "I'm not exactly sure," she added, smiling, "but I don't think I'm off by more than a couple of years.... I could never count."

After five minutes or so the man got up, went to get a vat, and began to scoop out amber-colored honey so thick he had to scrape it off on the side of the bucket. Isabel and I asked for a taste and he passed us a minuscule gob. The honey had a pungent tang that bloomed on the tongue, as if it were a condensation of all the flowers and wild-growing herbs on earth. When the bucket was full, he weighed it with an ancient-looking hand scale, the oldest I've seen, and asked the duchess to read the weight on the scale and calculate the price. She did so, then paid him, and he stood for a moment looking at the bills in his hand with a faintly bewildered expression. "*¿Estamos en paz?*" he asked finally. "Are we at peace?" She nodded.

"He's not used to money," she explained, driving back down the hill in the twilight, "he can't even read the scale. The country folk around here live by bartering—the way people were meant to live. He swaps honey for everything from wine to food."

In Seville the next morning, the morning before the fair, Isabel showed up unexpectedly with a determined expression and led me by the arm across town, to a short street where a pattern of tiles on the wall announced the dance academy of Juan Morilla. It was a place I'd been avoiding for a long time: more than 30 years ago Isabel and I split up and turned to two other people. She married a handsome businessman from Córdoba, and I fell for a *bailadora*, a flamenco dancer from Seville named Pepa, whose partner, Juan Morilla, was perhaps the greatest all-round Spanish dancer of his generation. Since that time, Isabel's husband and my Pepa, the two people we'd loved, had died, a fact that might be more touching if it weren't for the truth: we had both ceased to love them by then. The past, for each of us, carried with it a bubble of emptiness that was, in my case, sugar-coated protectively with nostalgia.

"Time you broke through," Isabel said, ringing the doorbell. "This won't hurt at all—*that's* what you're afraid of, isn't it?"

I was ready to kill her when the door opened and we were ushered in by a dancer to Morilla's office. Thirty-odd years is a long time not to see somebody, but the man who stood up, now in his sixties, bore a striking resemblance to himself at a younger age. After a while, Juan took out a suitcase filled with old photographs, among which was one of himself, Pepa, Isabel, her husband and me seated in a horse-drawn carriage in the April Fair—circa 1951 or

'52—when we were all in our late teens or early twenties. We'd
been outfitted for the occasion, the women in polka-dot flamenco
dresses with flounces, the men wearing dark suits with round
Córdoban hats, and we looked like a family of young Sevillans out
for a good time. There was a guitarist with us and the old photograph represented, for me, the beginning of what turned out to be
a passion for flamenco and *cante jondo* that has lasted all my life.
Juan took me into another room to see some of his young students
dance, and after half an hour I knew why I loved the intensity and
control of it, why I hated the vulgar, exported variety that fills
American stages and clubs with flying hair and fake emotion.
Flamenco has come back into fashion in the last decade, especially
for out-of-towners who want to join in the popular dancing of
sevillanas at the fair; many academies in the city teach it, but only
Morilla's teaches the real thing.

That night we ate dinner with Juan before going at midnight to
see the opening of the fair. A crowd had gathered expectantly at
the gate—the same crowd that waited in silence for the floats to
pass during Holy Week, but with a difference. Dark mourning
clothes and black mantillas had been exchanged for formal attire
of another sort: bright flamenco dresses, suits and ties with a jaunty
air. Expressions of reverence had been replaced by yearning and
wide-eyed anticipation—the look that acknowledges the April
Fair as a generous time of the flesh, the time of the cuckoo, the
time for falling in love. A hush fell and the people began to count
the seconds until, at midnight, a blast of fireworks was set off, followed by the illuminating of the entrance. Thousands of small
electric bulbs burst into bloom and the childish appeal of pure
spectacle—a series of arches towering high overhead—announced
the beginning of things. The crowd surged forward through the
darkness into the light, and the dancing began.

The phenomenon of the April Fair in Seville has never quite
been explained, mostly, I think, because it can't be: its effect is as
mysterious as that of Holy Week. Seville has had royal privilege
since 1254 to celebrate a fair and market, but a proposition to the
Town Council in 1846 made way for the fair as we now know it,

whose original purpose was the buying and selling of animals, crops and agricultural machinery. Given the character of the people, the closing of a deal was bound to be celebrated with a drink and a song, which soon became more important than the deal itself. Through the years this tradition continued to build until it exploded into its present form—a vast conglomeration of pavilions and stalls, most of them privately owned, where tens of thousands of people come to drink, pair up, and dance the four short couplets known as *sevillanas,* an 18th-century court dance not unlike a formal pavane whose distant origins are rooted long before that, in folk dance.

Today, the April Fair is a way of life: many of the people manage to stay up all night, sleeping on the wing for seven days. There's no official time for sleep because there's always something to do at the fair: a ride on horseback or horsedrawn carriage in the morning, an afternoon of bullfighting, the night for dancing, and *madrugada* (midnight to dawn) for churros and hot chocolate before you go home to change and start over.

The fair is the pinnacle of the annual bullfighting season, the Maestranza [also the name of Seville's bullring], when the best bullfighters and bulls in Spain come to Seville for two triumphant weeks for one or two *corridas* a day. Midway through, I began to go every afternoon. As it happens, I don't often feel about bullfighting as I do about *cante jondo,* since a bad fighter is little more than an incompetent butcher, but at its best it moves me, and

From Palm Sunday to Easter Sunday pious Seville loves the Virgin Mary and the holy purple, loves to pray and pay penance. Then comes feria.

Restraint and excess, the two halves of the national contradiction, the two warring traits which have shaped the history of these peoples are enshrined in the remarkable backflip which Seville performs every spring. The same city which wears pointy hoods and starves itself to show its devotion, then pulls on its party gear and stays awake for a week to celebrate the fact that the sap is rising. It is a week like no other....

You go to Seville in feria *because it is most like the Spain of your romance.*

—Robert Elms,
Spain: A Portrait after the General

*A*ndalucía awakens at the sound of tapping. The wooden stage welcomes Antonio and Lola for sevillanas. The guitarists lower their heads to better hear the sounds of their pizzicato and to allow the dancers a private moment to prepare their souls for the most passionate dance. Soon Antonio and Lola begin to move through the four parts, the coplas, that are the sevillana.

The Acquaintance: *Facing each other, Lola shows the swirl of her skirt and her ability to perform. Antonio flirts through his strong and clear tapping. Shy crossings end with a salute to the audience.*

The Awakening of Love: *The dancers' crossings become much quicker and more passionate, with Antonio leading very close turns, their faces two inches apart.*

The Social Presentation: *The dancing becomes cold for a few seconds, the dancers/lovers honoring the memory of their previous independence from each other. Now they begin the most difficult tapping; turning to face the audience and presenting themselves as a couple.*

The Promise of Eternal Love: *This is the dance of the consummated love. Antonio kneels in the eight crossings, and there is a clamourous applause from the many visitors at the* taberna *tonight.*

—Cristina Del Sol, *"Sueños"*

sometimes, when a great fighter has one of those rare days that bring man and bull together in timeless harmony, it achieves the mythological proportions of great art. The ritual itself, whose rules were fixed in the late 17th century, in the town of Ronda, has echoes that go back to pagan days in Crete, and something about it—the silent underbelly of all ritual—stirs something very deep if you don't close your mind to it, if you let it in.

The Seville bullring is the loveliest in all Spain, partly due to its proportions, partly to the color of *albero*, the sand that can be seen here in its purest form. Long ago, when I went to my first *corrida* in Seville during the month of April, the men in the audience all wore coat and tie, the women white lace mantillas over their heads, to show respect for the annual Maestranza ritual. Today the white mantillas have disappeared, but otherwise the dress code remains unchanged. The audience is the most knowledgeable in Spain, and on a sunny afternoon toward the end of the fair, I sat in the ring with Isabel and knew at last that I had no reason to be afraid of memories in Seville. Emilio Muñoz, a great *torero*, my favorite these days, was approaching a bull in total silence: the ring was packed with people, the audience so quiet you could hear yourself breathe. Muñoz moved with the strength and grace of a superb dancer, pressing forward, then seeming to gyrate into a series of turns—movements that managed to join his cape, his body and the huge lunging body of the bull into one living thing that flickered and trembled with light, the three suspended in time for an endless moment that denied and defied mortality. Then the bull stopped and the man walked away and the audience cheered in a way I hadn't heard for years.

That evening, Isabel and Juan and some friends joined me at the fair in a pavilion belonging to a family that raised brave bulls in the province of Huelva. We had a round of drinks, then some bowls of gazpacho—the cold vegetable soup made from seeded tomatoes, garlic, oil, salt, water and some crustless pieces of bread, all ground together in a mortar or blender. Once the creamy-seeming mixture is chilled, sprinkled with chopped vegetables and served, it appears to wash, cool and fill the stomach at the same time: it tastes like spring. Gazpacho, the name of which comes from an Arabic term for soaked bread, is not new; it's mentioned in Greek and Roman literature as a "drinkable food," and references to it appear in both testaments of the Bible. It is my favorite food in all of Andalusia, and I had a second bowl before the serious drinking began and people rose to dance *sevillanas*.

Somewhere between three and four in the morning, we were joined by another group of people—at five by another—and when the sky outside took on a color that was brighter than the paper lanterns or the electric bulbs, a glow as sharp and bright as Isabel's eyes, we were still dancing.

Peter Feibleman is a novelist and playwright. His works include the critically acclaimed novel, Charlie Boy, The Columbus Tree, *a novel set in Spain, and a play,* Cakewalk, *which opened in New York in 1996.*

✳

Spain in general and Andalusia in particular teaches us that you can have no real communal life unless you have focal and celebratory events throughout the year, in which the large majority of people in that community participate. That is because the only true basis of community is not supposedly enlightened self-interest but actual shared experience. This is much assisted by the preservation of pre-industrial feasts and saints' days and by a due attention to the rhythms of the seasons.

—Alastair Boyd, *The Sierras of the South: Travels in the Mountains of Andalusia*

NICHOLAS WOLLASTON

Quixote's Parable of Life

*In which a modern-day dreamer is inspired
to journey in Don Quixote's footsteps
on a quest through midlife.*

THE CHILDREN GREW UP AND DEIRDRE WENT TO EDINBURGH
University to work for a doctorate. In the spring of 1987 at the
Hall, after I had mended the water pipes that had frozen and burst
during the winter, and unblocked the drains that had overflowed
from excessive rain, and changed the oil and sharpened the blades
of the grass cutter, and watched the wild daffodils in the orchard
bloom and die, I settled down to read *Don Quixote*. And in the second week of May, a month before the general election, I flew to
Madrid and took a train to Manzanares in the middle of La
Mancha.

I gave myself four weeks.

May 14, Manzanares. At midday, getting off the train from
Madrid, I can't discover when there is a bus to Argamasilla de Alba,
40 kilometres from here. The man in the ticket office is no help:
trains are his business, not buses, and if there was ever a line to
Argamasilla it has been closed.

I don't mind, I'm in no hurry. It's a fine spring day, touched with
anticipation. I sense an emptiness ahead, stimulating and alarming
and all my own. Somehow, like my notebook, I must fill it.

Cervantes knew the feeling. In his prologue to *Don Quixote* he described the suspense before the words came: "Many times I took up my pen to write and many times I put it down, not knowing what to say." It's a familiar state: "Hesitating, the paper in front of me, elbow on the desk, fingers on my cheek, thinking…"

The station plaza is deserted. A taxi-driver dozes in his car, a dog lies in the sun by the wall. I walk over to a bench under the new-leafed plants and sit down with my rucksack. After ten minutes a bus comes into the plaza, from Albacete to Ciudad Real—no use to me. I must get to Argamasilla, my proper starting place. It was Don Quixote's home, though in the first sentence of his novel Cervantes was careful not to identify it: "In a village of La Mancha, whose name I don't wish to remember, there lived not long ago a gentleman…."

Don Quixote was verging on 50, younger than me, but I'm the same shape—tall and thin and bony—and I can guess his pleasure as he started on his journey across the plain, slipping away from home one morning unobserved, telling nobody of his intentions. He was happy to find how easy it was to begin.

A telephone rings in a box on one of the trees, waking the taxi-driver. He gets out to answer it, trying to hurry, and speaks for a while, too quietly for me to overhear; then hangs up. The dog stirs, stands up uneasily, yawns and hops over to the man to be stroked—it has only three legs. When the man returns to his taxi

> *La Mancha—originally Al Mansha, "the dry land" or the wilderness—was the Moorish name for the vast, parched plain that stretches from the mountains of Toledo to the Sierra Morena.*
>
> *[Miguel de Cervantes] Saavedra chose La Mancha as the setting for his masterpiece not only because he knew it very well personally but because it was then a backward peasant region whose very name was calculated to bring a smile to the lips of his sophisticated urban readers. But the 20th-century La Mancha is very different from the 17th-century one, for what was once a wilderness has become one of the great wheat-growing and wine-making regions of Spain, even though there are hardly any cities to speak of.*
>
> —Frederic V. Grunfeld,
> *Wild Spain: A Traveler's and Naturalist's Guide*

the dog comes to me and rubs its mange on my trousers. To get rid of it I go over and ask the taxi-driver, before he is asleep again, where the Argamasilla bus departs from. But he doesn't know—taxis are his business.

In the train from Madrid there were two Englishmen on their way to the Costa del Sol. One of them asked the ticket collector, "*Quelle heure—arriver?*" They were his few words of a foreign language and he didn't care that it was the wrong one, but tapped his watch and added in English, "Málaga, I mean?" In silence, politely, the Spaniard wrote the answer on a piece of paper.

I will do better, I hope.

A grey-haired man in a tricycle chair, winding himself along with hand pedals, comes at speed down a street into the plaza. He has no legs at all, he is unluckier than the dog. He could have been wounded as a boy soldier in the Civil War. He circles the plaza once, heeling over on his three wheels; circles it again and disappears up another street.

In the bar on the train I had a hunk of bread with dark raw ham, *jamón serrano*, and a beer, and now I feel sleepy and indecisive. I will see what happens, if I can keep awake. I should be alert for details and reactions, ready to scribble them down. But though I have a compulsion to follow Don Quixote through La Mancha and write a book, I can't yet tell its shape, I can only watch. It has its own existence and will emerge with the least nudging from me. Don Quixote spoke of a painter, busy with brush and canvas, who was asked what he was painting and replied, "Whatever it turns out to be."

I feel the same. Sometimes I have written a synopsis to be fleshed out later but this time the bones, ungainly, disjointed, like Don Quixote's, will fall together in a random way, assembled from my disordered thoughts.

I'm aware of two women approaching my bench under the trees, coming from the station. In wide black skirts they look like gypsies, one fat and one thin, their hair drawn back from their foreheads. They are handsome, confident, humorous, but not beautiful.

"*Buenas tardes*," they say and sit down with me, arranging their bundles. "Where are you from?"

"From Madrid." But I know they mean what country.

"He's American," the fat one tells the thin one.

"No, he's French," the thin one says.

I ask them about the bus to Argamasilla, and the fat woman lifts her eyes to the bright Manchegan sky: "The Lord, *el Señor*, knows." But the thin one says that the bus to Tomelloso passes through Argamasilla. They are going on it themselves tomorrow morning—there is a fiesta in Tomelloso.

When I ask if they are local people they laugh. They come from Mallorca, they go to all the fiestas in Spain, and they launch into a stream of incomprehensible language, laughing more—at me, I think. The fat one shuffles her big black-skirted bottom closer on the bench and asks for the price of a coffee for them both in the station bar. How much? Twenty *duros* will do—a hundred pesetas—and she drops my coin into one of her bundles.

A man walks from the station across the plaza to a block of flats. The fat woman calls to him and he waves back but, seeing me with them, he doesn't stop.

"My friend's lover," the thin woman explains and makes a sign of copulation with her fingers.

The fat woman laughs: "Yes, but he doesn't pay much."

It was two laughing whores at the door of an inn who set Don Quixote off on his first adventure. He rode up on his equally skinny horse, Rocinante, a grotesque figure in armour with a spear, and in his deluded vision—or his limitless imagination—they were beautiful maidens at a castle gate. At that moment a swineherd blew a horn to collect his pigs, which for Don Quixote was a trumpet call from the battlements to herald his approach. Reality wasn't good enough for such a man, and after their first fright at this curious visitor the two women got the idea. Amused by his madness, flattered by his gallantry, they would be princesses for him, not whores. It was a new way to please a man.

Travelling through La Mancha in Don Quixote's company, it will be hard not to catch his twisted vision of things or be infected with his fantasy. Through La Mancha: through life itself. I take Cervantes's book, the first modern novel, to be a parable of life— everyone's, but especially a writer's. So fact may slide into fiction sometimes, and the truth be stretched.

The two women of Manzanares extract what fun they can from me, as well as my hundred pesetas, then go back into the station for their coffee. A man standing in an empty cart pulled by a mule comes into the plaza, shouting something unintelligible. I get up and walk into the town, where I learn that the bus to Argamasilla tomorrow leaves not from the station but from the hospital.

On the top floor of the Mesón Sancho, commemorating Don Quixote's earthy, ever-realistic squire Sancho Panza, I find a room with a window among the roof tiles, and late in the evening have supper in a bar owned by a

D on Quixote, perceiving their alarm, raised his pasteboard visor, and displaying his withered and dusty countenance, accosted them gently and gravely: "I beseech your ladyships, do not flee, nor fear the least offense. The order of chivalry that I profess does not permit me to do injury to anyone, and least of all to such noble maidens as your presences denote you to be."

The wenches kept gazing earnestly, endeavoring to catch a glimpse of his face, which its ill-fashioned visor concealed; but when they heard themselves called maidens, a thing so out of the way of their profession, they could not restrain their laughter.

—Miguel de Cervantes Saavedra, *Don Quixote of La Mancha* (1605/1615), translated by Walter Starkie

toothless old man whom I can't understand. My Spanish is bad, but at least I have teeth for it.

From the TV in the corner I discover that there are celebrations in Madrid today for the king's and queen's 25th wedding anniversary. It was mine and Deirdre's also, in Spain last summer. We didn't drive through the streets in a coach like these two, but drank Spanish champagne with one of our sons and a few friends on the terrace of a rented house, with olive trees stacked on the Andalusian hills and the sea in the distance.

I still marvel that we have been married nearly half my life and much more than half of Deirdre's. Though I have never dedicated a book to anyone, and she won't like this any more than the others, it is for her. It's the least I can do—a gesture of what I used to call my love, in memory of hers.

After a *copa* of brandy with the toothless man I sit for half an hour in the main plaza. This is the time of the *paseo*, the nightly social stroll, and half of Manzanares is on parade. V. S. Pritchett said that the Spanish treat the street as their place of entertainment, like a drawing-room. A pram is parked close to the floodlit fountain for the baby to be kept happy by the illuminated jets, the incandescent froth. What bemused ideas do they convey? Astonishingly, in this small town in the middle of Spain, a black woman in a purple dress shaped by her African body goes tripping smartly across the square.

Opposite stands the church, bathed in electric light. Nothing is symmetrical or architected in that glowing holy edifice, yet it rules the plaza with its age, dignity, haphazard disproportions. The people driving past in new cars, the couples kissing on the benches, the baby's gossiping family, all know it. They are nothing to that accumulation of human love. Swifts scream across the darkening sky, and pigeons flop in and out of their nesting niches on the church, impatient for the floodlights to be switched off, and the black woman comes tripping back, and the baby is pushed home, the fountain still splashing in its eyes, and I have another *copa* in a bar on my way back to the Mesón Sancho.

And one more. And then a final one.

I'm still not clear what my purpose is, beyond catching tomorrow's bus to Argamasilla de Alba. The vagabond life on the roads of La Mancha gave Cervantes a formula for his book. And Don Quixote himself, stepping out of the pages of the second volume to criticize the first, which had already been published, said the author must have written it down gropingly, without method, letting it turn out anyhow.

The future will be conjured from the present and the past with, I hope, an extra essence to transform it. To Don Quixote—the

Knight of the Sad Countenance, as Sancho called him—that essence was life itself: the untruth that enhances truth.

Nicholas Wollaston has contributed to many British publications and written books of fiction, biography, and travel, including China in the Morning, Winter in England, *and* Tilting at Don Quixote, *from which this story was excerpted. He lives in England.*

*

In *The Tragic Sense of Life*, published in 1912, Miguel de Unamuno puts his faith not in any "actual flesh-and-bone philosopher" but in a creation of Spanish fiction, Don Quixote, whom he believes comes closest to epitomizing the positive spirit expressed by Spaniards in crucial points in their history:

> There is one figure, a comically tragic figure, a figure in which is revealed all that is profoundly tragic in the human comedy, the figure of Our Lord Don Quixote, the Spanish Christ, who summarises and includes in himself the immortal soul of my people. Perhaps the passion and death of the Knight of the Sorrowful Countenance is the passion and death of the Spanish people, its death and resurrection. And there is a Quixotesque ethic and a Quixotesque religious sense—the religious sense of Spanish Catholicism....
>
> —Miguel de Unamuno, *The Tragic Sense of Life in Men and Nations*, as quoted by Jimmy Burns, *A Literary Companion to Spain*

PART TWO

SOME THINGS TO DO

KEVIN GORDON

Bulls Before Breakfast

To "stand the bulls" in Pamplona
may be excitement enough.

"I'M FLYING TO PAMPLONA SUNDAY TO RUN WITH THE BULLS," I said one muggy July morning two summers ago.

My friend Barnaby Conrad was silent for a while. "Even I've never been *that* crazy," he said at last. "I like it a little more civilized: one bull at a time charging me in the safety of the ring."

In the late 1940s, Barnaby fought bulls beside the great matadors Juan Belmonte and Carlos Arruza. He also wrote a stack of books about bullfighting that I read wide-eyed as a kid. Those books eventually led to my yearly treks to Spain for the barbaric, addictive, thrilling spectacle of *los toros.*

"Just be careful," Barnaby said. "My son broke three ribs running in the *encierro.*"

Encierro, meaning "enclosure," is the term that Spaniards use for the running of the bulls. The word doesn't conjure up much of an image, which is typical of Spanish understatement. But inside Pamplona's "enclosure" are six, 1,200-pound fighting bulls, seven trained steers and thousands of lunatics careering for their lives along the town's tunnel-like streets. Just for the hell of it.

Running the bulls through the streets was originally the only way to get them from the corrals at one end of Pamplona to the

151

bullring downtown for the afternoon's *corrida*. One morning several hundred years ago, some foolhardy fellow thought it would be a thrill to dodge in front of the bulls as they ran. Believe it or not, others agreed and the *encierro* was born.

A typical *encierro* lasts for only a few minutes, though some have gone on for more than twenty minutes. After the running, the bulls are let into pens near the rings; they all die later in the day during the fights.

The week-long fiesta, held every July, is supposed to honor the patron saint of Pamplona, San Fermín, but like many Spanish festivals, its religious origin has been lost somewhere along the way. Only Spaniards ran with the bulls until 1926, when Ernest Hemingway's *The Sun Also Rises* was published. Much of the novel was set amid the abandon of San Fermín, and from then on, the festival was internationally famous and foreigners took part.

I reached Pamplona, set in the Basque country of northern Spain, on July 6, the first day of the fiesta. Looking resplendent in the requisite whites and a red kerchief and sash, I made my way through the crowds in the main square.

After checking into my hotel, I thumbed through several brochures with hair-raising photos of the *encierro*. Sure, I was ready to risk life and flabby limb on the town's cobblestone streets, but I didn't want to be *stupid* about it. How to avoid impalement?

The answer: ask around. I started with the American fiesta veterans lounging in the hotel lobby. "Talk to Carney," they said.

"Talk to Carney," said the English-speaking foreigners at the Windsor Bar.

"Talk to Carney," I remembered Barnaby advising me.

I talked to Carney.

I found him holding court at the Bar Txoco (pronounced CHO-ko), which borders the town's main square. Matt Carney, an American, was considered the best foreign bull-runner in Pamplona, a title he'd held for more than twenty years. He'd had his share of gorings, including one through the chest, but had continued to run inches from the horns. He divided his time between a cottage in Ireland (where he wrote novels), an apartment in Paris (where he modeled for European magazines) and the noisy bull-rings of Spain.

Matt was mesmerizing; he attracted a crowd as a magnet attracts iron filings, and I knew that next to San Fermín, he was the fellow I wanted by my side when the bulls came bearing down.

I took a seat in the outer circle of Matt's admirers, ordered a glass of Tío Pepe and listened slack-jawed as seasoned bull-runners swapped stories of near misses—and direct hits.

One young American named Kelly demonstrated how a bull's horn had pierced his stomach, punched through some vital organs, narrowly missed his spine and popped out the other side.

He snapped his fingers and said, "It happened just like that!"

Just like that, indeed: a month later, he'd hobbled out of the hospital.

"I had a pretty good run this morning," he added. "Stayed with the horns for a good twenty yards."

One of the first Americans to take part in the fiesta of San Fermín was artist David Black, who discovered Pamplona in 1950. At the time, he was a student in Paris; now he's in his sixties and lives on Majorca. Black, along with Matt Carney (who died in late 1988), served as the inspiration for Harvey Holt, the main character in James Michener's The Drifters.

Not surprisingly, quite a few notables have put in appearances at the festival, including Orson Welles, James Jones, William Styron, James Michener, Margaux Hemingway, Darryl Zanuck, Geraldo Rivera and ABC news correspondent Robert Trout. Although most of them only stood the bulls, Rivera actually ran and was knocked over. Ironically, Ernest Hemingway never ran in the encierro, *but he stood on the sidelines with the best of them.*

—Charles Leocha, "Raging Bull," *Travel & Leisure*

I shook my head in disbelief. Everyone in this town acted like a character in an adventure film. I sipped my sherry and listened, enthralled, to tale after surreal tale of man's alarming capacity for nonsense. And yet, inexplicably, I wanted to become part of it.

The group started breaking up, and I cornered Matt. We chatted for several minutes, and I told him how much I wanted to run with the bulls. "Maybe for your first time you should stand the bulls," he said.

"Stand?"

"Yeah. You're right in the thick of things, but instead of trying to dodge men and animals, you stand to one side when the bulls charge by," Matt explained. "It's what I do now that I'm getting up into my sixties. I only *run* with the Miuras."

Said to be the most dangerous breed of bull, Miuras killed the great Manolete and several other famous matadors.

"For your first time, why don't you stand with me tomorrow morning?" Matt asked.

I laughed in relief. "But I don't want to be in your way."

"You won't. During the *encierro*, it's every man for himself. Meet me in front of the *ayuntamiento* (town hall) at five minutes to eight."

Five to eight? The run begins at eight sharp. I arrive at *movies* fifteen minutes ahead of time.

"Isn't that cutting it close?"

"Plenty of time," he chuckled, disappearing into the crowd.

I slept no more than twenty minutes that night. Every time I closed my eyes, bulls chased me. Never mind the brass band under my hotel window that played every piece in its repertoire. Twice.

Pamplona in the early morning showed signs of the previous night's carousing. Knots of revelers stumbled along the dewy cobblestones, halfheartedly greeting the new day, which, for them, had begun hours before. The dingy veterans were soon outnumbered by fresh reinforcements. Many of the runners in the crowd were bouncing around to limber up their leg muscles.

At five minutes to eight, I scanned the bobbing faces at our meeting place. No Matt. Four to eight.... A minute later I felt a hearty slap on my back, and I turned around to see him smiling at me from beneath a red, white and blue headband. His long gray hair was pulled back à la Willie Nelson, but minus the pigtails.

"Can you spit?" he asked.

Spit? I'd spent the last half-hour drinking about a gallon of water, and my mouth was still as dry as a Manhattan apartment in winter. I couldn't work up enough saliva to lick a postage stamp. I had all the classic symptoms of fear that bullfighters suffer before going into the ring, including one called the Big Fear Leak (all that water has to go somewhere).

"If you can spit, you should run," Matt suggested.

"I think I'll stand with you as planned."

We jostled our way past the ornate *ayuntamiento* to the corner of Mercaderes and Estafeta Streets. I looked around anxiously at the stone walls, steel shutters and wooden barricades in a last minute search for a hasty retreat.

"Where's our out?" I asked.

"There isn't one," he said and smiled. "We're all right as long as a bull doesn't get separated from the herd. That's when they become angry and defensive and will attack anything that moves."

I looked at my watch. One minute to go. Then I looked at Matt. The smile was still on his face and he seemed like a man listening to Vivaldi.

Bang!

The first rocket meant that the holding pen, a quarter-mile away, had been opened and the bulls released. (They'd been moved from the corrals to the pen the night before.)

In 1994, eleven runners, including two Americans, an Australian, and a New Zealander, were gored. Sixteen others were crushed in the crowd or trampled by bulls and required hospital treatment. Thirteen people have died this century in Pamplona's bull run.

Other casualties are caused by less traditional activities, the most famous of which is the so-called Angel's Jump, invented by Australians who come to Pamplona just to drink. They hurl themselves off a sixteen-foot fountain into the waiting arms of equally inebriated companions, who often fail to catch them. Head injuries are common but they have not slowed the tide of Australians and other foreigners from trekking to San Fermín.

—Tracey Ober, "Wild Fiesta Brings out Basic Animal Instincts," Reuters

Bang!

The second rocket meant that the last bull had cleared the gate. The shorter the time between rockets, the better. The bulls were in a tight pack this time with no dangerous stragglers.

Right after a young American got speared just up the street, a Pamplonese man told me he was a total cretin because "everyone knows that if you fall down—for any reason—you should just cover your head and stay down and let the bulls jump over you." Never, ever, not even if Ross Perot becomes President of Germany and bungie-jumps off the Reichstag, should you try to get back up before the bulls have passed.

—Doug Lansky, "Getting Down in Pamplona"

I glanced down the street and saw the runners. They were jogging—playfully. Then, as if someone had turned up the pressure on a garden hose, there was a sudden burst of speed from the next wave of runners. Finally, the fastest group came. They were wild-eyed and going full tilt.

The onrushing crowd parted slightly and there they were. The bulls. Backs bobbing, horns wagging, raw power.

I gaped at the bovine explosion as it thundered past. The herd took a sharp right onto Estafeta, slamming heavily into the wooden barricade as it rounded the turn and galloped the rest of the way to the bullring.

All except one.

The last bull lost its footing on the slippery stones and flopped onto its side, skidding to a stop about ten feet in front of me. The creature seemed as surprised as I was. It blinked in bewilderment and then, rolling over onto its knees, looked me straight in the eye. Here was half a ton of solid muscle, with horns as long as a man's arms and as sharp as stilettos, about to snap me in two just like a breadstick.

I stood stock-still remembering what Matt had said. Someone shouted "*Toro sólo!*" to warn the unsuspecting runners bringing up the rear. (They'd stood by while the bulls blasted through.) A man darted past the animal, hand outstretched, taunting death.

Suddenly, the bull lurched to its feet, aiming its horns at the daredevil. The runners, who'd stopped dead in their tracks when the behemoth hit the street, jerked into action and took off up Estafeta. The bull, seeing the movement, lunged after them.

Screams and cheers broke the tension, and for the first time in what seemed like a long time, I breathed.

"Pretty dicey, huh?" asked Matt. "Come on. Let's head over to the Txoco and see how the other guys did."

I was hooked. It's true, I'd only stood the bulls, but now I felt ready to spit *and* run.

When the Pamplona papers came out the next morning, there I was—in a color picture of my first close call with a bull. I looked like a statue standing in a doorway, and just steps away was the bull, lying on its side and looking for all the world as if it were about to take a nap. A friend who saw the photo christened me *El Niño del Toro Cansado*—"The Sleepy Bull Kid."

Kevin Gordon is a writer and artist who has galleries in Madrid, New York, and Denver. The very next day after his "stand" in Pamplona re-counted here, he ran with the bulls and has returned to run year after year.

✷

I opened the newspaper recently to a chilling photograph of a bull killing a 22-year-old American tourist in the streets of Pamplona, the first death in fifteen years of the annual festival. The news brought back a powerful memory from 1970, when I bummed around Europe with a copy of *The Sun Also Rises* in my bag—a dangerous book for any 18-year-old on the loose. Sure enough, I ended up in Pamplona.

On the first morning of the *encierro,* I ran at the front of the pack, separated from the bulls by several hundred yards and plenty of fellow runners. It seemed easy, and I wondered why my father, a bullfighting expert, had warned me that the *encierro* was more dangerous than fighting a single bull in a ring. The second morning I started with the experienced San Fermines near the back. Jacked up with adrenaline and the narcissism of youth, I wore the red beret and neckerchief emblematic of that ancient rite of machismo. At the cannon's boom we took off, sprinting with cool bravery over the cobblestones. People cheered us from the windows above.

Near the bullring, runners suddenly bunched, blocking the way. People shouted and darted into doorways. "*¡Los toros!* Here they come!" Panicked men pushed and shoved to stay ahead of the horns. When we entered the tunnel that led to the ring, a man fell in the darkness, tripping others. Pushed from behind, I fell onto a mound of struggling, cursing bodies. Dozens piled on top of us. The bulls thundered into the tunnel and climbed our human logjam. Crushed under the weight of men and half-ton bulls, I gasped for air and prayed to God. Time slowed to a crawl. Then, suddenly, men scrambled to their feet and careened wildly toward the light outside the tunnel.

I rose to my knees, sucking in air. My shirt was torn, my red beret now one of dozens in the sand. I saw stars. Then I froze. To my left a black bull had fallen to his knees. In a moment he might rise and slam me against the wall. He swung his head my way, and I grabbed his right horn, pulled myself upright, and sprinted into the ring. Vaulting the *barrera* to safety, I felt a sharp pain in my ribs. Blood trickled from my elbow.

In the ring's infirmary a nun cleaned me up and shot me full of penicillin. She was telling me where to have my ribs x-rayed when five shouting men carried a man into the room. Blood spurted from his upper thigh. They lowered him onto the table, and someone in a white coat scissored away the trouser leg. The nun shooed me out the door. Outside I realized my wristwatch was gone, along with my adolescent delusion of immortality.

I returned to the ring to look for the watch. Behind the *barrera,* lying in the sand like a detail from a Dalí painting, lay a set of upper dentures still glistening with saliva. *Someone will need these,* I thought. I picked up the teeth and placed them on the edge of the *barrera.*

Stiff and bruised the next day, I sat in a café and read the *Diaro de Navarra,* which said that 33 people had been injured in the running including "the foreigner, Barrady Conard" (sic). The newspaper also said a man had died, a carpenter with a large family. Until the very end, it said, the dying man implored his friends to go back to the arena to find his new, very expensive, false teeth.

—Barnaby Conrad III, "In Pamplona"

Package Tour Blues

Amid hordes of tourists on the Costa del Sol,
a traveler goes in search of a good time.

"WELCOME TO MÁLAGA, WHERE THE LOCAL TIME IS HALF PAST noon and the outside temperature is thirty-four degrees centigrade. We hope you have enjoyed..." Blah blah blah. This is no time for corporate patter, let's go, Spain awaits. At least, Málaga airport awaits. A brand-new Málaga airport, a large, caramel-coloured structure, cosily monumental in the new vernacular style. It looked like it had been designed by Albert Speer in consultation with Prince Charles. We hundreds descended on Baggage Reclaim in a cool, cavernous hall where the ceiling was yellow, the walls and pillars cream and the marbled floor butterscotch. We were waiting for our luggage in an air-pocket in a sci-fi helping of Instant Whip.

Out in the crème caramel arrivals area, we were greeted by a phalanx of reps. The wonderful thing about a package tour is that you don't have to worry about how to work a foreign country; you don't need to get anxious about where to find the train or how to pay the bus-driver, because it's all taken care of. The Thomson woman pointed me through the door to another Thomson woman who pointed me to a bus ten yards away. In case we'd been fazed by the heat or, against all odds, found the wrong bus, there was a name-check of the two dozen or so of us on the coach by a third Thomson woman, the one who would be guiding us through the pitfalls of being driven to the hotels of our choice.

The hotel I had chosen was last on the itinerary, so I was to gain the full benefit of our guide's commentary, which had kicked off with an extensive welcome speech, followed by many words of warning about time-share touts and then by a full weather report. Meanwhile, the coach swung out into the race-track of the N340. Extensive improvements and the construction of subways and bridges for pedestrians have transformed the main thoroughfare of the Costa del Sol. It used to be the most dangerous road in Europe, with an annual average of 30 accidents per kilometre. Now it's merely one of the most dangerous roads in the world. As we careered along towards Torremolinos, I tried to forget that the most dangerous stretch of all is between the airport and Torremolinos. (Because of Brits, fresh from the car-rental office, driving patriotically on the left.)

Outside, there were surprising mountains in the background and a foreground cluttered with billboards in fields. The adverts of a consumerism which is supposed to be blandly international all proclaimed that we were abroad—Ducados, Whisky *¡con música!*, Zumo, San Miguel. Inside, there was the relentless monologue of our guide, who was now pointing out objects of interest with an enthusiasm for detail usually reserved for legal documents.

"Obviously, *on* the left, another hotel and some very badly parked cars. And *to* the right, you will see some blocks of flats as we enter the famous town of Torremolinos. Lots of shops, and lots of people, *as* you can see, many of them Spanish, who all take *to* the beach *on* a Sunday and park their cars very badly. Now, past the souvenir shop *on* the left and *down* the street we'll be coming to our first stop, so *all* of you who are booked *for* the Don Pedro, get ready to disembark *from* the coach and your hotel rep *will* be waiting for you."

It was the badly parked cars that were our eventual undoing. Somehow, our driver had manoeuvred up a side-street for the fifth drop-off. I suppose the two people booked there could have walked the small distance to their hotel from the main street, but that must be against regulations. Thus we found ourselves making a 90-degree turn in a lane where deft double parking would have made it hard for a tricycle to change direction. Something like a 57-point turn later, the driver conceded defeat, and one of the four passengers left on the coach, a short man in his fifties, lost his rag.

"Seventeen pounds surcharge I paid to get an earlier flight," he told me through clenched teeth, "and what's happened to my extra bit of time? It's gone down the bloody toilet. Seventeen pounds for the privilege of being stuck in a bloody coach going no bloody where."

"Still, it's only getting on for an hour we've been here," I replied brightly. "And we've got a whole fortnight to look forward to."

"You might. I've got a bloody week. I was hoping for a swim this afternoon."

My expressions of sympathy only stoked his ire. The next time he spoke, fury got the better of his syllables.

"Stuck on blood bus. Blood diculous."

The other two passengers were a couple in their late teens who were evidently here for a fortnight. They were content to look on with slack-jawed exhaustion as our driver climbed down to remonstrate with the owner of a double-parked van. Finally, the van-owner reversed down the street, allowing us to move off and out towards

It seems that a few weeks before, during a very busy evening, two Gypsies who had been drinking at the bar created a bit of a disturbance. In a short time, someone went upstairs to use the bathroom. They found that most of the essentials were missing. Sawed right off at the wall and hauled away. The barman could only guess that during the disturbance, other Gypsies, friends of the two at the bar, had slipped upstairs and taken away the toilet and the sink. In Spain, Gypsies are blamed for everything, but I had never before heard them blamed for stealing the bathroom.

—Ann and Larry Walker,
A Season in Spain

Fuengirola, as our guide launched into an extensive attack on thieving Gypsies for whom we had to be on the look-out.

Some time later we had made it to the seafront, where we inched towards a large, red hotel, the destination of the furious man who beetled off to check in and prepare for what would now be his evening swim. Three wasn't enough of an audience for our guide, it seemed, and we crawled the last few yards to the final hotel in silence.

It was a grey-beige amalgam of two buildings shaped like three-penny-bits and joined by a two-storey base. One building rose eight storeys above the two-storey base, the other sixteen. It had looked intriguing in the brochure. In real life, it was ghastly.

I didn't feel disappointed. Scared is nearer the mark. How was I going to spend two weeks here on my own? Would the view compensate for the vertigo if my room was on the sixteenth floor? Why were the young couple still slack-jawed? Did they share some nasal complaint? Preoccupied by queries and doubts, I was ushered into reception behind the young couple who, with the exertion of carrying their suitcases, were not so much breathing as snoring.

I checked in and received a jolly leaflet telling me that a "welcome guestogether" for new arrivals would be held tomorrow in the Ceramic Bar on the first floor at midday. I was then led to my room by a porter who listed precariously to his left as he strained to carry my suitcase. Fortunately, we climbed only a couple of flights up a spiral stairway before the porter lurched to the right. He was taking me to the emergency exit. No. There was a white wooden door on the left. The porter ushered me in and promptly ran away.

My first reaction was to laugh. My second was to wonder when exactly this room had been converted from a store cupboard. It didn't even reach to four walls. It was triangular, with a loo tucked into the cone. I was going to stay for two weeks in a slice of pizza. The loo itself was minute but it seemed as spacious as the veldt compared to the bedroom. That contained two walk-in wardrobes only a very thin toddler could have walked into. A bedside cabinet nicked from a doll's house. A chair. And a bed—a bed shorter and narrower than the one I slept in when my room at home had Noddy and Big Ears wallpaper.

It was clean, though, and the floor was done in marble. And the decor wasn't bad—plain white walls added to the rustic touch of the wooden door. A less rustic touch there was the lock, of such bulk and ferocity it wouldn't have disgraced a flat in Harlem. In addition, I saw, after parting the curtains (period pieces from the '70s these, all beige blobs and lime-green circles), there was a small balcony which afforded a view of the adjoining rust-coloured fire-escape and noisy back-street.

I lay on my bed and recalled how I had ended up here. Booking this fortnight only last weekend had been the result of my clever ruse to get a place on the cheap but, as young Nikki at my local travel agent's soon found out, there were no last-minute bargains. And precious few single rooms. Several hours at her computer yielded a room in something like the Hotel International Splendide in Marbella, a snip at £1500 for two weeks. Or the Hotel Dreck along the coast, understandably under-booked since not even the brochure could conceal its resemblance to a prison with awnings.

"Of course, it's more difficult to find a place for just..." Nikki had said. "But since you're going on your...And there's usually a supplement if you're..."

"What supplement?"

"Well, any hotel will charge at least £50 or £60 a week extra for...for those who don't have..."

"For singles?"

"Well. Yes. Singles. And naturally there aren't many single rooms."

"Can you give it one more go?"

She did, and struck lucky with this place. "It's very reasonable, really," Nikki assured me. "Three stars, which means it'll be all right, and half-board at £563, which includes your £7 a day single supplement."

"Blood in sand."

"Well, it's either that or the International Splendide. Or the Dreck."

"I'll take it."

✳

I came to at half past nine. It was the longest sleep I'd had in years and it left me feeling not full of zip and go but as sluggish as a drugged captive. In TV movies and the like, drugged captives spend a maximum of fifteen seconds regaining consciousness, then rub their eyes, shake their heads, untie knots, immobilize guards, and make good their escape. At a quarter to ten, I was still practising the parting of my eyes and lips.

A ten o'clock deadline for breakfast forced me out of bed and on to the floor. Using the bed as leverage, I pushed myself upright. The Earth's gravity had increased appreciably overnight. With cowed back and stiff ankles I hobbled the tiny distance to the bathroom, where a series of slow and trying ablutions signally failed to provide me with vim or verve. Three minutes to ten. With the ease and grace of a Dalek on the parallel bars, I yanked on a t-shirt and hopped into jeans.

I scampered excitedly downstairs like a small boy on Christmas Day. That's a lie, but somehow I made it to the restaurant by ten. The place was chock-a-block with couples and families.

I was 34, there was no alternative, I could handle this.... Oh God, oh God, oh God.

There were—how could it be otherwise?—no empty tables, so I attached myself to the end of a table occupied by a family, all of whose five members had, I soon guessed, just had a row. Nobody was having eye contact with anybody, especially me. I sat down and toyed awhile with my napkin to demonstrate that I was happy and comfortable with my lot before realizing that breakfast, like dinner, was entirely self-service. I slunk out of my chair and joined the queue at the buffet.

Huge jugs of fruit juice. Rows of cold meats. Rows of thin rectangles of yellow cheese. Rows of senile hard-boiled eggs. A shambles of diced frankfurters. Heaps of bread and rolls. Hillocks of cornflakes and muesli. Eating first thing in the morning, I don't get it. You're just out of bed, for goodness' sake. A normal person's breakfast is two very strong cups of coffee and two cigarettes and, if needs be, a second course of a very strong cup of coffee and a cigarette. However, having queued on automatic pilot, I found I was carrying a plate, so I decorated it with two slices of salami and a rectangle of yellow cheese. Coffee. I had to have coffee. And to have coffee I had to join another queue, at a machine that skooshed out hot, coffee-style liquid.

Back at my table, each member of the family was still inspecting shoes, plates and middle distances, so my best jerk's ingratiating nod-and-smile combination was to no avail. I played with my plate of things, if only because I had to do something while I waited for my coffee-style liquid to cool. Having swigged that down, I paused for as long a time as I could manage, then got the hell out of there. In the safety of my room, I sucked mightily on a cigarette, then sighed heavy sighs while contemplating the loneliest number, then slumped on to the bed where I sat, rocking backwards and forwards, groaning and swearing into my hands, just in time for the maid to barge in.

Encouraged by her presence standing guard at my door and the prospect of more coffee, I left my room and the hotel. The outside world was bright and hot and full of people. A minute's walk away I discovered an attractive café where I set about regaining my composure and ordered in my best—in fact, only—Spanish a *café solo*. There followed the highly unlikely event of someone greeting me as if they knew me.

"Hello again."

I swivelled round to see that the table behind had been taken by the furious man from the coach. What luck! A chum!

After we had exchanged pleasantries, I thought it an opportune moment to indulge in a little banter. "Glad to see that you've recovered your temper," I said with a smile.

"What?"

"It's just that the last time I saw you..." My voice trailed off as his previously sunny expression was replaced by that of a staunch defender of the faith, goaded beyond endurance by heretics.

"I must say, it's a lovely day, makes a change from rainy old Blighty, don't you think, here's hoping it stays like this for the fortnight, I should cocoa."

The babbling seemed to work to the extent that he replied to it. "I'm only here for a week," he said.

"Of *course* you are. This your first holiday here, is it?"

Apparently contented again, he settled back into his chair. "Oh, no. Been coming to Fuengirola for the past ten years. We loved it down here."

I noted the pronoun and tense he'd just used while taking my first sip of coffee. That turned out to be black and viscous and apparently laced with cocaine, and the furious man turned out to be a widower of only three months' standing. He admitted to having trouble sleeping but was astonishingly stoical about his bereavement, so I risked asking him if he didn't mind coming back to a place permeated with painful reminders of his wife.

"Oh, no. I've got happy memories of Fuengirola. Very happy. And I've got friends here as well. Just been to have my haircut from the barber I always go to up the road there. Had a good conversation, him in Spanish and me in English, like, but we got by. And I'll be seeing my drinking buddy tonight. He's Spanish as well, but he's got a bit of English, especially swearing, and what more do you want, eh?" His laugh burbled with nicotine then gave way to a cough.

I asked if he had any tips about things to do here, excursions, for example. A mistake.

"They're a bloody rip-off, that's what they are. You take that trip they advertise to the market and then Mijas. Nineteen hundred pesetas, is it? Bloody rip-off,

> *As you reach the mirador on the cliff over the glistening sea you hear the characteristic sounds of Andalucía: the screech and twitter of swallows overhead, faint high-pitched voices from the street, a distant strain of flamenco, the haunting panpipe of the itinerant knife grinder, the muffled whump of the Mediterranean on the rocks below, and the church bell from the plaza chiming the hour. Before the dying chime has faded, a motorcycle with no muffler rends the reverie and a pair of jackhammers begin their daily assault on the remains of the old house across the street. It is morning on the Costa del Sol.*
>
> —Allen Josephs,
> *White Wall of Spain:*
> *The Mysteries of Andalusian Culture*

more like. The market's only ten minutes' walk up the bloody road and you can get the bus to Mijas your bloody self and it'll only cost you fourpence bloody ha'penny."

Aha! something to expose! I thanked him for this inside information while he paid for the coffee that he'd drunk in one fierce go. He was off to the beach, he announced. Another bloody rip-off there, he could tell me, charging for the sun-loungers and parasols, bloody rip-off. I was to watch out. With that, he marched off, leaving me to drink three more *café solos* that gave me a strange, buzzy sensation and the heart-rate of a television newscaster.

It was approaching midday when I remembered that the welcome guestogether reception was being held at twelve. I ran back to the hotel where I sprinted up the stairs, down the stairs and up the stairs again. Did first floor mean ground floor or the floor one above the ground? And did the mezzanine count? I ran round the floor one above the ground until I came across a room that contained a large display of ceramic fish, ceramic crustaceans, ceramic mermaids.... Perhaps this was the Ceramic Bar.

Inside there were ten pale people waiting in pairs. I was sure I'd heard voices from the corridor but silence fell as I rushed in. I sat down next to the slack-jawed couple and smiled. Almost imperceptibly, they shifted away. No one said a word. Time wore on. A middle-aged woman fiddled noiselessly with her handbag. More time wore on. This was now the most excruciating silence I had experienced since Miss Muir demanded to know which of us in Primary Three had done that dirty drawing on the blackboard. I wiped the sweat from my hands. Mental strength was required to survive this. I embarked on the task of recalling the nicknames of all the clubs in the Scottish Second Division. I had reached number eight (Stenhousemiur, the Warriors), when the silence was broken. A middle-aged man opposite started to whistle softly through his teeth. The tune he was whistling was "Please Release Me."

In the fullness of time, a sturdy rep bustled in with an armful of brochures.

"Hello, everyone," she said with great breeziness. "Everyone settling in okay?... That's great. Right, then. Could you pass round these brochures, please? Right, then. My name's Jane and if I could just tell you that I won't be your rep; that's Trevor, but he can't be here today, and he'll be happy to deal with any queries or problems that you have, all right? Fine."

True to form, Jane proceeded to warn us about time-share touts and explain everything to us. Where the restaurant was and how to work the buffet. Where the telephones were and how to call home. How to change money and how to post postcards. Which buses to take and from where. That Trevor could be found every morning at his desk in the lobby and that we'd to be nice to Trevor because he was new. That we could haggle at the market but not in the shops. That there were lots of excursions to choose from, but that, since our hotel was nearby, we should avoid the organized trip to the weekly market and Mijas and save money by going on our own. Bang went my scoop.

With that Jane wished us a happy holiday and bustled out. I had planned on exchanging a few words with the slack-jawed couple but they had moved an appreciable distance away by the end and had, in any case, now fled the room. I was also ready to give my other fellow-guests my most chipper nods and smiles. No chance. They'd all scooted off, some of them chatting and laughing. I lingered long enough to wonder if this was how lunatics felt when they travelled by bus.

Ho hum. It was a perfect day for a little wander about town. Well, what else was I going to do? Pop out for lunch with some pals? Throw a party? I walked thoughtfully down to the lobby and out again to the promenade. I decided to head east this time. I set off with the air, I trust, of a man with a mission, or at least an appointment.

Of the throngs of foreign visitors to the Costa del Sol, the British by far outnumber the rest. Still, a full 50 percent of suncoast revelers are actually Spanish.

—LMc

To the left was a marina and then the beach which held large groups of Spaniards, some pink Britons, and volleyball nets. At regular intervals there were also restaurants, all of which had rowing boats outside, rowing boats filled with sand and topped by small fires grilling sardines impaled on sticks. To the right were hotels and then pastel-coloured apartment blocks whose ground floors were occupied by eateries and drinkeries: the Waterfront Bar, Ronnie's Café Bar, the Montego Ice-cream Parlour, El Bogavante (*cocedero de mariscos y freidura*), the Restaurante Chino La Suerte, Steve 'N' Kate's, Bonnie 'N' Clyde's. And how cheering it was to see that the Skandinaviska Turist Kyrkan's neighbours were something called the English Manila Bar and Bunters self-service carvery bar.

The most prominent feature of all was the heat. I slipped off my t-shirt and was pleased by the absence of catcalls. (My legs were sticking to my jeans but that I'd have to put up with.) About a mile east of the hotel, I decided I had grown bored with the going-for-a-walk-for-no-particular reason game so I turned round, to walk, for no particular reason, back in the direction of the hotel. I told myself I was doing myself some good (exercise, ozone), a theory lent credibility by the tedium this jaunt involved.

To feel that I had earned my lunch, I went beyond the hotel and Scoffers—as far, you will be impressed to learn, as Ladybirds live music bar. This was adorned by boards urging me to come in and relax, and boasting that Ladybirds was "as featured on Grampian Television" and that it offered "burgers curries scampi salmon." Other boards announced that appearing tonight was "the one and only Rochdale cowboy, Mike Harvey," that tomorrow's act was "Direct from Blackpool, the Colyers," and Thursday's "Mister Personality, Dave Ellis." However, these were all evening performances, and Ladybirds at one-thirty in the afternoon was as empty as my diary.

The danger with having so many places to choose from was to reject them all. I didn't like the seat covers in one pub, another had a waiter I didn't much like the look of, a third I spurned because there was a lovey-dovey couple at one of the tables. Finally, I plumped for Sam's English Breakfast Bar, a curious name for several reasons, one being that almost all the British places I'd seen so far made a big point about serving a full English breakfast all day. (Why? Search me.) Hoardings here advertised "The Best Tea By

The Sea (All Served In 'Pots' With Biscuits)," Cream Teas, and Sinful Pancakes. Another hoarding claimed, "There's only two places to eat—Sam's and your Mum's," so I had to suppress another attack of loneliness as I selected my table, which was soon covered in a plate filled with a Sinful Jamaican Pancake (stuffed with banana, jam and Tía María—I can recommend it) and a glass of San Miguel.

Replete and refreshed, I settled down to study the brochure Jane the sturdy rep had handed me. It was, the cover said, my "complimentary resort guide from Thomson," and it was full of interesting and valuable pieces of information. I now knew, for example, that the Costa del Sol normally enjoys 326 days of sunshine a year. And that the Spanish for bank is *banco*. I also learned how to say "Good morning," "Good afternoon," and "How much is it?" in the native tongue. Excellent. The list of translation of Spanish signs meant that I could now go, with complete confidence, through an open door at an entrance, find a lift and ascend to a lavatory, know which one was the gents, and recognize if it was vacant or engaged. Great stuff.

My early-evening shower was something of an event, particularly because the shower-head proved to be non-detachable. As a result, rinsing involved adopting a series of muscle-man poses under the trickle of water which was as much as the shower granted. Ten minutes of contortions washing myself and twenty minutes of psyching myself up meant that I was ready to face another meal in the restaurant. This time it would be far easier. I'd get to know some people.

Wrong. I felt as popular as a sex offender. A waiter conducted me, pityingly, to an empty table, whence I looked on as mums bantered with sons and husbands joshed wives. I had the cow and chips, since you ask. And a glass of beer, which could only have stigmatized me further since no one else was drinking. Oh, there was a bottle of wine at one table, shared among six adults.

Only 23 more meals here to go.

The long hours before that night's cabaret (flamenco by Isabel

Márquez) I whiled away in a supermarket, where I bought a bottle of much-needed brandy for bedside consumption, and in a couple of cafés where I watched the world, his wife and his children go by. After a time, I joined the procession of people for an evening stroll. It seemed to be the thing to do. And, if you were Spanish, the thing to do in an extended family group with toddlers strewn strategically across the width of the pavement, and at a maximum speed of one mile an hour.

The slowness of the collective pace condemned each pedestrian to be at the mercy of the vast population of haranguing street traders. Because they only preyed on couples or family units, I was distinctively immune from the terrible pest of the time-share touts, and I was evidently too old for the disco leafleteers, but even I didn't escape the pitches of the caricaturists, the painters of soft-focus portraits, the beggars and the youths who specialized in weaving beads through hair. Nor was there any escape in the bars, where shoe-shine men would be on patrol, ready to buff and polish your espadrilles, where women would try to sell you fans or rugs or shawls. Then there were the young African guys who were reputed to live in ruins outside the town and just about kept body and soul together by selling belts and bangles and fake Rolexes. (Some of them, I was to discover, had been adopted by British bars, where they were invariably known as Chalky.)

I arrived back at the hotel early enough to catch the finale of the cabaret's preamble, a youngsters' elimination game that required them to put a hat on their heads, then pass it on, and whoever was wearing the hat when the music stopped was out. The elimination games of my childhood always ended in acrimony and tears, and sometimes fisticuffs, but this one was conducted in a spirit of hilarity. I dunno. Kids these days...

The winner having been decided and warmly applauded by her rivals, it was time for the big show. The lights dimmed and the speakers belted out a tape of flamenco music, but the large audience had to wait. From my vantage-point at the back I could make out, at the emergency exit that doubled as the artistes' entrance, a costumed person in deep argument with a party who remained hidden from view. All was obviously not well with Isabel Márquez.

When the argument was finally settled, Isabel Márquez took to the stage. It transpired that Isabel Márquez was actually two men and two women, all four of them dressed in black hats, black jackets and tight, very tight, trousers with cummerbunds. And off they went, snapping their fingers, stamping their feet, throwing back their arms, twirling about in an almost-synchronized routine. This was followed by a solo performance—by, quite possibly, Señora Márquez herself—of a dance that mimed some catastrophe, I assumed, from the way she sped about the stage looking for help, stretched out her arms to fend off a terrible fate and then succumbed to same by collapsing in a decorous heap. Perhaps an aficionado would appreciate some wonderful significance in all this, but to me it looked like the dance equivalent of the kind of song Nana Mouskouri used to sing after giving a brief translation: "I am but a little shepherdess and my village has no water, and the gods they are cruel, and see, now the bull gores me."

After fifteen minutes of this, I knew that flamenco, or at least Isabel Márquez's performance of it, was one of those activities, like collecting stamps, horse-racing and coprophilia, in which I would never have the slightest interest. I repaired to my room and a companionable session with my bottle of brandy.

Harry Ritchie was literary editor of the Sunday Times *of London from 1993 to 1995 and now writes freelance. He is at work on a travel book about the last outposts of the British Empire, titled* The Last Pink Bits *and due for publication in 1996. He is also the author of* Success Stories *and* Here We Go: A Summer on the Costa del Sol, *from which this piece was excerpted.*

★

There they were by the hundreds—Americans, Scandinavians, British, French, German—all over 60, many enjoying their first Spanish holiday on the Costa del Sol, others returning a second or third time, still holding hands or linking arms affectionately after decades of marriage.

For many it was the adventure of a lifetime. They had worked hard for decades as laborers, educators, administrators, government officials, office workers, storekeepers. They had saved their kronen, pounds, francs, deutschmarks, dollars to buy new sport clothes and to enjoy the luxurious tourist hotels along the beaches.

The greatest gathering of hand-holders came usually after siesta late in the day along the beaches and main shopping strips. Rarely do we see openly such a general display of affection in such great numbers among the grey-and-white-haired couples along the California, Florida, or Cape Cod coasts. Was there a message and a lesson to be learned, we wondered, creeping close to the geriatric era as we were?

I thought back to the comment of the handsome white-haired gentleman in plaid bathing trunks, holding his pretty wife's hand, who bounded out of a hotel elevator, beaming: "Yes it is old folks home, geriatric row here, maybe, but isn't it fun?"

—Blythe Foote Finke, "Touching Improves a Vacation"

To the Alhambra

Specters of Moorish kings and visitors past
haunt Granada's legendary palace.

GRANADA RISES TO ETHEREAL SUMMITS, AND THE RUDDY STONE palace of the Moorish kings—the fabled Alhambra (meaning "red one")—seems to float over the city. Within clear view are the snow-covered heights of the Sierra Nevada, which in the words of Washington Irving "shine like silver" and "give Granada that com-

The Alhambra's Patio de
los Leones

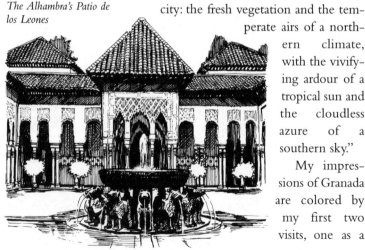

bination of delights so rare in a southern city: the fresh vegetation and the temperate airs of a northern climate, with the vivifying ardour of a tropical sun and the cloudless azure of a southern sky."

My impressions of Granada are colored by my first two visits, one as a student when, alone and with a copy of Washington Irving's *Tales of the Alhambra* under my arm, I climbed from downtown Granada, sweltering in August's heat, into the hills of the Alhambra; there everything was verdant and lush, thanks to the Arabs who had guided the waters of the Sierra Nevada through canals, irrigating the land and creating tranquil pools and gurgling fountains. The air cooled, the sound of rushing water was all around me, and I was transported into another world, unchanged since the times of the Arab caliphs.

I paused every so often to catch my breath and read from Washington Irving, putting myself in the mood for the visit that awaited me.

> While the city below pants with the noontide heat and the parched vega trembles to the eye, the delicate airs from the Sierra Nevada play through these lofty halls, bringing with them the sweetness of the surrounding gardens. Everything invites to that indolent repose, the bliss of southern climes, and while the half-shut eye looks out from shaded balconies upon the glittering landscape, the ear is lulled by the rustling of groves and the murmur of running streams.

I leafed through the chapter of "Legend of the Moor's Legacy," which describes Peregil, the water carrier, bringing icy water down from the sierra in jugs wrapped with fig leaves, and I appreciated the thirst for cool water and the passion for fountains that the Moors, coming out of the African desert, must have had.

When I finally reached the Alhambra I was confronted with a solid and powerful mass of stone, every bit the fortress it was meant to be, but certainly not how I imagined the Alhambra to look. But once I entered I was astonished by the splendor that greeted my eyes. Here were two large rectangular courtyards around which the palace rooms were clustered. There was delicate, lacy plasterwork on the walls, and even though the polychrome painting had faded, the floral and geometric patterns were no less compelling. Arab calligraphy, also traced in the plaster, carried the words of the official

ℳore than 4,000 words of Arabic origin grace the Spanish language today. A word beginning with "al-" or "az-" is often a clue, and Arabic is especially common in vocabulary associated with architecture, agriculture, and public administration. For example:

alcalde	*(from the Arabic* qadî 'juez) *judge or mayor*
alcazaba	*fortress*
alcázar	*(from the Arabic* al-qasr) *castle, palace, or fortress*
alguacil	*(from the Arabic* wazir) *peace-keeping officer*
alquilar	*(from the Arabic* kira) *to rent*
azúcar	*sugar*
gazpacho	*(Arabic for "soaked bread") cold, tomato-based soup often containing pieces of bread*

Names of many Spanish landmarks and towns are also Moorish. Alhambra, for example, comes from the Arabic Al Qal'a al-Hamra, translated variously as "red fort," and "the red one." Andalusia derives from al-Andalus, meaning "land in the west," and Granada comes from the Moorish word Karnattah, meaning "hill of strangers"—although granada also means "pomegranate" in Spanish.

—LMc

Alhambra poet, Ibn Zamrak, as well as texts from the Koran, and the repeated words "Allah is Great."

The Patio de los Arrayanes was serene, reflecting the towers of the Alhambra in its elongated pond. In the Hall of the Ambassadors (Salón de los Embajadores), next to the courtyard, I saw intricately wood-inlaid (*artesonado*) ceilings and walls covered in colorful ceramic tile. In the Patio de los Leones, twelve stylized lions encircled a fountain around which a veritable forest of 144 slender columns arose. Marvelous honeycomb stuccowork in unimaginably complex designs was on the ceiling of the Sala de las Dos Hermanas (Room of the Two Sisters) and the Sala de los Abencerrajes, both entered through the patio. Bubbling fountains created music all around me. I could hardly believe the magic the Moors had wrought, and was particularly struck that something so seemingly fragile had survived the centuries.

The powerful impression the Alhambra made on me that first time did not, however, prepare me for another experience I had there several years later when I returned with my family.

We had toured the Alhambra in the morning, a bit disappointed because the crowds robbed us of the calm needed to fully appreciate the tranquillity that the Alhambra was designed to convey. After dinner we could not resist climbing just once more to the Alhambra to experience its mystery by night. To our surprise it was open, and we were ushered in, but warned that closing time was in ten minutes and the lights would go out. Our voices dropped, our steps slowed; we were awestruck by the sight before us. Four people were sitting on the stone floor in silence, gazing upon the still green waters of the Patio de los Arrayanes pond, which reflected gracefully carved columns. Everyone was lost in revery, and we immediately succumbed to the mood. It was a religious, almost mystical, experience.

So spellbound were we that we failed to notice that other visitors had disappeared. At precisely midnight, all the lights were extinguished and the Alhambra was enveloped in total darkness. We clutched each other and took tentative steps in the direction from which we had entered. Now I could vividly imagine Washington Irving's terror during his first night alone in the palace:

> A vague and indescribable awe was creeping over me. I
> would fain have ascribed it to the thoughts of robbers
> awakened by the evening's conversation, but I felt that it
> was something more unreal and absurd.... Everything
> began to be affected by the working of my mind.

In the Sala de los Abencerrajes, where an entire family of opponents to Granada's king were beheaded, and whose blood, it is said, can still be seen in the fountain, I could almost hear the clanking chains and the murmurings that legend tells are the spirits of those so ignobly massacred. After what seemed an eternity, we were escorted out. But ever since that unforgettable evening I know that to completely capture the enchantment of the Alhambra, a visit at night, in relative solitude, is absolutely essential.

The Moorish kings lived, it would seem, in idyllic surroundings, but there were bloody battles taking place around them, and
the fighting among themselves approached civil war. By the 15th
century it was obvious that the
Moors were losing their
foothold in Spain. As the
Catholic Kings took control of
Moorish Spain, Granada's rulers
isolated themselves in the well-
defended Alhambra, which became a self-contained fortress
and a city in itself. Even when
summer's heat sent the kings in
search of more temperate cli-
mates, they merely transferred
their residence to the cooler,
higher elevations of the romantic
summer palace of the Generalife
in the Alhambra complex. But
the signs were irrefutable: the
Moorish domination of Spain
had come to an end.

*The Alhambra was used by
the conquering Christians
as a debtor's asylum, a hospital, a
prison, and a munitions dump, and
it is only in our own times that
they have placed upon the ram-
parts of that golden fortress the
haunting appeal of De Icaza's
blind beggar:*

Dale Limosna, Mujer,
Que no hay en la vida
        nada
Como la pena de ser
Ciego en Granada.

*Alms, lady, alms! For there
is nothing crueler in life
than to be blind in Granada.*

    —Jan Morris, *Spain*

Boabdil, the last Arab ruler of Granada, en route to exile in the
mountains of Las Alpujarras, turned around for one last glimpse of
his beloved Granada and tearfully exclaimed "*Allah Akbar*!" and
with a deep sigh bid farewell to Granada. His hardhearted mother,
Aixa, showed nothing but contempt for her son: "You cry like a
woman for the kingdom that you could not defend as a man," she
reportedly exclaimed. This spot has ever since been known as El
Suspiro del Moro—the Sigh of the Moor.

Despite the imposition of Christianity in Granada, the Catholic
Kings were obviously charmed by the Alhambra and left it relatively untouched. The impressive central mosque [down in the
town of Granada], however, was des-troyed and a grand cathedral
constructed in its place. Because of the great symbolic significance
of the fall of Granada, Fernando and Isabel had special affection for

Granada. "I hold this city dearer than my life," said Isabel. They chose to be buried here in a special chapel of the cathedral. Their grandson, Charles V, later built a magnificent Renaissance palace within the Alhambra grounds, and although it is by any standards an exceptional building, it is much too stern to be contemplated in the same breath as the sensual Alhambra. Charles did, however, appreciate the beauty of the Alhambra, reportedly exclaiming when he saw it, "Pity on he who lost it." And echoing the biting words of Boabdil's mother, he added, "She was right to say what she did and the king wrong to do what he did; because if I were he, or if he were I, I would take the Alhambra as my grave rather than live without my kingdom in the Alpujarras."

In 1976, the Argentine writer Jorge Luis Borges visited the Alhambra. Borges was blind, but he drew on memory, history and his sense of smell and touch to evoke the palace. In his poem "Alhambra" Borges lets his hand feel its way over the smooth surfaces of the marble, he listens to the murmuring of the streams, smells the sweetness of the lemon blossom, before recalling with sadness King Boabdil's final defeat.

> *Your gentle ways now*
> *depart,*
> *your keys will be denied you,*
> *the faithless cross will wipe*
> *out the moon,*
> *and the evening you gaze*
> *upon*
> *will be the last.*

> —Jimmy Burns,
> *A Literary Companion to Spain*

Penelope Casas lived in Spain for several years, and has spent the past 30 years exploring the country and leading tours with her husband, a physician who was born in Spain. She has written about Spanish food and travel for The New York Times, Gourmet, Connoisseur, *and* Condé Nast Traveler, *and received the Spanish National Prize of Gastronomy and the Medal of Touristic Merit from the Spanish government. This excerpt was taken from her book,* Discovering Spain: An Uncommon Guide.

✷

Visitors to the Alhambra share a restriction: they must walk by a door that forbids them entrance. Beyond this door once lived the man largely responsible for their presence here. Above it a plaque in Spanish reads:

"Washington Irving wrote in these rooms his *Tales of the Alhambra* in the year 1829."

If, like me, you try the doorknob, it will not budge. If you ask a guard for admittance he will tell you that it is not possible.

Irving had been in Spain four years with the American legation when he set out by horseback on May 1, 1829, from Seville to Granada. Shortly after his arrival at the Alhambra, dissatisfied that he was not dwelling within the heart of the Arabic palace, Irving tells how he came upon the very door that now denied me admission. It was locked.

Irving sought out the key, an easy task as the entire Alhambra was supervised by Doña Antonia Molina, known as Tía Antonia.

Tía Antonia unlocked the door. Stretching before him Irving saw four connecting rooms built 300 years earlier by Charles V as a temporary apartment while his nearby palace was under construction. The rooms were a mess. The walls held nearly obliterated frescoes whose rampant graffiti included what Irving refers to as the "insignificant names of aspiring travelers."

"I'll take it," Irving said....

My whining campaign paid off. Somehow the authorities conceded that my avid curiosity about what lay behind the locked door might possibly be more than quixotic. In addition, they were getting very tired of me. Right now, standing before me, the current manifestation of Tía Antonia had the key in hand. In time-honored melodramatic fashion, the lock refused to turn. Finally, after much labor on Antonia's part, the key moved. She opened the door.

First there was blackness. Then Antonia pulled open a shutter, followed by six others. Light streamed in. The four connecting rooms were empty. My mouth fell agape, an idiot expression to match my astonishment. Antonia told me that damage to Charles V's paneled ceilings had forced the authorities to place all the furnishings in storage. I had spent so much time soliciting admission that the question of what the rooms contained had never come up.

Within these empty, desolate rooms, I found myself in Irving's situation (give or take a few intrusive orange and citron branches) when he first looked from the windows of this apartment.

Now, as then, the apartment lacked only an occupant.

"I'll take it," I said to Antonia.

—Robert Packard, "Behind the Alhambra's Locked Door,"
The New York Times

CHARLES N. BARNARD

A Ramble through Barcelona

*Genius, madness, and joy abound
in the Catalán capital.*

I SIT IN A BEACHSIDE RESTAURANT ON THE EVENING OF MY
arrival—shoes off, toes wiggling into the warm sand, a cold carafe
of so-so white wine sweating into the tablecloth. The humid
breeze from the Mediterranean Sea that laps the coast of this city
in northeastern Spain carries a bouquet of scents: seafood, fish dry-
ing, squid frying, and…what else? Do I detect North Africa? A
man wearing a black velvet suit and a ruffled white shirt is playing
familiar Spanish tunes on a guitar as he moves between rows of
weathered, rickety tables placed all atilt on the beach. Two young
women stroll on the sand, supple bronze sculptures in black bathing
suits. Three container ships stand silhouetted on the pink-twilight
horizon, dislodged city blocks that have floated away to sea.

It is that quiet hour when the last of the day's beach people pick
up and scuff home and when too-early-for-dinner tourists like me
show up in this old working-class neighborhood called
Barceloneta. It is already 9:30, but I should know that in Spain one
does not even think about dining until 10:00. A few couples at
nearby tables keep me from being altogether alone, however. I nibble green olives and crusty bread with the wine. The proprietor is
a cheery character who assures me that his is the best paella in

town. Soft chords from the guitar accompany the quiet lapping of a slack tide.

It is a contented moment, knowing I am here for as long as I wish.

I go to see Antonio Gaudí's 1910 apartment building that has been affectionately nicknamed La Pedrera (the Quarry), expecting I know not what—and finding I know not what: a seven-story building that flows glacially around a corner, its architecture that of an amusement park fun house, all staring eyes and laughing mouths and peephole windows and beetle-browed balconies; waves upon waves of stone, a surf of a building on which great entanglements of ornamental wrought iron seaweed are snared. Standing tall on the roof is an encampment of giant ventilation towers masquerading as merciless-looking guardians, all helmeted and armored with mosaics.

The man is mad; Gaudí is mad. I am upset. Imagine getting away with something as outrageous as this over 80 years ago! Or even today. But it's not just mad, is it? Not really. I'd better come back and look again.

La Pedrera

Las Ramblas is the street everyone talks about, writes about, tries to paint or photograph. Barcelona has other more refined avenues, but in corporeal terms, this one is the city's jugular, or its windpipe, or perhaps its colon. It was once a stream, paved over long ago. I find it on my map, a wide, tree-lined slash running...no, promenading...from the harbor straight inland. Almost a mile long, I see. But length and width are not the measure or the meaning of Las Ramblas.

I walk toward the harbor from the top end. The broad center of the street, a thoroughfare between rows of old plane trees, is the paseo for people; motor vehicles must use two narrow roads on either side.

Las Ramblas is seamless for pedestrians: no intersections, just a continuous flow. In the first hundred yards I find metal chairs arranged in rows for watching the passing parade. I'm too curious to sit down just now. I come to the sector where bird sellers set up their forest of steely wire cages. Parakeets, canaries, arrogant things that look like ravens, and small birds, all noisy, all shrilling. The birdmen sell tropical fish, too, and sometimes tortoises.

A few blocks after the birds come flower displays and cactuses and then sidewalk cafés with color posters illustrating syrupy, silly drinks, and everywhere bookstalls and newsdealers—enough of these to supply the needs of Western Europe in all its languages and all its perversions, it seems. Las Ramblas is a bazaar. It is a river of people who parade and flaunt, provoke and solicit and perform.

This is just my first-day ramble on Las Ramblas. As it turns out, I will repeat some part of this walk every day while I am here. The more often I explore, the more I find elegance—fine old hotels, palaces, the opera—that is obscured by contemporary sordidness. Today I simply gawk—and arrive finally at the harbor and the Christopher Columbus Monument, which faces the Mediterranean. There is an elevator to the viewing platform near the top. Another time for that perhaps.

So (unfolding my map) I'm getting a sense of priorities here. There is Gaudí (a lot of Gaudí), and there is Las Ramblas, and then there is the Barri Gótic (Gothic Quarter), which I should see next—the ancient heart of the city, a labyrinth of narrow streets that crook about among Roman walls with imposing stone towers. The cathedral at the center, La Catedral de Santa Eulàlia, is square, not cruciform, in shape, with soaring spires and a peaceful cloister where a fountain trickles and guardian geese strut about displaying the aloof, detached look of clerics.

The Barri Gótic is not a Spanish village for tourists, but a time within a time, an original city within a newer city where a particular fraternity of citizens live and work and eat and shop and know each other as neighbors.

Within this stony precinct, near the cathedral, is a small square named Plaça del Rei (Plaza of the King). It was here that Ferdinand and Isabella received Columbus upon his first return from the New World. Now the square, with a temporary wooden stage at one end, is used for drama and concerts in the summer. I arrive as a rock group is setting up for a performance. Microphones and control boards and headphones and guitars are being linked by a veritable snake pit of wires—all the demonic paraphernalia of musicians costumed as a motorcycle gang. Amplified fragments of songs are rehearsed—heavy metal ricochets off ancient stones like sonic graffiti. Disinterested old women in housedresses hurry through the square, ignoring the scene, stepping over wires, carrying fresh bread and fish and groceries from the market for supper. Young women, chic in tiny black dresses with gold belts and matching shoes, enter the square with boyfriends and excitedly look for seats for the concert.

Barcelona seems tolerant, flexible, worldly. It welcomes rock and rap and punk while honoring native Catalán Pablo Casals. It supports an opera house. It enjoys the endless controversies about the madness or the genius of Gaudí, it preserves history, it builds for the future.

Picasso was not born in Barcelona, the guidebooks explain, but he spent some of his early years here, and now 2,500 pieces of his art are the capital of the Museo Picasso. It is in the Barri Gótic, not far from where the artist once lived. I wondered, as I walked through the galleries, if Picasso would like this place. Photographs so often picture him in baggy shorts, surrounded by such a chaos of creativity, such a personal flea market of paintings, sculpture, and pottery. His museum is a hushed funeral home by comparison, a memorial, a scholarly chronicle of his evolution as an artist. A prison for art, too, complete with dour-faced guards.

In Barcelona the juxtaposition and layering of periods can leave a visitor with dissonant, seemingly irreconcilable impressions. A stolid bourgeois conservatism is joined to a fierce Catalán desire for independence (and sometimes a passionate anarchism). The city is as much about unity in difference as those Gaudí facades covered with collages of broken tiles (the technical term for this ancient practice is trencadís) *in which various patterns, colors, textures, and styles jar with one another but also harmonize. This city is medieval, fin de siécle, and futuristic all at once.*

—Jed Perl, "Barcelona Dreaming," *Vogue*

Ordinary people actually have everyday conversations and debates about art and architecture in Barcelona—at lunch, perhaps, or even in bars at night. Not surprising; the city is an architectural exhibition, from Roman to Gothic to Mies van der Rohe. The man in the street understands and uses the terms neoclassicism or Greek Revival or art deco as part of a local lingua franca. Everywhere I hear the word modernisme, too. It is the equivalent of art nouveau in France. It describes the explosions of artistic expression that took place here at the turn of the century.

The seeds for that blossoming were planted in the 1830s, during a period of Catalán prosperity. A wealthy new bourgeois class was born with a vision of a new Barcelona, larger than the one defined by the medieval boundaries of the Barri Gòtic. During the 1850s, most of the walls surrounding the district were taken down, and Ildefons Cerdà, a Catalán engineer, created an ambitious expansion into the relatively flat plain around the old city. This would come to be known as the Eixample, meaning "Expansion," with broad new streets all arranged in a huge grid, and an enlightened provision for green space. It was the beginning of Barcelona's Renaixença (Renaissance).

Wealth and talent combined to make the Eixample one of Europe's architectural and residential showcases. Architects such as Gaudí, Domenèch i Montaner, Puig i Cadafalch, Jujol, and Valeri, all created stunning buildings in the area. Riotous ornamentation, brilliant mosaics, rich stained glass, wrought iron sculpture, the textures of tile, wood, marble, and stone—all combined in forms that defied the conventions of the time.

Back to Las Ramblas for another evening's entertainment. A man is selling three white kittens from a cardboard box. He asks 200 pesetas each, about two dollars. An enraptured girl holds one of the leggy, mewing little creatures aloft and pleads. Her date, shaking his head in feigned resignation, counts out 200 pesetas.

I hear the faint recorded music of the flamenco, accompanied by staccato heel-stamping. A costumed woman is dancing, solo, for the entertainment of sidewalk café patrons. She is passionate and pretty and passes a tambourine with a smile for her tips. The tourists love her; Cataláns ignore her.

I stroll on. A man is making a wire sculpture of a ten-speed bicycle from one continuous filament of brass, his hands twisting and pulling with only the occasional aid of pliers. He produces a five-inch bike in about two minutes. Two hundred pesetas, Señor.

Barcelona, city of artists.

> *In one's first brush with Gaudí's genius, it is not so much propriety that is outraged as one's sense of probability.*
>
> —Evelyn Waugh, *Labels: A Mediterranean Journal* (1930)

If there is a single symbol of Barcelona, the city's premier logotype, the familiar image on countless postcards and on the covers of countless guidebooks and brochures, it is unquestionably the unfinished church known as the *Templo de la Sagrada Familia* (Temple of the Holy Family). Started by an ecclesiastical architect in 1882, the project was taken over by Gaudí in 1883. In the 43 years that preceded this great, loony man's death in 1926 (run over by a tram while crossing the street), he overwhelmed the structure's Gothic beginnings with bizarre improvisations, including an assortment of chimney-like towers. Although it is not completed, La Sagrada Familia remains his most monumental work. It is also his tomb. I will go have a look.

Four of the towers (those originally designed for tube bells) have a porous, ventilated appearance, like incinerators. They stand against the sky, each topped with a colorful curlicue of mosaics, the final flourishes from a pastry chef's frosting tube. (Salvador Dalí said Gaudí had no taste—which is what made him a genius.)

At ground level, the site is an incomprehensible collection of symbolism and architectural styles—and idle, rusting construction machinery. The East Facade depicts the nativity. The West Facade, conceived by some of Gaudí's young followers, who resumed work on the church in the early 1950s, depicts the crucifixion and death of Christ, but in an altogether new style. The result is a structure that is some Gothic, some Gaudí, some stark modern—an architectural camel, a project designed by a committee. I ask if Barcelona considered trying to complete the project in time for the 1992 Olympics. "For the Olympics of 2092, perhaps," I was told. "Even if Gaudí were still alive, the work would be unfinished. He used to say that his Client was not in any hurry."

There are some things a visitor is absolutely expected to see in certain cities. In Barcelona the tourist "must" that is second only to visiting La Sagrada Familia is to witness—or even join—the sardana dancers in a public square on a Sunday evening. Inasmuch as this stately public performance falls considerably short of being exciting or colorful, its local significance requires a friend's explanation. I listen as I watch. We are standing together in the Plaça Sant Jaume, the square where the city hall faces the Catalán Government Palace.

Long, long before the sardana was ever danced, there were

Phoenicians, Carthaginians, Romans here. My friend related the history with blah-blah-blah speed...andnextcametheVisigoths MoorsandFranks.

By the 9th century Barcelona was an important walled city, ruled by its own noble families. By the 14th century, more than a hundred years before there was a Spain, these Catalans had built a thriving maritime empire that included Sicily and Sardinia. They achieved a distinct identity with their own language and customs, including the sardana.

The custom of dancing the sardana survived until 1939, when Franco decreed the suppression of all vestiges of Catalán culture, including the language and the sardana. Not until the dictator's death in 1975 did Catalonia once again become a country within a country. Dancing the sardana was an immediate symbol of liberation.

As my history lesson progresses, so does the ritual of the sardana. Musicians gather, unfold wooden chairs, set up music stands. They play; dancers pile their pocketbooks and shopping bags on the ground and form circles around them, holding hands and executing a series of small steps. The dancers, I see, are truly anybody, Barcelona citizens and tourists alike, all ages, today mostly women. Anyone may break into one of the many circles and increase its size and number. The music is romantic, rhythmic, courtly. The dancing goes on for one hour, then another. Passions never seem to rise. If these people are making a political statement, it is low-key. One wonders why Franco bothered to ban such a tame pastime.

Barcelona's great central food market, La Boqueria, is located about midway along Las Ramblas. It is closed on Sundays but springs to life every Monday morning. Within its railroad-station-size enclosure of iron and glass, there are hundreds of stalls, each an individual family business, selling fruits, vegetables, wild mushrooms, the meat of cows, lambs, birds, and horses. Also, at the heart of the market are piles of what must be every type of edible fish and crustacean that lives in the Mediterranean: an exhibition of silvery fish scales, scarlet claws, rubbery white flesh, curious shells, and slippery intestinal shapes. La Boqueria should be listed among the city's great museums, the one most alive, brilliant with all the colors of nature, scented by spices and pungent cheese, glistening with mountains of ice, chattering with barter, an agora that Barcelonans insist will never be replaced by one of those—the word is spat out as an epithet—supermarkets!

Sometimes I stop in twice a day. To feel the cool shade. To inhale. To listen. To have a morning tallat (coffee with a splash of milk) at the small market bar, El Pinocho. I allow myself just one churro, a stick of sweet, deep-fried doughnut dough. Later in the day I may stop to buy almonds to go with a beer on Las Ramblas. Or, at any hour, I come to the market to admire Barcelona's beautiful women, for they are always here in great numbers.

I observe rituals when I travel. If I have enjoyed a city, I will have a last dinner in the same restaurant where I had my first. By going back to the beginning, I see where I have been.

My return to Barceloneta is bittersweet, for I have learned that my beachside restaurant will be torn down. But for now I savor another carafe of so-so white wine, another best-paella-in-Spain, and listen to a Gypsy guitar.

I take one more look at my beat-up map of Barcelona, limp from use now, coming apart on the fold lines, full of notes and arrows and question marks and coffee stains—symbol of an intense, wonderful affair, a love letter I will read over and over.

Charles N. Barnard's work has been appearing in major U.S. magazines for 47 years and he's "still trying to get it right."

*

Following the advice of friends who'd shot slides of it, but couldn't remember in which country it was, I had searched for the Sagrada Familia church in Switzerland (sic) in 1960. It's hard to believe now how unknown outside Spain Gaudí's architecture still was 35 years ago.

Years later I finally found it in Spain, sitting on a blank and dismal plot of land in the middle of urban sprawl. Papers, metals, cans and refuse, the detritus left on open city spaces, lay about on rocks and lusterless dirt. The church itself looked like a leftover from some medieval conflict, unfin- ished, ill set—or—like an Everest or Annapurna or Kanchenjunga moved by man from the Himalayas unto the flatness of a city block. Its spires lifted into the clouds, its lofty spaces were as if molded from lace, some of its cavelike-dripped-in-stone doorways opened into nothingness. Piles of lime, brick, and stone lay about in the courtyards.

They were trying to finish it. But without the soaring imagination of its creator, the new parts were like rectilinear paste-ons: stiff, four-square. I wanted to cry: Stop! Just stop! Plant some grass! Trees! Let it go. Why does everything in this world have to be "finished"?

—Jan Haag, "One Sketch of Spain"

G. Y. DRYANSKY

Having It All

*Ibiza's good old days of hippie mellowness
are gone—or are they?*

PATRICE SAID HE SAW PEOPLE COPULATING UNDER THE BUBBLES. IT
seemed to go with the mood. It was plausible, but from where we
stood, up where three cannons
had been shooting streams of
foam for an hour onto about a
thousand young people packed
together, all I could make out
was a lot of writhing to the beat
of the house music. People were
dancing, with the foam rising
over their heads, and I wondered
if they would drown. It was six-
thirty in the morning. And here
we were, red-eyed, catching up
with the new Ibiza, my wife,
Joanne, and I....

> *T*he Balearic Islands (Illes
> Balears) *lie in the Medi-
> terranean Sea off the east coast,
> with Ibiza closest to mainland
> Spain. Named by Greek invaders
> for the* ballo *(Greek for sling) be-
> cause of ancient inhabitants' talent
> for catapulting rocks, the islands
> comprise a province and an au-
> tonomous region that also include
> Majorca (with the province's capi-
> tal, Palma), Menorca, Cabrera,
> and Formentera.*
>
> —LMc

We were years beyond the is-
land we'd earlier known and loved, when morning after morning
at this hour in Ibiza harbor the overnight ferry from Barcelona dis-

charged waves of immigrants from mainland and mainstream in leather, beads, and embroidery.

Flower children, painters, writers, aspiring saints, confirmed rogues, and, with all of these, the world's most blithe peasants had coinhabited Ibiza in weird harmony, each group in its own space—the term had just come into fashion. They called it the "magic island" back then in the '60s and '70s. And now these people, the "clubbers," were calling Ibiza their "disco island"—and magic as well.

Suddenly now, Martín, a lithe African-American known in Spanish as "the master of the dancers"—who looked like he could dance better than anyone writhing below his platform—took the microphone and told the night-long dancers they were dirty. Sprinklers gushed water, and the pulsing music switched to "Singin' in the Rain."

We left at about seven-thirty. They were still dancing, and it was still raining inside the discotheque Amnesia, beside a road on Ibiza I had traveled years ago when Amnesia's packed parking lot had been a pasture and the disco a farmhouse.

Patrice Calmettes was our guide to the clubs. He lives on Ibiza part of the year, but he is a Parisian, like Joanne and me, and, like us, he'd known the white nights of Paris, when around four a.m. Régine used to serve spaghetti to the stragglers sculpting conversations they'd forget when they finally got to sleep but would find again in Françoise Sagan's latest novel.

Writhing in foam near dawn was something else. Joanne and I eschewed getting foamy and wet at Amnesia, but earlier we'd done our little share of dancing at El Divino, Pachá, and Ku, and after Amnesia we still had at least one more club to visit. Near eight, while a red ball of sun rose from the waters of Playa d'en Bossa, we ate pastries and drank coffee with the group that had gathered there for a breather. Then we went down the road to Space. It was full daylight outside, but the night was artificially preserved inside. And the dance floor kept filling up. Patrice, Joanne, and I decided, though, that sleep might at last be in order....

We'd begun our crawl right after dinner, at about one-thirty in the morning, at the Dome, a bar near the harbor of Ibiza town. A crowd in costume had sat silently drinking soft drinks. Men in wedding dresses, women in tights, top hats, tails, and platform combat boots. A transsexual acquaintance of Patrice's came by and showed us the most beautiful breasts on the island—by his/her own account. There were real children in the arms of parents who looked like figures from a Mardi Gras float. The silence was impressive. It made me think of soldiers about to land somewhere dangerous. Later I came to understand that a lot of these people were just chilling out—they'd been dancing through much of the day and the night before.

El Divino, decorated by a man who designed sets for Fellini, was an airy, elegant place opening onto the harbor of Ibiza, with striped poles and awnings that brought on vague thoughts of Venice and of *Death in Venice.* A supper club, Pachá was bedlam. It was flower-power night, and people in '60s hippie clothes were writhing to the Rolling Stones: about three thousand souls, including one go-go girl in a cage, wearing just a net, who was about seven months pregnant. Ku was somber. It had fallen out of the clubbers' favor. People moped around the big swimming pool in the great hangar of a place. Amnesia was, as I said, wildly foamy....

Joanne and I went back to La Ventana, our hotel in the Old Town, and got some sleep before the five o'clock lunch hour at Las Salinas beach. We'd known Las Salinas when there was just an empty strand of pale sand, the saltworks, and a tiny hotel running electricity off a generator. The saltworks and the hotel were still there—along with row on row of cabanas swarming with house music.

At the concession called Guarano, people were bobbing over their salads while a disk jockey danced around his equipment. At the piece of beach called Malibu, the music flowed over fat long-haired blond German men in strings, lying buns-up, face down, like '50s TV wrestlers who'd just lost....

Joanne decided to wait at Guarano. I walked beside the water and rounded the cove to the beach called Es Caballet. Beyond a

ruined Moorish tower were the sea-washed formations where the
Phoenicians are said to have quarried stone for their tombs and
where the late performer Divine liked to bathe his huge flesh in
the cavities they'd left, as if in a bathtub. Next came the gay nud-
ist part of Es Caballet: hundreds upon hundreds of naked men
until, as the beach went on, nude women began to blend into the
crowd, and then people in bathing suits as well, couples of whom
one person, either the man or the woman, had decided to preserve
the privacy of his or her privates.

And all these people indeed blended together, all their choices,
as they lay about in peace or swam or talked on a hot beach in
September. As scenes go, it was eloquent. I didn't say elegant, but
it spoke to me and it interested me.

These were not my people. But here was what a day of peaceful leisure looked like in one much-sought-after place in the
Western world at the end of my century. I knew that many of the
clubbers are the charter-ticket version of Saturday night Bridge
and Tunnel people who punch computers year-round to pay for a
nonstop week of frenzy, and that some are a lost generation drift-
ing forever to where on earth the music is going, the way another
generation followed vibrations of Aquarius from Ibiza to Morocco
and on to Goa and Kathmandu. Yet I remembered what Paul
Richardson, who wrote a fascinating book called *Not Part of the
Package: A Year in Ibiza,* had told me on the phone from London
before I left for the island: "The thing everyone in Ibiza has in
common is tolerance."

So I had come back to see the new Ibiza, armed with tolerance,
the virtue that had also defined Ibiza back in those days when the
religious Ibizenco peasants were renting their farmhouses for next
to nothing to half-naked hippies, and bringing them flowers to
boot. Tolerance is inseparable from Ibiza's magic. But it is only
part of it.

The next day we went into the country and found our old
Ibiza, quite magically still there. The same landscape, not breathtaking but endearing: toast-colored fields and low pine hills, olive

groves and almond orchards defined by porous volcanic-stone walls. We passed the whitewashed geometric Ibizenco farmhouses, the *fincas* that were said to have inspired Le Corbusier. Ibizenco women in straw hats and black dresses were gathering figs in their gray aprons, or shaking almonds out of tall trees with poles. The way they always had.

Sandy Pratt, ahead of us in his dinky white Renault R-4, spun pungent dust as he turned onto one of Ibiza's good old bone-rattling dirt roads. It was nice to be spending time with Sandy again.

Like Sandy, Joanne and I had never been flower children, although maybe some of our best friends had. We'd already chosen the profession of observer, which separated us from movements. We and our two kids loved Ibiza for the sun and the clean water. It was cheap—Third World prices a short flight from Paris. The food you got easily—fresh fish and salads and lamb—was good, and the atmosphere was, all in all, what people then called mellow. We took a house for a few summers, right on the water at Es Canà, near the village of Santa Eulàlia. Our one close neighbor was a retired Norwegian sea captain who reminded you of Lord Mountbattan, a very distinguished man; he counted hippies among his friends as well.

Sandy owned Sandy's Bar in Santa Eulàlia. Having come to the conclusion that drinking was the one thing he knew much about, Sandy shocked his distinguished Irish family by giving up the law he'd read at Trinity College to tend bar on this island in the Baleares. When someone writes the history of watering places that helped define their time and place, Sandy's Bar must be included, along with, say, the Cedar Tavern in Greenwich Village and the Dôme in Paris. And so must Sandy.

I said earlier that Ibiza was in some measure a rogues' island—a tradition that came as a corollary of tolerance, I suppose. I don't know of a port anywhere else that has a monument to pirates like the one in the harbor of Ibiza. (They'd saved the island in the 18th century by defeating other pirates).

Sandy's attracted such notables as Elmyr de Hory, the suave art counterfeiter, and the witty Clifford Irving, who, after doing a book on Elmyr's exploits, went on to do time for creating a counterfeit autobiography of Howard Hughes. The rogues rubbed shoulders at Sandy's Bar with Robin Maugham, Terry-Thomas, Laurence Olivier, Howard Sackler, and a lot of painters and writers. We used to go for an evening drink with the kids—they'd have gin and tonic without the gin. It was the mellow sort of place you could take children.

lmyr de Hory's life was immortalized in Orson Welles's 1975 film, F for Fake, shot partially on location in Ibiza. Welles called the film a "pseudo-documentary about forgery and illusion."

—LMc

Sandy created the tone. More than the tone—the disingenuous but not blasé culture of the place. He sold the bar to an ice-cream parlor a dozen years ago, when the village of Santa Eulàlia had turned into a high-risen town. He became the island's great landscape gardener, working on all the best conversions of farms to estates. But Sandy's manner was his first great artistic achievement. Reserve, ease, discretion. Nothing but true evil seems to rile Sandy. The other old-time Ibiza émigrés consider his mellow way their ideal. I've heard him called "our guru," but I've never known Sandy to give lessons. We were happy to see him busy in his current profession.

Sandy took us up the back roads to initiate us into the new Ibiza of hidden luxury. Forget the gleaming black Jeeps, with the big dogs trained to stand sideways in the back, that belong to the Germans who hang out at the manicured marina of sleek Ibiza Nueva. If you want to see luxurious rusticity, follow the dust-covered R-4s like Sandy's up the wash-board roads. They'll lead you to some *fincas* without electricity or running water, where a painter or a writer is enjoying the simple luxe of not having to work for anyone else—or, just as easily, to some farms that are now properties with tennis courts and swimming pools. Ibiza is just 140 miles from North Africa, and the island's geometric white *fincas* follow centuries-old plain Moor-inspired designs. These days many of them have been expanded into million-dollar properties, like the one Joanne and I once decided not to buy for US$20,000.

Sandy, who lives in the hills but has been spotted more often than he admits at the disco Pachá, pointed out that rich people were now forgoing Marbella for Ibiza, where the benefit of wealth is not bristling social standing but choice and ease. Marbella, I recalled, was now riddled with in-group animosities and troubled with crime. On the other hand, Ibiza, Sandy argued, had in a few ways become easier than before.

"You can have everything here now," Sandy said. "You want an elegant restaurant meal, you have it. You want to dance all night, or you want to retreat into the country, it's here." And every place on the menu, he might have added, is very close to everywhere else in miles but very self-contained. At one time or another the island had been under the sway of Phoenicians, Greeks, Carthaginians, Romans, Moors, and, finally, Spaniards. Historians call Ibiza a "crossroad of civilizations."

In our time, you might argue that the word "lifestyle" has replaced "civilization." And Ibiza is a bright crossroad of lifestyles.

Sandy has a friend named Smelja, formally known as the Princess Michailovitch, who has moved from the country to Ibiza Nueva. We went to visit her, anxious to see what living was like in Ibiza's new version of Monte Carlo, the first attempt at a golden ghetto on the island. The neighborhood went up in the '80s on the shore of the capital town, Ibiza, along with the Botafoc marina. It is full of expensive apartment buildings—postmodern notions of grandeur with marble lobbies and the usual radiators—resembling concrete high-rises.

The Princess was satisfied with her stunning view of the harbor, her terrace and marble floors, and a well-designed entry in which to hang her fake Modigliani signed by Elmyr in his own name. She's past 70, and Ibiza Nueva appeals to her for the comfort. But Ibiza, she insisted, would always be the island where she learned how to live from flower children, soon after the day she arrived in the harbor in the '60s, recently widowed, wearing a Chanel suit and white gloves.

"I gravitated toward them," she said, "and they taught me serenity. They taught me to live without a clock."

Sandy and the Princess are Ibiza persons. And so is Patrice, who has been living part of the year on the island since 1975. Patrice is a talented photographer, but he also spent a good part of ten years having a telephone affair with his Paris neighbor Marlene Dietrich, whom he never met face to face. Ibiza people are quirky, talented, endearing nonstrivers. And the island persists in bringing out a bit of the hippie in anyone who gets seriously attached to it.

Did the hippies, as the Princess contends, give Ibiza its magic, or was it waiting there for them? Jean-Claude Friedrich, who owns El Divino, having made a bundle in California real estate, and who was a long-haired idler on Ibiza seventeen years ago, told me that an unidentified flying object had been spotted on Isla Vedra, the great wedge of rock just off the southwest coast. "Nothing special, right?" he said. "Except that it happened two thousand years ago and was written about in Phoenician and Roman papyruses."

Should we believe the story? Should we believe Patrice when he tells us that Tanit and Bes, ancient deities, still rule the island? Bes is a god of recreation, inspiring joy, erasing sorrow, whose roots go back to Egypt. Because he is often represented as a dwarf standing on a snake, Ibiza people say he is responsible for there being no venomous or feral wildlife on the island, nor poisonous plants.

Tanit is the Carthaginian goddess of fertility and love. Maybe because of the favors of Tanit or of Bes, or of both, Ibiza was a holy island for the Carthaginians. They conveyed their dead here to be buried, creating just outside the now-three-thousand-year-old town of Ibiza one of the greatest necropolises in the world. Some people believe that the whole island is honeycombed with tombs. "The clubbers are dancing on graves," Patrice says. And if we believe some of the hippies who still live in the hills of Ibiza, the unnumbered graves are emanating messages of joy and love.

Go figure. But if you do, figure the living Ibizencos into the equation as well.

People who live on rugged islands in the Mediterranean tend to be ornery and wary, like mountain people elsewhere. They've been invaded and had to retreat into the brush too many times in their history to be gregarious outside their villages and clans. Ibizencos are no Milquetoasts—no one could say that about a people who had the habit, until well into this century, of firing a charge of powder at the feet of a young woman to declare a marriage suit.

The Civil War was fought as viciously here as anywhere in Spain. But when I think of Sardinians and Corsicans, for example, I find the Ibizencos downright serene, and although they've been screwed over and over on real estate deals and have learned to screw back, I think you will still find them friendly and charming.

For what happened to part of Ibiza after flower power faded, blame mammon. A lot of developers tried to rival the mass tourism of nearby Majorca. Joanne and I had heard so much about the 747s loaded with holidaymakers that we expected to see the worst on our return. We were happy to note that only San Antonio, which had always seemed a displaced piece of the Côte d'Azur, Ibiza town, and Santa Eulàlia had undergone serious urbanization. And here and there, country roads that once deadened at naked bays now led to tall hotels.

For the rest, the recession in Europe had stalled the tourism offensive. Hotel people on Majorca and on Ibiza who were not filling their rooms were using their influence to stop further building, we were told. The new buzzwords for the future were "upscale" and "ecological."

Joanne and I went back to see the little house we used to rent on the bay in Es Canà. There were walls around all but the sea side of the property, and the sea view was partly blocked by an unfinished mammoth glass-and-concrete designer manor, the budding pride of some "Movida" millionaire, whose fortune may have gone bust with "*La Movida.*" There were many other new houses as we walked a few hundred yards farther along the shore to what had driven us away from Es Caná the last summer we'd stayed there.

It was a low row of apartments. Apartments! we'd said at the time—*no way*! The summer after, we took a finca in the hills with no electricity (but with a swimming pool). But now our once-alien apartments were covered with bougainvillea, the courtyard behind lined with mature palms. The German summer tenants were almost all gone. The view of the sea from the balconies was unquestionably as good as ours had once been. We looked at each other and had the same thought.

La Movida—literally, the movement or scene—refers to the period following Franco's death when a slumbering, deprived Spain awakened. Spaniards began to indulge in the nightclub scene as well as all the hip designer paraphernalia, new expressions of art, and daring fashions that money could buy. In general La Movida *meant doing everything in a more stylish, sophisticated way.*

—LMc

The next day we left La Ventana, our friendly hotel. It was beautifully located in the Old Town but too lacking in air to match our memories of Ibiza. And we moved back to Es Canà, into this row of apartments called Albatross, where there was a fine swimming pool, the beach just below it, the bougainvillea, the palms, and the view and the sound of the sea from our balcony.

At US$60 a night for a whole cheerful three-room suite, it brought to mind, all the more, the good old days.

We swam, we relaxed, and we ate, sometimes at a sophisticated new place or at one of the *típico* restaurants that people now call Ibizenco restaurants but which we remembered were places the Ibizencos created for the foreigners. No matter, their concept is unbeatable. It comes down to a flowered terrace with tables, where there is also a man with slabs of various meats and an ax and a charcoal fire. There's good local bread and aioli to put on it, olives, potatoes, salad, and good Spanish wine to go with your grilled steak or chops or suckling pig or chicken. The first time I ate in a *típico* restaurant, I thought that if ever I wanted to be a restaurateur this would be how I'd go about it. Good meat, an ax, and a fire....

We drove a lot. San Carlos was still the same tiny village where you'll drive into the wall of the lovely church if you are absent-minded when the road turns 90 degrees before turning 90 degrees again toward Anita's bar. At Anita's there were still weirdoes hanging out—some of the same people who turn up at the handicraft market at Las Dalias restaurant down the road still nicknamed Cape Canaveral for the number of spaced-out people there.

At the point on the shore called Pou des Lleó, there was a strip of beach, a bay with fishermen's boats in wooden cages, a tiny snack bar...and down the road a little pension, with two spotless little Ibizenco children playing outside. They were dressed like American kids, but they spoke only Spanish and Ibizenco, and so did their parents, the hoteliers who were inside, where a television was playing to an empty, spotless, wood-lined barroom. The little brochure on the bar boasted of *ambiente familiar*. We asked to see a room. It was nicer, with its whitewashed walls and new tile bath, than either our apartment or the room we'd had at the trendy Ventana. How much? Half pension for two: US$48. A double with breakfast: US$29.68. The menu boasted of fish. "Local fish?" I asked. "*De las rocas,*" the woman answered. From clean water near here. The fish known as rockfish in the Mediterranean feed off smaller fish and algae in the rocks close to shore. As pollution has killed off the algae and small fry, rockfish have become rarer and rarer. They are prized for their flavor.

We were leaving the next day and not ready to move all over again for one night, but we came back to the *pensión* and the restaurant Pou des Lleó for dinner. For fish: a *parrillada de pescado*—a variety of about ten grilled fish for the two of us. And it was wonderful. I looked at what a Spanish family was eating at a table next to ours, the family meal of the pensión. Something between a soup and a risotto, with great hunks of crab, followed by a saffroned fish stew. It all smelled wonderful. I had some almond-paste pie and more wine than I should have, considering the winding dark roads ahead. We made it safely, though, to Es Canà and went to bed with the sound of the tide lapping close to our balcony.

I have a friend, the writer Ted Castle, who liked to say in the '60s, "These are the good old days." They are now, on Ibiza.

G. Y. Dryansky has been the European editor of Condé Nast Traveler *since its inception. He has written for publications such as* Vogue, Esquire, *and* Architectural Digest, *and his books include the novels* Other People *and* The Heirs.

⋆

By the drinks table was a tableau of artists. One of them, an Englishman called Timothy, had shoulder-length white hair, a black suit and satin scarf, and an accent redolent of Old Chelsea. "I haven't painted for eight months, you know, I'm going through what you might call a dormant phase," he announced to no one in particular.

Beside the wheelbarrow with its cargo of coals I talked to Katerina, a dead-ringer for Eastenders' Pauline with the same weary smile and nicotine hair, but with the addition of a long Indian-cotton skirt and a thick line of kohl around both eyes. There was a commotion over by the drinks' table, and shortly the crowd parted to admit Timothy, who was complaining bitterly about the cold. Still clutching his glass he lay down on the ground in front of the wheelbarrow and rested his feet on the edge, within inches of the fire. He was wearing black espadrilles. The cry went up: it was a happening! A piece of free spontaneous expression, just like in the '60s! "No no no," shouted Timothy protestingly from his position on the ground. "It's not a happening—I'm simply warming up my feet."

—Paul Richardson, *Not Part of the Package: A Year in Ibiza*

Classroom by the Bay

*In Puerto de Santa María, learning Spanish
can be a game of charades.*

THE MOST NERVE-RACKING MOMENT OF MY FORTNIGHT'S SPANISH
course was telephoning my host family to tell them when I would
be arriving. Because I had studied Spanish for a couple of years at
school, I was under the delusion that I still had some grasp of the
language. But twenty years is a long time, and after spitting out the
vital information that I was arriving on their doorstep at four o'-
clock the following afternoon, I found that my vocabulary had
shrunk to "*¿Es OK?*" and "*No comprendo.*"

Nervously, I rang the doorbell the next day. Mari Carmen and
her husband, Rafael, leapt out to greet me and I gingerly put out
my hand to shake theirs. "Oh, you are so English," she said—in
Spanish—clasping me to her and slapping two big kisses on my
cheeks.

Like so many host families, Mari Carmen clearly enjoyed looking after students in her large rambling villa. There were three of
us lodging at the house: Margherita and Karin, both Swiss and in
their mid-twenties, and myself. We were all new arrivals and, after
dinner, Rafael and Mari Carmen, who spoke no English or
German, launched into conversation with us, helped by sign lan-

guage, a dictionary, and the eldest son, also called Rafael, back for the weekend.

El Puerto de Santa María provides the perfect setting for learning Spanish. It is a small town of baroque buildings and sherry bodegas on the Bay of Cádiz, untainted by package tourism. Our school, the Estudio Internacional Sampere, stood in the centre, occupying a converted house in a garden shaded by lemon trees.

"Write an essay of 60 words on your first impressions of Spain," said the flyleaf of our assessment paper. No chance. I was relieved to see several others hand in blank exam papers and indulge in the more interesting occupation of eyeing up their neighbours. At 35, I was one of the youngest, but outside university holiday periods (it was now October) the school attracts a mixed bunch. Our intake included the new Madrid manager of Finnair, a French film editor, and assorted Swiss and Germans for whom learning a new language is a fun way of spending a holiday. But it looked as if I was in for two weeks of hard work without English-speaking companionship.

We were six in the absolute beginners' class, held in the afternoons: Margherita and Rita, Swiss nurses; Jurgen and Heinz, German engineers; and Brigitte, a Swiss student. Stern but kindly Milagros pummelled grammar into us for the first two hours, then Emi—who could have been a professional comedian—took over and used some hilarious party games to get us talking. No English is spoken and the use of dictionaries frowned upon. Instead, if we didn't know a word, we piped up "¿*Qué significa...*?" and Milagros and Emi would act out charades accompanied by a gabble of explanation that became more intelligible as the days passed.

The Sampere family has more than 30 years experience in teaching Spanish and originates its own textbooks and class exercises, which are brilliantly conceived. There are no sessions in a language lab because, as the school's director, Cristina Sampere, says, "You can switch off in a lab, but you can't hide from a teacher who is asking you questions." By the end of the first week we had the present tense, a dozen irregular verbs, and a heap of vocabulary and useful phrases under our belts. It certainly helps if you have previously learnt a language at school and know how the parts of grammar and syntax work. And a few Spanish evening classes beforehand would also be a confidence-booster. But Jurgen, who spoke only German—and arrived totally unprepared—managed to keep up with the rest of us even though he was out on the town every night.

Back at our digs, Mari Carmen reinforced what we had learnt. Chattering away all the time, she would gently correct our grammar as we struggled through our first sentences and, on the rare occasions when we said something difficult correctly, reward us with a big smile and "*Muy bien.*" It was like being a child again. Guiltily, we also sneaked help with our written homework, leaving in a couple of mistakes in case Milagros smelled a rat. We were sleeping ten hours a night as the strain took its toll on our ageing brains. But there is no easy way to learn a new language and, although there are places which offer more casual tuition, the rewards are far greater if you suffer a little.

However, it certainly wasn't all work and no play. My mornings were spent on the beach. At night I met Rita, Heinz and Anya, a fellow journalist, who very kindly spoke in English for my benefit. Our favourite venue was La Resaca (which aptly translates as "the hangover"), a *sevillana* dance hall, where local Gipsy families wearing catsuits and gym shoes danced with great sensuality, their movements endearingly mimicked by wide-awake toddlers. We slotted in a fair bit of sightseeing, too. Seville is just 90 minutes away by train,

S paniards have great linguistic kindness, in that anyone with a minimal supply of Spanish discovers conversations being put together for him, being turned into small language lessons for his benefit.

But so kind are Spaniards that their talk will often limp along in sympathy with any stranger making heavy weather. In the village, this comes to be something of a problem; Joaquín, the mason, for instance, has done so much building for newcomers to the language that when he is explaining anything he cannot help breaking into a kind of baby talk, which his workers now all imitate.

—Alastair Reid, *Whereabouts: Notes on Being a Foreigner*

Cádiz a half-hour ferry ride across the bay, and the famous Andalusian riding school is up the road in Jerez.

By the end of my second week we had learned the past tenses and the "I am going to…" construction, opening up a new world of conversational possibilities. Cristina Sampere reckons it takes a month to master elementary Spanish and two months to attain a good working knowledge. I dropped in at Torremolinos on the way home, ready to impress in a resort where English is the *lingua franca*. In a bar I asked for a glass of *fino*. The waiter, assuming that I must mean *vino*, wearily came back with: "*Blanco o tinto?*" I explained that it was *fino* sherry I was after.

His eyes lit up: here was a tourist who spoke Spanish. We fell into conversation about the bullfight on the telly (I had mugged up on my bullfighting vocabulary after visiting the ring in El Puerto) and I found myself asking questions and understanding the answers. I was impressing even myself.

Gill Charlton is a travel writer and editor who has visited more than 60 countries. She has written for a wide variety of newspapers and magazines and edited the travel pages of The Illustrated London News, Woman *magazine, and special travel supplements for the* Telegraph Magazine. *She is now the travel editor of the* Daily Telegraph *and the* Sunday Telegraph.

★

Passing each other on the street, Spaniards will greet each other with "*Adiós*" instead of "*Hola.*" The way they see it, because you are passing *by* one another, a farewell is in order, not a salutation. The emphasis is on the parting, and they are saying "Goodbye"—or literally, "Go with God." One could view this as linguistic pessimism, but I think rather it reflects a cultural awareness of mortality, a recognition that indeed you may never see the person again and that it is important to take the opportunity to say goodbye and wish him or her well.

—Lucy McCauley, "The Language of Greeting"

MARSHALL KRANTZ

Nocturnal Madrid

*As Hemingway said, "Nobody goes to bed in Madrid
until they have killed the night."*

MIDNIGHT AT THE PUERTA DEL SOL, THE CENTER OF MADRID, THE
center of Spain, and there's a hellacious traffic jam. It's a week
night, and it's perfectly normal. And while the traffic-bound
Madrileños clog the square, their footloose countrymen crowd the
sidewalks, working their way from *tasca* to *taberna*, itinerant revelers all.

No doubt the majority of Madrid's three million-plus people
turn in at a reasonable hour, as befits proud, hard-working members of the European Union. But the myth, sustained by a healthy
dose of reality, persists that Madrid is a city most awake at night—
all night. It's not for nothing that Madrileños are called *gatos*, cats,
for their nocturnal prowling habits.

Spaniards like to say, politely yet with a whiff of superiority, that
Americans live to work but Spaniards work to live. So for this
American reared on Puritan values ("Early to bed, early to
rise...."), coming to terms with Madrid's *joie de vivre* was not easy,
especially when so much of it took place well past my bedtime.

Fortunately for me, Madrid nights begin in the afternoon, with
a siesta. That's the secret to survival. So after a nap, with dinner still
a few hours away, I met my companions and set off through the

narrow streets of Old Madrid in search of snacks, the famous Spanish *tapas.*

We didn't have to look far. It seemed that every other storefront housed a bar. Madrid's eating and drinking establishments are so numerous and varied that Madrileños cut a fine distinction between them, something like Eskimos supposedly having eight different words for snow. They go by the names *tasca, taberna, mesón, cervecería, café,* or *restaurante.* Madrileños even have a separate name for the outdoor cafés that spring to life during the summer: *las terrazas,* the terraces.

We ducked into the first place we chanced upon, a *tasca,* the quintessential Madrid *tapas* bar. A long, wood bar dominated the small room. There were no bar stools and only a few tables and chairs. Patrons packed the place, and were wreaking convivial havoc upon it, and themselves, with a blizzard of eating and drinking and loud talking. The din was truly impressive.

Barely keeping up with the barrage of orders, the bartender furiously worked the beer tap handle while another man slapped little plates of *tapas* on the bar: olives, almonds, cured ham, sauteed squid or shrimp, and *tortilla española,* a quiche-like potato omelette served in slices at room temperature.

It was a well-lighted place, and clean, except for the floor just below the bar, which was literally papered with crumpled napkins. Trashing the floor is an old custom, one that keeps boys with brooms employed throughout Madrid.

Madrileños go bar-hopping from about seven to ten, or eleven, when it's time for dinner. Or they may just go on snacking all night.

My American companions and I, in fact, chafed at the ceaseless victualizing to which our Spanish hosts subjected us. All we ever do is eat, we complained. But we failed to understand that eating and drinking are secondary concerns. The main course at any Spanish meal is conversation.

Conversation is so important that Madrid institutionalized it long ago. It is called *la tertulia,* meaning social gathering or salon.

Friends or colleagues meet regularly to discuss business, politics, art, the art of living, or maybe just to gossip or talk about sports.

After conducting our own impromptu *tertulia*, we steered our way deeper into Old Madrid, pausing briefly at Plaza de Santa Ana, a small square with a large appetite for partying. The numerous bars around Plaza de Santa Ana attract loads of university students. On this night they spilled out the doors of Cervecería Alemana and onto the plaza. Cervecería Alemana is also traditionally a favorite with bullfight aficionados, so it's no surprise that it was also a haunt of Hemingway.

Fortified once more, we pushed on to Plaza Mayor, Madrid's most famous landmark. A masterpiece of Renaissance architecture, Plaza Mayor lies at the heart of Old Madrid, which is the Madrid the Hapsburgs built in the 16th and 17th centuries when Spain was at its height of power. The rectangular plaza is enclosed by ground-level shops set along arcades, and on the succeeding floors by 78, three-story homes with more than 475 small balconies. The bronze, equestrian statue of King Philip III that stands in the cobblestone plaza provides a convenient rendezvous for young Madrileños, and an object of irreverent humor. They joke about meeting under *los huevos del caballo,* the "eggs" of the horse.

The area around Plaza Mayor is renowned for its rustic, subterranean taverns, called *mesones*, or *cuevas*, caves. Student minstrels dressed in traditional costumes often wander between *mesones* such as La Tortilla, La Guitarra, and Las Cuevas de Luis Candelas, which is named after an 18th-century rogue-about-town, whose last words before dancing on the gallows reportedly were, "Be happy, my beloved city." Judging from the *sangría*-enhanced gaiety at the Luis Candelas tavern, it appears generations of Madrileños have slavishly heeded his words.

In centuries past, royalty and other noted personages stole through the dark streets for secret trysts at dimly lit taverns. According to legend, Goya met the business end of his lover's jealous husband's dagger outside a *mesón*. Madrid's movers and shakers, including the royal family, still frequent Old Madrid.

Our dinner took place uptown in the modern Madrid of sleek office towers and fashionable shops. A pricey dinner and cabaret show at the Meliá Castilla, Madrid's largest hotel, drew Madrid's affluent, who exited their BMWs wearing Armani and furs. The show featured a Las Vegas-style revue with an Iberian twist, a flamenco number slipped into the American-pop lineup.

D o not move too fast. Take a cue from the Madrileños. This is not Paris or New York, remember. It is only six o'clock. There is the whole night ahead.

That is the great secret of a long evening of eating and drinking in Madrid without facing bankruptcy or temporary physical disability. Move slowly, nibble, sip. The evening is long and there are miles to go.

—Ann and Larry Walker,
A Season in Spain

The generous display of skin—though less than a Vegas show—represents the sexual and cultural freedom that erupted in Spain after Franco's death in 1975. Called *La Movida,* the Movement, it was led by, among others, filmmaker Pedro Almodóvar, he of *Women on the Verge of a Nervous Breakdown* fame.

With midnight fast approaching, we strategized about how to spend our own a.m. hours. We could dance the night away—*El País* lists nearly a hundred clubs and discos open after three a.m.— or we could retire to yet another bar, or perhaps attend a *zarzuela,* a Spanish operetta.

We also had our choice of jazz, salsa, or even karaoke, but with our taste for flamenco tantalizingly whetted, we opted for Faraloe's, one of several clubs in Madrid dedicated to Andalusia's fiery music. But Faraloe's was virtually empty when we arrived. I thought we'd made a mistake. Perhaps we had come on the wrong night.

We were merely early.

We ordered drinks and a few more *tapas,* and soon the club began to fill. I was delighted to see that the audience would be almost exclusively Spanish, since I had heard that flamenco clubs in Madrid primarily cater to tourists, with shows long on slick commercialism and short on gritty, Andalusian soul. But Madrid is a city of immigrants, from other parts of Spain; they cleave to romantic reminders of home.

Prior to the show, the audience members indulged in a bit of do-it-yourself flamenco. They jammed the club's small stage to dance daring *sevillanas*, which remain consistently popular in Madrid despite the post-Franco rock and pop invasion from the United States and the rest of Europe.

The show began close to one. As flamenco purists will tell you, the guitar playing and the dancing, as artistic and exciting as they are, are subordinate to the singing. For it is the singing that most powerfully expresses the tragedy of the Gypsies, in whose culture flamenco is rooted.

Spaniards have created an artificial time zone to suit their lifestyle. Although Madrid is west of London, its clocks are set to continental time. So in late June, when it's eleven p.m. in Berlin and Madrid, the Madrileños are watching the sun set while the Germans have long since been in darkness.

—Marshall Fisher,
"Walking after Midnight"

The music and dancing brought shouts of appreciation from the audience, but the singing held it rapt. The singer, a wiry, middle-aged man with angular features and wavy black hair flecked with gray, strained his voice into tortured, attenuated notes, cries of pain made music. His passion overwhelmed the audience; his every vocal nuance twisted it into ever tighter knots of raw emotion. It was a stunning performance, and the audience exulted when he was through.

The strains of flamenco followed us out the door. We late-night novices had acquitted ourselves respectably, but fatigue overtook us before we could achieve the traditional end to a Madrid night: eating *churros* dunked in hot chocolate at dawn at the classic Chocolatería de San Ginés near Plaza Mayor.

Our taxi sped along Madrid's main boulevard, Paseo de Castellana-cum-Recoletos-cum-Prado. The lights that had shone earlier in the evening on the magnificent sculpture of Cibeles and her lion-borne chariot in the eponymous plaza were now dark. By four a.m. the midnight crowds had thinned to sparse clumps of pedestrians and freely flowing traffic.

But as the cab turned onto Plaza de las Cortes, I saw a sight that for me embodied the sweet joy of this nocturnal city. A man in a tuxedo and a woman in an evening dress suddenly emerged from the legendary, belle epoque Palace Hotel, where Jake and Brett drank martinis in *The Sun Also Rises*. Arm in arm, and engaged in easy conversation, they swung down the street toward Old Madrid.

I could see chocolate-soaked *churros* in their future.

Marshall Krantz writes about travel and culture from his home in Oakland, California. His work has appeared in numerous publications, including The Washington Post, *the* Los Angeles Times, *inflight magazines, and travel guidebooks.*

★

"When I first came to Madrid in 1954," [the cab driver] shouted back to me over the buffeting rush of hot air pouring through the open windows, "there was no traffic. There were hardly any traffic lights. It wasn't necessary. No one had cars. Now you can't move for traffic."

When I noted that we were indeed moving, and at a breathtaking rate, he grew sulky and insisted that this was an unusual day. I soon learned that most Madrileños take a secret pride in the awfulness of their city's traffic, as a kind of proof of their arrival in the modern age. The quickest way to make a Madrid native peevish is to suggest that the city's traffic is no worse than London's or New York's.

—Bill Bryson, "The New World of Spain," *National Geographic*

ELIZABETH ROYTE

A Sanctuary in the South

*Spain has transformed a legendary hunting ground
into one of Europe's finest wildlife preserves.*

EARLY ONE GRAY FALL MORNING, TWENTY OF US CLAMBER ABOARD
a big Land Rover bus: high-school kids with hairdos and attitudes,
women in perfume and suits, a man with an infant—all a bit subdued. The motor kicks to life with a noise that could deafen a
snake. Revving up and bouncing over obstacles in his path, our
guide heads for the high, mobile Atlantic dunes that form Doñana
National Park's southern littoral. Shaped by the *foreño*, the pre-
dominant southwesterly wind, the dunes shelter in their lee another ancient dune system, anchored by vegetation. Extending into
the park, this stable upland is habitat for red and fallow deer,
weasels, mongooses, badgers, polecats, wild boar, and lynx, among
other animals.

Out on the beach, flying past clammers at 50 miles an hour,
the guide points out shorebirds. He turns north at the mouth of
the Guadalquivir, and suddenly pine needles blanket our path.
Deer scuttle from view as children cry out, "*¡Ciervo, ciervo!*"
("Deer, deer!") and shutters snap.

After several miles through wild olive trees and umbrella pine,
we stop at the edge of the salt marsh and get out of the bus for a
look around. The wind whips through our hair and light jackets,

213

heightening the eeriness of this desolate plain. A kite circles over-head. A wild boar with two black piglets crashes through the bushes.

For 3,000 years, this coast, the short Costa de La Luz, has been a human causeway. Waves of invaders (Phoenicians, Greeks, Carthaginians, Romans, Moors) flowed across these beaches, plundering Andalusia's riches, creating port cities like Cádiz. This is where Spain's empire builders set sail: Columbus in 1492, Cortés in 1504, Magellan in 1519. This is where the conquistadors sent home Mexican loot, galleons groaning with the gold that financed Spain's 16th-century grapple hold over the Western world.

I look toward the north, where the dry mud flats extend as far as the eye can see. The ground is cracked into polygons of gray-green putty. Hoofprints—a deer, a boar?—lead out several yards to some withered, stumpy vegetation and then turn back to the forest. Somewhere out there the Guadalquivir flows through its momentarily shallow channel, marking the edge of the salt marsh. With jocular enthusiasm, our guide lectures on the marsh, its size, the changes each season brings, the rich diversity of life in edge habitat (the zone between wet and dry lands), and the biological intricacy of the three different adjoining ecosystems.

For all its natural assets and grandness of scale, until recently most of Doñana, a 173,000-acre wildlife preserve, could not be seen and thus appreciated. Visitors are closely restricted. They may walk through designated areas, armed with maps and guides to the flora and the fauna, study ex-

Spanish lynx

hibits at interpretive centers, or sign up for the Land Rover tour, which stops at designated observation sites—the only times passengers may get out.

Doñana National Park shelters more than 250 species of birds and countless thousands of each species. In the spring it teems with ducks, egrets, flamingos, pelicans, spoonbills, and storks on their way north from Africa. In the fall they reappear on their way south. Without this haven, Scandinavians and other northern Europeans might never see their favorite migrants again.

The park is not only essential to the life cycles of more than half of Europe's migratory birds; it also harbors an immense variety of permanent residents—wild boar, otters, partridges, quail, ducks, red deer, the nearly extinct Spanish lynx, and Spain's rarest bird, the imperial eagle. At one point, you could even spot wild camels wandering about sand dunes that had served as settings for the film *Lawrence of Arabia.*

Doñana got its name from Doña Ana, wife of the duke of Medina Sidonia, the ill-fated commander of the Spanish Armada. The duchess built a palace, the first of several, that attracted numerous royal hunters and guests, including Goya, who spent the spring of 1797 here painting his reputed mistress, the duchess of Alba.

The wilderness that is historically called Coto Doñana, meaning Doñana Game Preserve, is a roadless area that juxtaposes three strikingly different ecosystems: coastal dunes, wet marshes, and dry uplands. This variety, combined with a gentle climate, great size, and strategic location between two continents, accounts for the astonishing diversity of wildlife. Equally astonishing is that hardly anybody tried to protect all this until recent times. In the early 1960s the land developers set out to condo-ize Doñana with the same mindless energy that had already gone far in blighting Andalusia's nearby Costa del Sol. The forces of progress called for draining Doñana's salt marshes, carving a highway across the wilderness, and building a resort along the coast. Then to the rescue came Prince Bernhard of the Netherlands, who launched the World Wildlife Fund to save Doñana. In 1965 the fund persuaded the Spanish government to preserve Doñana as a national park.

Today the park receives more than 250,000 visitors a year. The park's managers guard their fragile turf as zealously as a lioness does her cubs. They've limited visitor access to the interior to an official tour, which lasts four hours and covers perhaps one-fifth of the park's acreage. Still, even a fifth is well worth seeing.

Its proximity to Africa is one of the principal reasons for the wealth and variety of the Doñana's birdlife. Birds with large wingspans, such as the eagles and kites that abound here, cannot fly across water for long distances because they require thermal updrafts for the long glides that allow them to rest their wings during migrations. Hence they cross the Mediterranean at the three points—the Dardanelles, Gibraltar, and Tarifa—where the intervening straits are at their narrowest. For those making the journey from West Africa, the marismas *of the Doñana are a logical, indeed essential, resting place and hunting ground.*

—Frederic V. Grunfeld,
Wild Spain: A Traveler's and Naturalist's Guide

The park has six walking areas. One, along the dunes, can be reached on foot from Matalascañas. A new marsh site can be reached by Land Rover, and an area in the pines can be reached by a boat tour leaving from the town of Sanlúcar de Barrameda, on the east bank of the Guadalquivir. Though visitors may spend as much time as they like here, overnight camping is prohibited.

"These are very sensitive ecosystems that don't tolerate the presence of people," says Eduardo Crespo, assistant director of Doñana. "We have the only breeding colony for tree-nesting spoonbills in Europe. We have fourteen breeding couples of Spanish imperial eagles; there are only a hundred couples in the world. We have a strong percentage of the Iberian lynx population, and we don't want to take the risk of letting people get too close to a population so near to extinction." The philosophy is admirable; but for visitors accustomed to the easy access of American parks, this is all rather frustrating—wilderness limited to bus stops at viewing boutiques, a sort of shopping mall of nature.

Even so, a wilderness experience isn't the point. People visit Doñana more or less the way they would a zoo, walking on circumscribed paths, buying snack foods, and snapping pictures of the larger mammals. Until these new areas opened up, there were no backcountry trails, no remote spots that invited gentle communion with nature.

Spaniards have apparently not yet begun to feel particularly concerned about their country's natural heritage. "We are 25 years behind the social situation in the States," says Crespo. "Your parks are very old; we have some old parks here, but the whole idea of nature conservation is foreign to Spain." Even decades after the end of Franco's repressive dictatorship, Spain is not politically arable enough for "green" reforms to take root. Litter mars the roadsides all around Doñana and its environs, and chain-smoking visitors (Spaniards still adore cigarettes) must be reminded not to toss live butts over the combustible landscape.

Asked if his goals for Doñana resembled the American model of conservation, Crespo says, "In some aspects, yes. But one thing we cannot practice in Europe is what we call conservation through abstention. We don't have your enormous areas that can be left untouched." Centuries of human use—hunting, fishing, grazing—also make a shift in values difficult. Having always exploited the wilderness as a commodity, the people living around Doñana are now being asked to conserve it as a treasure house of biological diversity. This does not always go smoothly.

Inevitably, it seems the park is under threat from development. Even at current levels the drain on the water supply is severe, and made worse by pollution of the Guadalquivir by pesticides and Sevilla's industry. Several lynx have also been killed by traffic on the road to Matalascañas. More serious are the proposals for a huge new tourist center to be known as the Costa Doñana, on the very fringes of the park. Pressure by national and international environmental bodies has resulted in this project being shelved, but the threat remains, much of it stemming from local people who see much-needed jobs in the venture.

—Mark Ellingham and John Fisher, *Spain: The Rough Guide*

"People who live near the park cause more problems than any other visitors," Crespo says. "They feel that their ancestral rights aren't being considered. For years there was no regulation whatsoever—complete chaos. Now the people say, '*El parque es nuestro*'—this is our land. We don't want people from Madrid coming here and managing it."

As the bus rolls noisily over the dunes, looping back to the Atlantic, our group is strangely quiet. The high, pristine mountains of white sand seem miles deep. Juniper, savin trees, and grasses fill and stabilize the low swales in between, called *corrales*. Few of us have seen anything quite like this before, so much untrammeled ground; indeed, Spain has only 60 miles of unspoiled coastline. In the distance the sea looms, and though we slalom up and down dunes it never seems to get closer. Strange patterns mark the sand. We guess at snakes, mongooses, the dragging feet of raptors on the kill.

As we swing back onto the paved road to Acebuche, the main information center, our guide points out one final bird, but few bother to look up at the sky. Perhaps we feel numbed by all the information we've absorbed; perhaps it's the strangeness of the landscape. Eduardo Crespo has seen this kind of nature fatigue before.

"Doñana is a myth, a legend," he says, puffing on a cigarette. "People think of it as a large, wild piece of untouched territory. They don't think of the interdependence of living creatures here—humans included. They're not ready to understand the ecological importance of this flat place." Still, no one is disappointed. The camera buffs take a few final shots from the Land Rover, and when the guide turns off the engine we stand and applaud.

Elizabeth Royte, a freelance writer based in New York, has written for Harper's, The New Yorker, *and* The New York Times Magazine, *among other publications.*

⋆

When my husband Brooke and I were in Spain, we found ourselves in the Doñana National Park, one of the last remaining wetlands in Europe. We were there during spring migration, so we were able to witness waves of birds from both the European and African continents.

The wetlands happen to be on the edge of a beautiful town called El Rocío. We went on a Sunday morning to see the flamingos and the spoonbills. On the edge of the marsh is a beautiful whitewashed adobe *santuario*. An old woman handed each person a large candle. She said, "Light this candle with your desire in mind, let your desire pierce your heart, and take it home with you."

The people lighted their candles with their desires in mind, then moved into an alcove to put their candles onto a huge iron rack. In this white-tiled room with a statue of the Mother of Dew, each person stood next to their candle and tended to their desire, watching while the wax melted. When the wax had melted sufficiently to make a ball of it, each person took the wax home as a talisman.

The room was searing—there had to be hundreds, even thousands, of candles, all burning at the same time, with people attending to their individual desires. It was wonderful. Brooke said to me, "My desire is melting into everyone else's." And that was precisely the point: when you're in that collective space in a ritualistic way, there is no way your desire won't merge with everyone else's desire. They are the desires of our highest selves....

Once again the dance, that sharing of breath, that merging with something larger than ourselves. One plus one equals three—that third thing.

—Terry Tempest Williams, in *Listening to the Land: Conversations About Nature, Culture, and Eros* by Derrick Jensen

Never Look Back

*A hike up mainland Spain's highest peak can be
a challenge of extremes: baking sun
and plummeting temperatures.*

I WAS THREE WEEKS TOO LATE FOR THE *ROMERÍA*, THE ANNUAL
midnight trek to the top of Mulhacén, the highest peak in mainland Spain. During the night of 5 August each year, Andalusian
pilgrims climb the 11,420-foot mountain in honour of the Virgin
of the Snows. These noctural ascents have at least one advantage—
they avoid "red runs," or long periods of walking in direct sunshine. For me, ability to endure red runs (Mulhacén can only be
walked without snow-gear in summer) would decide whether or
not I'd be joining Abdul Muley Hassan, the penultimate Moorish
king of Granada, buried on the heights of the mountain that bears
his name.

Treks usually begin from Trevelez. Some 40 miles by road from
Granada, this is Spain's highest village, with steep streets perching
on a hillside 4,700 feet up the Sierra Nevada range. Our trek,
though, began lower down and several miles farther south, at
Orgiva. Here I joined eight fellow trekkers, at the house of Carole
Donovan, our guide, who has lived in the region for the past
twenty years.

The first evening meal was so quiet that I wondered whether
it was the start of a group therapy session, rather than a trekking

holiday. Who would confess their inadequacies first? We all had our reasons for trekking in the Sierra Nevada, but no one was letting on. I had an altitude problem: I'd only ever walked in England's Lake District before, nothing on this scale. My first inkling that I might be a little out of my league came during some pre-dinner map reading. "I presume these contours are accurate?" Jane, a cheerful researcher from London, asked Carole.

The next morning, after catching a bus to Soportujar, we took to the sierras along a river valley. Following narrow mule tracks, we climbed our way up scented hillsides, through a perfume of wild mint and thyme. Great expanses of forest and wildflowers are sustained by melting snows from the peaks flowing through channels built by the Moors centuries ago.

It was about twenty minutes before I found myself trailing behind my companions. Until I caught up with them at the lunch stop my only companions were yellow-and-turquoise bee-eaters. Ahead of me, my fellow trekkers were taking it all in their stride, among them an eye surgeon, an anaesthetist, a computer programmer and a librarian. Wordless, with heads bent, they moved with quiet determination like silent pilgrims. Penitential garb, however, was replaced by garish fleece jackets, backpacks and hiking boots.

Only when you are at the back do you realise the advantages of being at the front on trekking holidays: longer breaks when the group stops, and someone behind you to notice if anything falls out of your backpack. During the week-long trek the only time I was at the front was when sitting beside Alessandro, our driver on the three-hour journey from Málaga airport to Orgiva.

Cabra montes

At times it seemed as if my fellow trekkers perhaps wanted to scale Mulhacén to get over some terrible personal tragedies. During the first afternoon's climb the link between trekking and psychology was hinted at when Richard, the anaesthetist, offered me some fatherly advice: "Never look back," he said. "Only forward." I wondered if the trek would begin to echo the plot of *Apocalypse Now,* and if as the journey progressed, my companions would become stranger and less communicative.

On the second night we stayed in Carole's isolated *cortijo* (farmhouse) in the Soportujar forest, amid hundreds of king-size pine cones. Plumbing was non-existent, so I sluiced myself in the freezing flow of a nearby river. Later, to pre-empt any complaints about my snoring, I tied a plastic water bottle to my backside to prevent me from sleeping on my back.

We left at sunrise the next morning. Ascending the high ridge of the Sierra Nevada, we soon spotted the long curving horns of the *cabra montes,* the shy wild mountain goat of the Alpujarras, the southern slopes of the high sierras. We managed to walk within 100 feet of the animal before it ran off.

A third of the way up, Sue, the librarian, decided to turn back. Andrew, an enviously superfit 29-year-old, offered to escort her to the road where she could catch a lift back to Orgiva. Four hours later, as the rest of us scaled the upper slopes, vultures circling overhead, I wished I'd joined her. But I struggled on, reminding myself that after Switzerland, Spain is the most mountainous country in Europe. I'd also begun to confuse Exodus, the trekking agency that had organised our trip, with a famous voluntary euthanasia organisation. "No, that's Exit," one of my companions reassured me.

Temperatures had dropped and the varied flora of the lower slopes gave way to surreal, monochrome hillsides. The strange, moonscape-like quality made it easy to forget how close we were to the welcoming Moorish towns of the Alpujarran valleys below.

When we eventually reached our dormitory at the Refugio Félix Mendes at eight p.m., I headed straight for the nearest bottom bunk. I'd had enough of climbing and walking for one day. I felt vindicated during that evening's meal when two of the most experienced trekkers admitted it had been one of the hardest day's walking of their lives. At last we were one, united in the insane expressions of exhaustion that only trekkers have after a tough trip.

Keeping a safe distance from the sheer drop of Mulhacén's northwest face early the next morning, we followed an exposed ridge to the summit. We had been promised panoramas at the top; views stretching as far as Morocco and over to the central plains of Spain. Unfortunately, the mist even denied us a glimpse of Granada and the Alhambra just a few miles north.

From the top of Mulhacén we took an eastern descent via the Siete Lagunas (Seven Lakes) down to Trevelez, famous for its local air-cured hams, dried by exposure to alpine winds. Now, a descent of Mulhacén would be easier than going up, right? Wrong. Going down was harder; less time to appreciate the scenery and more concentration required. Take your eyes off your next foot-hold and you might lose your balance.

The next day, time off in Trevelez coincided with market day. While others embarked on a five-hour trek of the 7,700-foot Penabou nearby, I relished my freedom. Taking a stroll through Trevelez's cobbled streets, I was admiring the flower-filled balconies when a *señora* tending to her plants unwittingly watered me. She waved an apology before rushing inside.

In Trevelez's main square you soon realise that there can never be a Spanish branch of the Noise Abatement Society. Like many towns in southern Spain, there seems to be some unofficial rule that transistor radios must blast to distortion. Only when a Civil Guard truck passes is there any attempt to lower the volume.

The following day our descent from Trevelez took us through spectacular gorges. Berber refugees from Seville first settled here in the 12th century, and later the area was the Moors' last stronghold in Spain before they were driven out by Ferdinand and Isabella. After the fall of Granada some Moorish families remained in the villages to teach their complex irrigation systems to Christian peasant colonies from Galicia and Asturias.

En route to Pitres, we travelled through Pampaneira, Bubión and Capileira, the charming white villages of the Poqueira Ravine, all with flat-roofed houses clinging to steep mountainsides. Snow-capped mountains competed with the brilliance of the white-washed villages below.

After checking into a hotel in Pitres's spacious main square, we sipped early evening drinks at a bar opposite a white parish church. We were in perfect time to watch Pitres come to life in an effortless blending of generations that only Spain manages so well. Mothers strolled into the square hand-in-hand with their well-dressed daughters, while a man carried his laughing young son under his arm like luggage. Love of children here is matched by a respect for the elderly from youngsters.

On the next table several old men were playing dominoes, slapping down pieces and commenting on their moves in raspy voices. "What do the women do when their men play dominoes?" wondered Jean, one of my energetic companions. Once again, I noted how trekking was like psychology: we came seeking answers and ended up asking questions. So what if the questions weren't always profound; neither were the answers. Next time I make the trek I'll take a mule with me for moral support. He might make better sense of it all.

Max Wooldridge was born in England in 1966 and worked a variety of bum jobs before he turned to writing. He won The Observer's *inaugural Young Travel Writer of the Year Award in 1988, and his work has appeared in* The Independent, The Mail on Sunday, The Times, Time Out, *and* The Observer. *He recently completed a guidebook to Brittany and for his next guidebook—on Ireland—he hopes to cycle around the entire coast. He lives in south London.*

★

Spain, at 195,000 square miles, is roughly the size of Thailand, Turkmenistan, Yemen, Papua New Guinea, Cameroon, or Sweden.

—Larry Habegger, "A Shepherd's Geography"

S. IRENE VIRBILA

Savoring San Sebastián

*In this corner of the Basque country, people treat the sea
like family and everyone knows how to cook.*

A FEW WORDS OF SPANISH IS ALL I CAN MUSTER. NOT A CHANCE I
spoke Basque, so we compromised. The taxi driver spoke Spanish, I
spoke Italian—and we managed. "Terrible traffic," he commented as
we rode along at a pace just slow
enough to glimpse the city, lit up
like a birthday cake in the dusk.

As we rode through streets
lined with handsome belle
epoque buildings, a cheer went
up from somewhere on the other
side of the river, and fireworks
showered gold and silver. "Soccer
match," he said. "San Sebastián
against Barcelona." Of course.

Though it was already late
October, it was still balmy, and
the darkening streets were filled
with people out for the evening
paseo. That's a promenade in the grand old sense, and as soon as I
checked into my hotel I wanted to be out in the crowds.

*"Before we go any fur-
ther," he said after I
had introduced myself as someone
who was traveling around Spain,
"I must give you a word of advice.
You should try not to talk about
the Basque country as if it were
Spanish. Of course, you're a foreigner, and no one would really
mind, but it makes a better impression if you always distinguish
between Spain and Euskadi."*

*—Michael Jacobs, Between Hopes
and Memories: A Spanish Journey*

Just twelve miles from the French border at Irun-Hendaye, San Sebastián, or Donostia as it's called in Basque, is the cultural center of Spain's Pais Vasco, or Basque country. Euskadi is the Basque name for the whole of the Basque country, which also includes the provinces of Baja Navarra, Labourdie, and Zuberoa in France. For centuries, San Sebastián has been dubbed "the pearl of the Cantabrian Sea," but its real heyday was at the turn of the century. Today the city retains much of its belle epoque splendor.

It all started in 1845 when doctors advised Queen Isabella II to spend the summer at Playa de la Concha. At the time, San Sebastián was a modest fishing village in the shelter of Monte Urgull, famous for the exploits of its fishermen and whalers, and for the beauty of its three beaches: La Concha, Ondarreta, and Gros. With the queen came the court and aristocracy, who transformed the town into an elegant summer resort on a par with Nice or Biarritz. Broad, tree-shaded avenues were soon flanked with stately art nouveau buildings. Lovely walks were laid out and parks and gardens planted.

San Sebastián's elegant *paseo* wraps around La Concha all the way from the turreted Town Hall to Miramar Palace at the other end of the scallop-shaped beach, a little over a mile away. With its white cast-iron railing and ornate lampposts, this sea walk has become the city's drawing room, the place where everybody appears at least once a day. Young and old couples stroll arm in arm. Mothers parade their be-ribboned babies in high, old-fashioned carriages. Friends meet to talk, leaning over the railing to watch the scene on the beach below, or rolling up their pant cuffs to wade in the surf, keeping up a conversation all the while. Nobody worries about whether they're dressed for the beach. Off come the shoes. Women simply hitch up their skirts and carry their high heels in their hands. Teenagers play Frisbee or practice baton twirling, while young girls in long Sunday dresses and satin bows draw messages in the sand.

People here treat the sea like family. These are fishermen after all. Every day you see the same men fishing from Zurriola Bridge and the banks of the Urumea. They might be wearing stone-washed jeans and running shoes, but they haven't left their berets behind. It's no big excursion to go fishing or go to the beach. Students do their homework sitting beside the sea. Men take the morning paper down to La Concha to read. It's so easy to slip off your shoes and go strolling along the beach for a few minutes. A few hardy souls even go swimming year-round.

The evening *paseo* usually ends in the narrow streets of La Parte Vieja, the old quarter, where every other doorway seems to be a bar or small restaurant serving up some of the best *tapas* in Spain. Here the theme is overwhelmingly seafood: toothpicks skewered with rounds of pimento-stained octopus or chunks of tuna topped with anchovy, olives and sweet onions. Plates of the fragrant raw-cured *jamón* (ham) share the bill with grilled green peppers and codfish *tortilla*.

Wash it down with Basque beer or *txacoli*, the local white wine, splashed into wide tumblers. The idea is to have a glass here, a few *tapas* there, and move on from place to place. It's like one big party, spilling out into the street every night. The Basques love to eat, and food is a big part of the culture. It is also what draws so many Spanish and European visitors to San Sebastián.

With all the bars shut tight

The bit about the Basques being Europe's sole surviving aboriginals may sound like precisely the kind of mythology made to sustain terrorist groups, but it isn't only the angry young militants of ETA [Basque separatist group] who believe it. Most scholars now seem to accept that their language (which sounds half way between a smoker's cough and a stutter) is the only one on the continent to predate the Indo-European influx from the East three thousand years ago.

That their blood type with its unique preponderance of Rhesus-negative points to the same conclusion, as does a marked difference in cranial shape and a complete lack of migration mythology. Basically it seems that the Basques, secure in their impenetrable redoubt, surrounded by wooded mountains and hugging the Atlantic, are indeed very different from their French and Spanish neighbours and from any other peoples anywhere.

—Robert Elms,
Spain: A Portrait after the General

the next morning, I could hardly recognize the streets where I'd nibbled my way the night before. Kids were playing soccer against the church wall. Hundreds of bird cages were hung outside the windows, and songbirds and parrots called from balcony to balcony. I wandered into the Museo de la Ciudad in the former convent of San Telmo to learn more about Euskadi and its ancient culture. Though it goes back at least 50,000 years, the origins of Euskadi are still a mystery to scholars. Among the most interesting exhibits are the museum's collection of ironwork, wood carving, handwoven textiles and fishing implements.

One unique feature of San Sebastián—and Basque culture—is its *sociedades gastronómicas*, or gastronomic societies, private clubs (men only) whose members cook for each other several times a week. Walk down Calle 31 de Agosto, the only street to survive an 1813 fire, and you'll pass several doorways closed off with folding screens. "*Privado*" the signs read. No one knows for sure just how many of these clubs there are in San Sebastián—some say as many as 100. In a city of 175,000, that's a very serious interest in food.

In the company of Juan José Castillo, chef/owner of the venerable Casa Nicolasa, I visited two of these private clubs. Castillo is a member of Gaztelupe, where a card game was in progress in one corner, while several amateur chefs were just donning their aprons at the bank of stoves in back. As Castillo explained, "Executives and doctors sit down to table with plumbers and fishermen here, and everybody uses the familiar '*tu.*' The only rule is no politics, but discussions about this or that recipe can get just as heated."

Members at the next club, the famous Gaztelubide, were cooking up a storm. Every burner was occupied, and enthusiastic cooks showed off local specialties such as chicken in sweet red pepper sauce, squid in ink sauce and *merluza* (hake) with clams. It looked wonderful. A long banquet table was set for that night's guests: a Georgian choral group. Celebrated *toreadores,* politicians, actors and musicians have been lucky enough to be invited to dinner—including "Cantinflas," Adlai Stevenson, and Kirk Douglas.

Some of the more modern clubs are allowing women as equal

members, but this is very new. Men here are just learning to spend some of their leisure time with their wives.

One effect of the gastronomic societies is that everyone—but everyone—knows how to cook. Nowhere else in Europe do you see so many men shopping at the market. Food is such an important part of Basque life that the principles of cooking are taught in the schools, along with the Basque language and other aspects of Basque culture. All this goes a long way toward explaining why the Basque country, and the province of Guizpucoa and San Sebastián in particular, is said to have the best cooking in Spain. When Queen Elizabeth visited Madrid, it was a San Sebastián chef—Juan Mari Arzak—who was invited to cook for her. And when four chefs were named to represent Spain in the Common Market's Eurotoques, all four were Basques.

The food is important, of course, but that goes without saying. It is as obvious as the importance of breath, of the heart beating. In fact, the quality and variety of food are so important to the Spanish, that they spend a higher percentage of their disposable income on food than any other industrial nation in the world. Food doesn't cost more in Spain than in France or Canada or Australia—the Spanish simply demand better food and a greater variety of food.

—Ann and Larry Walker,
A Season in Spain

When Arzak pays his daily visit to La Brecha market, he's as much a hero as a soccer star. Stall after stall here is filled with eye-catching food—everything from wild pigeons and fat grain-fed hens to smoky Idiazabel cheese from the mountains, musky wild mushrooms and fragrant honey. The fish market has its own imposing stone building in back. And what is offered for sale here is astonishing in its variety. Huge whole fish, tangles of milky squid, silvery anchovies and lively lobsters with their claws taped shut are displayed like diamonds in Cartier's windows.

"The best fish in Spain—the best fish in Europe!" Arzak asserts. "Basque cooking lets the quality of the ingredients shine through undisguised, and what we have available to us is remarkable. In a radius of 100 kilometers we have fish from the Cantabrian Sea, mushrooms and game from the Pyrenees, vegetables from the Navarra Valley, and wines from Rioja, plus *foie gras* and Armagnac from southwest France."

Originally my plan had been to use San Sebastián as a base for exploring the rest of the Spanish Basque country, but I got a little distracted. I slipped into the rhythm of San Sebastián so easily, it was hard to think about leaving just yet.

Every morning I would get up and walk along the Urumea, cross a bridge to the Gros district, then meander back across the Zurriola Bridge in front of the opera house for a *café con leche* at the café on the corner. Sometimes I took my pastry with me as I walked, sort of companionably tagging along behind some Basques, along the Paseo Nuevo, which hugs the base of Monte Urgull, stopping to feel the spray on my sleepy face and watch the waves break into a thousand fragments on the rocks. I had every intention of taking the steep walk up the beehive-shaped hill, but I somehow never got around to it.

Something was always going on at the port: kids learning to sail, marching bathtub-size sailboats up and down the stairs to the water; or a lady selling crabs and paper cones filled with rosy shrimp and tiny sea snails. Or I could visit the Aquarium and see the enormous skeleton of a whale captured in the bay in 1878. On most days, I watched the boats come in with their cache of fish.

La Concha's perfect sweep of waves always beckoned. I walked in the sea, sometimes all the way around, past Miramar Palace and along Ondarreta Beach to the modern steel sculpture called The Comb of the Winds. After a lunch at Akelare, a restaurant perched on the far side of Monte Igueldo, with a spectacular view of rolling green hills and the sea beyond, I finally saw the light and decided to rent a car for the day. The next day. All I had in mind after a lunch of Pedro Subijana's magical Basque cuisine was a delicious siesta.

So the following day we set off for Guetaria, a fishing village about fifteen miles west of San Sebastián. The road passes Orio, a village famous for its oarsmen, and Zarauz, a sprawling resort town, on the way. Fishing boats painted red, green and white, the colors of the Basque flag, bobbed in Guetaria's tiny port. The narrow streets of the town above were filled with the seductive smell of grilled fish. Every little restaurant featured a blackened iron grill set on sturdy legs just outside the door, where people were enjoying an alfresco feast.

We spent the rest of the afternoon driving up in the hills above to see the vineyards that produce the famous *txacoli* wine, and steep in the view of azure sea and green hills scattered with dazzling white farmhouses. All around the bounties of Basque country beckoned, but I decided to save them for another time; for now, the sweet surprises of San Sebastián were enough.

S. Irene Virbila is the restaurant critic for the Los Angeles Times. *Before moving to L.A. just in time for the late, great earthquake, she spent fifteen peripatetic years traveling and writing about food, wine, and the good things of life. Her work has appeared in* The New York Times, *the* San Francisco Chronicle, The Wine Spectator, Food & Wine, *and other publications.*

✳

San Sebastián lives with the problems that the ETA presents in quite a remarkable way, never seeming to deny that they exist, yet never allowing them to drown out the attractions of this splendid town. The Basques are far too proud of their pearl to allow it to become subsumed by the swamp of the struggle. In many ways the refinements, the splendours, the sheer civility of San Sebastián act as the most powerful advertisement for the Basque cause, a beacon of an ancient civilisation which has achieved a great cultural maturity.

—Robert Elms, *Spain: A Portrait after the General*

LISA MELTZER

* * *

Toro, Torero

Matador and bull re-enact
an ancient pagan ritual.

JOSÉ IGNACIO TOOK MY CUP AND DIPPED IT INTO THE BUCKET OF *sangría* at his feet. "You just wait for the next one," he said. "The first two matadors were of no consequence. The next one is local, but he's getting famous in other parts of the country." José placed the cup back in my hands as the third bull galloped out of the corral gate.

A group of us had bought cheap tickets in the "*sol y sombra*," only we ended up on the very edge of it, right next to "*sol.*" The *sol* at that moment was beating down on my head. The *sangría* tasted cool.

Your first fight is incomprehensible. I had been to several fights by then, and I'd heard a lot of people say they hoped the bull would win. But the bull never wins, even if the matador is gored to death, an event Spanish television loves to show over and over through the remainder of the season. The bull always dies. And contrary to what you hear, the meat is sold in the shops the next day. As José put it, "What are they going to do, bury it?" He also pointed out that before the fights the bulls at least led good lives, roaming the hillsides freely. On trips in the country, I'd seen the unsuspecting black *toros bravos* dotted over hillsides, ignorant of the fate to which their easy lives were leading.

The bull ran around the ring twice before the *picador,* high on his horse, dug his long spear into the back of the bull's neck. A cruel and erotic gesture, a man thrusting, a stream of blood running down the bull's glistening flank.

Three *banderilleros* came next, each one raising two thin, arrow-like sticks, like overgrown toothpicks, pinching them into the bull's flesh on either side of his neck before dashing away again.

They were like the clowns in the circus, only more serious. Three of the six arrows stuck, their colorful tips bouncing as the bull ran, a little slower now, a little heavier.

"José, no more," I pleaded as my friend took my cup from me yet again. The crowd was talking, eating *bocadillos* of *tortilla española* and *jamón,* drinking wine, laughing.

I held the cup that had been filled over and over again, and I waited for the *sangría* to hit. I watched the *banderilleros* going around and around the ring and the bull.

I watched the bullfighter finally emerge, costumed in turquoise and silver. I watched the matador and the *toro* begin their dance, the red cape a stage curtain flicking and soaring. If you speak Spanish you can learn

> *There'd been a bullfight the day before at La Maestranza, and María was off to get* lengua de toro *at the butcher's, a special one in town that was always mobbed the day after a* corrida.
>
> *I thought of those bulls, after their customary final parade around the ring, dragged by horses, being taken off somewhere beyond the spectators' view to where the white-aproned butcher waited. He would hold onto the torsos of the animals, still warm, some without ears or tails, having been awarded to a matador for a good performance. I thought how he would slice clean the already silenced tongue, cut out the white, fleshy mass and wrap it in brown paper to sell to Spanish women cooking* lengua de toro *for the midday meal.*
>
> —Lucy McCauley,
> "The *Pensión María*"

a lot from the old men who attend the bullfights all season just as Americans get season tickets to baseball games. The younger generation often scorns the bullfights as inhumane. But the old men will tell you what it is about, and you will feel why you must return. It is not just about a bull and a man fighting in a ring, nor is it about glory. It is from our dark past, a pagan ritual. It is us as we fight our way through life trying to understand. Life and death, *toro* and *torero,* devil and God, man and the beast within man. That is what they told me.

After many passes with the cape, the matador at last unsheathed his sword and waited. The bull stood motionless in space before him, his flanks black with sweat and blood, his chest heaving breaths one by one, each one measured backwards now away from the last.

"The *toro* must not suffer," explained José Ignacio. "It is a bad fight if he suffers. It is bad if the matador takes too long." José put his hand in front of my eyes.

"What?" I asked, and pushed his hand away so I could see.

"Blind," he said, dropping his hand. "The bull is blind by now. From the blood and the tension and the noise. He is not used to this. He has never interacted with a human before today. The blindness is a comfort to him. It makes it less complicated. It begins to prepare him for his trip away from us."

I watched the bull. I watched for the moment that would mark his exit. The bull was charmed still by some unseen power possessed by the matador, and the matador waited, listening with his whole self.

And when that moment fell into place, like a form at last coming visible, he pulled back ever so slightly, a final arc, and as the bull pulled in its breath, he sprang forward on his toes and plunged the blade of his sword between the blades of the shoulders and it sank in to the hilt.

"*¡Bravo! ¡Bravo!*" shouted the crowd, everyone leaping to their feet, their voices rising on the "o." "The bull is dead!" José yelled through the noise.

"But he's still standing," I argued. "How could he be dead?" The cheers died down and I waited with the *torero* and the crowd for the *toro* to fall. But he didn't fall. He stood, stubborn and refusing, at the edge of sun and shadow. We stopped drinking the *sangría*. We stopped eating the *bocadillos*. We stopped holding the wine flasks above us and letting the sweet wine arc into our mouths. We stopped talking and looking around at the crowd.

The *torero* stepped forward. He took away his own protective distance, charming the *toro* no longer with his magic red cape and peacock colors. He did not forget himself—his respect for the power and cunning of the bull—but he stayed with him for that moment. There was no space left between them. The *torero* put one hand on a horn. The bull's breath seemed caught, suspended, waiting for something else, some final word. The *torero* took his other hand and put the flat of the palm on the broad black space between the *toro's* two blind eyes, and he rubbed it in circles. He whispered something to the bull, some secret that at last allowed the animal to heave one great final sigh and give up this world and the bullfighter who had brought him to this point, and us in the stands watching, and the fields where he had stood and run in sun and rain. And as the sigh was breathed out, he fell to his side.

The cup had appeared in my hands again, and as the bull heaved and fell to the ground and the crowd roared, the *sangría* hit, and I was drunk and there were tears streaming down my face. Something had been drawn out of me, too, charmed until I was half blind, and the tears brought me to some other place, away from the ring, away from my friends and the *sangría* and the blood of the bull. I thought I didn't see it happen; I thought I must have blinked, or looked away, or sipped from my cup.

The crowd was cheering wildly. The ring attendants tied ropes to the bull's legs that were then tied to the horses. The horses dragged their brother, suddenly lighter, suddenly skimming across the dusty surface of the ring, across to the other side and back through the corral gate. The dust was hastily smoothed back down with rakes, and the crimson rivulets of blood were lost to me.

"*¡Bravo! ¡Bravo!*" the crowd was yelling, and I was yelling with them. For a brief, liquid flash, I heard against my cheek the mur-

mur of the *torero* as he pressed his palm between the *toro's* eyes—
life, death, *toro, torero,* devil, God—and the *toro's* hot breath whispering back as he fell.

*Lisa Meltzer is a freelance writer and editor. She spent a year and a half
traveling through Spain, learning Castilian Spanish and teaching English.
She has edited popular children's and young adult fiction for several years
and is at work on a collection of short stories. She lives in San Francisco.*

★

The *torero* was caught between an unpredictable beast and the demanding
attentions of the crowd: consequently he risked his life the whole time.
The danger he faced was the essential stuff of his profession: with varying
degrees of courage and skill he courted and calculated it simultaneously
employing a more or less sure technique for evading its consequences.
Each fresh fight was a work of art, and gradually I came to discern what
qualities gave it meaning and, sometimes, beauty. There was much that I
still missed, but both Sartre and I had definitely become fans.

—Simone de Beauvoir, *The Prime of Life* (1962)

Quixotic Adventures

In which our hero shouts into the mouth of the cave,
and other events worth recording.

MAY 16, TOMELLOSO. THE BUS LEAVES BEFORE DAWN. A HARE CROSSES the road in the headlights. Slowly, like a stage after the curtain goes up, the land grows visible. The plain begins to fold and wrinkle, turning into low hills with lagoons lying in the slits between.

At Ruidera, where the bus drops me as daylight breaks, I have a coffee in a bar. Two men drinking *aguardiente* for breakfast silently eye the thin, bald foreigner. I leave my rucksack in the bar and walk through the village; walk for hours along the line of lagoons, the way Don Quixote came, in the cool, grey, clouded morning.

A big fish jumps—the pike of Ruidera are famous. Waterbirds splash and quack in the reeds, cuckoos call over the lagoons. And such nightingales! I stand under the poplars while they drench me with song. This is a Spain I haven't heard of. Nobody comes along the road—I have the morning, the lagoons, the nightingales to myself.

By midday I'm walking up into the hills, through clumps of rosemary to the Cave of Montesinos: a rustic picnic bench, a litter bin, a notice for tourists pointing to the cave—a crack slant-

ing down into the hillside, perhaps the shaft of an old copper
mine.

Don Quixote found the mouth choked with thorns, wild figs,
brambles. When he slashed at them with his sword a flock of crows
and jackdaws flew out, knocking him over. A lesser man would
have taken it as a bad omen but Don Quixote tied on a rope,
prayed for God's help and the protection of his mistress, the lovely,
matchless Dulcinea, to whose love he dedicated this dangerous adventure, and began the descent. He only wished he had brought a
bell so that Sancho Panza, paying out the rope and making a thousand signs of the cross, would know he was alive. "God be your
guide," Sancho called as his master vanished into the dark, "and
bring you back safely to the light of the world."

Don Quixote climbed down, shouting for more rope till there
was none left. After waiting a while Sancho pulled the rope up.
Don Quixote returned to the surface, his eyes shut, and had to be
shaken and slapped before he stretched his limbs, as if waking from
deep sleep. What had he seen in that hell down there?

"Hell you call it!" he cried. "You have snatched me from the
sweetest life, the loveliest vision that man has ever had. Now I
know that the pleasures of this life are a dream—they pass like a
shadow, they wither like flowers in the field." He had found himself in a meadow—a madman's fantasy, Sancho thought—where a
wonderful castle was revealed, with battlements of crystal, the
scene for unimaginable episodes of romance and chivalry. He believed he had spent three days in that enchanted land, and had had
a glimpse of Dulcinea.

Sancho knew that Dulcinea was an uncouth village girl, far
from lovely, and told his master he was talking nonsense.

"Sancho," Don Quixote said, "I know you too well—it's because you love me that you speak like that. You have no experience of world affairs, so anything you don't understand seems impossible. But the time will come when you will believe what I saw
down there. The truth allows no argument." And Don Quixote,
though mad, was incapable of a lie.

This afternoon I go a short way down into the cave and shout, "Don Quixote!" hoping for an echo or perhaps a frightened bat—even a sight of Dulcinea—but nothing happens. It isn't a pleasant place, I don't stay long, but I don't doubt the reality of Don Quixote's vision. Reality, for him, was the illusion that led him into action.

On the long walk back the nightingales are silent. Instead, blue dragonflies slide through the bushes by the lagoons. At Ruidera the bar is shut, with my rucksack locked inside. I rattle the door and a girl comes out with it from the next house. The early morning quiet is forgotten as a motorbike rally tears through the village. On their huge machines the drivers and their pillion girls, hair streaming, wear their crash helmets strapped to their arms.

May 30, Tembleque. At times also I wish I had a companion. Don Quixote had his Sancho Panza and—a real presence, a real woman—his Dulcinea. But there is a need to be self-centered and another person has other needs. To be alone is to be vulnerable, exposed only to oneself and one's own imagination.

Two Moroccan families in big estate cars with Paris number plates, loaded to the ground, have parked for a picnic behind the petrol station. Children are sent off to squat in the ditch while

*Q*uixote was a man of great heart, great courage, great generosity, and an understanding of nothing in this life, but a perfect understanding of his ideal life, his interior life. His love, his pride, his honor knew no limits. When he enjoyed, he enjoyed hugely with no thought of the next hour, let alone tomorrow; when he suffered, his suffering knew no limits and was inconsolable, would never end.

His companion, Sancho, was his mirror image because mirrors reverse. He was not intelligent, but cunning; he couldn't read, but he understood the world; he was cynical, yet totally trusting once his confidence was won. He was willing to compromise to avoid a fight; his honor was flexible. He began thinking about where he would find his supper before his breakfast was finished. Together, Quixote and Sancho represent two sides of the complex Spanish character.

—Ann and Larry Walker,
A Season in Spain

veiled women tear loaves of bread apart and the men escape to the bar for coffee. At a table outside, buffeted by the draught of passing lorries, I'm joined by a threadbare man in a black cap, carrying a plastic bag, who asks for money. He kisses the hundred pesetas I give him before dropping it in the bag; then picks up my *El País* and reads it aloud, slowly, sitting beside me.

The bus from Madridejos to El Toboso takes me through vines, barley, wheat, more vines. The fields are becoming poorer, the villages more silent and faceless. Even the bus is nearly empty. After a soldier gets out at a lonely crossroads I'm left with one other passenger, a girl who talks non-stop to the driver in a throaty voice loud enough to reach the *sierras* (I remember Sancho's story of Dulcinea shouting from the church tower, being heard far away in the field) and tries to bring me in.

We pass a small lagoon with a café beside it and signs, not very lively, of water sports; and later a string of salt pans. Outside a village there is a row of wooden doorways into the hillside.

"Are they houses?" I ask the girl in the bus.

"Caves," she tells me.

"Do people live in them?"

She laughs: "Long ago."

We discuss Tembleque, Toledo, London, and I ask her about El Toboso. "*Muerto*—dead," was what Benito, the young bar owner who gave me a lift two weeks ago, called it. This girl uses another word, one I don't understand, but from the sound and shape of her lips it's worse than death.

A small white chapel stands in the fields, more like an Asian pagoda than a Spanish church. Children are kicking a ball against it. Under a tree a dozen men and women are having lunch. The summer has occupied the land, each day is a few degrees hotter.

Don Quixote rode into El Toboso at midnight, hoping for the blessing of his incomparable Dulcinea who lived here. The village was asleep, there was no sound but the barking of dogs, grunting of pigs, mewing of cats, braying of a donkey. "Sancho, my son," the knight said, "lead me to Dulcinea's palace. Perhaps we shall find her awake."

Sancho was at a loss, knowing only a peasant girl in a cottage. And was this the time for knocking up people? Were they a pair of pimps, going round the whorehouses at all hours? They began to quarrel, the knight admitting he had never been inside Dulcinea's palace in his life, though he adored her, and his squire confessing he had no idea who Dulcinea was. "Sancho, Sancho!" his master cried. "There's a time for jokes and a time when they fall flat." But a young farmer, on his way with two mules to start ploughing before dawn, couldn't help: "I don't believe there's any such lady in the place."

Cunningly, though touched by his master's madness and becoming unsure of Dulcinea's reality, Sancho said they shouldn't be found wandering round El Toboso at night. They went back into the countryside and hid in a wood till daybreak, when Don Quixote told Sancho to return alone in search of Dulcinea and beg her to receive her knight. Sancho mustn't be frightened at such beauty, but watch her slightest move, her nervousness, her colour, her voice—anything to betray her secret feelings. "Trust me," Sancho said, and rode back towards El Toboso, leaving the knight full of muddled, melancholy thoughts.

Sancho too was troubled, and sat down under a tree to ponder. He was being sent to look for a nobody—for a princess as dazzling as the sun, living in a palace. The people of El Toboso would beat him up if they found out. His master ought to be in a strait-jacket, and he himself was no better—even more of a fool to follow him. But Don Quixote mistook one thing for another, black for white, windmills for giants, so he might be persuaded that the first girl he met was Dulcinea. And if he didn't believe it, Sancho would swear it.

In the afternoon, riding on donkeys, three girls from the village came along the road. Sancho hurried back to Don Quixote, who was sighing a thousand sighs of love.

"What luck, Sancho?"

"Your lady Dulcinea is coming out to meet you with two others. Come on—you'll see them in a blaze of gold, all clusters of pearls, diamonds, rubies, brocade, their hair to their shoulders like sunbeams in the wind, on three fine horses...."

"Holy God!" Don Quixote cried. "What are you saying? If you're cheating me..." His squire must be trying to cheer him with false hopes. "I can see nothing," he said when they emerged from the wood. "Only three village girls on donkeys."

"Nonsense! Rub your eyes! Pay homage to the lady of your dreams!" Sancho dropped to his knees and addressed one of the girls: "Queen, princess, beautiful duchess!—may your high-and-mightiness be pleased to receive your captive knight who stands there turned to stone...." Trying to convince his master he almost deceived himself, while Don Quixote knelt beside him in confusion at this moon-faced, snub-nosed wench.

"Out of the way!" she shouted. "We're in a hurry!"

She must be bewitched for him alone, Don Quixote thought. This ugly peasant, treated by Sancho as a princess, was an insult to his imagination. Years of hoping for the impossible—more deeply hoped for, being impossible—couldn't be wiped out by bleak reality. "Oh perfection of all desire!" he began. "Pinnacle of human grace! Sole remedy for this afflicted heart!..."

"Tell that to my grandmother!" she yelled. "You think I want to listen to that crap? Out of the way!" Kicking her donkey into a trot she fell off and Don Quixote ran to pick her up. But she jumped on the donkey's back, far from ladylike, and sped away with her friends.

"Look what my enemies have done!" the Knight of the Sad Countenance cried. "Not just transformed her, but turned her into that hussy. And even robbed her of the sweet scent that comes from a life among flowers and perfume—I got a whiff of garlic that stank to my heart."

The hypocrite in Sancho, or the coward or the liar or the half-quixotized Sancho, joined in: "The swine! I'd like to see them strung up by the gills like sardines. Wasn't it enough to turn those pearls of eyes into acorns and her golden hair into a bristly cow's tail, without meddling with her smell? Though to tell the truth I never saw any ugliness about her, only beauty, and it was set off by a mole on her lip, with some long red hairs like threads of gold."

"Then she must have another one to match it on the fat of her thigh," Don Quixote said. The true Dulcinea, whoever the one in real life might be, was a creation of his mind and he was free to see her as he pleased. "Nature has put nothing on Dulcinea that isn't perfect. If she had a hundred moles like that, they would shine like stars. But I didn't see it, Sancho—I'm the unluckiest of men!" It was his most tragic moment.

In El Toboso this afternoon the sun bounces from the white houses and dusty streets. After a drink with a few olives in a bar I walk through the little town. A museum, "Dulcinea's house," is fitted out with massive furniture of the period, walnut chests and tables, wine jars, a big double bed, an ox cart in the backyard and a wine press made from a single tree trunk. The Cervantes center, where they keep copies of *Don Quixote* in 30 languages, is locked, but I'm too lazy to knock up the caretaker. There are texts from the book written in tiles on the street corners and the usual grotesque statues of the knight and his squire.

I feel a growing resentment at the bony, knobbly, ineffective figure of Don Quixote, a sense of personal insult. That bundle of shreds and patches is too like myself. It brings back the anti-imperialist demonstrations in China 30 years ago where the long-nosed scarecrow being ridiculed by the crowd was uncomfortably familiar. Sometimes I was recognized as a genuine example and laughed at in disbelief.

I find a shady place where I can sit out this soporific afternoon. There is almost nobody about. A priest, a boy, two girls, an old man walk past. A church bell strikes each quarter-hour for an hour, two hours, while I sit under the trees. Someone starts a motorbike and roars away into the distance. The old man walks past again. I think I can hear the jingle of a fruit machine reaching through the heat, but it may be an echo in my empty head. A quarter of an hour later the old man comes back, keeping time with the church clock. In another quarter of an hour he is back again.

"*Buenas tardes,*" I say.

At once he tells me about his cataracts, in both eyes. Then he wants to know where I am from, and I tell him. "The children learn English, French, all those things in school now," he says. "We were never taught them."

I ask him where I can stay in El Toboso. There is no *fonda* or hotel here, the nearest is the Venta of Don Quixote five kilometers away on the main road from Madrid to Valencia. The old man tells me to go to the Martínez brothers' bar where someone will find me a room. "You have no companion?" he asks. "You shouldn't travel alone—it's bad for you. You need someone to talk to. Even Don Quixote..."

I half think I might sleep out in the open, but later I go to the Martínez bar. A big card game is going on, with spectators watching over the players' shoulders, more popular even than the TV. Some of the older men wear short black smocks. A lunatic in a peaked cap and uniform jacket covered with military badges stamps his boots and salutes me—a pale descendant of Don Quixote. I salute back. He begins to shout. The barman hisses at him. He shouts louder. Everyone hisses and the barman gives him a beer to keep him quiet. I have a beer too and ask about a room. I can have supper here, they say, but not a bed. The man next to me tells me to try the house at the end of the street, the last door on the left.

I go there and knock once, twice, three times, banging and ringing a bell, louder each time. I like El Toboso, I want to stay here. At last an old woman, Antonia, opens the door.

"Yes, yes," she says, "I was expecting you—you want a bed for the night, I know."

How did she know?

"The girl on the bus from Madridejos is my nephew's wife— she told me about you. They all come to Antonia."

She locks her door and leads me back down the street, past the huge old convent of the Trinitarias to another big building, also monastic with high walls, its lower windows heavily barred; through an archway into a court with a fountain where children are playing and a woman is hosing the plants; up a staircase in the corner to the second floor, into a modern flat.

"It's my brother's," Antonia says. "He's working in Madrid."

I have a room overlooking the court, better than in any *fonda* or hotel. Next door is a Japanese—I can't escape them: here, in a small Manchegan town, the only other foreigner is a Japanese. He speaks no English and almost no Spanish. Over the roofs the sun drops behind pink-grey clouds towards Toledo, the crickets start chattering in the roadside thistles, and night comes with a sharp chill. On such a night Don Quixote and Sancho Panza rode into El Toboso in search of Dulcinea.

I go back for supper at the Martínez bar, at a table next to the card players: *sopa de cocido,* a big salad, two pork chops and fried potatoes, bread and as much wine as I can drink, with a coffee, for 650 pesetas—value and friendliness and general happiness around—better still when I'm praised for my terrible Spanish. Off the tourist trail the people are very polite, untouched by the rough and ready manners elsewhere. George Orwell wrote that the Spanish have "a generosity, a species of nobility, that do not really belong to the twentieth century." The common idiom for the pronoun "you" is still what Sancho called his master, "your honor," without any irony at all. And whatever his humiliation, Don Quixote stayed dignified and courteous.

Nicholas Wollaston also contributed "Quixote's Parable of Life" in Part One, "The Way of Quixote" in Part Three, and "Where Quixote's Fortunes Fell" in Part Four. All of these stories were excerpted from Tilting at Don Quixote.

*

In the days of Cervantes there were two classes of writers; sedentary writers, like Lope de Vega, who were attached to the place where they lived and rarely left it, their contacts with the external world being through their fellow countrymen; and the vagabond writers, globe-trotters such as Cervantes became, who, whether owing to their own personal impulses or to the caprices of destiny, found themselves compelled to roam the different countries of the world seeing new faces and observing new customs.

In Cervantes' case this tendency to be always on the move was established early, through the misfortunes of his father. Miguel was born on

Michaelmas [September 29, the feast day of St. Michael the Archangel] and baptized on October 9, 1547, the fourth child of a poor *hidalgo*, Rodrigo de Cervantes, a physician without diploma who suffered from acute deafness and whose adult life consisted of dreary wanderings from village to village in flight from creditors.

—Walter Starkie, Introduction to *Don Quixote of La Mancha,*
by Miguel de Cervantes Saavedra

PART THREE

GOING YOUR OWN WAY

LOUIS DE BERNIÈRES

Seeing Red

In a Spanish tomato war, catharsis.

I AM A BOSOM FRIEND OF THE MATURING SUN, BEING NEARLY 40 and autumn my favorite time of year. In England in the early morning there are heavy dews on the grass that soak insidiously through the leather of one's shoes, the temperature settles to a soft warmth that has just the slightest suspicion of a chill, and the apples fall to the ground, revealing themselves to have been partially explored already by finches and wasps.

Autumn has its pitfalls as well as its windfalls, of course. Perhaps the largest problem is knowing what to do with the glut of vegetables and fruit from the summer's harvest. One thing you can do is pile the surplus into huge heaps and have a festival. In August on the Isle of Wight, just off the south coast of England, they hold a garlic orgy. There was a time, fewer than twenty years ago, when only nostalgic immigrants and anarchist intellectuals ate garlic in England, but European travel has so transformed our palate that there now exist intransigent fanatics who are convinced that garlic is a greater part of the meaning of life. I confess that I am one of these people; I have been known to put garlic on my poached eggs in the morning, and I fully understand why the people of the island see fit to crown a queen for the day and wheel her about in a carriage shaped like a giant bulb of garlic. This is entirely sane and reasonable. In Braga, Portugal, they have a ceremony in which they pass leeks around for one another to sniff; and in Porto, another town in Portugal, they have a rather less dignified celebration in which they thwack one another with the same vegetable. Before writing off the Portuguese as idiosyncratic, however, readers are advised to peel off the outer layer of a leek and try both rituals for themselves. The leek really has a pleasant smell, and it is ideal for the cathartic striking of people without hurting them very much.

But Spain tops all of Europe with its multitude of appealing fiestas. It is important to note that the Spanish are not in the business of fabricating folklore for the benefit of the tourist industry. Visitors are supposed to make do with silly songs like "O La Paloma Blanca" and "Viva España" in the armpits and orifices of otherwise pleasant places like Málaga and Fuengirola, whilst the traditional rites go on elsewhere as they have always done, solely for the entertainment of the natives. In Seville the girls would come out in the evenings to dance *sevillanas,* and the people of Ulldecona would still perform weekly passion plays during Lent, whether or not there were any cameras to snap them.

I have had firsthand experience of this cheerful disregard for the potential of tourism. I was off to Buñol to witness La Tomatina, a particularly picturesque fiesta fortuitously developed to celebrate autumn and its overabundance of tomatoes. I telephoned the Spanish Tourist Office in London in order to ask about it. "Oh," said the man, "there so many fiestas in Espain, all Espain is one big fiesta."

"So you don't know anything about the fiesta in Buñol?"

"I think is in Balencia. I gib you number of Municipal Tourist office in Balencia."

There was an animated conversation in the Valencia office as they discussed the correct answers to my garbled questions. Yes, it was on the 31st of August. Yes, Valencia was the nearest airport. No, there were no hotels, campsites, or *pensiones* in Buñol. "But don't worry, Señor, because nobody will be sleeping anyway, okay?"

✳

It was 104 degrees when I arrived in Valencia, and the people were feeling unjustly persecuted. I was repeatedly informed that it was supposed to be cool in the evening and that it was never this hot. "This is not natural," they exclaimed as they mopped their faces. Of course in August most of the Spanish go on holiday to somewhere nice and cool, such as Galicia, and leave the hotter areas to bewildered and sweltering tourists from northern Europe, who wonder why there's no one about and why there are actually dogs asleep in the public drinking fountains, up to their necks in water.

I was a little hotter than most, given that the extractor fan for my hostel's air-conditioning system was right outside my room and was blasting hot air straight into my window. Take my advice: don't book room 104 of the Hospederia Pilar; you will boil in your own blood like some peppery Eastern European sausage. Even in the relative cool of the streets (105 degrees) the humidity was so extreme that one expected to see shoals of lugubrious cuttlefish swimming past one's eyes on their way to the sea. I quaffed one and a half liters of water with each meal and bought more in the market, resigned to the curious way in which I am accompanied by freakish heat waves whenever I travel. In Crete once, in the early spring, it was so hot that I was forced to run like a commando from the shade of one stone to another as I attempted to admire the palace of Knossos, and the skin on the top of my head peeled off within a single day. In Cephalonia, I suffered a wondrous heatstroke that left me so delirious I could not determine whether I was freezing cold or frizzled to a cinder. I declare that Valencia was peanuts by comparison, and whilst the city snored at siesta time I patrolled the somnolent streets on my own like the mad dog and Englishman that I am.

At night it was simply too humid to sleep, so I read tirelessly, relishing the aftertaste of the wonderful cuisine. Four travel tips: 1) You can't get a *paella* unless there are at least two of you. I spent a lot of time looking for spare people who wanted *paella*. 2) There is a dish called *conejo al ajillo*, which consists of whole cloves of garlic roasted with potatoes and rabbit. It makes your urine smell of garlic for three days and leaves you feeling so ecstatic that you don't care that you can't sleep and are being gnawed to death by relentless and invisible mosquitoes. If you don't like garlic, or disapprove of extreme happiness on religious or moral grounds, try the grilled sole. It will make you only very happy. 3) If you want the very best service, including free liqueurs and bonbons, just place a notebook at the side of your plate and make the occasional note in it. The proprietor will suspect that you are a restaurant critic and will act accordingly. 4) People taking photographs of their meals are not critics; they are from the United States.

When I was not eating, I made sincere efforts to find out about the tomato festival in Buñol. In the municipal tourist office there was a young woman with beautiful eyes and a mocking demeanor who told me that I should inquire at the regional tourist office at the railway station. The young man there told me that La Tomatina was in fact only one part of a weeklong fiesta in honor of a saint, and that the tomato part was the result of a wedding that took place 31 years ago at which the guests forgot to eat the salad. They were too

> *As our second bottle of Tío Pepe neared the bottom, dessert would arrive—an orange or banana for each of us, chaste on its white plate beside a small knife and fork. In my crude American way, I would peel and eat the fruit by hand. Gabriel [my Andalusian friend], like a craftsman, would pare the orange so as to leave a perfect globe of meat beside a spiral of peel that could be returned to the seamless sphere. Or he would prong the banana near the stem, slit the peel lengthwise, free the flesh, then part it along its longitudinal seams, leaving three strips of banana in elegant parallel. Setting aside his implements, he would rip the orange with his hands and cram as many sections as possible into his mouth. Eyes watering, cheeks bloated, masticating hysterically, he would choke down the dessert in spasms like a snake. Easing his throat with a last sip of sherry, he would lean back in his chair and pronounce, "Once you've shown that you know proper form, it doesn't matter what you actually do."*
>
> —Bruce Berger, "Memories of Gabriel," *American Way*

replete to eat it and too inebriated to be sensible, and so they threw it at one another. He told me that now the occasion actually begins with somebody climbing a pole to retrieve a ham, and I was reminded that in Portugal one does the same thing, except that there is a dried, salted cod at the top. He said that Buñol's population of 9,000 swells to 30,000 for La Tomatina, and don't wear any nice clothes, because it's traditional to have them ripped off you.

I soon learned that the history was not so clear; someone else told me that a cartload of tomatoes had overturned in the town about a hundred years ago and that, since the fruit was now spoiled, the people decided it would be fun to throw it at one another. The man in the newspaper shop said that in fact (and he should know—he has a relative there) it has always been traditional in Buñol for neighbors to throw things at one another during fiesta. Someone else told me that in truth La Tomatina arose out of a violent argument. What was agreed upon, however, was the fact that it had been banned under Franco, who, like all dictators, hated people to enjoy themselves. Apparently the Guardia Civil used to turn up to ensure that the fiesta was not happening, and then, after they had gone, the fiesta happened. Clearly, the "facts" about the fiesta were not forthcoming, so I decided to wait until I arrived in Buñol to separate myth from truth.

I left for Buñol at 8:00 a.m. on the day of La Tomatina. My train carried me at a sedate pace past an enormous necropolis, dark citrus groves, vineyards, fields of rich, red soil, and toward the breasted hills in which the town reclines. I was starting to feel apprehensive about my destination based on my observations of Valencian tomatoes, which are approximately the size of a baby's head. I was certain that someone would be killed. If this were England, there would be hooligans putting stones and razor blades inside the fruit. There was indeed an ominous message from the mayor in the festival program, which I'd picked up in Valencia: "We request that persons be respected; it is absolutely forbidden to bring glass bottles into the plaza, to destroy shirts, to annoy people with water bombs. Also we ask that tomatoes be squashed in the hand before they are thrown." I knew that it has always been the custom to throw *globos de agua* (balloons filled with water) at fiestas, and that in some South American countries the local thugs had taken to putting them in the freezer first. I began to worry about surviving intact.

I reached Buñol three hours before La Tomatina was scheduled to begin and made my way to the plaza that was to be the site of the event. The town is dominated by a large and ugly cement works and is divided by deep, jungly chasms containing tiny streams, carpeted and curtained in swaths of blue convolvulus. Prickly pears sprout with insouciance from the rocks, and the alleys between the houses consist of ramps and steps that form an unfathomable labyrinth, out of which there is no escape unless you single-mindedly decide to take any route that goes downward. To climb back up, you need iron lungs and the calf muscles of an Andean Inca.

It was clear when I arrived that people had already made preparations for the festivities: the houses along the only important street were draped with plastic sheeting. I planted myself in the middle of the tiny plaza and continued my study of the fiesta program. It revealed that the week's festivities were, most curiously, like any village fete in England, though much scaled-up and with greater emphasis upon bands and orchestras. Just as in Britain, there was a committee of efficient women in charge of the whole event, curious sports, fireworks, karaoke, football, a procession of carts, junior and senior fishing contests, a chess competition, a dog-obedience trial, tennis, cycling, and 24-hour ping-pong. In England we would have competitions for cake and jam and fruit rather than for *paella* and *gazpacho,* and we would place less emphasis upon religion. We might raise money by throwing wet sponges at the vicar, while in Buñol there are processions and offerings of fruit and flowers to St. Luis Beltrán and Our Lady of the Unprotected. Buñol is also superior in that it has not only a fiesta queen (this year it was Señorita María Eugenia Estepa Saez) but no fewer than fourteen beautiful and implacably wholesome maids of honor. I would have married all of them on the spot, either simultaneously or in sequence.

The plaza filled up slowly, and soon the whole street was packed in both directions, mainly with the youth of both sexes in about equal numbers but also with tiny children and intrepid representatives of older generations. Behind me two little boys filled a plastic bag with water from the public drinking fountain, swung it about their heads, and soaked me from head to foot. As it was again 104 degrees, I was profoundly grateful, and anyway I knew that I would be able to get them later. Next to me a group of friends began to tear one another's t-shirts. I moved away a little. A band of people with painted faces stretched banners across the street in order to protest a toxic-waste incinerator. A disabled man in a wheelchair passed by with a plastic bucket sensibly planted atop his head. A man in a bandanna ambushed a policeman and stole his badge. There ensued a good-natured scuffle, which the policeman won. The kids began to act up for the TV crews that were setting up in upper windows, where they thought that they would be safe. At 10:00 a.m. a man in a van appeared to hand out free wine from a barrel and complementary meaty pastries. For some reason the climbing of the pole to fetch the ham was canceled, and a group of young men paraded the pole through the street in protest. Three policemen tried to turn them back but then gave in.

It was now far too hot for those who were not in the shade, and they began to chant, "*Agua, agua, agua,*" to the two men and the woman standing on a platform just above our heads. So what if water bombs had been specifically forbidden? The people were begging to be soaked. There was a swift discussion, and then hoses were turned on the folk below, who clambered to get onto one another's shoulders in order to be better sprayed. They began to chant, "*Olé, olé, olé, olé, olé, olé.*" In Britain this is the favorite refrain of the more moronic variety of soccer fan, so I couldn't bring myself to join in, though it did remind me of *aioli,* which is a particularly nice garlic concoction from the south of France. Buckets

of water began to be emptied on us from upper windows by
kindly old gentlemen who in more glorious days would have been
down below in the thick of the melee. They were acclaimed and
begged to work faster. Sweatshirt and t-shirt tearing now became
de rigueur, and the sodden rags were hurled high into the air,
where they snagged on telephone wires and power lines and the
wrought-ironwork of balconies. An Asian camera crew made the
mistake of trying to film in the middle of the crowd. They had
taken the precaution of covering their camera with plastic, but that
didn't stop the Spaniards in their vicinity from pelting them with
soaked morsels of clothing. They backed away with nowhere to
go, holding up their hands for mercy, and the crowd began to chant
again. At first I thought that we had been infiltrated by radical
Socialists, because the new chorus had the same rhythm as "The
people united will never be defeated." But no, they were chanting,
"*Ea, ea, ea, el Chino se cabrea.*" I'm not sure, but I think that this
means, "Hey, hey, hey the Chinaman's getting pissed off."

Friendly inhabitants turned hoses on us from the rooftops and
were cheered and applauded. We were all hysterical with happiness
before we had even seen a tomato. We began to chant, "*To-ma-tes,
to-ma-tes, to-ma-tes,*" clapping on the first and last syllables; we
wanted tomatoes more than we wanted to be rich, more than we
wanted world peace, more than we wanted eternal youth. In Chiva
and Requena they probably heard us insisting upon tomatoes, and
in Venta Quemada I expect that tiles and chimneys toppled from
the roofs. It was like a striptease; the authorities were holding back
deliberately in order to stir up our excitement. "*To-ma-tes, to-ma-
tes...*" Our fists punched the air in unison, and it occurred to me
that this was what it must have been like at a Nuremberg rally. (If
only they had chanted "*tomates*" instead of "*Sieg heil.*")

Suddenly there was an explosion behind me that nearly caused
my soul to leave my body, and then a horn sounded far away. The
street's narrow and winding nature kept the vehicle's approach hidden from view. Moments later, a huge dump truck was upon us, its
bed filled with tomatoes. On top of it were a dozen or so tossers,
who were hurling the truck's contents at us. Some of them were

wearing diving masks because they knew that we would just throw the tomatoes back. I got a tomato thrown at full strength in the nape of the neck and another in the chest. So much for being the detached observer with a notebook.

The truck passed by, and I felt a little disappointed. It had been fun, but it hadn't lasted long, and the tomatoes were already squashed to a pulp.

Then another truck rolled through, and more fruit hurtled down at us. Water continued to pour from the hoses above. What had been a generous shower of tomatoes suddenly became an alarming hailstorm. I tried to be clever and catch the ones that had my number on them but very soon gave up. One tomato after another crushed itself against every part of my anatomy, some with a sharp stinging slap and others with a decadent and relaxed sperlosh. I realized that there was absolutely not the slightest chance of coming through unscathed, and I threw my Britannic reserve to the winds. I knelt down and scooped tomatoes into my t-shirt; my neighbors promptly pillaged them as I stood up, leaving me just enough to practice mortar-bombing a fat man by a wall. How much more satisfying it is when an accurate lob descends vertically upon an unsuspecting soul than when one bowls a victim over with a baseball pitcher's velocity and ferocity.

There was another truck, and the alarming hailstorm transmogrified instantaneously into a red tornado. As the flurry of projectiles intensified, it became physically impossible for the senses to register details; individual tomatoes blurred into a whirling system of scarlet curves that crossed

> *There are times when passion will achieve results where self-control has failed, and when anger will serve to fire the blood of caution.*
>
> —Antonio de Solís,
> *Conquisto de Méjico* (1684)

and cascaded. They flew with such rapidity that it was like watching the discarded straw flying from the back of a harvester. I grew wild-hearted and exhilarated.

Another truck sounded its horn, a deep blast like that of a ship in fog, and passed through the crowd. Our red tornado became an inexorable hurricane. It was becoming difficult to stand upright in so much slush and with so many wet missiles impacting from every possible direction. We blotted out the sun and sky with our remorseless fusillades and barrages. Water continued to sluice down upon us from roof and window. We staggered blindly with juice in our eyes and our feet spread wide for balance. When we caught one another's glances, it was with the complicitous and conspiratorial glee of mischievous children. Drenched in that stupendous slurry, we had abolished all distinctions of sex and age and country; we had achieved the extreme mutuality of a glorious and liberating madness.

There was another truck, and then I lost count. I was sliding and slipping, I was having a battle with a pair of twins, and I'd gone deaf in one ear because it was filled with pulp. I had peel up my nose, and my eyes were smarting painfully. I groveled ignominiously on the pavement, grabbing ammunition from the very hands of others. Somebody stuffed a handful of gloop down the front of my shorts. It was a fierce amazon who in daily life was undoubtedly dignified and sophisticated. I gave chase but lost her when I fell over. Somebody stood on me. I flung pulp backwards over my head, and they got off. Next to me an unfortunate middle-aged man was groping on his hands and knees for a shoe that he had lost beneath four inches of roseate splosh. I squashed a good two pounds on the heads of the two little boys who had soaked me earlier. I was now so completely drenched in juice that even my unmentionable parts began to sting horribly. My shoes were full; I had become one vast squelching mound of pulped tomato. A girl next to me burst into tears because someone had hurled a tomato into the side of her head at close range, and she was led away by a friend. I joined in the general effort to pelt the TV crews in the upper windows and balconies, and was in turn splatted by those behind me on the wall above the fountain. Semi-naked bodies in ripped and rended clothing whirled and wheeled and fought and collided. It was merciless; it was all against all without fear or favor. I could not recall ever having had so much fun.

The program said that at 1300 hours there would be a cleanup followed by a *"siesta popular,"* and accordingly there was another startling explosion at exactly one o'clock. To my amazement we all stopped fighting. I had assumed that we would be too far gone in hysteria and bacchanalian frenzy to obey any signal from the authorities, but the truth was that after an hour of total war we all were wholly exhausted. We stopped kicking slush at one another and returned to a normal state of consciousness, only to be astounded and amazed by the scene that we thousands had created among us. Anyone who has seen *Apocalypse Now* will remember the parts where everybody and everything is soaked in blood and gore. That is nothing compared with what we now beheld. The houses were splattered up to the roofs with tags of peel and flakes of flesh. Beneath us the street ran above our ankles with tomato puree. It was a sight from a slaughterhouse, a true picture of a prodigious biblical massacre, a benign catastrophe of epic scale.

People emerged with implements that looked like giant croupier's pushers and began to shove the copious pink slush down into the sewers. I took off my shirt and wrung a torrent from it. Some of us were helpfully hosed down by the folk who came out to clean their streets and houses, but somehow I missed out. And then there was a miracle, no doubt wrought by St. Luis Beltrán himself, a miracle that passed me by, I suppose, because I am not a Catholic. The crowd actually disappeared and then reappeared in sparkling clean clothes. I was dumbfounded. I was the only one left who was caked from bald crown to soggy shoelace in congealed fruit, and I was, as the Spanish saying goes, caught with my arse in the air.

I am used to feeling ridiculous (I have two sisters, after all), but I have never felt so shamefaced as I did when I discovered that I was the only one on the train back to Valencia who looked like an escapee from a charnel house, and the only one to wend his disheveled way back through the most public and chic part of Valencia under the superior gaze of café habitués who no doubt were remarking to one another, "He can't be a Catholic, he isn't clean, looks like the saint missed him. With shapeless shorts like that, he must be British."

I feared that I would not be allowed into the Hospederia Pilar in my hideous state, but a cleaning lady took pity on me and ran off to fetch my key. In my room I assessed the damage: camera full of juice, all body hair congealed with peel that had solidified in the heat, shoes full, socks hopelessly stiff and unremovable, white cotton underwear pink, notebook irretrievably dissolved, legs already aching to the point of agony. I suppose that in repeatedly gathering up ammo I must have done the equivalent of a couple hundred squats.

I left Spain deeply impressed by the Pantagruelian orgy in which I had taken part. Everything at La Tomatina happened exactly on time and just as planned—"a fabulous technical achievement on the part of the Red Cross, the Guardia Civil, and the local police," as one reporter put it. And this is odd when you consider that it was also the most consummate example of frenzied Spanish anarchy in which anyone could possibly wish to become embroiled.

It seems that a committee whose members are granted the honorific of "*tomatero*" provide the military efficiency and punctilious dedication that propel the event. The twelve *tomateros* have their own version of the fiesta's creation myth: they explain that it all began as a prank involving a salad at lunchtime one day in 1944, and profess themselves impressed by the way in which the festival now involves 10,000 people. Except that one of the papers says it was 20,000, and the man in the tourist office says it was 30,000. Furthermore, the man at the newsstand says that in fact the tomatoes come from Extremadura, because the local tomatoes are too big and you cannot grow enough of them. He says that we threw 11,000 pounds. *Levante* states categorically that the tomatoes come from Cáceres and that there were 200,000 pounds, while *Las Provincias* says that it was 260,000 pounds. It was five truckloads, says the newsdealer; four truckloads, says *Levante*. All I know for sure is that it was certainly enough tomatoes to inundate half a mile of street to ankle depth and to keep 10,000 or 20,000 or 30,000 *franctireurs* gleefully slinging fruit for an entire hour, an hour that ended with all of us smiling inanely, our hearts full of a strange and inordinate affection for one another, replete with that conviviality so prophetically recommended by the mayor. "Let us create a collective climate of civility and urbanity which will substitute for the heat of summer the warmth of human cordiality," he had written in the program, and yes, we did a good job of that, if I do say so myself.

Let me work it out: I'm nearly 40, and I'll probably be too decrepit to participate by the time I'm 70. That means I can return to La Tomatina about 30 times. That might be enough, I suppose.

Louis de Bernières was born in 1954. After four disastrous months in the British Army, he left for a village in Colombia where he worked as a teacher in the morning and a cowboy in the afternoon. Since then he has been employed as a car mechanic, a landscape gardener, and a teacher of truants. His most recent novel is Corelli's Mandolin *and his first was* The War of Emmanuel's Nether Parts. *He now writes full-time and lives in London.*

✳

In five things he greatly delighted: dry wood to burn, an aged horse to ride, matured wine to drink, old friends to frequent, and ancient tomes to read.

—Alfonso of Aragón (1073–1134), *Melchior de Santa Cruz,*
Floresta Española

Letting Life Happen

A small island village embraces this traveler—and he learns
to love bananas in all their creative renditions.

I LAY BACK IN THE WARM OCEAN AND FLOATED, LOOKING UP AT A cloudless gold-blue sky.

This was perfection. Two days earlier, fleeing a cold Spanish winter, I had, impulsively, loaded my VW camper aboard an enormous ferryboat and plunged southward through Atlantic storms to the Canary Islands, those remote volcanic blips off the Sahara coast of Africa.

To be sure, my impetuous escape seemed a little bit crazy. I had little in the way of cash—just about enough to return the 700 or so ocean miles to mainland Spain. I knew no one in Gran Canaria, where I had alighted, and had no place to stay except for my faithful camper. I didn't know how long I planned to stay or where to go next.

And yet, the island spoke to me. Gently but firmly. "Stay," it said. "Just stay and see what happens." For a person who loves to be on the move, it seemed an odd proposition. But the voice inside sounded so certain, so totally clear. "Stay. Stay and let things happen."

And so that's what I did. And once I allowed myself to let go, things literally arranged themselves and I stood around watching like a delighted spectator as my life on Gran Canaria was fashioned gently before my eyes.

Although the Canary Islands were referred to briefly by Pliny the Elder as the Fortunate Isles, little was known about these remote volcanic outposts until the arrival of explorer Jean de Bethencourt in 1402, who came with plans to establish colonies for the Spanish crown. The Guanches, the islands' only inhabitants, were rousted out of their cave-dwelling languor and eliminated long before Columbus's brief but famous stop-over here on the way to the New World.

Gran Canaria and Tenerife experienced the first great surges of tourist-resort development in the 1960s. Little Lanzarote followed later and now boasts a handful of beach resorts below its moonscape hinterland of volcanoes, lava fields and "black deserts" of sand and ash.

More remote and undiscovered are the tiny islets of Gomera and Hierro, where dense rain forests and terraced mountains mingle with high sheep pastures, towering volcanoes and hidden lava-sand beaches. Nobody could tell me much about them or the other outer islands of La Palma and Fuerteventura. I planned to visit them all once I had gained my shore legs after a few days in Las Palmas, the capital of Gran Canaria.

But things didn't quite work out that way.

As I drove out of Las Palmas, the map of the island open but ignored on the passenger seat, I let my camper take the narrow island roads at whim. It seemed to know where it was going as we climbed high up the slopes of the largest volcano, Valcequello.

I stopped in a pretty mountain village for *tapas* in a tiny blue-

Some say the Canary Islands are the peaks of Atlantis, the fabled island that sank beneath the sea, and that the Guanches were its last survivors. A people of mysterious origin, the Guanches were almost exterminated before they yielded to Isabella and Ferdinand's rule in the 15th century; not long after, plague and famine wiped out their race entirely.

—LMc

painted bar with a vine-shaded patio overlooking the whole island. Here? I wondered. But I kept on moving.

I drove past more villages with lovely little churches and tiny plazas enclosed by neat white-and-lemon stucco buildings, past banana plantations on terraced hillsides, past vast fields of tomatoes and small vineyards. Huge sprays of bougainvillea burst from roadside hedges. The scent of wild herbs rose from the tiny fields sloping down to the ocean.

A tiny cottage appeared with a stone roof in a cleft between two rocks. It had everything: vines, bananas, a small cornfield, two donkeys, blue shutters, and a view over cliffs and black volcanic soil beaches and ceaseless lines of surfing ocean.

Here? I wondered. But still I kept moving.

At dusk, I parked on a patch of grass below the volcanoes. I had some bread, cheese and sausage, and a glass of brandy, and settled down to sleep feeling utterly at peace. Someone else was orchestrating this trip and that was just fine.

Early the next morning as I sat on a rock watching the sun come up, I looked down and saw something I'd not noticed the night before: a tiny white village huddled on top of a rocky promontory that jutted like an ocean liner straight out into the Atlantic. It was different from anything else I'd seen on the island. Most of the villages were straggly affairs, scattered over hillsides like blown confetti. But this place looked light and strong and enduring on 100-foot cliffs. A long flight of steps climbed up to it from a track.

There was no road through the village, just a sinewy path with cubist houses packed together on either side and ending in an area of level rock at the end of the promontory. I could see laundry blowing in the morning breezes; the hillsides below rose steeply from the rocky beach and were smothered in banana trees. It looked completely cut off from the rest of the island. A true haven. Mine!

Somehow the camper groped its way down from the volcano, bouncing and wriggling on cart tracks cut through the brush. I saw no one as we descended.

Close up, the village looked even more dramatic. Scores of white-painted steps rose up the rock to the houses that peered down from their cliff-edge niches. Children were playing in the dust at the base of the steps. They stopped and slowly approached, smiling shyly. A rough hand-painted sign nailed to a tree read "El Roque."

"*¡Hola!*"

The children grinned. "*Sí, sí, hola. ¡Hola!*"

One of the larger boys came over and shook my hand. And he wouldn't let go. He tugged and pointed to the steps.

"*Mi casa*—my house. You come."

It was an invitation and I accepted.

We all climbed together. The smaller children straggled in a line behind me; I felt like the Pied Piper and even my wheezing at the end of the 130-step climb had a pipe-ish sound to it.

I've never seen a place quite like El Roque before or since. The lime-white cottages clustered tight in medieval fashion on either side of a six-foot-wide stone path that twisted and roller-coasted up and down, following the idiosyncrasies of the promontory's rocky top. I passed a couple of shops the size of broom closets that doubled as rum bars for the men. Crusty bronzed faces peered out curiously from shadowy doorways. Old women, shrouded in black, scurried by.

About halfway down the wriggling street we paused outside of the larger houses facing a ten-foot-high carved wood door decorated with etched brass medallions. The older boy, obviously one of the leaders of my pack of frisky followers, pushed at the door and a panel squeaked open. The rest of the door remained solidly in place.

We entered a dark lobby with bare blue walls and a richly tiled floor. The boy took my hand and gestured to his followers to stay back at the main door. We moved deeper into the house where it was even darker. Then he opened a smaller door and the sunshine rushed in, blinding me.

We were in the living room, simply decorated with small tapestries, a broad oak table on bulbous legs, topped with two fat brass candlesticks encased in wax drippings. Eight dining chairs were placed around the table, their backs and sides carved in high baroque style with vine leaves and grape bunches. Straight ahead were three large windows looking out over a bay of black sand edged by banana plantations and, beyond that, the great cone of Valcequello. The room was filled with light. The windows were open and I could hear birds—canaries, I thought, by their flighty chattering, and mourning doves issuing soft cooing sounds.

The boy's name was Julio. He called out and I could hear someone coming, the swish of sandals on tiles. I was still mesmerized by the view until a figure stepped in front of me and gave a slight curtsy. She was utterly beautiful. "My sister," said Julio in slow English. "She is named María."

The door opened and the room suddenly became much smaller. A great bear of a man entered, hands as big as frying pans and fingers like thick bananas. A bushy mustache covered most of his mouth and curved down, walrus-like, at either side. His hair was as black and bushy as his mustache. A long scar reaching from forehead to jawbone gave him a dangerous look but his eyes were the gentlest blue, shining, exuding welcome without words.

Julio stood up, rake-straight, María gave one of her curtsies and vanished again and I rose to meet the man. "Papá, this is Señor David."

Tomás Feraldes could speak no English but during the next half hour or so I had one of the richest conversations I have ever had with a stranger. His words rumbled from deep in his chest, like boulders tumbling down a ridge. His son acted as interpreter and we talked in baby-language of everything—the village, the banana plantation upon which all the villagers depended for their livelihood, the ocean, the wonderful variety of fish you could catch from the promontory cliffs, the history of Gran Canaria, and the great pride of the islanders in their little green paradise.

"We are of Spain but we are not of Spain," he told me. "We are Canary people. This is our land. This is our country."

The brandy flowed. Little dishes appeared—*calamares* in lemon and garlic, big fat fava beans that we squeezed to pop out the soft flesh, spicy mixes of tomatoes and garlic with chunks of lime-marinated fish, sardines, island cheese, and more brandy.

Then Julio turned to me.

"My father says you will stay here if you wish."

"Here? Where? In this house?"

"No—in another place. My brother's home. He is away in Madrid."

"Where is this house?"

"It is very close. My father says you will come to see your house now. If you wish."

I now knew I had no control over anything. I'd followed my inner voice and let things happen and they were happening so fast and so perfectly I had no wish to impede the flow.

We were outside again in the narrow street. The children were still there, and off we all went, Pied-Piper fashion again, wriggling between the houses. We

To their great relief at times of world turmoil, the Canaries see themselves as largely inconsequential in the affairs of the world. After I'd gone what I considered too many days without seeing a newspaper, I asked a British resident of Tenerife what was happening in the rest of the world. He looked at me blankly, then explained in simple terms he hoped I'd understand: "People in the Canaries don't pay attention to outside news—they know that no matter what happens in the world, it's unlikely to affect them."

—Richard Homan, "How Tweet It Is; Great Bird-Watching in—Where Else?—The Canary Islands," *The Washington Post*

walked right to the end of the promontory where we all stood on the edge of the cliffs, watching huge waves explode 50 feet in the air and feeling the vibrations through the rock.

Julio nudged me. "This is your house." He was pointing to a small square building, the last house on the rock, white and blue, with a staircase leading up to a red door. On the flat roof I could see plants waving. There were windows everywhere overlooking the beach, the volcano, the broad Atlantic.

Grinning like an idiot again, I followed him up the stairs. He unlocked the door and we walked into one of the most beautiful rooms I have ever seen. Light filled every niche. On the left was a small propane stove, a sink, a big working table and four chairs with straw seats.

The living area was simply furnished—a few scattered rugs, armchairs, low tables, lamps and empty shelves, hungry for books. I could see the bathroom tiled in blue Spanish tiles and then another staircase leading up and out onto the roof with views over everything—the whole village, ocean, mountains, bays....

It was a dream.

"You like your home?" Julio was watching my face.

"Julio, this is the best house I have ever seen."

Moving in was splendid chaos. Every child in the village came to help me carry my belongings from the camper (it looked so tiny from the top of those 130 steps) to the house at the end of the village—clothes, sleeping bag, books, cameras, food, fishing rod, cushions, towels—and my guitar. When the children saw it, they went wild. Compared with the island *timpales,* this was a brute of an instrument, a battered Gibson with a rich deep tone. They were all shouting something at me. Indispensable Julio stepped in again.

"They say play, Señor David. Please."

Oh, what the heck. "Skip, skip, skip to m'Lou..."

I'd used the same song before on one of my journeys and it had worked wonders. The chorus is simple, the melody obvious, and even if you can't get the words straight you can hum and la-la all the way through it. Which is precisely what they did.

Twenty-three little voices sang lustily at the bottom of El Roque's steps, bouncing around in the hot afternoon sun. High above, a crowd of villagers gathered by the wall at the top of the rock began clapping, and then the kids started clapping. Soon the whole bay rang to the sound of this crazy ditty that was utterly meaningless to them and perfect for this impromptu getting-to-know-you celebration on this, my first day in El Roque.

It was four months before I left Gran Canaria. I even managed to tempt my wife, Anne, to put aside her work for a while and join me in my island home.

The villagers were delighted. Once they realized I was married, all attempts had been abandoned to match me up with one of the many eligible females in El Roque (no, Julio's sister, María, was already spoken for). And on the day Anne arrived I invited the whole village to the house for a celebration. I had no idea what a Pandora's box I'd opened with this innocent little gesture.

I'd asked everyone to come over in the evening after their long workday in the banana plantation. Any time after six, I said. Anne and I had prepared some platters of bread and cheese and opened bottles of island wine and rum. Then at 6:30 precisely, there was a knock on the door. It was Julio (he'd long since appointed himself as my social secretary and general factotum).

"Please come. We are all welcoming your Mrs. David."

Anne and I walked out on the platform at the top of our steps and looked down. Faces! Scores of laughing, smiling Canary faces staring up at us, clapping, singing. And everyone was carrying something—we could see cakes, pans of broiled fish, a sack of crabs, banana branches, straw baskets of tomatoes, bottles of wine, more cakes....

"Everyone who comes to the house must bring present," Julio told us. "It is our custom."

I have no idea how we got the whole village of El Roque into our tiny house, but we did. The kitchen, the living room, even the roof was jammed with villagers—many of them we'd never met. Anne and I were buoyed like froth ahead of the surge onto the roof, and we never made it back to the kitchen to serve the simple dishes we'd prepared. Someone carried up the *timpales* and the guitar and off we went into a spree of folk songs that set the whole house bouncing long into the night.

What had been intended as a one-time "Welcome to Anne" occasion became a regular weekly event for the rest of our stay. Every Thursday evening there'd be a "folk-fest" gathering at the house that would leave our voices hoarse and our kitchen table bowed with food. The problem was not in feeding the multitudes but in actually getting rid of all the fish, sausages, tomatoes, bananas, cakes, and wine before the next session on the following Thursday.

The most difficult items were the bananas. They'd bring whole branches with as many as 150 firm green bananas hanging from them. We tried every way we could think of to use them—banana bread, banana cake, banana crepes, banana omelet, banana purée, banana soufflé, fried bananas, banana with garlic (interesting experiment there), and even fish with baked whole bananas. And we still ended up with huge surpluses.

Aside from the rent we insisted on giving Julio's father each month, we were living a cash-free life. We were utterly happy in our village and had no real desire to go anywhere else on the island. I found great satisfaction in painting again, something I'd let slide, and Anne discovered a previously unknown gift for knitting enormous woolen shawls in bright colors.

Every couple of weeks we'd pack a box of these new creations, leap into the camper, and drive the 30 or so bumpy miles back into Las Palmas to sell our work to bored tourists with lots of money and very little to spend it on. Not that we needed the money. But it was rewarding to see people willing to pay real cash for our rooftop creations.

The residents of El Roque were a hard-working bunch. Up by five every morning, the men moved off quietly to tend the banana plantations on the surrounding hillsides while the women cleaned every part of their houses (even the outdoor steps and the pebbles on the main path through the village) before baking, washing, cooking, buying from the peddlers and fish vendors who passed through the village every day. No soap operas or siestas here. Just the solid, daily, dawn-to-dusk ritual that should have left everyone worn out, but in fact seemed to have just the opposite effect.

Our village had dignity, pride, and constant pep. If there were family problems, we never saw them. If there was malicious gossip and back-biting it must have been taking place well off the main path that we walked every day. If there was infidelity and illicit romance, it was done with such craft and guile as to be unnoticeable.

El Roque was a true home, and we became as close to the villagers as our natures could allow. We went fishing and crab hunting with the men (the latter at night with huge torches of reeds dipped in tar that drew the crabs from the rocks like magnets). We worked in the banana plantations, we picked mini-mountains of tomatoes, we painted portraits of the villagers and gave them as gifts, we learned how to prepare the romantic sauces for Canary Island fish dishes, and we even learned to love bananas in all their culinary variations.

In the end, the village brought us a peace and creative energy that we had never experienced before and have only rarely enjoyed since. El Roque is a touchstone for us both—and a place we have vowed to return to one day.

David Yeadon has written and illustrated sixteen travel books, including New York: The Best Places, Backroad Journeys of Southern Europe, The Back of Beyond: Travels to the Wild Places of the Earth, *and* Lost Worlds: Exploring the World's Remote Places. *He lives with his wife, Anne, in Mohegan Lake, New York.*

✳

There is a sense in which all Spanish villages are interchangeable: they have in common a manner of being, a vantage point, and, in this present Spain, a plight. Having lived in four separate villages, I think I would feel at ease in any—in its rituals and hierarchies, in its dingy, loquacious cafés, in its human rhythm. Spanish villages bear to each other family likenesses. It is only when one gets to know a village by name—landscape, houses, people—that it becomes a quite separate drama, a web of connections and commitments, even of argument.

—Alastair Reid, *Whereabouts: Notes on Being a Foreigner*

CALVIN TRILLIN

Abigail *y Yo*

The author pines for a linguistic epiphany.

I SUPPOSE YOU COULD SAY THAT ABIGAIL WAS LIVING OUT MY FAN-
tasies, if you were the sort of person who liked to rub it in. Abigail,
my older daughter, had decided to spend the semester studying in
Madrid. In long letters and Sunday telephone calls, she filled us in
on her life in Spain: sunny afternoons at the boat pond in El
Retiro Gardens, a weekend spent at the annual fiesta of a tiny village in Galicia, long discussions in the dormitory of a Spanish
friend she had met in the subway and sometimes referred to as *la
amiga del Metro.*

"It sounds absolutely terrific," my wife said one Sunday on the
telephone, just after Abigail told us how exciting it was to be able
to understand lectures in Spanish.

There was a pause in the conversation—a pause that I, in playing the role fathers have traditionally played in expensive long-distance conversations with college-age children, might have been
expected to fill with "Well, OK. Fine. Goodbye." Instead, I said, "I'd
like to tell you how I feel about all this, Abigail, but I don't know
the Spanish word for 'envy.'"

I might have known that word. I might have known a lot of
Spanish words. When I was in Spain just after college, I had the

opportunity to remain in Madrid for a year to study, and I didn't take it—a decision I think about often, in the way a businessman might reflect on his decision to pass up that patch of scrubland that is now occupied by the third-largest-grossing shopping center west of the Mississippi.

I was serious about Spanish. I was never serious about French. Sure, I still exchange sour remarks with a Paris taxi-driver now and then, but my public announcement that, more or less as a matter of policy, I do not use verbs in French was widely taken as an acknowledgment that I could no longer be considered a diligent student of the language. I never made a systematic attempt at Italian, and I have simply ignored German. Spanish is my foreign language.

More to the point, Spanish is not my foreign language. In my good moments, I've been able to say what I need to say in Spanish, although not in a way that is likely to attract compliments on my grammar and syntax. In my bad moments, my attempts to speak Spanish have a lot in common with my attempts to speak Italian, which is to say that they lean heavily on gestures. I have always had trouble understanding Spanish; there have been times when a paragraph of Spanish sounded to me like one long word.

Even when I seem to be doing pretty well in speaking Spanish, I can run out of it, the way someone might run out of flour or eggs. A few years after I passed up the chance to stay in Madrid, some friends and I went to Baja California to mark an occasion I can no longer remember, and I became the group's spokesman to the owner of our motel, a Mrs. Gonzáles, who spoke no English. Toward the end of a very long evening, as I listened to her complain about some excess of celebration on our part, I suddenly realized that I had run out of Spanish. It wasn't merely that I couldn't think of the Spanish words for what I wanted to say. ("I am mortified, Mrs. Gonzáles, to learn that someone in our group might have behaved in a manner so inappropriate, not to say disgusting.") I couldn't think of any Spanish words at all. Desperately rummaging around in the small bin of Spanish in my mind, I could come up with nothing but the title of a Calderón play I had once read, to no lasting effect, in a Spanish-literature course.

"Mrs. Gonzáles," I said, "life is a dream."

She looked impressed and, I must say, surprised. She told me that I had said something really quite profound. I shrugged. It seemed the appropriately modest response; even if it hadn't been, it would have been all I could do until I managed to borrow a cup of Spanish from a neighbor. Eventually, I came to look back on the experience as just about the only time I had been truly impressive in a foreign language.

> *ince he could not speak more than a few words of English and since his French, while fluent, was even more unintelligible than mine, which was not fluent at all, I attempted to resurrect my illiterate Spanish, a language I had picked up between frontline actions in 1938. Most of it consisted of such pragmatic phrases as: "I'm wounded," "It hurts very much," "Left leg," "Where's the toilet?" "How much?" "I'm hungry," "In the balls."*
>
> —Alvah Bessie, *Spain Again*

Every few years, I work up the energy to hurl myself again at the Spanish language, in the hope of making the breakthrough that people who learn foreign languages are always talking about. The evidence of my failures clutters the house—the Spanish-language tapes jammed in the back of a drawer, the absolutely guaranteed three-volume teach-yourself-Spanish course that falls from the highest shelf in the closet as I fumble for a suitcase I thought I might have stashed up there some years ago. It has often occurred to me that I'll never speak Spanish. People who spend a lot of time around newspapers are afflicted with the ability to imagine what is sometimes called the drop head of their obituary—an obituary large enough to call for a drop head as well as the main headline has traditionally been the principal side benefit of the trade—and the drop head I have sometimes imagined for me is "Monolingual Reporter Succumbs."

Sometimes, though, I think my Spanish breakthrough is somewhere on the next cassette. When I decided to visit Abigail in Spain this spring, I decided at the same time to give Spanish one more try. For a few weeks, I spent an hour a day speaking Spanish with a young woman from Spain who was teaching at New York University. In Spanish, I told her a lot of things about America— how the wheat got to Kansas in the 19th century, for instance, which is probably something that nobody in her town in Spain speaks about very often—and she told me that I did not appear to know the difference between *por* and *para*. I think I learned a lot about Spanish from her, although I continue to believe that no one truly understands the difference between *por* and *para*. I bought one of those pocket computers that translate from Spanish to English and back. On the plane to Madrid, I was carrying my Spanish-English dictionary, my translating computer, a copy of *The Old Gringo* in English and of *Gringo Viejo* in Spanish, an issue of a Madrid newspaper called *El País*, and a volume that I would have to name if I happened to be among those asked by some literary journal to list their favorite books of the year—*301 Spanish Verbs*. In the interest of moderation, I had passed up *501 Spanish Verbs,* by the same author, but I felt overequipped anyway. I felt like some Wall Street hobbyist who, upon deciding he might like to do some biking around the city, immediately buys a fourteen-hundred-dol-lar Italian racing bike, a pair of imported leather biking gloves, three kinds of pumps, and the sort of clothing that might be seen on a competitor in the Tour de France. I was prepared. When I ar-rived in Spain, I intended to speak Spanish. I intended to under-stand Spanish. I had a fallback position, of course: Abigail speaks very good English.

"Just give me a little hint of what it's about," I said to Ginny. Abigail and I and Ginny, a fellow-student of Abigail's at the Instituto Internacional, were in a *tapas* bar off the Plaza Mayor, eat-ing a sort of seafood salad and a pile of tiny fried fish. We were dis-cussing a Cervantes play called *El Retablo de las Maravillas,* which Ginny and some other American students were going to put on at the Instituto the following week. I was hoping that by having Ginny give me some idea of the plot I could avoid getting off on the wrong foot when I saw the actual performance. What I dreaded was finding myself, just before the final curtain, suddenly disabused of the notion that I had been watching a play about the early days of major league baseball.

> *I found myself not just learning Spanish but being changed by it, behaving differently in it. For one thing, Spanish is a more extravagant and spontaneous language than English and must be delivered with a precise vocabulary of gestures; now I gesticulate while speaking English. Spanish proved liberating, in a way; I found I could grow vociferously angry with much more ease in Spanish than in English, and I fell into making proverbial utterances, as Spaniards do, just because they serve the language almost as punctuation.*
>
> —Alastair Reid, *Whereabouts: Notes on Being a Foreigner*

Abigail didn't seem concerned about being able to understand the play. Basically, Abigail could understand Spanish. It hadn't come in any blinding flash, she said. At some point, she simply realized that she had been taking in what was said by the contestants on a television game show that the family she lived with watched every Monday night—*El Precio Justo,* a two-hour Spanish version of *The Price Is Right.*

My record in attempting to understand Spanish theatrical works was not encouraging. As far as I could remember, I had last sat in the audience of a Spanish production, game but bewildered, in Vermont, where many years ago, I spent several weeks in the summer Spanish program at Middlebury College. The Middlebury summer language programs are renowned in the field; I must be one of their rare failure stories. The summer I was there, Middlebury had half a dozen programs—each of them using a language not simply as the language of instruction but as the language that students were expected to speak in the dining hall and the dormitories and on the playing fields. The students were virtually all Americans, many of them high-school language teachers working on their master's degrees, but within days most of them had fallen into the stereotypes then identified with the countries whose languages they were studying. It was common to refer to, say, those studying French as "the French"—and to take it for granted that they would spend a lot of time criticizing one another's accents. "The Russians" were stiff-necked and basically impossible to deal with when it came to assigning hours and tables in a shared dining hall. If a great horde of people, all of them looking perfectly capable of singing loud drinking songs, burst into the local tavern together, one of the regulars was bound to mutter, in English, "Jesus, it's the Germans." I can't actually remember what "the Spanish" were noted for, but if my own experience is any guide I'm afraid it may have been indolence.

This time though, I was serious—which was why I wanted Ginny to give me a little head start on *El Retablo de las Maravillas*. She seemed willing. "It's about some Gypsies who come to a village and scare the villagers," she told me. "The villagers are kind of conformists, and the Gypsies say, for instance, that all smart people can see rats on this screen. So all the villagers say they can see rats."

Ginny fell silent and began poking around in the seafood salad for one of the less suspicious-looking creatures.

"That's it?" I asked.

"Well, I don't want to give away the whole plot," she said.

I was somewhat comforted by the knowledge that when I saw *El Retablo de las Maravillas* I would have more stage Spanish under my belt. Abigail and I had decided to spend the weekend in Barcelona, and a young friend of ours who was living there, Anya Schiffrin, had promised to take us around to some of her favorite attractions—none of which, I suspect, would have made a list compiled by the bureau of tourism. I knew that on Anya's tour we'd be seeing the show at an old music hall and at the sort of night club where the entertainment is provided by the waitresses and the barman and, now and then, an inspired amateur from among the evening's clientele.

By the time we took our seats that Friday night at the music hall, a place called El Molino, I was feeling that the first two days of my latest attempt at speaking Spanish had gone pretty well. In both Madrid and Barcelona, I had used only Spanish at the hotel—I knew that virtually everyone involved spoke English, but I pretended that I was at Middlebury—and I hadn't ended up in the broom closet. I had chatted fairly easily, if briefly, with some of the vendors at La Boqueria, Barcelona's stupendous public market, where Abigail and I exhausted our Spanish adjectives expressing appreciation of a sandwich made by rubbing tomatoes on the inside of a toasted baguette and then loading it up with fresh anchovies. The unfortunate episode at lunch—when I spoke to the waiter, he replied to Anya—was something I had decided to accept as a small but temporary setback.

El Molino turned out to be an appropriately rococo old vaudeville house with two tiers of ornate boxes overlooking the orchestra seats. It was painted almost entirely red—what seemed to be dozens of coats, resulting in the kind of shiny finish that certain expensive decorators put on the dining room walls of rich people in Manhattan. Although the audience sat in conventional rows of theatre seats, drinks were served, and the price of admission was folded into the price of the first drink. To accommodate the drinks, there was a narrow counter running along the backs of the seats in front of you—a menace as well as a convenience, Anya warned us, because if the man in front of you absent-mindedly put his arm around his wife's shoulders he'd be likely to put your beer right in your lap.

The show at El Molino featured chorus girls wearing a staggering array of costumes that I would describe, in general, as having too many feathers in some places and not enough in others. There were also chorus boys, although that term probably reflects insufficient respect for their age. Most of the production numbers had people in feathers moving in unison on the stage—dancing in the sense that Rex Harrison in *My Fair Lady* was singing. During feather changes, pairs of comics came out to do sketches that required nearly constant leering. The themes of the production numbers were established by ever-changing backdrops. Anya apparently noticed a puzzled look on my face when, in front of a backdrop that was difficult to identify except for a street sign that said "Via Veneto," a woman sang a song to a man while being accompanied, more or less, by eight or ten chorus girls who were dressed in something suggesting Latin-American peasant women—although I can't say I've ever actually seen a Latin-American peasant woman wearing a rug on her head. "Every day, she's heard the voice of a man, and she fell in love with him through the voice, and that's him," Anya whispered. "Why the costumes I don't know."

The audience at El Molino—certainly including our party—was enthusiastic, but I wouldn't claim that I actually followed what was being said onstage. I had the same problem the next night at the Bodega Bohemia, where the only entertainer who didn't carry drinks or wipe down the bar during the other acts was the piano player—a gray-haired old gentleman in a business suit who looked like a retired high-school principal returning to accompany the senior boy's choir, just to keep his hand in. In both places, people spoke rapidly and used a lot of slang and double-entendres. I explained to Anya that I was working, at best, with single-entendre Spanish.

Anya told us that it had taken her two or three trips to catch on to the patter at El Molino herself. Abigail reminded me that in Barcelona I had enjoyed a triumph or two in comprehending ordinary, non-leering Spanish. At lunch one day at a little seafood place in Barceloneta, the dock area, the proprietress, a jolly friend of Anya's, had told us why she avoids long trips on boats or airplanes: she believes that an accident could easily put her in the water, she can't swim, and she therefore assumes that she would be eaten by sharks. As I was telling Abigail that those precautions sounded sensible enough to me, I realized that they had been presented to us in Spanish.

I didn't feel that my Spanish had been tested on some of our stops. That had certainly been true at a dance hall Anya took us to after Bodega Bohemia—a vast place where a number of the most lavishly dressed ballroom dancers seemed to get along just as well without partners. At the event we attended on Sunday, a *sevillana* festival at the Barcelona bullring, I don't think anyone could have made out all the lyrics blaring from the huge loudspeakers on the stage. In the ring, thousands of Andalusians, most of them people who had come to Catalonia for factory jobs, danced and sang and waved green-and-white Andalusian flags for seven or eight hours. Some of the participants were in the sort of clothing that Americans associate with flamenco dancers, but some of them had got into costume by wearing green jackets or green hats; looking out on the crowd, I had to shake off the impression that I had come across a horde of Boston Irish who had been taken suddenly and implausibly with a passion for melodramatic dancing.

As we drove from the *sevillana* festival to our final meal in Barcelona, I told Anya how much we had enjoyed our tour.

"Oh, no!" she said. "I forgot to take you to the museum of the dead, where they let you sit in the hearses."

"Not to worry," I said. "It's always nice to save one treat for the next visit."

I understood the taxi-driver who drove us in from the Madrid airport when we returned from Barcelona. We talked about Americans and Russians. He said that Americans were more open than Russians. I thought about telling him how the Russians had behaved when they had to share the dining hall at Middlebury, even though I was quite aware that those Russians were not real Russians. When you're uncertain in a language, there's a temptation to use what you've got. The taxi-driver told me not to worry about not understanding the comics at El Molino; he said Catalans didn't talk right. The taxi-driver spoke excellent Spanish himself. It occurred to me that if I were put in charge of the government broadcasting system in Spain the first two announcers I'd try to hire would be the taxi-driver and the proprietress of the seafood restaurant in Barceloneta. She might even be willing to come to Madrid for the broadcasts, since you don't have to fly over any water to get there from Barcelona.

The conversations at the restaurant and in the taxi had been brief, of course. The real test was whether I could understand a lecture given by one of Abigail's professors. Abigail told me that the lecture in her politics class would be about the period in the late '50s when Franco's regime gradually began to change—a period that happened to coincide with my first visit to Spain. She was, I later realized, giving me a little head start. In class the next morning, I sat next to Abigail. I thought I was ready. I had spent some of the previous evening thumbing through *301 Spanish Verbs.* The professor began. He spoke beautifully clear Spanish—better, even, than the taxi-driver's. He spoke about the technocrats coming into government and about the role of Opus Dei and about the mystery that persists as to why Franco permitted the sort of economic development that he must have known would lead to an expanded middle class and demands for more freedom. I took notes.

"I understood everything," I said to Abigail at the end of the lecture.

Abigail said that she was proud of me. "I knew you could do it," she said. "Maybe you ought to come to my history class tomorrow. You could be on a roll."

I understood history, too. I was gaining confidence. I did pretty well in conversation with Abigail's *amiga del Metro* and at dinner with the family Abigail was living with. I was beginning to think that if I were staying on until the next Monday I might be ready for a crack at *El Precio Justo.* The dramatic piece at hand, though, was not *El Precio Justo* but *El Retablo de las Maravillas.* On the night before I left Spain, we took our seats in the Instituto's auditorium for the performance.

Total immersion in a foreign tongue is highly therapeutic. There are some Britons who find it desperately hard to achieve self-expression, and thus lead a satisfying life, in their own land; perhaps this is particularly true of those endowed with an introspective and romantic nature. But in a new clime, equipped with another language, their personalities undergo a sea-change. They sprout their new tongue like a beard and strut more confidently on their new stage. French or Spanish words and ways assume extraordinary, almost magical significance because they are the instruments of release. The convert becomes more popish than the Pope, frequently annoying his host country by his pedantic passion for its history and ostentatious familiarity with its way of life.

—Alastair Boyd,
*The Sierras of the South:
Travels in the Mountains of Andalusia*

I couldn't understand it. I couldn't understand it at all. For one awful moment, I was convinced that it was being done in a language other than Spanish. When it was over, all I knew about it was that some Gypsies came to a village where the peasants were rather conformist, and told the peasants that smart people would be able to see the rats on a screen.

"What was that about?" I said to Abigail at the end of the play.

"I don't know," Abigail said. "I couldn't understand it."

At first, I thought Abigail was just trying to make me feel better, but then it turned out that her friends hadn't understood it either. Later in the evening, I talked to Abigail's history teacher—a native of Majorca who had appeared in the same play in high school—and she said she'd had some trouble understanding the play herself. That did make me feel better, although I was pretty sure that the history teacher had never been in doubt as to what language was being spoken.

The history teacher and I were speaking Spanish, of course. I decided that *El Retablo de las Maravillas* had been a special case. So was El Molino. Of course, you could argue that a lecture at the Instituto Internacional on politics or history would also amount to a special case—if you were that sort of person. The professor, after all, has organized the material systematically, and is accustomed to speaking to foreigners, and is dealing with a subject rich in cognates. That's not the way I look at it. When I think of those lectures, what I remember is an encounter I had with a couple of American students after Abigail's history class. Abigail had suggested that I not accompany her to her history-of-art lecture ("Don't press your luck"), and I was on my way to the Metro.

"You're Abigail's father, aren't you?" one of the students said.

"We saw you in history," the other one explained. "We thought you must be really bored sitting there, unless—Do you understand Spanish?"

I hesitated for only a second. "Yes," I said. "Yes, I do."

Calvin Trillin is a writer for The New Yorker, *a syndicated columnist, and a contributor to periodicals such as* The Atlantic Monthly, Harper's,

Esquire, *and* The New York Times Magazine. *He is the author of*
many books of nonfiction, including If You Can't Say Something Nice
and Travels with Alice, *as well as novels and short story collections.*

✳

The power suddenly went out. Upon investigation at our neighbors' (a
mother and daughter) the outage seemed to be limited to our apartment.
Then the daughter asked me what seemed like an unusual question.
"*¿Tiene hambre?*" (Are you hungry?) To which I replied, "*No, no tengo*
hambre." (No, I'm not hungry.) If my memory serves, this exchange was
repeated at least two times. At which she laughed heartily and showed me
a copper wire. "*¿Tiene Ud. alambre?*" (Do you have some wire?) It turned
out that replacement wire of that sort was essential for repairing the fuses
in this apartment, which was accomplished (regularly) by tying a new
piece of copper wire to both ends of a ceramic mold.

—Erland G. Anderson, "Centering on Seville"

All Aboard the Puffer Train

*Bilbao to Córdoba by rail offers a smoky taste
of the country.*

THE VOYAGE FROM PORTSMOUTH TO BILBAO HAD BEEN A PASSAGE
of dreams for someone who gets sick on a waterbed. The Pride of
Bilbao had done herself and my stomach proud, neither having
taken any sudden turns. How to continue the land journey to
Córdoba in equal comfort? By bus or by train?

"Train," said the young woman in the tourist office on board
ship. "It's almost double the price. But the train, señor, is much
more comfortable."

The man at the railway station said (as well he might): "Look,
everyone in Spain smokes, the buses have no windows and no air-
conditioning. The buses never leave on time, and it's eighteen
hours of sweating hell from here to Córdoba." OK, OK. I would
take the train.

Boarding an hour before departure, I gave a helping hand to a
grunting, sweating lady with a snappy dog and two boxes of wilt-
ing vegetables. "These carriages aren't made for humans, at least
not of my size," she said. "But what's a poor woman to do when
all the buses are full?"

It was now that I felt my first twinge of unease. I was even larger than she was. If all the buses were full then perhaps the train would be empty?

"Not a chance," she said. "It's August—all the Spanish are travelling."

To where?

"Anywhere they have family."

My cabin was clean and empty. It was also very, very small. In a space no more that two metres by two were two rows of four seats facing one another, the seat-backs set at 90 degrees. I stowed my bags on the upper rack, praying that seven other people would not be carrying as much as I, cursing that I hadn't taken a sleeper for £20 more. I tried out the seat. It shifted a mere five degrees into the "sleeping position," leaving my knees firmly pressed up against the seat opposite. I made my way along the still-stationary train to the dining car, where I had been assured a first-class dinner would be served. The menu, bound in red leather, was handed to me even before I had squeezed into the space between the peeling Formica table and the uncushioned wooden pew.

A three-course meal weighed in at about £22. How much for a bag of crisps and a Coke then?

"Cheap," affirmed the waiter. "But then you can't sit here; this is for eaters only." I was the only person in the dining car. The waiter hesitated. "OK," he winked, "but you'll have to forget that I let you sit here. It could cost me my job."

The waiter departed and the ticket collector arrived, in full dress uniform. He, too, winked as he clipped my ticket. "Enjoy your meal. Looks like we'll be leaving on time." His emphasis did not bode well. The waiter returned with Coke, crisps—and a bill for £6. We left Bilbao four seconds late. As I made my way back to my seat I was enveloped by a pall of cigarette smoke; the corridor was lined with smokers. Wasn't this a non-smoking section?

"The cabins are non-smokers; the corridors outside the cabins...those are the smokers," said one coughing puffer. "You're wondering where the smoke goes?" he said. "This is where it goes...." He pressed a green button next to a sign that said: "DO NOT DEPRESS THIS BUTTON UNTIL THE TRAIN IS AT A FULL

STOP." The door whooshed open, landscape flew by, and the smoke flew out into the evening; he pressed a second button. This had a different sign, which said: "THIS BUTTON MUST BE PRESSED IF THE DOOR IS OPENED WHILE THE TRAIN IS IN MOTION."

After the Greeks, Spaniards are the heaviest smokers in Europe. About 40 percent of adults in Spain smoke, compared with 25 percent of adults in the United States. A recent article in the Economist *shed some light on why:*

"Having inflicted tobacco on Europe, Spaniards were the first Europeans to become addicted to the weed. An English traveller noted in the 1830s that a Spaniard without a cigar looked 'like a house without a chimney.' The most popular books in Spain a century ago were described as 'tiny, with blank pages': they were books of cigarette-papers. Basque refugee children taken to England in 1937 startled their hosts by asking for cigarettes."

—LMc

I found my cabin; the door was closed, the curtain drawn and there was no handle on the outside. I knocked politely; then not so politely; then rudely. Unseen hands forced it open. "Come in and shut the door," a woman growled. "That smoke will kill me if this journey doesn't!"

We arrived at Burgos twenty minutes late. Even before the train stopped, passengers were scrambling along the platform, grabbing at the door handles. One of my companions had an explanation for this apparently insane behaviour. "It takes two hours from Bilbao to Burgos and the train is supposed to stop for half an hour in Burgos," he said. "But we're only going to stop for ten minutes so we can make up the time." He warmed to his subject, became misty eyed with nostalgia. "In the old days, when the Generalísimo made the trains run on time or else, trains didn't stop at all. People tried to board them as they whizzed through the station."

Sure enough, we left Burgos on time, bound for Madrid: journey time four and a half hours, station time one and a half. I was coming to understand how an eleven-hour journey might actually take seventeen. Railway timetables in Spain contrive to give journey times only, with no mention of stops, along with an "estimated time of arrival." Time for some shut-eye.

When I awoke it was stiflingly hot; the corridors were full of whispering, peering, smoking people. The train had stopped in the middle of nowhere.

"The engine has blown up," said someone.

"No!" said another sagely. "One of the wheels has a puncture."

I suggested that someone open the doors and let some air in.

"There's no electricity," they said.

I pushed the green button anyway. The door whooshed open and the smoke whooshed out. People clapped in relief and patted me on the back. Doors up and down the train were whooshing open as fast as the good news could carry; people were jumping into the dark countryside, relieving themselves, smoking, chatting.

A conductor came up. "You shouldn't have done that," he said. "Now you will see how difficult it's going to be to get everybody back on. We shall certainly lose one or two."

Why had we stopped in the

My traveling companion was a notorious transportation maven and set on experiencing the AVE, Spain's high-speed train. "What extra we spend on the AVE ticket, we'll save on the hotel," Todd insisted. "It's so fast we can do Seville in one day and be back to sleep at our friends' in Madrid that night."

What we forgot was that our friends' typical Madrileño lifestyle was a poor fit with the concept of the seven a.m. train. Dinner at ten, to the bars by midnight, dancing until six, then of course churros and hot chocolate. Barely time for Mamen to drop us off at Atocha, Madrid's train station.

As we pulled out of Atocha, the video screen above us came on and presented us with the sight of beatific Spaniards relaxing on the AVE. There was actually a plot: an attractive couple, crisscrossing on the AVE between Madrid and Seville, leave notes for each other on the train and in Atocha lockers and finally rendezvous for a late-night dinner. All made possible by high-speed rail!

Todd, beside me, was oblivious, forehead and nose squeezed against the window, snoring. I didn't last much longer. The next thing I knew we were filing out of the train in Seville.

—Marshall Fisher, "High-Speed Snooze"

middle of nowhere, I wanted to know. "It's the engineer's family; they're late. Also, the engine seems to have blown up. But never worry, once we get to Madrid we will leave it on time." And—against the odds, against logic, against time itself—we did, by means of a stop of a mere eight minutes in the Spanish capital.

I was on a fast learning curve when it came to Spanish rail travel. Two lessons in particular are worth sharing. First, it is wise to bring along your own water. The canny old woman in my cabin with the huge hamper on her knees had brought gallons of the stuff. By the time we reached Córdoba she had sold 60 bottles, several of them to me. My second nugget of insider knowledge concerned the toilets. Inevitably the one nearest my cabin was a ladies'. So was the next one, and the one after that. While I was standing cross-legged, wondering what to do, a man pushed past me, reversed the hanging sign to reveal the figure of a man on the other side, and disappeared inside. Simple really.

We arrived in Ciudad Real nearly thirteen hours after leaving Bilbao. The train had picked up time. We had the luxury of fifteen minutes' leg-stretching time on the platform. Córdoba was now a mere four hours away.

As soon as we pulled out of Ciudad Real, one of the young women took down her bags and placed them by the door. "I'm making a fast getaway in Córdoba," she said. "I'm not staying on this train a second longer than I have to." Unfortunately, many others had the same idea. The corridor filled rapidly with luggage and people. Every so often the shout would go up that Córdoba was in sight; each time the crush of people surged and ebbed, and each time it was a false alarm. Finally, we passed the sign saying "CÓRDOBA" and the train slowed. A huge hurrah went up, bags were shouldered, hair pomaded back, jumping positions assumed, and a little man arrived in the carriage to make an announcement: "Ladies and gentlemen, we will have one whole hour to detrain in Córdoba. This train will arrive on time and, as is usual on Spanish trains, leave punctually for Málaga." And so it was that we rolled slowly and early into Córdoba.

Eli Silas originally contributed this story to The Daily Telegraph *but is out of touch with the newspaper. We have been unable to locate him; if anyone knows of his whereabouts, please let us know.*

✳

If you've never seen Córdoba's mosque, you can't imagine what it is; no picture can capture the appearance nor describe the sensations. Here, wherever you turn, are red- and-white-striped double arches on marble columns—hundreds of them, leading you down aisles that branch off in many different directions. The mosque is like a maze, and it's quite possible to lose your way. Some say the arches recall oases of palm trees. "Besides their spectacular appearance, the combination of brick and stone in these arches cleverly allows for expansion and contraction in accord with weather conditions," Feliciano tells us. "Strangely enough, they serve no structural purpose and do not support anything; they are purely decorative."

Begun in the 8th century and enlarged over the years, the mosque was finally completed in the 10th century....

Suddenly, for the first time, we notice something different in the distance through the sea of striped arches. To our amazement it is a full-blown cathedral, buried, almost lost in the immensity of the mosque, its steeple (sheathing the original minaret) and Gothic arches piercing the mosque's flat roof and ascending skyward. Feliciano has deliberately steered us clear of the cathedral until the end. For although mosques all over Spain were wantonly destroyed in a fit of religious fervor after the Reconquest, and churches built on their sites (Sevilla supposedly had a mosque to rival Córdoba's), La Mezquita of Córdoba, in accord with the city's inimitable ecumenical style, was the only one to survive. The cathedral was built within the mosque in the 15th century, apparently much to the dismay and protestation of Cordobeses, who treasured this unique example of Moorish artistry.

Even Charles V, who had approved the construction of the cathedral (without having seen the mosque), was dismayed when he finally came to Córdoba and saw how the Moorish temple had been compromised by a cathedral of minimal artistic worth. Indeed, the contrast is unfortunate: this dark, austere, and laborious monument of Christendom is in direct conflict with the poetic lightness and grace of the mosque. Its only redeeming quality, aside from its marvelous choir stalls and some other artistic details, is the unique experience of seeing two cultures and religions side by side and the realization that it is precisely the construction of the cathedral that saved the mosque from destruction.

—Penelope Casas, *Discovering Spain: An Uncommon Guide*

Walking to Santiago

On a 500-mile pilgrimage, the journey
is surely its own reward.

THERE WERE WILDFLOWERS EVERYWHERE: MEADOWS OF KNEE-high clover dotted with foxglove, cowslip, and patches of red campion. It was early still, and the fields were deserted. My pack was light, the grass was soft underfoot, my spirits high. It was going to be a fine day, I told myself; if only I knew where the hell I was. But whatever way I turned my map—upside down, around in circles, on its side—there was no escaping it: I was completely and utterly lost.

I had walked for two hours through the meadows of the foothills of the Pyrenees before I found the Basque farmer. Bereted, overalled, and jowly, he was leaning on his staff at the edge of a beechwood, watching a pair of collies drive his sheep swirling into their pens.

"I'm looking for the way to the Spanish border," I said. "I'm trying to get to the abbey of Roncesvalles by nightfall."

"Where have you come from?" he asked suspiciously.

"The foot of the pass—St-Jean-Pied-de-Port."

"And how did you get *there*?" he asked. He was not a man to be put off easily.

"From Oloron," I said. Then, proudly, I added: "I walked."

"You started your journey in Oloron?" he persisted.

"Not exactly."

"Where from, then?"

"Toulouse."

"YOU HAVE COME FROM TOULOUSE?" he asked, raising his voice. "BY FOOT?"

"Yes," I replied, feeling suddenly rather pleased with myself.

"*Pourquoi?*"

"I am on a pilgrimage," I said. "I'm going to Compostela."

"Compostela? In Spain?"

The farmer shook his head.

"You are a priest?"

"No."

"A monk?"

"No."

"A seminarian, perhaps?"

"No."

"Then why are you going on *pélerinage?*"

"For a holiday," I said. "For a change."

"You are doing this," continued the farmer, a look of increasing amazement spreading across his face, "you are doing this for pleasure?"

"I suppose so," I said, my spirits beginning to fall somewhat.

"Then," said the farmer, "it is quite simple. You are a madman."

"Honestly, I…"

"A sane man," continued the farmer with almost De Gaullian finality, "does not walk across Spain for pleasure."

"No?"

"*Non.* I live next to Spain and I should know. Your footpath is on top of that hill. Good day."

There were a number of occasions during the following weeks when I wondered if the Basque farmer could have been right: perhaps you do have to be a little dippy to elect to walk several hundred miles across the mud bake of the Castilian plains when you could equally well hire a car. And, of course, every long-distance walk has its bad moments: the blisters, the squalls of rain, the sprained ankle, the closed hotel at sunset.

Yet looking back now, for every moment of despair there were a hundred of ecstasy. You can never forget those beautiful Spanish evenings—a soft breeze blowing through the poplars, the irrigation runnels bubbling by your feet, the gnarled old olives creaking in the night, and a churchtower—the destination that night—dividing the horizon ahead. The journey to the tomb of Saint James at Santiago de Compostela—a journey that in the Middle Ages was undertaken by more than half a million pilgrims every year—was, according to the 16th-century traveler Andrew Boorde, "the greatest journey an Englishman mae goe," and much the same remains true today.

For the Camino de Santiago, the great pilgrim's road, is still a magnificent route, a five-hundred-mile-long footpath leading through some of the most stunning and unspoiled scenery in the world. If you choose to make the pilgrimage in the authentic manner, by walking it or riding it on horseback, you still take the old original track, along which tens of millions of other pilgrims have passed before you, a road whose cobbles have been rubbed as soft as sea pebbles, rutted by Roman carts, polished by passing horseshoes. You see exactly the same sights, feel the same pains, as generations of previous pilgrims—men like John of Gaunt and Saint Francis of Assisi, women like Chaucer's formidable Wife of Bath. In a very real way you become part of the road's history.

But equally, if you have neither the time nor the energy to take medieval transport and elect instead to go by bicycle or in a car, the modern asphalt road will still let you see some of the most extraordinary churches, sculptures, and objects of religious art to come out of the European Middle Ages.

Like all the best things, the pilgrimage to Santiago began with a dream. Or, rather, two dreams.

The first dreamer was Charlemagne, the Holy Roman emperor who in the late 8th century reunited most of Europe in the

Carolingian Empire. It is said that in the year before his death he had a vision of a starry road in the sky that crossed France and Spain and reached toward the end of the world; and he heard a voice saying:

"This is the path of Saint James and I am that apostle, servant of Christ, son of Zebedee, brother of John the Evangelist, whom Herod slew, appointed by God's grace to preach His law: look you, my body is in Galicia, but no man knoweth where, and the Saracens oppress the land. The starry way signifies that you shall go at the head of a host and free that land, and after you, people in pilgrimage will follow until the end of time...."

So Charlemagne led his host to Spain, vanquishing the Saracens and following the Milky Way into the misty wastes of Galicia. When he came to "*Finis Terrae*" (from the Latin for the "end of the Earth"), he walked straight out onto the waves. Then a boat appeared, the same mystical boat that centuries before had carried the body of Saint James from Palestine, and it took Charlemagne out into the open ocean. There, he stood on the prow and hurled his spear into the deep.

Thus northern Spain was freed from the Moorish yoke. But for all these Carolingian heroics, the body of Saint James still lay undiscovered in its resting place. And for that discovery to be made, a second vision was necessary.

It was given to a hermit named Pelagius, who lived a life of prayer and austerity in the damp mountains of Galicia, eating only honey and wild grasses. One day Pelagius was tucking into a plate of delicious greenery when all of a sudden he saw a new star appear in the sky, accompanied by fragments of strange celestial music. He reported this vision to Theodomir, his bishop, who in turn called out the local people, who armed themselves with picks and shovels. In a deserted place in the hills, directly underneath the star, the stone tomb was discovered in a dank and echoing cave. Within it lay a body, its head intact, sweetly perfumed, and on the ground lay a letter:

"Here lies Santiago, son of Zebedee and Salome, brother of

Saint John, whom Herod beheaded in Jerusalem. He came by sea, borne by his disciples...."

A small church was built on the site, and from the beginning it attracted pilgrims. Later the church became a monastery, and a town grew up around it. The town was named Santiago de Compostela, St. James of the Field of the Star.

Of course, modern academics will have none of it. Saint James never came anywhere near Spain, they say, either in his life or after his death. The story is probably a clerical fraud dreamed up by the monks to attract donations: or if not, it was simply the result of a monastic muddle, with some ignorant scribe who was copying out the Acts of the Apostles confusing the Latin for Jerusalem *(Hierosolyma)* with the Latin word for Spain *(Hispania)*. What's more, so the academics contend, the name of Compostela has nothing to do with stars and a lot to do with a derivation from the Latin *compostum*, from which we get the phrase *compost heap.*

Even the tradition of pilgrimage, they argue, is simply a memory of some orgiastic pre-Christian bondage cult that used to organize illicit visits to nearby Cabo Finisterre, where cult members got up to no good among the menhirs and dolmens on the seashore. It is from this cult that Saint James inherits his emblem, the scallop shell: long before the Vatican converted scallops into the emblem of Christian pilgrimage, worn by every footsore traveler to Santiago, the shell was the Roman symbol for the vagina and the emblem of the pagan love goddess, Venus. It was worn by devotees of esoteric classical cults in altogether different contexts and, so it seems, for altogether different purposes.

The modern pilgrim is free to choose whichever of these two versions he cares to believe: the dull and scholarly or the romantic and mythical. For myself, I was quite happy to suspend my critical faculties for the duration of the pilgrimage, and at the end I said a prayer at what I like to believe was the tomb of Saint James. Moreover, I walked the road with a *coquille St-Jacques*—a pilgrim's scallop shell—around my neck. Although (disappointingly) it did not elicit any indecent propositions from beautiful Spanish girls au fait with Roman erotic symbolism, it did awaken in every village I passed through a deep reservoir of old-world goodwill toward itinerant pilgrims. After twelve hundred years, you would have thought that the novelty of passing pilgrims would have worn off in villages along the route; yet, strangely, it is not so.

Old men out in the fields polling their olive trees would stop what they were doing and politely bow to you; village priests would offer you their blessing and ask you to pray for them at the tomb of Saint James. In village bars, the owners would round off my bills to a convenient decimal. One hotel owner solemnly presented me with a bar of chocolate: "¡*Hombre!* My son is your age," he said, holding me in a firm Iberian grip. "He did the pilgrimage last year. Now he is in Salamanca, studying for the priesthood."

Most remarkable of all was the hilltop village of Cirauqui, a little to the south of Hemingway's beloved Pamplona. Even from afar, the village looked different. The widows had done their best to make the place cheerful: put cages full of birds—canaries and cockatoos—out onto the windowsills and loaded their balconies with snapdragons and nasturtiums. The village had red-tiled roofs and white-washed walls, and as I sat in the shade of the village church, beginning my picnic lunch, I was abducted by a gray-haired, prickly-chinned old lady and carried off to her house with cries of "*peregrino*" (pilgrim) and "Santiago."

Like every other house in the village, it was wind-worn and crumbling; above its door was hung the escutcheon of some long-extinct don. Inside, the furnishing was dark and frugal: a solitary

> *He was Belgian and had walked all the way from his home. When Louella asked him why he was making the pilgrimage, he replied that he had worked as a schoolteacher for 40 years and had been married for 35 of them. On retirement he found himself suddenly at home with a wife to whom he had nothing to say. Following the Way of St. James, he wrote to her each day and she to him at postes restants. It was, he said, like a honeymoon all over again and they were in love once more.*
>
> —Robin Hanbury-Tenison,
> *Spanish Pilgrimage: A Canter to St. James*

picture of a bleeding Sacred Heart hung on the wall, and there was a strong scent of beeswax polish and mahogany. I sat down next to her sleeping husband in the kitchen, and while her grandchildren climbed all over me, course after course of an enormous peasant lunch was put on the table. A vast salad, soaked in local olive oil, was followed by a huge plate of ham and eggs, suspended in a welter of tomatoes; this was followed by a succession of other courses, including a strange confection of morels, and brought to a close by bowls full of ripe Castilian fruits. The feast was washed down by wine from the old lady's own small vineyard.

"You do have an awful lot of grandchildren," I said, as twelve of them tumbled among the remnants of the meal.

"There are ten more at school," she replied, beaming proudly.

After the lunch was finally finished and the dishes cleared, the old lady sat back and asked me where I was from—Germany perhaps?

"Scotland," I said.

"Where is that?"

"Near England."

"England...*Londres*," said the lady vaguely. Then her face lit up. She rose and indicated that she wanted me to follow her. I was led into the pitch darkness of her shuttered bedroom. She scuttled off into a corner, returning with a magazine cradled lovingly in her arms.

"*Londres*," she said, opening the pages at a much-thumbed center spread and pointing at a picture of an elegant blonde. "*Londres*," she said. "The city of Lady Di."

Of course, it was not always like this. Hospitality varied from place to place.

In the Middle Ages, the pilgrim who braved the heights of the French Pyrenees would be rewarded on reaching Spain with the medieval equivalent of the New York Hilton. The monks of the abbey of Roncesvalles would wash his feet for him on arrival; he would be offered an actual bed in a heated dormitory; free meals would be offered during the period he was resting there; a picnic would be given to him for the next part of the journey; and if all this proved too much for the amazed traveler, he would be given a decent burial, in consecrated ground.

Today the monks at Roncesvalles—whose monastery was founded specifically to look after pilgrims—are too busy flogging knickknacks to tourists to take much interest in modern pilgrims. Having read about the provisions made for medieval pilgrims, you come down from the cold gray mists of the Roncesvalles Pass expecting great things. And indeed, there is still a dormitory—but it is very cold, entirely without linen, and, far from having your feet washed, there is no provision even for hot water. You are not fed nor provided with a picnic, and you are thrown out at nine o'clock the following morning.

To make matters worse, the villages around Roncesvalles are some of the most inhospitable in Spain. The houses are shored with buttresses and pierced with windows no wider than a lancet; their stones are rarely smaller than the average-size coffin. Half farm, half castle, half church, the houses of Navarre are old and solid and easily defensible. They are deserted but for packs of howling, wolflike dogs and hobbling, black-clad widows: it is as if some terrible plague had descended and carried off the men, the children, and the cats. Torn posters cover the village walls. There is no sound but for some ill-oiled door creaking on its hinges in the wind.

The first week of the trip had been dogged with rain and thick Pyrenean mists. In Navarre, however, the sun was scorching. The midday heat quivered over the vineyards, driving me off the track and into the narrow shade of the roadside cypresses. One afternoon I decided to take a siesta in a haystack. I was exhausted: that morning I had risen early and walked from the last conifers and pastures of the hills to the olive groves and cornfields of the plains. It was hot, and I lay down and enjoyed the new sounds and smells: almond blossoms and buzzing flies, rock roses and blue columbines, the grating of amorous grasshoppers and the woodland cackle of a golden oriole.

I had been dozing for no more than half an hour before I was wakened by the unlikely sound of chanting male voices. Two dark, burly men were heading toward me with enormous backpacks on their shoulders. They were each holding something in their right hand, and as they drew closer I could see that these were rosaries. The chant was the Roman Catholic prayer, the Hail Mary, in Italian.

Oscar and Giuseppe were pilgrims from a village near Turin. Giuseppe was a farmer; Oscar had just been laid off by Fiat. Both had sons training for the priesthood, and Giuseppe had a brother who was a Trappist monk; both had undertaken the pilgrimage out of strictly religious reasons. They joined me on my haystack, and Giuseppe took off his shoes. His feet were red and swollen; one sported a pustule the size of a small football.

"You will cripple yourself if you walk with feet like that," I said. Giuseppe grinned, pulled a toothpick out of his shirt pocket, and began to pick at his molars.

"Seriously," I said, "you should rest them, at least for a day or two."

"We must cover at least 40 kilometers a day," he replied. "We have less than three weeks to get to Compostela. I have to get back for the harvest, and Oscar needs to look for a job."

"If you are in a hurry, you could take a bus for a bit of the route," I suggested.

"No," replied Oscar firmly. "This is a pilgrimage."

"What difference will it make?"

"I need a job and I am going to ask Saint James for one. If he knows what I have suffered, he will not refuse me."

Oscar was dressed in sneakers, jeans, and t-shirt, indistinguishable from a million other 20th-century Europeans. But his beliefs were those of a medieval peasant. Carrying a backpack two or three times the weight of my own, he had already walked more in that week than I had in the previous two; and the pain he was inflicting upon himself and his friend was quite deliberate. After the polite, lukewarm piety with which I had grown up, I found the robust faith of the Italians strange—and oddly attractive. Their approach to the pilgrimage would have been quite familiar to Aymeric Picaud, and maybe even to Chaucer's Wife of Bath.

I walked with the Italians that afternoon, scrambling along the track in an effort to keep up with them. We trudged from village to village; sometimes the road sank into the ground, as if cut down by some fast-flowing river, down into a tunnel of overgrown scurvy grass and wild poppies. Dry-stone revetments held up the vine terraces above. Below, the walls were like a section of an archaeological excavation—dotted with shards and skulls, an old pilgrim's charm perhaps, the discarded rubbish of a millennium of travelers.

Up in the open again, church towers were rarely out of sight, and we descended down paths corkscrewing through shallow hills along avenues of poplar and cypress. Sometimes our footsteps would fall in time with the dull thud of mattocks on dry earth, as villagers turned the soil around their vines.

Everyone knows what each must do and performs his or her (or its) task without much comment. Wyn and Claudy walk the compliant mules laterally through the woods until the slope affords easy passage for the animals. The Spanish engineer, Augustín, and I carry down the packs. We clamber back up and help the others down.

By the time our band reconvenes on the other side, we have what now passes for conversation.

"Whoo, shit," says Claudy.

"Yeeeoooo," says Augustín.

"Hooooo," I say.

"Heee-haaw," says Ultreya.

"Okay," says Val.

And we walk on.

—Jack Hitt, Off the Road: A Modern-Day Walk Down the Pilgrim's Route into Spain

We were taken in by the Fathers of the Reparadores [at Puente la Reina] and given bare bunks in their pilgrims' hostel. There was no food and no hot water, but the Italians did not seem to mind. They kissed the pictures of Il Papa on the wall and hung their rosaries on the bars of their bunks. Their only grouse was that the monks refused to give them Holy Communion until the next morning.

When I awoke at eight o'clock, the Italians had long gone. I thanked the monks and made my way to a bar, where I ate breakfast. Then I headed off along the old cobbled track, alone again.

As I walked I wondered how far Oscar and Giuseppe were representative of the pilgrims who had walked the road over the centuries. Certainly, many of the modern pilgrims whom I talked to were motivated as much by the wish for a holiday as by any religious urge, and there is evidence that quite a lot of medieval pilgrims must have felt the same way. Andrew Boorde, who left us the fullest English-language account of the journey, was certainly no saint. He was very skeptical about the relics he saw at Santiago and, moreover, ended his days in London's Fleet Prison, accused of living with three women simultaneously.

Nor do other records give the impression that the medieval pilgrimage was all piety and long faces. Those who could would travel in some style. They brought their own musicians with them and passed along the road in a litter, or *palanquin*, serenaded by viols, tabors, and harps, interspersing visits to the more attractive shrines with visits to tournaments and other noblemen, allowing time to try out Spanish delicacies—Galician shellfish or the fine wines of La Rioja.

The poorer classes, then as now, traveled in groups, drank a great deal, and made a lot of noise:

> "They will ordain beforehand to have with them both men
> and women [including those sorts of women] who sing
> wanton songs; and some other pilgrims will have with
> them bagpipes; so that every town they come through,
> what with the noise of their singing, and with the sound of
> their piping, and with the jangling of their bells, and with
> the barking of dogs after them, they make more noise than
> if the king came their way, with all his clarions and many
> other minstrells...."

One thinks also of Chaucer's pilgrims, crooks virtually to a man, what with the corrupt Miller, the lecherous Wife of Bath, the worldly Prioress, and particularly the loathsome Pardoner selling relics that were supposedly the ossified remains of great saints but were in fact "pigges bones." It was people like this who gave pilgrimage an increasingly bad name as the Middle Ages progressed, and at whom the famous saying was directed: *Ir romera y volver ramera* ("Go a pilgrim, return a whore").

And yet it is undoubtedly true that when mass pilgrimage first became popular in the 11th century, it was inspired first and foremost by devotion: people really did believe in saints' relics, that they had a spiritual power and could act as divine go-betweens in the quest for personal salvation. Today when we read of the warehouses full of "true" relics stored up by monasteries across medieval Europe—those gallons of the Virgin's Milk, forest of fragments of the True Cross, jars full of Our Lord's Breath, and even His Holy Foreskin—the collections seem more comic than anything else. But to the simple Christians of the Middle Ages, relics held out the promise of an authority superior to man's and were, as a 2nd-century Greek writer put it, "more valuable than refined gold." Moreover, people believed that the places in which relics were kept were invested with magical properties—the ability to heal earthly sickness and wipe clean a soul besmirched with sin—and many were prepared to travel vast distances to experience those powers.

> *After dinner we went over the mountains of Luciana, and stopped at the town of Piedrabuena, a fine country, near a large ridge of mountains. There is no danger of thieves in Spain. As you stop in towns or villages, you may leave five hundred pounds worth in your coach all night, without any danger; but the* banditti *on the mountain or in large woods are dangerous.*
>
> —John Macdonald, *Memoirs of an Eighteenth-Century Footman* (1790)
>
> NOTE: *Macdonald was footman to William Dalrymple's great uncle, Major William Dalrymple, during his travels in Spain in 1774.*
>   —LMc

My pilgrim friends Giuseppe and Oscar spoke with the authentic voice of early medieval pilgrims. But at the end of another day's walking, I saw a work of art from the 12th century that to me expressed the feelings and fears of medieval pilgrims better than anything I had ever previously seen or read.

The church of San Miguel in Estella is a great fortress of a building and is reached by a massive, almost Wagnerian flight of steps. Inside, it is as dark as night. Narrow, arrow-slit windows emit only the minimum of light; above, massive masonry vaults groan under the weight of stone; it is cold and empty and silent but for the tread of feet on flagstones. It is an awesome sight—yet nothing affects one so much as the great north portal, emblazoned with some of the most frightening sculpture I have ever seen.

It is flanked by a line of martyrs who grimly grip the instruments with which they were tortured. With their severe expressions and hanging-judge eyes, they look as intolerant and autocratic, as stiff and as Spanish, as a line of Guardia Civil. If these are the men who are going to be the jury at the Last Judgment, you think, the sentences are going to be far from lenient.

Yet the martyrs are nothing compared with Christ, sitting Enthroned in Majesty at the center of the tympanum. He is as still and unmoving as the eye of a hurricane. Yet around him swirls a typhoon of cherubim and seraphim, holy women and beasts of the Apocalypse, bunches of grapes and man-headed animals, Babylonian griffins and coiling snakes—the images becoming ever more anarchic the farther removed they are from the calming influence of Christ. It is a simple and effective idea: without God, life becomes gruesome and hell-like; moreover, there is another idea implicitly linked to the first. In the twisting, tortured forms of the self-devouring man-beasts, evil is shown as a kind of human insanity, a mental condition. Hell is not so much heat and torment as a kind of terrible apocalyptic bedlam.

The vision is deeply troubled, harrowing, and pessimistic. The portal shows the nightmares and forest fears looming large in the psyche of medieval man. It shows him tortured by doubt in this world and living in continual fear of damnation and hellfire in the next. At the end of the day, it was that fear that led men to leave the comfort and safety of their homes and take to the pilgrimage roads in search of divine forgiveness. It was fear, not hope, that inspired the first pilgrims to Compostela.

After Estella, you head through low, hilly country to Burgos, one of the most windswept cities in Spain. There you enter a wasteland.

K̲urt said he didn't mind when he arrived. Walking the Camino was easy in spite of blisters, wet feet, aching shoulders and the like. Life was reduced to its basics: eating, sleeping, and walking. It left your mind free. There was an unmistakable air about Kurt that I came to recognise as the "pilgrim look." People encountered in remote mountains or on desert crossings sometimes have it too. It comes, I think, from being alone with one's thoughts for long periods, while one's body is being disciplined by long hard activity. Possibly the "pilgrim look" reflects something of the inner struggle, or maybe it reveals a new sense of purpose or awareness, but however one interprets it, it is a less guarded expression than people usually present to the world.

—Bettina Selby, *Pilgrim's Road: A Journey to Santiago de Compostela*

For the following two weeks the pilgrim passes through strange deforested plains—bleak, flat, austere, and desolate—wearying both to the feet and to the spirit. It was always an empty and inhospitable area, although today the traveler is unlikely to see what once was a common sight: a pack of wolves descending to devour the bodies of pilgrims.

It takes at least a fortnight's walking before you come to León, where you are rewarded for your labors by a night in the Hotel San Marcos—one of the great hotels of Europe: once the headquarters of the Crusader Knights of Saint James, now a flagship of the Spanish *parador* chain.

From León, you pass briefly through more clement Mediterranean regions, full of vineyards and olives, until you move up into the hills of Galicia. For me, a Scot, it was a kind of homecoming: suddenly I was back among Celts, back among the rain clouds, back in a country where the rocks blossomed with strange gray lichens.

The change from the olive groves of Castile was very sudden. In the morning at Villafranca I had still been in the heat of the plains. But at Herrería, I had turned left off the road and immediately crossed some invisible barrier. Suddenly the dust turned to mud, and soft mosses began to creep up the dry stone walls, over-loading the bows of the trees and hanging heavily off the branches.

The people changed too: the narrow Castilians gave way to thickset farmers in knitted cardigans and flat caps; in the bars they ate in silence, cutting up their chops on wooden plates with knives that looked as if they had been stolen from some abattoir. They drank wine from tumblers, and the air was heavy with woodsmoke, cigarettes, and the primeval charcoal stink of grilling meat.

The women also seemed to thicken out: as I passed through muddy farmyards I would be watched by silent, broad-bosomed matrons in aprons and pinnies. They would be carrying meal out for the hens, shepherding their children in for supper, or sternly calling their dogs to back away from the pilgrim. Sometimes I would meet them carrying in fodder for the cows, their faces lost under great mountains of hay.

The monks were in their fields, planting cabbages with the air of old Edwardian gentlemen playing croquet. There were fifteen of them: plump, elderly men in matching blue overalls and wide-brimmed straw hats, and as they raked the earth and carefully placed the cabbages in neat lines, the abbot shouted encouragement from his seat on the side of the field; you knew he was the abbot because he was wearing a heavy pectoral cross and bright green Wellington boots. When the cabbages were in place, the abbot squatted down on his hams to make sure the line was straight, as if sizing up the angles before sending his ball flying firmly through the hoop.

Father Domingo, the guestmaster, detached himself from the clerical chain gang and came to meet me at the side of the field.

"*Peregrino?*" he asked.

"*Sí.*"

"Follow me," he said; and together we headed toward the monastery gates, I with my staff, he with his rake.

I was educated by Benedictine monks in an English public school in Yorkshire, an experience that was enough to put anyone off monasticism for life. Yet on this journey I grew to love the monasteries I passed by: they seemed marvelous towers of solid

ivory, abodes of faith, wisdom, and learning marked out from the
outside world by their calmness, their lack of haste. Each monastery
had a different quality to recommend it. One might distill an unusual liqueur, some rich brew flavored with wild herbs and derived
from a medieval recipe carefully guarded in the monastic library.
Another might make strong goat's cheese, or pottery, or have cloisters carved with tangling Romanesque vine scrolls.

In medieval times, the pilgrim to Rome came down from the
heights of Tuscany to be rewarded with a view of the city's magnificent walls, looping over the seven hills. The approach to
Jerusalem was an equally suitable climax to so long a journey: that
last wonderful stretch of road up from Emmaus threading up
through the pine trees and oleanders.

In comparison, the first view of Santiago was always unremark-
able; even the Romans seemed to have been unimpressed, for the
river you cross is named Lavacolla, derived from the Latin for "arse
wipe." Yet to arrive at any destination that you have longed for has
its rewards. I was in a fairly bad way. I was unshaven, and none of
my clothes had been washed for a week. I smelled. More seriously,
a blister on the ball of my right foot had gone bad and I had a pronounced Quasimodo limp. Just to arrive, just to cease walking,
seemed enough.

The outskirts of Santiago seemed strangely deserted. It was only
when I neared the towering cliff face of the cathedral that the
crowds thickened, and then they did so dramatically. Suddenly
police cars were everywhere, and so were policemen, keeping the
crowds back with metal crowd gates and machine guns. I asked a
passerby what was happening. The king, Juan Carlos, was about to
arrive in Santiago. Where was he staying? In the Hostal Los Reyes
Católicos. The same hotel at which I had a reservation.

I was within seconds of perfectly mistiming my entry to the
hotel. Having fought my way through the police cordon, waving
my reservation slip, I limped up to the door of the parador seconds
before His Majesty. Smooth functionaries in gold brocade had

time to secret the embarrassing specter away in a corner and hide his stinking rucksack. There was a fanfare of trumpets, and the king entered the magnificent hostel, originally built by his predecessor, King Ferdinand, for the shelter of pilgrims. On this occasion, understandably enough, they were rather less welcome. At breakfast I found an ally in the waiter:

"These kings," he said disdainfully. "They make such a mess. We get so many of them here."

I laughed, thinking he was joking. But he was quite serious.

It was midafternoon before I had exhausted the novelties of my hotel room: baths, linen sheets, a laundry service, even a bidet in which, in the absence of any more suitable use, I soaked my aching feet. Washed, shaved, and scented, with a fresh change of clothes, I headed out into the square to finish my journey.

The hotel was still surrounded by limousines and their attendant hordes of chauffeurs, policemen, and photographers. But the area in front of the great cathedral, built on the site of the original small church, was now empty but for a small group of pilgrims like myself. A Belgian bicyclist was dancing a small jig on the cathedral steps. Another pilgrim, a young bearded Spaniard whom I had previously met

Inside the body of the church we found ourselves captured, as pilgrims always must have been, by the gracefulness of the space around us, the perfection of Romanesque architecture at its apogee. It is through this space that, on special occasions, the giant botafumiero—*the largest incense censer in the world (made in 1602)—is swung to the eaves by eight men pulling on a rope. The purpose is to disperse the smoke of the fragrant burning gums and spices as widely as possible through the church, but the spectacle is one of pure theatre, an uplifting treat for the pilgrims, a heart stopping and dangerous reminder of fear on childhood swings when the world turned upside down. Once, long ago, the* botafumiero *is said to have continued its sickening swoop above the bowed heads of the congregation and flown out of a cathedral window; perhaps it will happen again.*

—Robin Hanbury-Tenison,
Spanish Pilgrimage: A Canter to St. James

near León, appeared to have virtually expired beside the portal; one old lady dropped a coin on his lap as she passed.

Inside, the cathedral was almost pitch dark. Rolling Romanesque arches thundered forward on massive feet toward the shrine—a huge baroque construction that filled the space normally occupied by the *coro*. It was an extraordinary object, a forest of wooden pinnacles and stalactites, dominating the nave like some hugely enlarged cuckoo clock, the image of Saint James filling the little cavity normally reserved for the bird. Yet in the night blackness of the nave, the shrine took on a strange quality of gilded magnificence. We pilgrims queued up beside a staircase, waiting to be admitted into the space behind the statue, as excited as a group of children waiting for a ride on a fairground roller coaster.

For the pilgrims of the Middle Ages, the bones of Saint James were the supreme relics of Europe, the most powerful miracle workers and sin cleansers in Christendom. Even Aymeric Picaud, the author of the 12th-century pilgrim's guide, normally so rude about all things Spanish, was forced into awestruck admiration:

"His whole body is there...divinely illuminated by heavenly carbuncles, endlessly honoured by divine fragrant odours, decorated with the brightness of celestial candles and unceasingly honoured by angelic adoration...."

We pilgrims clutched our staffs, burly young men hobbling forward like old women. One by one, we climbed the stairs up into the darkness and there threw our arms around the statue, hugging it close. What should have been a hugely embarrassing exercise was, in the circumstances, oddly moving. The statue was cold, hard, and solid, yet it felt quite natural to squeeze it as enthusiastically as if it were your girlfriend, and it responded to the cuddle with a satisfactory rattling noise.

Then the stairs led down again, down, down, deep down into the crypt, to a dim, bare, round-arched, flagstone space furnished with a single kneeler. Here I knelt before a grille and looked forward. A few feet away, through a narrow passage, a small chamber was lit with dazzling brilliance. There, encased in solid silver, sat the reliquary that contained the bones of the saint.

Logically, I knew it was a fairly slim chance—though far from impossible—that the bones were those of the fisherman Jesus first picked up beside the Sea of Galilee, James the son of Zebedee and Salome. But irrespective of their identity, I felt that the bones had been imbued with sanctity and importance through the pain of the tens of millions of pilgrims throughout the ages who had traveled thousands of miles to pray at the kneeler at which I now knelt.

So, despite having long dropped the habit, I did pray there, and the prayers came with a surprising ease. I prayed for the people who had helped me on the journey, the priest who had blessed my stick, the innkeeper who had refused payment, the monks who had given me food, and the cobbler who had mended my torn shoes. And then I did what I suppose I had come to do: I prayed for my fiancée and for the success of my forthcoming marriage, now only a few weeks away.

Then I got up, climbed the steps, and walked back, under the great incense-darkened vaults of the nave, under the triple portal and the old rose window.

Outside it had begun to rain.

William Dalrymple is the author of In Xanadu *and* City of Djinns: A Year in Delhi. *As a travel writer, he continues a family tradition begun by his great uncle (x8), Major William Dalrymple, who wrote* Travels through Spain and Portugal in 1774 *(1777). He was brought up in the same house in Scotland that the major was, and now divides his time between London and Edinburgh. He is married to the artist Olivia Fraser.*

*

In medieval times, the route did not end in Santiago. People wanted to see the end of the world, and that meant travelling further to the west. There was no America then, no Cuba, the world could have been flat with steep edges; it was all mystery, waiting there to be discovered. If you walked westwards you could come to the end of Europe, to the place called Finis Terrae in Latin, Finisterre in Spanish and Fisterre in Gallego.

We caught a bus to Fisterre which left us in the old village with more than a mile's walk uphill to see the end of the world. There were pilgrims, with rucksacks and staves and scallop shells around their necks, just as tanned and pleased with themselves as the pilgrims I had seen in León when I started my journey. The hills on the promontory which overlooked the end of the world were wild with gorse and heather; as we walked up we could see small fishing craft like silver specks in the bay below....

In the years before 1492 you could have stood here contemplating the deep blue sea and the flat earth and the hot sun in the brilliant sky, knowing that you had come to the end of things, speculating what was beyond: great wealth and unimagined possibilities or nothing, the abyss that these same waves had touched or come close to. And then the turning back: the walk homewards, away from the setting sun, in the direction of the dull east, and all the places to revisit, and all the time in the world.

—Colm Tóibín, *The Sign of the Cross: Travels in Catholic Europe*

COLM TÓIBÍN

Demons and Dragons

At a festival that did not exist during the Franco era,
the author reflects on Catalonia's legacy and rebirth.

I REMEMBER THE STRANGE HUMIDITY DURING THAT FIRST
September in the city. I remember the rancid smells and the constant noise as steel shutters were pulled up and down. I remember
the sound of cars and motorbikes reverberating against the old
stone buildings, the footfalls and voices which echoed in the narrow streets. It was 1975, two months before the death of General
Franco. I was twenty years old and had just arrived in Barcelona.

The buildings on the Ramblas, the long tree-lined walk between the Plaça de Catalunya and the port, were as different as
each face which sized you up for a split second before it passed.
The Ramblas, busy all the time, was a whole new world to wander in and discover. The kiosks selling newspapers and books
were open day and night. During the day one stretch had kiosks
selling flowers, another had kiosks with animals for sale. People sat
at the outside tables for hours on end staring at passersby.

I knew no Spanish, but I understood that the Ramblas had its
own customs, its own rules. The prostitutes, for example, didn't
seem to come up from the port beyond a certain point. Also nobody seemed to be going anywhere in particular. Most people
seemed to be idly strolling. On Sunday mornings families filled

the Ramblas, walked up and down under the shade of the plane trees. I tried out each bar. I stood at the kiosks and tried to decipher the newspaper headlines and the titles of books.

One night, while close to the Cathedral, I strayed into a small square through a narrow alleyway. It was quiet and dark and hidden away. One of the walls had been badly damaged by shrapnel or bullets. Nobody came through the alleyway while I was there and there was no sound except a trickle of water from a small fountain in the middle of the square.

I began to haunt the old city. I could hardly wait for darkness to fall, when the lamps would be lit high up on the walls, and the streets would become shadowy, ghostly. This was the late medieval world of master craftsmen, stonecutters, masons, sculptors and architects surviving intact in the middle of a city.

When I found work as a teacher and decided to stay for a while, I began to study the language and by January I was confident that I had made some progress. One evening I was invited for supper to a small flat in the Gothic quarter. My fellow guests were natives of the city. As the conversation went on I realised that I couldn't understand a single word they said. All the nights spent poring over the niceties and oddities of Spanish grammar had been in vain. It was only when someone apologised to me for speaking in Catalán, and thus excluding me, that I understood the problem.

They and their family and friends, they explained, all spoke Catalán as a first language, although they were fluent in Spanish as well. Most of them couldn't write the language, however, and few of them had ever read a book in Catalán. It wasn't merely spoken, they explained, in villages and remote places. It was the language of the prosperous classes in Barcelona. Franco had banned the public use of the language in 1939.

Catalán, I discovered, isn't a dialect of Spanish, nor of Provençal, although it has close connections with both. Some words (*casa* for "house," for example) are the same as in Spanish; other words (*menjar* for "eat") are close to French or Italian. Most of the words for fruit, vegetables and spices are completely different from the Spanish words. The way of forming the past simple is like no other language; the way of forming the past continuous is more or less the same as in Spanish; the way of forming the past subjunctive is the same as in Italian.

Catalán is a pure Latin language. There are no Arabic sounds. Thus the pronunciation of the word "Barcelona" does not have the "th" sound as used in the series *Fawlty Towers*. Catalán sounds are harsh and guttural. The language is full of short, sharp nouns such as *cap* for "head," *fill* for "son," and *clau* for "key"; and similar-sounding verbs: *crec* for "I believe," *vaig* for "I go," and *vull* for "I want."

By the time I began to learn Catalán in 1976 I didn't just need it in order to follow the conversation at dinner parties, I needed it to know what the crowd was shouting in the streets, to read the writing on the walls. In that year the language which had been the preserve of the city's middle classes and which had, since the Civil War, been used mainly indoors now took to the streets with a vengeance.

From 1931 to 1939 Catalonia had its own chief executive and legislature, and bilingual legal and education systems. More than a thousand Catalán-language newspapers and magazines were published. Catalán schools were among the best in Europe, astonishingly humane and advanced by comparison with what normally passed for education in Spain. The eight years of autonomy were the fulfillment of a century of struggle. The full possibilities of an autonomous Catalonia were never realized, however. There was no time: five years after the period of autonomy began, the Spanish Civil War broke out.

—David Rosenthal,
"Thriving without a State,"
The Atlantic Monthly

By 1977 it was as though it had never been banned. The new Spain was prepared to allow Catalonia a certain autonomy and the Catalán language a certain official respect.

In January 1988 I returned to Barcelona. I stayed there all year and again for three months in 1989. People asked me if the city had changed; some of the changes were obvious, such as the street names which were now in Catalán only. There was more crime. But I still wasn't sure. On the final Sunday in September 1988, the last day of the Mercè festival, which had not existed in the Franco era, I felt at ease enough in the city, at home enough again, to look around me carefully, to take notes, and maybe take stock.

In the wake of Franco's death and the return of democracy to Catalunya, Barcelona experienced an outburst of militant linguistic Catalanism. Agitators demanded that the university teach only texts written in (or translated into) Catalán—a sure recipe for academic disaster, since most of Spanish literature (let alone English, French, German, or Italian) would have been excluded by such a policy, while the chaos that Catalán exclusiveness would have produced in the study of the sciences hardly bears thinking about. Mostly the fuss came down to the public as inconvenience, particularly when enthusiasts spray-painted street signs back into Catalán.

This militancy seems to be spent now. It holds out on the margins of intellectual life, but its energy is clearly lost in a time of transition.

—Robert Hughes, *Barcelona*

You could hardly move on the Ramblas that morning; the street was crowded as it had always been, but the stretch between the port and the Liceu Opera House was seedier than before. There was a sense that people who should have been in jail were walking about freely, a feeling that the police might swoop at any moment.

This was Picasso's stomping ground in the years when he lived in the city; this was where George Orwell, in May 1937, watched fascinated as the crowd built barricades with speed and skill. Now men stood around, watching and waiting while all around them street-sellers sold jewellery and rugs, cheap cassettes and Indian clothes.

The Ramblas began as a small stream, a seasonal river whose channel was used in the dry season as a roadway. In the 14th century as the city grew it was included within new walls, and then in the 18th century the stream was diverted and became the street which Federico García Lorca hoped would go on forever. Some of the buildings are from the 18th century: the Virreina Palace, near the market, was built in the 1770s, as was the Casa March, further down on the other side. But most date from the 19th century, including the Liceu Opera House, which was built in 1847 and rebuilt after a fire in 1861.

A few of the buildings were constructed in the style for which the city later became famous: using tiles, mosaics and floral motifs, mixing medieval images with the idioms of the art nouveau movement, with decoration and colour on the outside of buildings. L'Antiga Casa Figueres, for example, was first built in 1902, and is now restored and again in use as a cake shop.

Across the road one of the banks has bought and restored L'Antiga Botiga Bruno Cuadros, finished in 1885 with all the elaborate colour and subtle decoration of its original pastiche Japanese style. But these buildings stand out on the Ramblas; by the time serious money was available for building in Barcelona, the Ramblas had ceased to be fashionable, and was replaced by the Ramblas de Catalunya and the Passeig de Gràcia.

ederico García Lorca, born in 1899 in the vicinity of Granada, produced a number of outstanding works in lyric poetry, drama, and prose between his eighteenth year and the time of his death in 1936 at the age of 37. He was a pianist, the organizer of a dramatic troupe, and a distinguished folklorist of Spanish popular songs of great distinction.

Many stories are told of him. He was loved by the people. His murder by the fascist firing squad in Granada is perhaps as he would have wished it to be: to die on the horns of the bull—if a man does not put his sword first through his heart.

—William Carlos Williams, "Federico García Lorca," *The Kenyon Review* (1939)

The atmosphere changes once you pass the Opera House and the coloured tiles designed by Miró into the more stable and solid world of the flower sellers. People walk differently, the clothes are smarter, no one wonders if you are easy prey. It is relaxed, as you walk past the bird-sellers' stalls, towards the Plaça de Catalunya.

As always, there was a queue that Sunday outside Agut, the restaurant behind the Passeig de Colom on Carrer Gignsà.

Eventually it was our turn. As we sat down the couple at the next table were having a dessert of lemon sorbet with champagne poured all over it. The food looked good, the people animated and content, the waiters constantly bringing more wine and shouting orders into the kitchen.

The fare was traditionally Catalán. Agut's *escalibada* was particularly good: onions and green and red peppers roasted on the outside and then peeled and soaked in oil. The free-range chicken cooked with prawns came next in an old-fashioned ceramic dish, followed by profiteroles for dessert.

As it approached five o'clock there was a sense of hurry in the restaurant, a sense of expectation. Notices all over the centre of the city announced the *correfoc* for seven o'clock, encouraging people to wear old clothes and headgear, and asking those who lived along the route through which the devils and dragons would pass not to throw water on the participants. "Respect the devils and the dragons," one sign read. These had been put up by the authorities.

The festival had begun on Friday with a speech by José Carreras, fireworks over the town hall and concerts in the old city squares at ten o'clock. Maria del Mar Bonet, who in the 1970s had written one of the classic songs in Catalán against Franco's police, who had been arrested and held under the old régime, was now being paid by the municipality to sing in front of the floodlit cathedral, its spiky façade dramatic against the clear sky. She sang in Catalán, medieval songs of the troubadours, songs from the 12th and 13th and her native island of Majorca. I looked up once, distracted by something in the sky, and saw a seagull, flying towards the cathedral spire and hovering there in the floodlight, holding its wings perfectly still. It wavered there for so long that everybody began to notice it, and a small cry went up from the crowd.

On Saturday, in the late afternoon, the giants did their dance through the centre of the old city to the beat of drums. Every village and every district of the city kept its own giants and some took them to Barcelona for this festival. The giants' faces were wonderfully made, perfectly still and serene as they were marched through the streets: kings, queens, Moors, pirates, harvesters, noblemen, noblewomen, all of them more than fifteen feet tall, doing twirls and running for a stretch and then standing still so the small human carrying their weight could have a rest and a replacement could take over.

Sunday night was the highlight. Sunday night was going to be rough. You might get pushed and knocked over, or badly burned by the fireworks which would be attached to the dragons and the devils. The clock had been put back on Saturday night and by half past six, as the crowds went towards the Plaça de Sant Jaume, darkness was already falling.

The square had been fitted out with overhead cables laden with fireworks; in front of the entrance to the town hall a huge devil had been built of more fireworks. There were some old people in the square, and young children sat high on their parents' shoulders, but most of the people in the square were young, boys and girls in large groups, hats on their heads to protect themselves from the sparks, handkerchiefs at the ready to protect their lungs from the sulphurous fumes.

Five to seven: we waited close to the edge of things, away from the real centre of danger, not far from the van which the Red Cross had driven into the square. It was dusk now, and at seven it began: the whole square became a mass of bangs and small explosions, a line of fireworks caught and the noise zipped over our heads with a spray of sparks. The devil in front of the town hall lit up as though an electric shock had gone through it. And five minutes later it was over—the square was in darkness, the first bangs and thrills finished. Now it was time for the parade.

For one moment during the fireworks when the sound of the explosions was echoing against the old walls of the Plaça de Sant Jaume, I remembered the last time I had heard this square reverberate with explosions. In the years immediately after Franco died this was one of the places where the demonstrators would gather, and this was where the police would come in jeeploads, complete with batons and rubber-bullet guns and other weapons. I remembered this square in 1976 and 1977, the huge crowds gathering in front of the town hall, calling for amnesty, for liberty, for autonomy, the Communists, the Socialists and the Nationalists all united in shouting the same slogans. I remembered how frightened we were when the police would charge into the square wielding their batons, how everyone would rush to one of the exits only to find it blocked and then panic and rush towards another. I remembered one Sunday evening in 1977, how I kept looking behind me as I ran down towards Via Laietana and noticed that two policemen had fixed on me and were making ground. I darted towards Sant Just, and waited there, shaking with fear. I remembered another bright evening when I saw a circle of policemen in the square beating a young girl with batons, hitting her hard, with passion and temper, over and over. We all stood at a safe distance wondering what to do, no one brave enough to intervene.

During all the years of Franco's reign and for two years afterwards a plaque remained on the wall to the right of the huge door of the town hall, telling the citizens of Barcelona that "*La Guerra Ha Terminado*"—the Civil War had ended and the "red army" had been defeated. Out of this very door, as we stood in the square 50 years later, now came dragons of all shapes and sizes, as though emerging from the jaws of death, breathing fire and making their way across the square. Sometimes they lunged into the crowd, who shrieked in terror and pushed back to avoid the flame. Gangs of youths then ran at the monsters as though to attack them, and tried to hold them back as the devil or dragon attempted to get by. Each time a new fiery monster appeared another mock feud broke out. Soon we became braver and moved towards the centre where we could watch each demon emerge, some of them huge and scaly, others multi-coloured with fierce faces out of comic books. We left ourselves room to run if one of these decided to come after us.

One by one they came out, a procession of horrible and grotesque creatures. Their minders, holders and protectors were armed with sacks of fireworks and were prepared to stop without any notice, fix new petards into their launchers and let them loose on the unsuspecting and excitable crowd. The procession was to end at Passeig de Colom, and at nine o'clock the last big display of fireworks would be shot into the air at the statue of Columbus to celebrate the tenth anniversary of the parade. This parade had begun in 1979, just as the city was getting on its feet again after the long rule of the old dictator.

When all the monsters had emerged we walked down and met the parade again at Passeig de Colom. Here the youth of the city came into their own; groups of them stood under buildings imploring people on the balconies to throw water down on them. "*¡Aigua!*

¡Aigua!" they roared in Catalán and shouted with joy as bucketfuls of water were flung all over them. Others ran over to join the lucky ones who had found a willing balcony and they all revelled in the showers of cold water.

They were now attacking the devils and dragons with greater ferocity, and trying to impede the progress of those who carried the fireworks. But the parade was still making its way towards the statue at the bottom of the Ramblas without much trouble, until they started to sit down in front of it shouting in Catalán "*no passareu, no passareu,*" meaning "you will not pass." The torchbearers attacked them with their sparks and battles broke out, but these were mock battles: not once did

> *But I defy anyone to be thrown as I was among the Spanish working class—I ought perhaps to say the Catalán working class, for apart from a few Aragonese and Andalusians I mixed only with Catalans—and not be struck by their essential decency; above all, their straightforwardness and generosity. A Spaniard's generosity, in the ordinary sense of the word, is at times almost embarrassing. If you ask him for a cigarette he will force the whole packet upon you. And beyond this there is generosity in a deeper sense, a real largeness of spirit, which I have met with again and again in the most unpromising circumstances.*
>
> —George Orwell,
> *Homage to Catalonia* (1938)

anyone lose his temper or hit an opponent. Eventually, they were moved in time for the demons to get through to the statue of Columbus and see the fireworks shoot over the city.

The music started at ten. For the third night in a row bands played in the old squares and up on the hill of Montjuic which overlooked the port. There were crowds on the Ramblas now, pouring down into the metro, or walking up towards the Plaça de Catalunya, just sauntering, idling, waiting for the concerts to begin.

To the right was the Plaça Reial; the much-maligned Plaça Reial, reputed to be the source of all the crime now in the city centre, the place where the handbag-snatchers and the dope dealers hang out, the square where tourists and thieves and touts meet, but which respectable natives of the city stay away from. The square was built in a French neo-classical style between 1848 and 1860; in 1879 Antoni Gaudí designed the lamps in the centre, one of his first commissions. A fountain has been added, and there are tall palm trees. On sunny winter mornings—the winter sky is usually clear and sunny in Barcelona—the square can be very beautiful and in the summer you can drink beer and eat *tapas* until after two in the morning. But still, the place is seedy. In the early 1980s the municipality tried to clean up the square and at night police cars now patrol the perimeter. Then the authorities began to put on jazz concerts on Sunday nights; a trendy architect did up the buildings, and writers and singers were reputedly about to move into the square at any moment. Yet none of this has had the slightest impact on the indigenous population of the square, who haven't changed much since 1975. You still have to watch yourself there, and it seems that nothing will ever change in the Plaça Reial.

Yet on that Sunday night of the Mercè festival every seat at every outside bar was taken. For once the plan was working: the middle classes were sitting comfortably in the Plaça Reial. The waiter brought us glasses of beer, squid deep fried in batter and slices of lemon. All around us were Catalán voices. The same Catalans who had abandoned the Plaça Reial to the foreigners and the outsiders were back tonight, back in the downtown that they had learned to fear. This fear had been born not just in previous years when the sale of heroin had become rampant in the area, but in the years after the Cuban War at the end of the 19th century when there was desperate poverty; the years after the First World War when there was enormous unemployment and unrest; and the years of the Civil War, when the Anarchists held the city centre.

That Sunday night the Catalans were in the Plaça de Sant Jaume too, dancing to a band playing Viennese waltzes. There were more old people here; each generation seemed to have found its level on the last night of the festival. In the Plaça de Rei around the corner the music was more modern and cool, and this was where the fashionable people were, the people who would later move on to the fast-lane nightclubs, were now standing in the 14th-century square swaying slightly to the music.

A bar on the corner, an old bar with upstairs windows overlooking the square, was half-empty now, although it was a hot night and the square outside was full. Catalans and the citizens of Barcelona in general have very little interest in alcohol, will seldom have more than one drink in a bar, and will often nurse a Coca-Cola for an entire evening.

All over the city the music went on. On Friday night 180,000 people had gone to the free rock concert on Montjuic and tonight there were 100,000 people up there again; earlier, an estimated 100,000 had watched the dragons and devils on the *correfoc*, and the same number of children had taken part in various events in the city over the weekend, all the events were paid for by the town hall. There had been no arrests, no fights. The city was stable now, at peace. The squares were full of people as midnight approached. Barcelona was having a good time.

Colm Tóibín also contributed "The Legacy of War" in Part One. Both stories were excerpted from his book Homage to Barcelona.

✳

Modern Catalonia plays havoc with the concept of North and South—economically, technologically, symbolically. To the rest of Spain it has been, since at least the beginning of the Industrial Revolution, the North—wealthier, better developed, more efficient, more democratic, less priest-ridden, closer to Europe both physically and socially. It is a place where poor southerners go to work for higher wages. And many Catalans are, in fact, firmly oriented toward Europe and the rest of the world. Daniel and Elisabet, for instance, told me that they had each been to Madrid only once, he to get a foreign visa, she to demonstrate with other doctors against reductions in the national health-care budget. "I've been in San Francisco more that I've been in Madrid," Elisabet said.

— William Finnegan, "Our Far-Flung Correspondent: Catalonia,"
The New Yorker

Soleares

*The author remembers learning
the song of loneliness.*

I HAD MEMORIZED ONE SENTENCE IN SPANISH ON THE PLANE RIDE
over. "*Yo quiero aprender la guitarra.*" That was all I knew of the language. In fact, being young and having never been outside the
United States, I really did not believe that people actually spoke a
language other than mine. I was seventeen, just out of high school,
in love with the flamenco guitar, and never thought to prepare for
the experience of arriving in another culture.

First hearing flamenco guitar at twelve years old was for me like
being struck by truth. It was the way I wanted to express myself
and within its dark sounds in particular I felt at home. Though
flamenco guitar is not usually played by women, I never ques-
tioned this, or my ability to learn. Again, another fortunate quality
of youth.

When I read Don Porhen's wonderful book, *The Art of Flamenco*,
I knew where I was going—to Morón de la Frontera to study with
Diego del Gastor, the great Gypsy master guitarist who Pohren had
described so compellingly in his book. Also described was *cante
jondo*, the deep song, the vehicle that brings the *duende* to us, the
quality that transforms both the artist and the listener from the inside out. *Cante jondo* expresses feelings of loneliness, grief, and

tragedy. It is this deep song that is valued above all. Pohren had made it clear in his book that this could not be bought and sold at the marketplace. It could only be found by seeking out the flamenco way of life in Andalucía with the Gypsies. What would a culture that valued this deep song be like? I wondered. I had to find out.

Fortunately Pohren, who was then running a kind of flamenco camp at his *finca* outside of Morón, thought I was a boy due to my name. He might have discouraged me otherwise. Instead he sent me directions on a bar napkin, a small hand-drawn map from Sevilla to Morón.

I took the plane to Madrid. The train to Sevilla. The bus to Morón. I had my guitar. My map. One suitcase. It was 1968. It was on the winding dusty bus to Morón that I began to feel the pull of something foreign and comforting at the same time. Women in black. Low voices speaking a language I didn't understand. Afternoon in Andalucía. I fell asleep.

I woke up at the bus station and consulted my bar napkin. The Bar Pepe was at the center of this universe, and I began to climb the charming narrow winding streets. When I got to Plaza San Miguel, all of five minutes from the bus station, I found that Bar Pepe was a tiny hole in the wall drafted by a beautiful old church and a castle crumbling on the hill behind it.

I walked across the plaza and stepped down into the cool darkened bar, out of the afternoon white glare. I stepped out of the silent white afternoon down into a rampaging fiesta that had been going on all night.

I saw old men dressed in suit jackets, berets, and fanciful *pañuelos,* and women in nondescript knee-length skirts and blouses. This was not how I expected Gypsies to dress. No polka dots. And this was not what I imagined a fiesta to be, simply because my imagination was limited to what I knew. This was not a performance. This was life and music together. Alive.

It didn't matter that the words flew by my conscious understanding. This was a language of music communicating profound feelings. Diego sat in a straight-backed chair playing guitar for an older man who sang. There were no idle listeners. Each person in a close circle around the artists clapped, cried, or expressed encouragement at certain points. Even I, a stranger, was swept into Diego's *toque*.

I sat in Bar Pepe until dawn. The beginning of many long journeys of listening. If the walls of Bar Pepe could sing, some of the greatest flamenco moments would be recorded for eternity.

My first lesson was not what I expected. Real lessons never are. I had planned to take lessons from Diego del Gastor. I had watched him play in the bar all week. My heart had been opened by his music. I had sat at his side during an all-night fiesta where he had stroked my cheek and called me "*niña*." But here the message was still from the old to the young. Diego did not want to teach women the guitar.

Though I was young enough to be called *niña*, I was old enough to be viewed as a woman. Diego did not discourage me from studying, however, and suggested Juan del Gastor, his nephew, as my teacher. Diego had four guitar-playing nephews, all great musicians. Juan was my age exactly and had the most even disposition. This may have been a consideration in the choice.

My first lesson with Juan was the beginning of a friendship that has spanned nearly three decades. Since there is no written music, until my ear was more developed Juan translated all crucial information. But what is the core of the music? Does it come through technique, through rhythm, through the soul?

What a particular teacher communicates is his gift. What a particular student goes after is her search. What happens between them is a conversation, superficial or meaningful, depending on the chemistry. I have known Gypsy guitarists to teach purposely bad material in a lesson gone astray.

My first lesson with Juan went on for hours. It began in the afternoon at Porhen's *finca* and ended in the small hours of the morning at Bar Pepe. It covered a variety of styles and melodies as well as vocabulary, philosophy, and cooking recipes.

The actual structure of the lesson was like this: we sat chair to chair, face to face, guitar to guitar. Like looking in a mirror, you learn to read the teacher's hands backwards. "*Por favor, toca soleares,*" says the student. And if the teacher is in the mood for *soleares*, he begins to play.

"*¡Me gusta eso!*" I said as I heard a Diego *falseta* being played through Juan. A *falseta* is an original melody played on the flamenco guitar. Like jazz improvisation, it can be spontaneous and original. Over the years it will be developed in all its variations by the artist, as well as learned or stolen by others.

I wanted to learn *soleares*, the song of loneliness. I wanted to learn Diego's *soleares*. Famous for his *falsetas* of this form, I had heard it played all week. It was ringing in my ears. It seemed to grow from the very mountains surrounding the white town. Its *compás*, the rhythmic frame, was regal and its *falsetas* shimmered from Diego's right hand. And I was a lonely seventeen-year-old who had been touched, turned inside out, by his *duende* and *soleares*.

I still remember the first two *falsetas* I learned. They looked deceptively simple. When Juan played them they were full of life. When I played them back they were flat. I cringed.

"*Está bien,*" Juan would say, beaming, I think just in response to my efforts and from generosity of spirit. "*Eso es,*" he would say as I played it back for the twentieth time, engraving it into my memory.

The *falseta* flew from Juan's hands directly into my heart. But to come out again flying through my hands would take many years. The *compás*, the rhythm, has to be so much a part of the body that it is as natural as breathing. *Falsetas* do not live in a vacuum. They live in the home of *compás*. Without *compás*, they are plot with no meaning. Mindless chatter. With *compás*, the soul of the artist, and the grace of melody, the *falsetas* become a profound and intimate conversation.

Compás can be taught in many ways. Through clapping, through strumming, through counting, through osmosis. My most

powerful *compás* lessons were during fiestas where I would try to
stand next to Ansonini del Puerto. One of the great dancers and
fiesteros of the pure art, Ansonini would put his hand on my shoulder and squeeze the *compás*, the accents of *soleares*, for example,
falling on three, six, eight, and ten. He didn't count. He just
squeezed and when there was a great moment he broke into such
a heartfelt *olé*, it was its own deep song and lesson in listening.

As with *falsetas*, fiestas do not exist in a vacuum. The listeners,
the *aficionados*, are part of the creation. They receive and know and
love the music. For that time span, whether it be an afternoon of
spontaneous eruption or a planned evening party, the bond between the giver and the receiver is absolute and what's more, there
is no exit. It is probably this bridge that creates the energy
whirlpool of the fiesta. For that moment the gap between artist
and audience is spanned.

A not-good fiesta has its roots in what I call a lack of honesty.
Yet there is no finger that can be pointed. This lack of honesty becomes a collective responsibility. A wrong fiesta can push you out
of sorts for weeks. So I would tell myself the day after, "Be careful!
Know your fiesta beforehand." This however was a contradiction
in terms. A fiesta is so spontaneous, there is of course no way to
know. And the better the fiesta is, the worse the re-entry back into
one's everyday world.

Being in Morón de la Frontera in the '60s was one of those gifts
life occasionally offers that changes the course of the river. It was
a renaissance of flamenco. The flamenco Gypsy culture was still
unbroken. There was no crashing back into everyday life. This *was*
everyday life. Living opera. This was before the irrevocable change,
when a TV was put in the Bar Pepe to watch flamenco. Much later
the bar was torn down altogether.

When I returned to the United States after my first trip to
Spain, I was lonely without the *soleares*. I was alone without the
dust. In Morón, the clinking of a glass being cleaned in a bar
down the street before siesta was the beginning of twelve beats.
Any one moment had the potential for rhythm. And the air was
alive with *falsetas*.

Dorien Ross, Ph.D. is a writer and psychologist who lives in New York. She is the author of the novel Returning to A *(City Lights Books, 1995), which is based on her experience studying guitar and living among the Gypsy people in Spain. Her short stories and essays have been published in* Best American Essays, Tikkun, *and other journals and anthologies.*

✶

First comes the guitarist, a neutral, dark suited figure, carrying his instrument in one hand and a kitchen chair in another. He places the chair in the shadows, sits himself comfortably, leans his cheek close to the guitar and spreads his white fingers over the strings. He strikes a few chords in the darkness, speculatively, warming his hands and his imagination together. Presently the music becomes more confident and free, the crisp strokes of the rhythms more challenging. At that moment the singer walks into the light, stands with closed eyes, and begins to moan in the back of his throat as though testing the muscles of his voice. The audience goes deathly quiet, for what is coming has never been heard before, and will never be heard again. Suddenly the singer takes a gasp of breath, throws back his head and hits a high barbaric note, a naked wail of sand and desert, serpentine, prehensile. Shuddering then, with contorted and screwed-up face, he moves into the first verse of his song. It is a lament of passion, an animal cry, thrown out, as it were, over burning rocks, a call half-lost in air, but imperative and terrible.

—Laurie Lee, *A Rose for Winter: Travels in Andalusia* (1955)

Where the Bullfight Was Born

Built along a cliff, Ronda is old Spain at its most picturesque,
harboring legends of banditry and of one
particularly inventive matador.

PEACE, SO RELENTLESSLY DENIED TO THE TRAVELER ON THE COSTA del Sol, descends instantly when just beyond Marbella he turns off north onto the Ronda road. This is marvelously deserted. Ronda—kept short of accommodation, it is alleged, by a hoteliers' conspiracy—rids itself of the bulk of its visitors at the end of every day. A few cars passed me on their way downhill to the coast; otherwise there was little sign of life in these splendidly empty mountains.

Five miles short of Ronda I pulled in at a roadside café. It was precariously sited close to the slope of a steep valley, and a precious customer's car, unsuccessfully parked, had rolled fifteen yards downhill into a corral with some donkeys. From the organized life of an area now described as the California of Europe, I had suddenly crossed an invisible frontier into the improvised Spain of old. The man who ran the place made me an omelet of potatoes studded with mountain ham—very dense and dry, to be correctly eaten with the fingers. He poured himself a glass of bluish wine and sat down with me to share the view. A huge bird—eagle or vulture—flapped into sight over a nearby peak and planed down the valley. Why were there no houses? I asked him, and he said it was because this had been bandit country. There had been bandits in these mountains as late as the '40s, and one of them had ridden in here one night for what proved to be his last meal before falling into an ambush laid by the Civil Guards.

While this conversation was in progress, a large and handsome nanny goat had stationed herself at the back of my chair, and now with great delicacy and precision, she leaned forward, picked up a piece of my bread, and began to chew. "Hope the goat doesn't bother you," the man said. "She's a friend of the family. Often pays us a visit."

"She doesn't bother me in the slightest," I said. "She's a fine-looking animal. What's her name?"

The man seemed surprised. "Not being a Christian," he said, "she doesn't have one. We just call her 'the goat.'"

I thanked him, patted the goat on the head, and left. Ten minutes later I drove over the top of the *sierra* and down through the outskirts of Ronda, and the landscape burst into life. There were hens and pigeons and litters of scuttling black piglets in the open spaces. A mother snatched up her baby from the verge of the road, a horseman wearing leather chaps and a big hat gal-

The civilization of Andalucía is the oldest in the Western world. A thriving native culture along the lower reaches of the Guadalquivir River traded regularly with Phoenicia and occasionally with the Israel of Solomon some thousand years before Christ. Strong evidence exists that this culture, known as Tarshish in the Old Testament and as Tartessos in the Greek texts, ranges well back into the second millennium to the time of the Minoans, while some of the most recent evidence involving revised radiocarbon dating indicates megalithic cultures in an even earlier age.

—Allen Josephs,
White Wall of Spain: The Mysteries of Andalusian Culture

loped after an escaping cow, and a traditional turkey woman controlled her flock with a seven-foot whip.

The great Arab gate called the Puerta de Almocábar barred the way at the entrance to the town. It was flanked by massive towers, and through it a perfect white Andalusian street of matching houses curved up into the heart of Ronda. There are bottlenecks among gothic and Moorish buildings at the top of the hill, and, after that, a descent to the New Bridge over the theatrical gorge of the Río Guadalevín, and glimpses, through ornamental grilles, of cyclopean boulders rearing up three hundred feet from the trickle of water in the bottom. Across the bridge the town opens into the Plaza de España, a charming, if haphazard, square smelling of geraniums and saddlery, with shops like caverns, a coachman plying for country hire on the box of a vehicle resembling a tumbril, and men with sonorous voices calling the numbers of lottery tickets for sale.

Here, through a fine, ruined archway, is the town's parking lot, with the cars lined up under a backdrop of the old town over the river, its white houses crammed as on a seaside terrace along the edge of a five-hundred-foot precipice. On our side, across the road, Don Miguel's restaurant jutting out over the gorge at its narrowest and most fearsome point recalls a scene in Tibet. I asked the knowledgeable attendant about eating there, and he replied, "You could do worse. Personally, I never set foot in the place. I suffer from vertigo, and it makes my head swim."

In all it was a memorable first encounter. Here was a small corner of Spain miraculously preserved: hardly changed, or so it seemed, since the editor of *Murray's Handbook,* Richard Ford, a difficult man to please, wrote of it in 1880, "There is but *one* Ronda in the world," hastening to warn of children "fond of throwing stones from dangerous heights at an unprotected traveller."

By now it was 8:00 p.m., with the sun waning in power at the bottom of the sky, and an evening relucence diffused from surfaces of bare rock, and a nacreous speckling of clouds to warm the whiteness of the buildings. The best of Ronda, built along the edge of the Tajo gorge, rises to nearly a thousand feet, with the prospect at this hour of a vast amphitheater saturated with fading light, men on donkeys and mules immediately below among ancient, abandoned houses with trees growing through their roofs, a herd of sheep running as nimbly as cats, a threshing floor ringed with stones like a miniature Stonehenge, and in the distance the *sierra* being pulled apart, range from range, by the mist.

The Tajo provides the reason for Ronda's existence, for apart from this incomparable natural defense, why should it have occurred to anyone to settle here? Only the unreliable irrigation provided by the Guadalevín offers relief in an environment largely copied from African deserts. The cliff abetted the inhabitants in their struggle against marauding armies, but the living was poor. Before the new affluence promoted by tourism, Rondeños picked olives, raised pigs, and cured ham. Until after the war, day laborers might hope to find employment for a hundred days a year, and the daily wage could be as low as three and a half pesetas, at a time when there were nine pesetas to the dollar. The Andalusia of those days has been described as the poorest region in Europe, and there were Andalusians, as reported in the newspapers of the day, who literally starved to death. Hence the chronic and permanent banditry. Hence the garrote set up outside the Chapel of Los Dolores in Ronda, where desperate peasants who had taken to robbery were brought to be strangled in batches of four—as recorded in macabre fashion by the figures carved in the church's porch.

Tajo Gorge Bridge

Unendurable poverty, and its long legacy of hatred, determined the atrocious aspects of the Spanish Civil War in Andalusia. It is widely asserted that the cliff in Ronda was the scene of the episode described in Hemingway's *For Whom the Bell Tolls* in which local supporters of the Franco re-

volt were compelled by cudgel-armed peasants to run the gaunt-
let before being tossed over the edge. There is no clear-cut evidence that this actually hap-
pened, and the subject is avoided
in local discussion, but it is not
denied that many hundreds of
civilians were murdered in the
town. With its capture by the
Nationalists, Republican sympa-
thizers were punished, as elsewhere in Andalusia, with
extreme severity. Broadcasting
from Seville, the nationalist general Queipo de Llano had said,
"For every person they [the government supporters] kill, I shall
kill ten, or perhaps even exceed
that proportion." There is no
doubt that he meant it.

"Panem Et Circensis" were the
Roman recipes for civil peace,
and there can be no doubt that
even when bread was in short
supply in Spain, fiestas, the
Spanish equivalent of circuses,
were provided in abundance.

I arrived in Ronda halfway
through the annual festivities
conducted in September, which,
although scheduled in the handsome official program to take
place between the eighth and
fourteenth of the month, had in-

> *Carts were piled exactly as
> for a capea except that
> the side toward the river was not
> enclosed. That was left open. Then
> Pablo ordered the priest to confess
> the fascists and give them the nec-
> essary sacraments....*
>
> *"While the priest was engaged in
> these duties, Pablo organized those
> in the plaza into two lines.*
>
> *"He placed them in two lines as
> you would place men for a rope
> pulling contest, or as they stand in
> a city to watch the ending of a bi-
> cycle road race with just room for
> the cyclists to pass between, or as
> men stood to allow the passage of
> a holy image in a procession. Two
> meters was left between the lines
> and they extended from the door
> of the* Ayuntamiento *clear across
> the plaza to the edge of the cliff.
> So that, from the doorway of the*
> Ayuntamiento, *looking across the
> plaza, one coming out would see
> two solid lines of people waiting.*
>
> *"They were armed with flails such
> as are used to beat out the grain
> and they were a good flail's length
> apart."*
>
> —Ernest Hemingway,
> *For Whom the Bell Tolls* (1940)

flated by tacking a full extra week of jollifications onto the front.
What was on offer was a marathon of pleasure guaranteed in the
end to reduce revelers to a state of exhaustion. Every day of the in-

terminable two weeks was crammed with such attractions as displays of horsemanship, shows put on by folklore groups invited from numerous countries, a concert by flamenco singers, pageantry by lovely ladies in old-style costumes, a carriage-driving contest, military parades to the music of stirring bands, a pentathlon, an "interesting" football match, a bicycle race, a procession of giants and "big-headed" dwarfs, a comic bullfight in which aspirant *toreros* dressed as firemen would squirt each other with fire hoses, a *novillada* fought with young bulls, and the celebrated annual *goyesca*, in which all participants are attired in the bullfighting regalia of the 18th century.

Those who are still on their feet at the end of each long, festive day are expected to make a night of it at the *feria* outside the town, in operation from 1:00 a.m. until dawn. Here *casetas* (temporary cottages) are for hire, where families entertain their friends, sherry flows like a river in spate, and professional Gypsy dancers and guitarists can be called in to keep the party going.

Alarm is often voiced at the inroads made by expanding fiestas into the serious business of living. Here is Don Rafael Manzano, a former director of the Alcázar of Seville, on the subject of his city's spring fair—now, according to Don Rafael, completely out of control—which Ronda has set itself to imitate, if not surpass. "Until recently, only rich people with no work could stay up and enjoy themselves all night. Now everybody tries to. If the parents stay up, so do the children as part of their democratic right. The result is my own children fall asleep over their books at school. As a nation we are in danger of forgetting that there is work to be done."

The main attractions of the Ronda fiesta are staged in its bullring—the excuse for the fiesta itself being to commemorate the birthday of Pedro Romero, a Rondeño who became the most

> *There is one town that would be better than Aranjuez to see your first bullfight in if you were only going to see one and that is Ronda. That is where you should go if you ever go to Spain on a honeymoon or if you ever bolt with anyone.*
>
> —Ernest Hemingway,
> *Death in the Afternoon* (1932)

famous bullfighter of all time. Romero invented the modern style
of bullfighting, conducted largely on foot. At a time when life was
notably short and brutish, he lived until the age of 85, having faced
his first bull as a boy of 8, and killed some 6,000 animals in all.
Pedro Romero attracted the attention and admiration of Francisco
Goya, and the archaic costumes worn in the annual bullfight in
homage to both men are based on the paintings from his *tauro-
maquia* collection, in which some paintings depict Romero in
action.

Ronda's bullring, scene of so many of Romero's exploits, is one
of the oldest, the largest, and the most elegant in existence. Its ex-
terior—with the exception of the splendid baroque main gate,
featured in the film of *Carmen*—appears of massive African simplicity, giving the illusion of an enormous white, slightly flattened
dome dominating the center of the town.

The museum it contains offers a wide though eccentric variety
of bullfighting memorabilia, with occasional bizarre items such as
a matador's pantaloons displaying the blood-stained rent through
which the wearer accidentally skewered himself with his own
sword. Possibly the first bullfight poster to be published advertises
the appearance of Pedro Romero, who, it was promised, would kill
sixteen bulls with his *cuadrilla* that afternoon. Could captured
Barbary pirates have been forced to fight in the ring in Goya's day?
Several prints show dark-faced bullfighters in turbans and flowing
robes defending themselves somewhat hopelessly with their
swords. These prints, the captions assure us, are based not upon fact
but upon the painter's imagination. Nevertheless, one wonders.

Ronda is devoid of self-conscious displays of the trappings of
antiquity. The monuments of Roman, Arabic, and Gothic occupation associate in a comfortable and matter-of-fact way with the
buildings of our day: the Minarete de San Sebastián next to an
ironmonger's shop and facing the bakery at the top of the Calle
Salvatierra, and the princely façade of the Salvatierra Palace itself
at its bottom in an environment of bars. Everywhere history is
taken for granted. The permanently crowded bar called La Verdad
("truth") in the Calle Pedro Romero has an ancient Arabic in-

scription running all around the doorway leading to the kitchen. It reads, THERE IS NO CONQUEROR BUT ALLAH. A remarkable declaration of an outlawed faith in a town in which the Inquisition once ruled. So much is forgotten, so much overlooked.

José Páez, who has written a book and many newspaper articles about the town, accompanied me .on a final stroll through its streets. It was the last day of the fiesta, and there were girls by the hundreds in Sevillian-style costumes roaming in groups, clicking their castanets, dancing, and singing in their high-pitched voices. Sometimes a man went with them, banging on a drum as they passed from street to street, leaving no corner or alleyway unvisited, as if beating the bounds of the town. José agreed that what we were witnessing could only be the vestiges of some bygone ceremony, by which the town had been cleansed of evil influences. The dancers seemed moved by compulsion, communicating a little of this to onlookers in their vicinity. As the current of excitement took possession, women put down shopping bags and abandoned babies in prams to join in, and once in a while, a man correctly dressed for the routine of an office or bank would stop to dance a few steps. It was a moment when one saw the fiesta in a new guise, not merely as the vehicle of popular enjoyment, but— at least in part—as a ritual left over from prehistory, once seen as essential to the well-being of the community.

Our walk ended in the splendid and gracious Alameda del Tajo Gardens, laid out in 1807 by a mayor who hit upon the ingenious and wholly successful method of raising funds for this project by imposing stiff fines upon citizens heard to blaspheme. Ronda is full of wildlife, and here it was present in concentrated form. Enormous diurnal moths hung like hummingbirds in suspension before the flowers they probed with their long proboscis. José, a student of nature, has produced a most interesting theory after a study of the behavior of vultures, which infallibly appear every year at this time to circle in the sky for an hour or so before flying off. It had been at least 50 years, he said, since the horses killed in the bullring were dragged to the edge of the cliff and thrown over for disposal by the vultures. Every year, nevertheless, the birds brought their young here on their first flights, as he supposed, to pass on to them the knowledge of the place where once there had always been food in abundance, which might possibly be provided once again.

We strolled to the edge of the cliff. The sun had just set, and shortly, stripped of its light, the *sierra* would lose both color and depth. Within half an hour, night would suddenly fall, and the mountainous shapes, reduced to a sharp-edged cutout against the still-luminous sky, would come very close to the town, filling the gardens with the hootings of enormous owls.

"I regard this town where I was born as an earthly paradise," José said, "and although I have traveled in many countries, I always return to it with gratitude and relief." After a moment of thought, he added, "People come to this spot to commit suicide. Sometimes I ask myself, Why do they not look at the view and change their minds?"

Norman Lewis has written thirteen novels and ten nonfiction works. His Voices from the Old Sea, A Dragon Apparent, *and* Golden Earth *are considered travel classics, and* Naples '44 *is widely considered one of the best books written about World War II. His most recent works are* A Goddess in the Stones: Travels in India, *and* An Empire of the East: Travels in Indonesia. *He lives with his family in Essex, England.*

*

The Romeros were a clan greatly gifted in the arena, but Pedro Romero at Ronda excelled his kind. And when his choice [for a wife] fell upon a beautiful *gitana*, the consternation of his family was hardly greater than that in every house wherein dwelt an unmarried maid....

Ronda is famous for what happened a few months later. One morning, Romero mounted his horse and set out for Málaga, where a peculiarly glorious triumph promised to await him. For several hours he rode, thinking only of Elena. Then of a sudden his mare shied, stumbled, and fell heavily. No bones were broken but the hero's legs were bruised and stiff. There was no fight for him that day.

Painfully he mounted. His horse limped slowly home and the clock in the ancient tower of Ronda church struck midnight as he reached his doorstep. The house was tight shuttered. All was dark and silent. Romero knocked with the light tap Elena knew so well. In an instant her arms would close about him and every ache would vanish. But there was no movement within, though his keen ears seemed to catch the slightest stir in an upper room. Romero shook the door till it almost gave on its hinges. At last it opened. His wife stood on the threshold, all loving tenderness, but the peach of her cheek seemed white in the pale moonlight, and the arms that clasped his neck were trembling....

A Spanish chamber is not apt to be overfurnished. Elena's contained a bed, a chair, and in one corner a huge vat ready for the autumn pressing. The half-crazed husband wrenched off the cover and there within, squatted like a toad, was a human figure. One look Romero took. A dozen times he stabbed blindly with his knife, then turned on his fainting wife, caught her up, dashed down the stairs and on through the streets till he came to the terrifying brink of the chasm of the Guadiaro. There, pausing for one second, he hurled his shrieking burden into the void....

It was determined that Romero should be arrested and held for trial. But prison and the *garrote* were not to that hero's liking. Before another midnight sounded he was off to the mountains and enthusiastically accepted as chief of a band of brigands.

Of his further exploits my friends did not enlighten me, but the episode I have described has a remarkable history. For, in after years, one Prosper Mérimée listened to the Ronda story and revolutionized it. Romero was transmuted into José, Elena, immortalized as *Carmen*.

—Ellery Sedgwick, "Spain in Easy Lessons,"
The Atlantic Monthly (1952)

JEFF GREENWALD

A Moment in the Master's Presence

A writer's whirlwind tour is punctuated
by Pablo Picasso.

WE LEFT TANGIER THE 27TH OF MARCH, ON THE AFTERNOON OF a beautiful spring day. As the ferry began the short journey toward Algeciras I stood at the stern in second class, holding a cigarette (sometimes you just need to hold a cigarette), and folded my arms over the rail.

In front of me, due south, was all of Africa, still unimaginably huge and foreboding. To the west lay the Atlantic, choppy and black, curving like olive brine toward the horizon. Eastward rose the southern of the Pillars of Hercules (or the Knees of Aphrodite, an image that more closely befit my sense of consummation) and, beyond that giant outcropping of stone, the vast Mediterranean Sea.

To the north, Spain and the European continent welled up like a gigantic green fungus, frighteningly civilized, full of high-speed trains and racy ads for the United Colors of Benetton.

The ferry turned into a long, narrow bay. To the starboard, the Rock of Gibraltar—Aphrodite's right knee—bent toward the sky. *A rite of passage,* I thought to myself; but the monolithic landmark, bristling with smokestacks and radio antennas, seemed less a tribute to our long perseverance than a monument to Britannic voodoo.

We docked in Algeciras half an hour late. The train to Madrid for our connection to Barcelona left in fifteen minutes. Everything depended on our clearing customs immediately and getting to the station as fast as humanly possible.

But there was a hitch. When we presented our papers at immigration the Spanish officer confiscated Sally's Australian passport and tossed it without ceremony into his tiny vestibule.

"*No puede pasar,*" he declared without looking up. "You cannot enter Spain. Return to Tangier."

This was a surprise; the French consul in Tangier had assured Sally that her French visa was also valid for entry into Spain. A small detail, unfortunately, had slipped his mind: the diplomatic concession among France, Australia and Spain had expired five months earlier.

Sally begged and pleaded, but in vain. The agent wouldn't even look at us. Once every fifteen seconds he'd just shake his head and repeat: "Return to Tangier." I felt like we'd landed on a talking Monopoly board.

"Okay, here's what we'll do," she said. "You go on to Barcelona..."

"Forget it. There's no way I'm leaving you here. I'll go back too."

"*No.* You go on to Barcelona. Take a day or two to write. Leave a note at American Express, and I'll meet you as soon as I arrive."

"I can't let you do that."

"Why not?"

"Because...because...well, it's *Tangier,* for God's sake." The truth was, I couldn't think of any reason that wasn't patronizing, sexist or both.

"Go," she insisted. "Don't miss your train."

"Look." I motioned over to the main immigration office, where two uniformed men were smoking black tobacco. "Ask them. They're in charge; this guy's just a badge."

Sally nodded and walked across the now-empty customs room. The officers lowered their cigarettes. I watched her back as she charmed them. A minute later the agent who had taken Sally's passport was summoned; a minute after that she came skipping back, clutching her passport and waving both thumbs in the air.

We grabbed our packs and raced for the taxi stand. A driver named an extortionate price. Without bothering to bargain we tossed in our gear and sped off for the station, arriving on the dot of 9:15. The place was utterly empty, save for a single train. An attendant materialized, and I grabbed his arm.

"Madrid?"

"*Sí*...Madrid."

We leapt aboard as the train started moving. Seconds later we were pulling out of the station into the Spanish omelette sunset, leaving Algeciras, Africa and the Strait of Gibraltar behind.

Europe was a known quantity, and an expensive one; we had no desire to tarry long there. We planned to blow through Spain and Italy with the windy invisibility of a Pope's plea for peace, mindful of Sally's dwindling finances and my own obsessive compulsion to reach Turkey and make my way to Asia.

We could not, however, zip across Europe without paying homage to two cities, for there were sights in both Barcelona and Florence that I felt magically drawn to see.

Barcelona is a place where everything is straining at the edges. The city swells with intoxicating energy, bursting the seams of its thick Spanish wineskin. It's a city infectious with art, a fabulous city where the devil-may-care Catalonian spirit has exploded into full bloom. Nowhere else has a specific geographical resonance inspired so many artists—Miró, Picasso, and Dalí among them—to throw caution so fearlessly to the winds. Even the chocolate galleries are a revelation, their artfully sculpted birds, mammals and dinosaurs peering over the huge fitted cobblestones of the Gothic Quarter. We passed one shop that sold paprika in eight savory shades; another that offered only handmade candles; a third specializing in gold-ribbed fountain pens. Every artisan in the city seems consumed by the obsession to create a masterpiece. And scattered amid the storefronts and galleries stand the startlingly inventive cathedrals, *casas* and fountains of Antonio Gaudí, the wildly prolific and conceptually outrageous Catalán architect whose confectionery buildings rise and wriggle in fantastic shapes that we recognize, instantly and intuitively, from our dreams.

We spent hours in the Picasso Museum. It was a revelation to see Pablo Picasso's famous pigeon drawings, executed in 1890; for though it's quite common to look at what Picasso drew at fifty and quip, "My eight-year-old could do that," it's far more difficult to find the fifty-year-old who can draw as well as Picasso could at eight. It is said that Pablo's father, an accomplished painter in his own right, was so impressed by his son's early sketches that he handed his own palette and brushes over to the boy. "I will never paint again," José Ruiz Blasco declared in 1894. "I now dedicate my career to yours." Picasso was then thirteen. The relationship remained powerful, for many of Picasso's early works are studies of José Ruiz. The portraits convey dignity, strength and an enormous capacity for commitment, traits Blasco must have bequeathed to his son, who pursued the same career with unflagging passion for 85 years.

Picasso's mastery of line and color grew like a cinder cone. Hot new powers sprang from his hand with each passing month. By eighteen he had completed *First Communion*, an oil painting that compares favorably to the best work of Vermeer. The most impressive thing about him, though, is that he seems to have lived forever. He was a geological force, shaping the epoch of modern art.

Viewing Picasso's work always has a profound effect on me, calling up an almost unbearable nostalgia for the years when, before dedicating myself to writing, I concentrated on the visual arts. Looking at his bold, playful ceramics made me want to retire my laptop, move into a bright studio (in Barcelona, Oaxaca or anywhere the light is good, the food is cheap and the women have black eyes) and get my priorities straight. For the argument expressed by Picasso is that man lives to make visual art; that nothing we do, short of sex, can be half as vital or a tenth as much fun. (And they are by no means, as he delighted in pointing out, mutually exclusive.)

But my disenchantment with writing had little to do with Picasso. It was symptomatic only of my exhaustion. Unlike the suspiciously prolific Spaniard, I do not sip from a bottomless well of inspirational nectar. During the thirteen weeks of our voyage my relationship with writing had run hot and cold. There had been days when I'd felt completely fluid, and my prose poured forth like oil from a '72 Chevy Nova. Other times I'd been content to sketch out a scene, or a bit of dialogue, and let the day's work go at that.

Since Marrakesh, though, I'd been in a slump. Places were going by fast, and the real-time task of measuring the size of the world seemed beyond me. Sally and I had begun lapsing, not into culture shock exactly, but into fugues of temporal disorientation. We experienced the dizzy incredulity that comes from being whisked from country to country, culture to culture, in a period of time so compressed that there is no opportunity to digest one course before being compelled to devour another. Boarding the train in Algeciras, zooming off to Madrid for a connection to Barcelona, neither Sally nor I

> *A río revuelto ganancia de pescadores.*
> *It is good fishing in troubled waters.*
>
> —Fernan de Rojas,
> *La Celestina, Act II* (1502)

was able to comprehend that our journey had already touched the soil of nine countries and stirred the waters of three seas.

"This is not a trip about Being There," I sighed as we left the Museum. "It's a trip about *getting* there."

"It's about Being There while getting there," Sally parried.

She was right, of course. But when I turned on my laptop to seek that territory I found no There there.

As we were about to leave Barcelona I stopped at a covered bazaar to shop for fruit, olives and cheese. Sally waited outside, guarding our gear on the crowded sidewalk. She glanced up for a split second to locate me and her daypack was instantly stolen. Inside were her toiletries, spiritual books, and private journal.

After a brief display of rage and disbelief, Sally accepted the loss with good grace. "At least it was mine they took," she said. "I've got my passport and traveler's checks in my money belt. Your daypack has everything: your money, your camera…"

"… and my computer."

"Jesus." We stood helplessly by the curb, caught in a strange little eddy of grief and gratitude.

"If you'd gone back to Tangier," I reflected, "this never would have happened."

"That's right." She managed a laugh, and took the groceries in her free arm. "The blessings are always there. It's just a question of recognizing them."

Jeff Greenwald is a contributing editor for Wired *magazine and the author of* Mr. Raja's Neighborhood, Shopping for Buddhas, *and his most recent book,* The Size of the World: Once Around without Leaving the Ground, *the product of a seven-month trip around the world without the benefit of aircraft, from which this piece was excerpted.*

✳

I was riveted by Pablo Picasso's stark *Guernica*, his monumental cry of pain at the horrors of war, a gift from the artist that he would not permit to be sent to Spain until fascism ended. During most of the decades-long wait, *Guernica* was on loan to New York's Museum of Modern Art. I saw it there countless times. In its Madrid setting, placed well behind a wall of glass suitable for housing a whale, it seemed entirely new—more pertinent. I now saw that it was inspired at least in part by Goya's white-hot painting of the Spanish anguish during the Napoleonic Wars, *The Third of May, 1808.*

—Gordon Cotler, "Morning in Madrid," *Travel Holiday*

JILL BURBERRY

In a Majorcan Garden

Persistence pays off for one gardening aficionado.

IT TOOK ME THREE YEARS TO GET INTO ARAXA. PERHAPS THAT IS
as it should be. To an English ear Araxa sounds like a magical kingdom and my endeavours have the flavour of a zany folktale. Araxa
is the original name of an Arab garden in Majorca that is now
called La Raixa. I learnt about it in an article by Russel Page, the
international landscape artist who died a few years ago. He restored
the Alhambra gardens in Granada. In the article he also described
Al Fabia, a garden created by Benhabet when he was governor of
Pollensa and Inca. It fired my imagination and I made up my mind
to visit them.

My first opportunity was in 1987. I was staying in Palma,
Majorca, and Al Fabia is not far away. It was open to the public and
is easily accessible by car, or there is a train from Palma to Bunyola.
Al Fabia is an hour's pleasant walk farther on along narrow roads
between fields of orange and lemon trees.

Majorca was under Arab control from 902 A.D. until it was re-
captured by "James the Conqueror," of Aragón, in 1229. Benhabet
surprisingly welcomed James with a present: "Full twenty beasts
laden with barley, kids, fowls, grapes," Henry C. Shelley tells us in
Majorca, which was published by Methuen in 1925. An old guide-

book says he fell in love with a beautiful Christian girl. Benhabet laid out Al Fabia with the traditional eight terraces of the Moslem paradise. Happily the original design is unchanged and the garden still contains lovely pebble-patterned paths, pools and water effects. But the plantings I saw were old, overgrown and in need of renewal.

La Raixa is near Bunyola too, but it had been sold into private hands and closed to the public. In 1988, with the help of a map, I found the entrance. In fact there were two drives with gates. One had a "no entry" sign for cars and the other was marked "private." Once more I gave up. But last February I determined to try again.

Robert, a friend, offered to drive there and parked by the entrance that was barred to cars. We skulked guiltily along the winding lane past orchards of pale pink and white almond trees, which just that week had exploded into thousands of blossoms. Armies of olive trees, said to be around 1,000 years old, sprouted gargoyle-faced from their gnarled trunks. The regiment to our left was twisted and bent by the wind into a state of retreat. Those on our right were almost erect and apparently bewildered by victory. A buzzard wheeled overhead, dropping his prey and swooping to recapture it before it fell to earth.

At the top of the drive we came to a fine archway, built for Cardinal Despuigs. He acquired possession of the estate by marrying into the Sa Forteza family.

> *he natural beauty of Majorca was a solace to George Sand when she spent the calm of the year 1838 with her consumptive lover, Frédéric Chopin, watching his health and their romance bleed away. "It's a green Helvetia," she wrote, "under a Calabrian sky, and with the silent solemnity of the Orient." From the balcony of their cell in the Carthusian monastery in Valldemosa, she perceived the "immense, infinitely detailed and inexhaustibly varied" ensemble of sea and countryside and noted, "I should advise those who are consumed by artistic vainglory to look well and often at such scenes."*
>
> —G. Y. Dryansky, "Almond Isle," *Condé Nast Traveler*

It had previously been given as a reward to the Count of Ampurias for services to James and later to the Sacristan of Genoa who sent soldiers to help him. We went under the arch into a formally laid out drive flanked on both sides by broad terraces. On the right, lion masks set in a high wall spewed water. To the left was a charming pool and lovely views over the farmland and orchards we had just passed through. A dog barked savagely.

We braved the dog and went under another arch into a cobbled courtyard containing a well and the massive trunk of an ancient chestnut tree. A row of palm trees was almost leaning against one wall of the house. An elderly caretaker told us the house was private and that we could not go in. With the little Spanish I knew I tried to persuade him: "For three years I have come to Majorca just to see your garden. Every year I have found it closed. I am a gardener. Could I possibly see it?" The old man called to a woman in an upstairs room. We never saw her. She was probably his wife. She might have been the German opera singer who we were told had bought the estate for half a million pounds.

After a few words with her he pointed to a flight of stone steps that appeared to vanish into the house and said something in Spanish. Robert said that we were to go up. So we climbed two storeys of the vaulted staircase which led through to the other side of the building and out in the upper garden at the foot of a beautiful flight of Italian steps; a miniature of those at the Villa d'Este in Rome. At the top stood a statue of Apollo. The steps were lined with masked faces that once gushed water and whose mossy beards now dripped greenish moisture. There were stone vases on the balustrade and four rather broken muse-like figures, probably left from a hoard of classical treasures that Cardinal Despuigs brought back from Rome and displayed in his home. At the foot of the stairs, from either side, a lion looked down. One seemed to be laughing. The steps straddled the eight traditional terraces that originally led to the harem which no longer existed. It was sited in this totally secluded area for the protection of the women. The stairs and accompanying water effects, the formal terraces to our right and the narrower terraces to our left, indeed all the garden and its broken-down water courses were in desperate need of repair. We decided it would cost its owner another half million pounds to put right. But oh the pleasure in exploring it as it was!

From the top of the steps we walked along the left-hand terraces and found ourselves looking down on a man-made lake with a sheer drop on its far side. Three of its sides were straight like a huge water tank, but a wavy sculptured shoreline edged the path along the bottom of the hill. There were seats from which to enjoy the wide expanse of sky and pine trees rippling in the lake. A high waterfall tumbled generously into it. Concrete jetties stretched under the water, probably containing pipes and fonts for water jets. A broken aqueduct ran along the far wall graced by a terracotta figure of a boy in his Sunday best. One of his legs was broken. Through a gate stretched more terraces; probably also part of the estate.

However, there was still plenty to explore on our side. So we went on up the hill. Each terrace had a narrow path on the edge and against the hillside were neglected plantings that included cacti, pelargonius, agaves, yucca, lavender, montbretia, asphodel, cistus and deutzia; all gone wild. Towards the middle of the hill was a grotto. Within, a thick-set stalagmite had grown centimetre by centimetre, from centuries of dripping water, into the form of an old man. Beside him a stalactite pillar stretched from ceiling to floor.

As we followed layer upon layer of those terraces, magnificent vistas sprang into sight over the sheer edge of one face of the hill. An octagonal look-out tower was sited to take full advantage of the view. Its lower room was empty, but as I peered through the shutters of the upper storey I nearly screamed. For in the dim light I slowly made out four seated figures, sprawling around a dead fire. When my eyes had adapted to the darkness I perceived that the figures were papier mâché models probably left from a tableau created for historical effect in the days when the house was open to the public. I said nothing but watched Robert's reaction. He was silent for a few minutes. Then he raised his beret to the phantoms within.

Up again to the next building which was a chapel. Inside were an altar, a crucifix and the most rascally looking friar I have ever seen. He too was papier mâché. Stopping to regain my composure,

I looked on to the valley far below at what appeared to be a ter-racotta river. A closely packed flock of sheep hurried along the gulley, their recently dipped coats glowing rusty-brown in the sun.

On and up to yet another building at the very top. It was empty. In corners were stoops for holy water, and Arabic inscriptions ran above the windows. Had it been the home of a holy hermit? Coming down we took another set of terraces that from time to time met and interzigzagged with those we had already traversed. They offered different but equally delightful views.

On returning to England I found a book, *Mallorca the Magnificent* by Nina Lassey Duryea, at the Hispano and Luzo Brazilian Council library in London which contains a few pages which describe La Raixa as it was in its prime: "a mass of ver-dure—cacti, palms, plane trees, heliotrope, fifteen-feet-high roses, massed canna lillies beside dim pools, purple and white irises, nar-cissus, violets. A thousand perfumes mingle, and butterflies and birds play on the mossy paths. Everywhere is the sound of running water from runnels of yellowed marble six inches wide which ir-rigate the flowerbeds." Another passage continues: "Then one climbs up through lovely paths to the top of the hill, passing Moorish lookouts, and comes upon an artificial lake on the sum-mit." How could we have missed it? Is it still there? I must go back if it is.

Jill Burberry is a professional gardener for the Royal Parks in London and a freelance writer. Her interests include Islamic art, metalwork, and calligraphy.

⋆

We were displaying an architectural interest in a small house that had a fine Moorish doorway and brilliant green sun-shutters over its windows, when a little girl who was sitting on the doorstep rose and came shyly to-ward us. She was eating a slice of something that looked like bread and honey, from which she had already taken several large bites; her mouth was sticky with the honey. She stopped within a yard of us, smiled, and offered her slice to us.

Now it is the custom for Majorcans to offer to the stranger a share of their food.... In all innocence, because we wished to show our friendliness and to avoid hurting her feelings, we thanked her, took the slice and had each a small nibble.

The girl watched us, and when the second nibble had been taken a most disconcerting change came over her face. Her brown eyes opened wide and her mouth drooped at the corners; then her lips quivered and suddenly she burst into tears.

Clearly we had blundered. Her offer had been a mere gesture of welcome; she had not intended that we should accept it.

—Gordon West, *Jogging Round Majorca* (1929)

BARBARA SAVAGE

✦ ✦ ✦

Biking Cataluña

A pair of cyclists find themselves embraced
by Catalans at every turn.

IT RAINED THE MORNING WE LEFT BARCELONA. DOLLY AND SANTY
tried to convince us to wait and leave another day, but we assured
them that we had plenty of experience cycling in the wet. And besides, we yearned to be on our way. Our only concern as we ped-
aled out of the city was the Spanish drivers. Negotiating Spain's
single-lane back roads full of potholes and rocks would be tough
enough; we didn't need maniac drivers to make things worse.

Even with the rain, it felt great to be outdoors and pedaling, to
get away from the crowds, breathe the fresh air, and feel our muscles working again. We headed north along the Mediterranean
coast toward Cadaqués, a fishing village two hundred miles north
of Barcelona, where we planned to spend the next month or so
waiting out the remainder of the cold winter weather. The narrow
coastal roads between Barcelona and Cadaqués were steep and
winding, and we made good use of our extra gears, which took the
knee-wrenching strain out of climbing and allowed us to relax and
enjoy our spectacular surroundings. The rocky coastal mountains
were spotted with pines. Herds of goats wandered across the road.
Sandy beaches curled up at the foot of the sheer cliffs, and the

turquoise and deep-blue waters of the Mediterranean were sprinkled with fishing boats.

There was very little traffic on the roads. The deluge of tourists from central and northern Europe wouldn't begin to arrive for another three or four months, and the commercial traffic kept to the inland *autopistas.* The occasional trucks and cars that did pass us only added to our already high spirits. The drivers never honked impatiently or tried to squeeze past when they approached us from the rear. Instead, just like the folks in Washington State, they slowed down, shifted into their lower gears, and crept along behind us through the twists and turns until it was perfectly safe to pass. When they eased by, they always waved hysterically and called out words of encouragement.

The drivers weren't the only people who shouted and waved to us in Cataluña, the northeastern section of Spain. Whenever the Catalán farmers or villagers spotted us pedaling up the road, they stopped their work and yelled: *¡Estupendo! ¡Fabuloso! ¡Qué coraje!* or *Vaya con Dios.*

We took our time getting to Cadaqués, stopping at most of the beaches and pueblos along the way and talking with the people we met. At lunch time each day we would pull into a town or village and head straight for its open-air marketplace to buy oranges, tomatoes, and cheese, then hit the bakery for a loaf of crusty white bread, and one of the dozen tiny grocery shops for yogurt.

The marketplaces were always jammed with women, dressed in dark sweaters and skirts, who pushed and squeezed their way from one vegetable, fruit, meat, poultry, or cheese stand to the next, in search of the day's best bargains. Each woman pulled her own shopping cart, a nylon rectangular basket on wheels. The women bargained and gossiped and discussed the morning's local news at each stand, which made shopping a time-consuming process. Many of the women, trailed by their *niños,* spent an hour or more every day shopping at the marketplace and the stores around town.

When Larry and I pulled into a marketplace, scores of women closed in around us to see what it was that foreigners liked to eat. Spaniards were proud of their fruits and cheeses, and it always pleased them that we asked for Valencia oranges and goat cheese. And when they discovered that we could speak Spanish, they quickly set to work digging out of us all they wanted to know. The women standing closest to us did the asking, and our answers were passed along to those at the back of the crowd. Within a matter of minutes, every human in the marketplace knew where we were from, where we were going, how old we were, and what our marital status was. The women invariably asked if we had any children, and my response made them frown and shake their heads.

> *One fish-seller in the Boqueria market came to regard me as her personal property: she made it clear that I could only buy fish from her. She would lie in wait for me as I wandered from stall to stall and then pounce, demanding to know what I wanted, and insist that she had it at the best price. If I hinted that the prawns she wanted me to buy had been frozen, she would protest vociferously, calling people over to attest to the freshness of all the fish and seafood on her stall. She had me hooked.*
>
> —Colm Tóibín,
> *Homage to Barcelona*

"No children? What a shame," they would all mutter. Then someone would pat me on the arm and tell me not to worry, there was still time; the children would come.

We ate our lunches on the benches in the towns' tree-lined plazas, crowded with elderly Catalán men dressed in their traditional black berets, black pants, and dark sweaters. As soon as Larry and I pulled into a plaza, the old men would hobble over to examine our bikes and find out what we were all about. They usually asked if we were French, since the French were such bicycle fanatics and we were too fair to be Spanish. When they discovered that we were Americans, they would start in on how uncle so-and-so and cousin such-and-such had gone to the New World to seek their fortunes in places like Chicago, Miami, and New York City. The old Catalans talked about the Civil War and the atrocities Franco had inflicted upon Cataluña, while younger people discussed inflation, unemployment, and the Basque terrorists.

Each night we pitched our tent on a sandy deserted beach and fell asleep curled up in our warm down cocoons listening to the rise and fall of the swells and the splash of the waves against the rocky cliffs. In the mornings, before it was light, the muffled putt-putt-putt sounds of the fishing boats coaxed us awake, and we would climb out of our tent and watch the lights from the boats' huge kerosene lamps drift farther out to sea and the sun rise from behind the water's horizon. After stretching exercises and breakfast, we scrubbed our dishes with handfuls of sand and rinsed them in the sea while a salty breeze showered us with mist. The few fishermen still floating close to shore waved good morning to us, and the seagulls flew in to devour our scraps.

On January 26, Larry and I pumped over a ridge in the steep coastal mountains near the French border and glided down into the village of Cadaqués. We had visited Cadaqués several times in 1974, when we were working in Barcelona, and we figured it would be a perfect place to spend the next five weeks. The village was surrounded by terraced mountains and miles of jagged, unspoiled coastline, perfect for hiking. Its tough, proud fishermen had fought to prevent ugly, tourist high-rises, which littered much of the Costa Brava between the French border and Barcelona, from swallowing its tiny niche of the Mediterranean coast. And too, Cadaqués was home base for the surrealist painter, Salvador Dalí. Artists from all over the world journeyed to his village to live and work.

After we rolled into Cadaqués, we decided to look for a cheap *pensión* rather than pitch our tent on the outskirts of town, since we were expecting weeks of cold, rainy weather. We left our bikes at the waterfront and walked back along the steep, narrow cobblestone pathways that ran from the bay up into the hills. The pathways were lined by one- and two-story whitewashed houses; women sat out front in their wooden chairs, sewing and mending clothes. As we walked, I stopped to ask the women if they knew of any private *pensiones* where Larry and I could stay.

"I know just the place for you two," said one of the women who nodded and gestured for us to follow her. "I don't know if you know it, but Spanish *pensiones* are usually so noisy it's impossible to sleep in them. The Spaniards who live in them stay up late and talk loud and turn their televisions up loud. But this place is different. It's small and quiet and clean. It'll be perfect for you. You'll see."

Not far from Cadaqués, in Figueras, is the Teatre-Museu Dalí, a museum designed by the artist for his work. A row of enormous white cement eggs lines the roof, piles of truck tires act as columns, and the walls are pink stucco. Inside, a panoply of Dalí jokes awaits, including a room arranged to mimic the face of Mae West (her lips become an inviting red sofa). Dalí died in 1989.

—LMc

The woman led us up a pathway that opened into a courtyard with a stone floor edged by gigantic earthern flowerpots. The whitewashed houses that surrounded the courtyard all had varnished doors and wrought-iron balconies crammed with more potted flowers and cactus.

The woman rapped on one of the doors, and a short Catalán lady dressed in a black skirt and a dark-green blouse emerged. The two women jabbered together in their Catalán dialect for a couple of minutes, then the woman who had brought us introduced us to Señora Nadal.

"My friend here has a few vacant rooms she will show you. I'm going shopping now, but I'll be seeing you later. I live in the house across the alley to the left. Oh yes, and my name is Señora Casañas. *¡Adiós!*"

Larry and I followed Señora Nadal into the house adjoining hers, upstairs, and into a living room full of antique furniture. Huge earthen tiles covered the floor of the room, the walls were white-washed, and the balcony looked down onto the courtyard below. A long hallway led from the living room, past three bedrooms and a bathroom, into a large kitchen.

All of the bedrooms were vacant, and I chose the far one, with the window that opened onto the cobblestone alley behind the *pensión*.

Every morning, as soon as we got up, Larry and I went for a run along the waterfront to the end of bay. The first morning the village fishermen, preparing their boats and nets for their day at sea, stared at us curiously. We waved and smiled; they waved back, but hesitantly. The next day we waved and wished them good luck; they waved back more enthusiastically. The following morning they shouted and waved to us first. From then on the fishermen cheered us on every morning and stopped to talk with us whenever they spotted us in town.

Once, as we were coming back from a hike to the lighthouse, Lorenzo Riera motioned for us to sit down beside him on the wooden bench he was occupying. Lorenzo was one of the dozens of ancient Cataláns who spent each day following the sun from plaza to plaza. Neither Larry nor I had met Lorenzo before, so we were anxious to hear what he had to say.

"My house faces your kitchen window in Señora Nadal's," Lorenzo explained. "I've heard you two in there speaking Spanish, so I know you can understand me. I've seen you sitting in the plazas. You know all the right ones except for this one here. You should sit here after five o'clock and not over there in the Torradet where you usually sit. Anyway, I've decided you're all right. You're not like those other foreigners that are always getting wild on drugs. I'd like to talk to you."

"Fine," grinned Larry, "then why don't you sit right there and tell us something about yourself."

That, of course, was exactly what Lorenzo had in mind, and as soon as Larry made his request, a wide, toothless smile shot across the old man's wrinkled face. He patted his beret, then leaned his head into Larry's to get a better view of who he was talking to. Lorenzo's eyesight wasn't what it used to be back in the '20s when he was a young man.

"How old do you think I am?" he asked.

"Sixty," I answered. I was lying, but I knew 60 would please him.

"I'm 81 years old," he declared triumphantly.

"No kidding. You sure don't look it!" Larry whistled.

Lorenzo leaned back in the bench and smiled. He patted his beret again, and then he put his face back up against Larry's and continued talking. He spoke in a mixture of Castilian Spanish and Catalán, but we managed to understand most of what he said.

"I was a barber when I was young. That was a *very* long time ago. Back then, being a barber was terrible on account of the lice. I hated the lice," he muttered, shaking his head in disgust. "They were always in everybody's beard and hair.

"Thirty céntimos. That's what I got for shaving a fellow twice a week for a month. Nowadays 30 céntimos is worth nothing. Why there's 100 céntimos in a peseta, and you can't buy nothing nowadays with a peseta, except maybe a piece of candy.

"I worked hard all my life to make a living. Folks worked hard back then when I was younger, and almost everybody was poor. Back then, buying a cup of coffee in a bar was a big expense. But now it's all different. Folks don't know what hard work and poverty is anymore. They work less and have more money now, but they spend it all. Nowadays, instead of only buying a cup of coffee, you gotta have snacks first, and then brandy after the coffee. Yessir, folks are soft now. Why, if they had to work hard and didn't have much money, like it used to be, they'd probably all go off and shoot themselves."

Lorenzo paused here just long enough to move away from the shadow that was creeping up on his end of the bench.

"When I was young, Cadaqués was a whole lot smaller than this. But a lot of the old families are still here. My children still live here. They take care of me now that my wife is gone. I live with one of my daughters and her family, and she cooks all my meals for me."

Lorenzo hesitated again, this time to look at his watch. It was two o'clock, time for his midday meal.

"I'll eat a big meal now; salad, lentil stew, fish, and bread and wine, and then I'll take my siesta. I'm an old man now, and my children take care of me. That's the way it is in Spain. The children care for their parents when they get old. That's the way it should be. I cared for them now they care for me.

"Well, I've got to go now. My daughter doesn't like it when I'm late because the food gets cold waiting for me. Now you remember what I told you about this plaza here. You come here after five. This is the only place in Cadaqués that catches the last of the sun."

After biking around the world and writing Miles from Nowhere, *from which this piece was adapted, Barbara Savage died in a cycling accident in California. Her husband, Larry, and The Mountaineers, her publisher, established the "Barbara Savage/*Miles from Nowhere *Memorial Award" for the best unpublished adventure travel manuscript.*

✳

There was such a wind over the sea, such a wind howling that when I opened the balcony shutters they were nearly blown off their hinges and when I stepped out onto the large tiled balcony the wind whistled in my ears and blew so hard that I had to go back in and shut the window. I went back into the room, relieved by the quiet and the calm. It was a day for staying indoors.

The wind of Cadaqués, I learned, was called *La Tramontana*; it usually lasted for three days, but it could last longer and had already been blowing for two days. Who knew when it would end?

—Colm Tóibín, Homage to Barcelona

Leaving Madrid

*What do you do when your past becomes
like a foreign country?*

It is my last Christmas in Madrid, and we are throwing a party, Miguel and I, bigger than all the other parties we have thrown before. Candles flicker on a homemade altar; two couples dance to no music in the center of the room; in a corner someone lights a pipe. Miguel approaches from behind, leans into me, whispers in my ear, "Hey, Cinderella, want to dance?"

I shake my head. The smell of hashish mixes with the smell of the Christmas tree, the spilled beer, the marinated anchovies, the cigarettes, the sputtering candles.

Silently, I tiptoe out of the living room, grab my keys, and sneak out the front door of the flat. Without waiting for the elevator, I run down the six flights of stairs, open up the big, green doors of the portal, and stumble out into the cold.

It's my party, I think. *I can leave if I want to.*

A few taxis linger on the streets of Madrid; a few late-night partiers stagger home. It feels like snow. A white Christmas. My last Christmas in Madrid. White snow, black soot, a grey sky. The pipes will freeze. I'll have to order more coal from the coal store. "Some chips of wood, please, too." Much easier to light the stove.

I'll go to the brandy store and order more brandy. It will be cold outside, while we stay warm in.

I walk fast through the streets of Madrid. Past the *panadería,* the smell of bread coming out of ovens. Past La Luna Discotheque, people spilling out onto the street. I am wearing a dress that's black and full-skirted, like Cinderella. I imagine myself invisible and invincible.

I run up the Paseo del Prado. Bare trees line the avenue. I remember the trees as I first saw them three summers ago, full, lush, spanning like a canopy over the open-air cafés along the boulevard. I cut up Calle Alcalá through La Puerta Alcalá, *allí está,* past the *correos,* past the *Guernica,* past the Prado. In front of me, quiet and empty like a ghost town, El Parque del Retiro. The Park of Retreat.

I rub my hands against my cheeks, run through the big iron gates of the park, inhale the cold, feel my lungs expand. The sky is turning dark blue in the east. The kiosks and the *terrazas* are empty, closed. Chairs piled on chairs, piled on tables, piled on tables. No loud Americans asking directions, asking waiters in the park where the nearest English bookstore is, asking how long Franco has been dead. No eighteen-year-old American servicemen ordering gin and tonics in the middle of the park in the middle of the day.

Alone in the Park of Retreat.

I remember the park as I saw it the first time. It was the August that broke all previous heat records. Miguel and I wandered the city that August as if living a dream, the sun high and white all afternoon long. I watched the heat waves move like endless oceans in front of me. Whole families slept in the middle of the day, came out at night. Whole families, four-year-old children playing in the plaza at four o'clock in the morning. I never slept that whole August that broke all previous heat records. Spaniards slept during the day, but I couldn't sleep then; I wasn't accustomed to it. Instead I wandered the streets, navigated the oceans of airwaves, looking for anything that was open, a sign of life in the middle of the day, in the middle of Madrid.

That August I memorized a quote from Salman Rushdie's *Midnight's Children* as if it explained everything:

> Heat, gnawing at the mind's division between fantasy and
> reality, made anything seem possible; the half-waking chaos
> of afternoon siestas fogged men's brains, and the air was
> filled with the stickiness of aroused desire. What grows best
> in the heat: fantasy; unreason; lust.

In the Retiro that August afternoon with Miguel, a singer sang *Gracias a la Vida*. We gave her lots of money. "An unheard of amount for Spain," Miguel said. Then he took an eyelash from my cheek. "Close your eyes. Make five wishes." He joined his hands, each finger glued to the corresponding finger of the other hand, put the eyelash between one set of fingers. "Open your eyes," he said. "Remember your five wishes." Then he touched each set of fingers to his nose, making a semi-circle. "Wish number one, wish number two, wish number three. Wherever the lash be, the wish will come true for you." I cheated. I made it easy. In five different ways, I wished for the same thing: I want Miguel. I want you. I want the man sitting across from me. I want the man who gives unheard of amounts of money to a girl singing in the park. I want the man with my eyelash between his fingers.

I slow my pace once I'm in the middle of the park, breathless at the sight of the lake: calm, still, like smooth blue glass. The sky is turning a dark sky-at-dawn blue. The clock of the *correos* rings six times. It feels like snow.

All the rowboats are tied up to the pier behind the locked gate. I take off my shoes, hike up my black Cinderella dress, climb up the fence, hop over into the land of the boat man. The nearest boat beckons, black on the blue lake. I untie the knot, throw my shoes in the bottom of the boat, jump in. First, I row around the perimeter of the lake. Row to the middle of the lake, row around the middle in circles. The oars hit the cold water—slap, slap, slap— shattering in ripples the blue glass.

On the shore of the lake behind the fence, a family of Gypsies appears. A young girl leading a baby goat points to me in the middle of the lake. "*Mamá, mamá,*" she cries. "A lady in the middle of the lake. A lady in a black Cinderella dress, rowing in circles."

I hear the Gypsy women call out to me as they have done for three years. "*Oye guapa, ven aquí, guapa. Te digo el futuro, guapa. Ven aquí, te digo el futuro.*"

I look to the shore, but no one is there. The park is empty, quiet, still. "Wait a minute," I whisper. "If you can read the future, can you tell me anything about the past?"

I had never intended to stay in Madrid so long, but there was something intoxicating, addictive, about the city, and it wasn't just Miguel. It was the way Christmas lasted two weeks; the way everyone partied in the streets; the way the sky went on forever from the center of Castile. It was easy to stay in Madrid back then; the city opened her arms wide to me like a lover or a mother, took me in.

My second week in Madrid, I was at a café having *copas,* listening to a woman play Beethoven on a piano, a man across the bar staring at me. *Turn away,* I thought, *I'm not interested. Go away. I'm just a tourist. Not interested.* A moment later, next to me, the man asked for a cigarette. "Where are you from? You're not Spanish."

"American," I said, offering a Fortuna.

"No thanks. I don't really smoke. My name's Miguel. Ham sandwich please, no mayonnaise. That's all the English I remember. I was in New York once."

Go away, I thought, *I'm really not interested. Déjame en paz.* I was listening to a woman play Beethoven as I had never heard before. Her head never lifted from the piano; her thick, black hair cascaded down her back; her fingers pounded the keys.

After the concert the man said: "Can I walk you home?"

"No. It's okay. I'm fine."

"Please."

Twenty minutes later in front of a window, he grabbed my hand. "This is my window," he said. "I made this window." I didn't know what he meant. I looked closely at the glass; it looked like regular glass. "I'm an *escaparatista*."

An escape artist, I tried to understand.

"Not the glass," he said, laughing. "What's inside. The display." Inside the window were three mannequins, one gold, one silver, one black, wearing helmets, draped in golden mesh, holding pistols.

Perhaps more than in most places, it is necessary to be a bit open, a bit trusting in Madrid.

Madrid, like most great cities, is a state of mind. You cannot be in Madrid and act as if you are in Chicago.

—Ann and Larry Walker,
A Season in Spain

Is it a firearms store? A mannequin store? Do they sell hats?

"Watches," Miguel said, reading my mind. "They sell watches." On each mannequin, four watches, one on each wrist, one on each ankle, some with diamonds, others with rubies.

"It's my specialty," Miguel said. "Windows. Watches. Time."

My first job was easy to find. An agency in Madrid that hired Americans to go to companies or homes, teach rich Spaniards English. I felt like a prostitute, but it paid pretty well. Every morning I would go to Luis's office in a big, tall building in the rich part of town. "Conversation," I loosely called the class. "Your English, Luis, it will get much better if we just sit and talk. Tell me about yourself, Luis. Your family, your life in Spain."

"My life," he said, "it's good. We're happy, my family."

We talked about everything, Luis and I. My life, his life, the U.S., Franco, the sun, the heat, Halley's Comet. He invited me to his house to meet his wife and the twins they had adopted late in life. Once they invited me to their house in the mountains, where Luis told me his first language was really Bable.

"Bable?" I thought he was joking.

"Not many speak it anymore. Was outlawed under Franco. Is old language from Asturias. My people from Asturias."

Two years and Luis's English never got any better. My Bable improved slowly. "Hello, how are you?" I would say in Bable to Luis every morning.

*

By my first Christmas in Madrid, I was finally ready for the butcher. I had been for the first six months an unwilling vegetarian, intimidated by all that meat, cuts we don't eat back in the States. For two days I practiced what it was I would say when I got to the butcher. "*Dos filetes de ternera, por favor.*" Two veal filets, please. It sounded perfect. I practiced it in various ways. First, as if I were really Spanish: fast and hard, slightly slurred, slightly lispy, bored, as if going to a market that took up four square blocks of the center of Madrid was something I had been doing all my life. Then I tried it fast and angry, like he had kept me waiting too long. Finally, "*dos filetes de ternera,*" one last time, slow and sad, pathetic, like I was poor, like these 300 pesetas were all I had left.

When I got to the market, I circled around, visited all the familiar haunts: the cheese store, the produce man, the Gypsy garlic seller. Finally I approached the butcher. Whole piglets sat on the front counter. Someone had put dark, thick-framed glasses on one. Cow tongues hung in the front; intestinal linings in the back; half sheep heads, brains inside; bull testicles. I lost my nerve. "*Dos filetes de ternura,*" I said quickly, timidly, stupidly. One small switch of a vowel, and I had accidentally asked for "tenderness" instead of "veal."

"Would you like a little bit of love too?" The butcher looked at me and wiped his hands on the blood-splattered apron.

That next August, I moved into my very own flat in Madrid, a *buhardilla*, an attic apartment on Calle Atocha, two blocks from the train station. A small, green apartment with sloped ceilings, wooden beams, kitchen in a closet, no door to the bathroom, a coal stove for heat. Miguel helped me decorate. We searched the streets of Madrid, went to the flea market and the old part of town, found treasures for the flat: an antique chest, we cleaned and stained, then he varnished; an *armario*, a tall, wooden closet, long mirror in front, gilded angels on top.

The day I moved in, Calle Atocha was blocked off. "It's a memorial service," Miguel told me.

"Who died?"

"Nine leftist lawyers—eight men, one woman—eight years ago, gunned down in an apartment three doors away. Today, the government is putting up a plaque in commemoration."

I had to stand on a chair to look out the skylight of my *buhardilla*. All down the street, men, women, children dressed in black, carried red carnations, laying them down, throwing them at a door three doors away. My street undulated like a sea of carnations bleeding.

That night in my *buhardilla*, the attic like an oven, our bodies drenched in sweat, the moon in the skylight. A desire, unknown before, as if from a past life, inside me. I held on as if Miguel were God; he held on as if I were God.

I couldn't say what it was I felt; I couldn't even feel what it was I felt, as if I would explode in a million pieces if I tried to feel what it was I felt.

"The moon," he said. The light of the moon on our bodies shining through.

My second Christmas in Madrid: a whirlwind tour of Spain with Miguel. I started the day at the market, now so confident I even ate bull testicles. It was the day of *El Gordo,* the Fat One, the biggest lottery of the year. As a special present Miguel had given me a lottery ticket. "A traditional Christmas gift," he had said. "*Buena suerte.*" For weeks, I had been hearing in the streets of Madrid, like a refrain on all the corners, blind lottery sellers singing out, "*La lotería para hoy y para la Navidad.*"

The streets were deserted as I had never seen them before. On the way to the market I looked in the windows of overflowing bars. Whole families in the bars stared at televisions. On the televisions were two choir boys singing in choir voices the winning lottery numbers and the winning amount. "*Ocho, nueve, uno, treinta y dos, cuarenta,*" followed by "*Quinientos milliones, ocho cientos mil pesetas.*"

At the market I bought provisions for the tour of Spain: bread, cheese, *chorizo, aceitunas.* On my way home, the streets were still deserted, the bars still full, the choir voices of the choir boys echoing in the empty streets.

When I got home I checked my ticket. I imagined feeding all the Gypsy children of Spain with 500 million pesetas. My numbers didn't match. I didn't win anything.

Once outside of Madrid, Miguel in the seat next to me, the first thing I noticed was that the sky was doing things I had never seen a sky do before. The sky in Castile that winter was like a movie of a sky. Dark, black clouds, then suddenly billowy, white clouds; the sky alternated dark blue, light blue, grey, orange, red, purple; golden rays always shining through. We followed the sky wherever it led us: around Castile to pueblos guarded by stone walls, south to pastures with cows grazing, east to cemeteries, dark and overgrown, west to rolling hills topped with whitewashed windmills, like candles on a birthday cake.

He was huge, fat, blind, and I would say one-legged but I fear that is the addition of my imagination. I passed him every day on my daily jaunt around the Plaza Mayor; he hung out in an arched passageway close to both sun and shade. Over and over again he would shout at an extraordinarily high pitch the call to lottery riches: "¡Para hoy! ¡Para hoy! ¡Me queda El Gordo para hoy! For today, for today, I've still got the Fat One for today!" The sound still rings in my ears all these many years later, and I mutter it to myself at odd moments.

—James O'Reilly, "In Salamanca"

I had given Miguel a camera for Christmas; he had given me a camera for Christmas. Our first joint purchase. We took photographs of the windmills, the cows, the dark cemeteries, the walled pueblos. Afterwards, all the photographs looked like pictures of the sky with golden rays, dots of insignificance below.

Early New Year's Eve, we arrived at Vejer de la Frontera. A band greeted us on the main street of the pueblo. We searched out the pizzeria where Miguel's sister, Ana, worked. Inside, the pizzeria was alive with music, streamers, balloons, teenagers setting off firecrackers under chairs. "Welcome to Vejer," they cried. "Welcome to the strangers!"

Ana took us to her house on the outskirts of Vejer near the

coast, the southernmost tip of Spain, Africa eight kilometers away. The sky was misty, grey, dark; the air tepid. "Maybe tomorrow if the fog lifts," Ana told us, "you can see Africa from the front porch."

Her house was like a house I had dreamed of as a child: no furniture except one giant bed in the living room draped in a soft blue cover; a baby palm tree in every room reaching upward; pillows of all colors scattered across the floor like wild flowers in a field. Outside the front door, jasmine fell over the path onto the porch; two full-grown poinsettias, with red leaves like little bows, guarded the path.

"There's enough food, drink, and drugs to last a week," Ana told us. "You're staying 'til the Twelfth Day, aren't you? King's Day, I mean. When the three kings come. Want a line?"

The next day we were still up, the whole night spent in the pizzeria, dancing, lighting firecrackers, celebrating a new year.

"I'll take you to Zahara," Ana said. "The best beach to see Africa." I suddenly felt as if my greatest ambition had always been to see Africa, as if I would understand some great truth about myself, about life, if I could only see Africa.

We went down through a forest of pine trees that led to a rocky beach of sand and tar and driftwood. On the sand, Ana fell asleep. Miguel and I lay on the beach, sipping *vino tinto,* looking out into the mist that would soon lift to unveil the continent of Africa. The wind picked up and I tried to teach him an old Joni Mitchell song. "This must have been exactly where she was," I exclaimed as if it were a revelation.

"The wind is in from Africa.
  Last night I couldn't sleep."

He couldn't do the *w* for wind; he couldn't do the *couldn't.* Finally, we started to sing it in Spanish: "*El viento viene de Africa. Anoche no podía dormir.*"

I waited a minute, then I continued alone, "I got beach tar on my feet." I laughed. I thought this was the funniest thing I had ever heard. I didn't know the word for tar. It was all over our shoes. I pointed and asked him the word in Spanish.

About noon, the fog started to lift away from the ocean. It came in over us, swept through the pine forest, shrouding Vejer de la Frontera in a blanket of mist. The waves of the Atlantic crashed on the shores of Zahara. In the distance, out somewhere in the Atlantic Ocean, a brown land mass appeared. "¡*Africa!*" I cried. It was nothing but a big brown land mass. Yet inside me I felt something stir, some spark of understanding, some concept of the world in its totality, and my relationship to it. I was an American who lived in Madrid, who came to the south of Spain, who saw Africa.

We fell asleep on the beach, my head on Miguel's lap, tar on our feet, *el viento* in from Africa.

In July we moved in together to a generous flat overlooking the Plaza Santa Ana, twelve balconies to the calle. Friends who had gone to the States for a year left us with the flat. With it came a maid I never knew what to do with. *Purísima,* or the Purest One, I called her to my American friends. My house was cleaner than I had ever kept it. Not because Purísima did the work, but because I spent whole evenings before she came, sweeping, dusting, mopping. Not a single dirty dish in my sink. I wanted Purísima to like me; I wanted her to approve. She saw right through me. She knew I was an imposter, that I didn't really belong here. She told me I shouldn't go out with wet hair; I shouldn't go barefoot in the house; I shouldn't eat salad on a cold day, only soup. She came late; she left early. I gave her gifts and money at every opportunity. Miguel was growing marijuana in the back studio. I told her it was a special American herb for cooking. I knew she knew it wasn't. I knew that she knew I knew. Finally, I stopped coming home when I knew she would be there.

At Thanksgiving we threw a party for 35 people, everyone from the American school where I worked, friends and families invited. We cooked three turkeys; everyone brought food. Miguel made a table with plywood and sawhorses to sit 35 people. We covered it with sheets, borrowed candelabras, picked up chairs from the school, bought flowers, cleaned all the windows.

Before we ate, all 35 people at the table joined hands, gave thanks for our friends, our families, our lives in Spain. We said a prayer, remembered past Thanksgivings. At first it was beautiful, and then suddenly, to me, it all looked so strange: strangely beautiful, yet strangely out of place, like when someone you don't know, have never even imagined appears in your dream, and you don't understand what that person is doing in your dream. It was the first time I felt out of place being an American in Madrid. Purísima was right, I thought.

"This is the best Thanksgiving I've ever had." Someone squeezed my hand.

The next day, I went to a church around the corner, La Iglesia de San José, the church where once a year, people bring their pets for a special blessing from the Father. Winding around corners, down cobblestone alleys, thousands of Madrileños in line, holding in their hands, on leashes, or in cages, dogs, cats, parrots, canaries, waiting in line for the Father's blessing.

On that day, there were no animals, no people. I was alone in the church. I slipped 200 pesetas into the poor box, lit a few candles for good measure.

In a pew I knelt down and thought about Time, Miguel's specialty. I couldn't believe it had been three years. The passage of time here made no sense. The years slipped away and I never felt them pass. In a foreign country, time has no meaning. My past had become like a foreign country, my present like a foreign country, and I like the Atlantic Ocean in between, in a storm, crashing against opposite coasts, wave after wave after wave.

"Time," I said to Miguel when I got home. "It's about Time."

"I knew it would happen," he said. "We both knew it would happen." He moved to a window, looked down on the Plaza Santa Ana. "Don't go."

"I have to," I said. "My mother. My family. My life. Time. It has no meaning here. It's slipping away, and I can't even feel it pass."

∗

My last Christmas in Madrid. A week before Christmas, two weeks before I will leave Spain, we decide to have a party. We walk to the Plaza Mayor. It is a cold December night. We stop along the way at our favorite bar and order brandy after brandy. We eat fried calamari sandwiches in the Plaza Mayor, then join the Christmas merrymakers. In the Plaza Mayor, all the stalls are selling Christmas ornaments, lights, tinsel; one cider stall where men from Asturias pour cider from their right hands over their shoulders to a glass they hold in their left hands behind them. It is an art I have tried to learn for three years.

It takes us two hours to find the tree we are sure is ours. It is slightly sad, slightly lopsided, slightly absent of fullness. "Perfect," we say in unison.

On the way home, Miguel carries the tree as if it were a sword and he were Cervantes fighting windmills: swoosh, swoosh, swoosh with the tree. A window of a car is open; he accidentally swooshes the tree inside the window, powdering an old Señora's face. She opens the door and screams loudly at us as we run away laughing, "*Imbéciles, ¿qué hacen? Idiotas.*"

We run the rest of the way home. When we get home we set the tree up in a window looking out on the Plaza. We drink more brandy. We start to trim the tree.

The day before the party, I go to the Corte Inglés, the largest department store in all of Spain. The first dress I see is a black Cinderella dress, 28 eyelet hooks up the back, tight bodice, skirt flaring out. One hundred dollars. I can't afford it. I try it on. I am transformed: a princess of the night.

We splurge on food and alcohol. We order beer from the beer store, the young boy who delivers it now our friend. We invite him for a beer and a joint. His name is Chema; he lives in Vallecas.

I buy hundreds of raw anchovies. I spend the morning cleaning little anchovy bodies. Cut the heads off, slice the bodies down the middle, clean out the innards, wash, line up in a dish like little dead soldiers. Marinate in vinegar. Let sit. Add oil, garlic, parsley. Serve. Delicious.

We set up an altar, put the food and drinks on the altar.

On the lake in Retiro Park, I look again for the Gypsy fortune tellers, anxious for a sign of what's to come, scared to find out, relieved when no Gypsies appear. I row around the lake one more time before I bring the boat in, tie it up to the dock, and hop back over the fence. At the gate of the Retiro, I hail a taxi and head back to the party.

When I get home, Miguel looks at me questioningly. I mouth the words "El Retiro," and he nods. He knows I go there when I need to think, reflect, retreat.

Towards the end of the party, Miguel takes me to the kitchen. We refill the dishes. We talk. He tells me that he loves me. "We're soul mates," he says. "We share the same spirit; it's cosmic energy." He knows we'll be friends forever.

We come out of the kitchen, walk down the long corridor of our generous flat, past balcony number one, balcony number two, balcony number three. Turn the corner into the living room. Suddenly, the lights go off. Everyone in the room lights a sparkler and yells, "Surprise." I step back in the darkness, groping for a wall or a door, some support, finding only Miguel's body. In my ear, he whispers, "It's a party for you. *Buen viaje.*"

In the darkness, my living room is like a galaxy of shooting stars. "Close your eyes," Miguel says. "Make a wish."

Pier Roberts grew up in Oakland, California, where she has lived her whole life except for three years teaching English in Spain. She now lives in a small cottage near the Oakland freeway. When the traffic noise overwhelms her, she closes her eyes and imagines waves outside her window lapping onto a shore, and Africa rising up in the distance. Her work has appeared in publications including Catholic Girls, Bakunin, *and* Walrus.

★

I wondered whether my life would ever be the same after this day. I felt as if I'd known Pilar all of my life, but had no idea if I would ever see her again. I wanted to believe that her life, too, would be irrevocably altered by our meeting.

We made our way up Madrid's Paseo del Prado to the Puerta del Sol. We elbowed our way through the crowd of shoppers who filled the square. We wandered up Calle de Preciados and enjoyed playing the parts of young lovers. We even went into one shop and tried on engagement rings.

"What will you do when you return to London?" she inquired as we walked the wide boulevard. "Will you go back to your teaching?"

"Only for a while," I answered, surprised by the conviction in my voice.

Although I had been toying with the idea of quitting my job in order to travel around the world, I hadn't actually made it definite. "I'm not certain that I'll ever be satisfied teaching college students. And I think there must be more to life than this."

"I think so, too, but I am not certain where one finds this 'more.'"

At the train station, when it was time to go, Pilar walked with me onto the platform. As she stood there, her smile fading for the first time since I had known her, she reached into her handbag and pulled out a book of poems by Pablo Neruda and recited—all I can remember of it is this line, in her voice:

> Look for me for here I will return, without saying a thing,
> without voice, pure, here I will return to be the churning
> of the water, of its unbroken heart....

That was many years ago now. But hardly a day goes by that I don't think about Pilar. I wonder why I didn't stay with her and live out that romance. I wonder if she is sitting in a café in Madrid, looking across the square for me.

—Glenn A. Leichman, "Looking for Pilar"

The Way of Quixote

*In which the traveler confronts the good knight's windmill,
and other events worth telling.*

MAY 16, CAMPO DE CRIPTANA. IN THE EVENING THERE IS A WED-
ding, the bride and bridegroom posing endlessly outside the
church for the cameras—a photographer is more important than
a priest. After the flashbulbs someone lets off bangers in the crowd
and rice bags are thrown like bombs over the couple. Struggling
to a car with ribbons on the aerial, bumpers, door handles, they
fall into a bed of white flowers and drive away in a burst of satin
and petals.

After dark I walk up to see the windmills on a hill above the
town where they catch the relentless Manchegan wind, ten white
towers capped with grey, their sails ready to turn.

"What luck, friend Sancho!" Don Quixote cried as they rode
across the plain. "Look at those monster giants—more than 40 of
them! I'm going into battle, I'll kill them all."

"What giants?" Sancho asked.

"Over there, with long arms."

"Watch out, sir!—those are windmills."

"You know nothing about it," Don Quixote retorted. "They're
giants, and if you're frightened keep away and say your prayers
while I attack." He dug his spurs into Rocinante, ignoring

Sancho's shouts and the breeze that stirred the windmill sails: "Don't flee, you cowards!—it's only one man fighting you." Commending himself with all his heart to Dulcinea, putting up his shield, urging Rocinante into a gallop, he charged the first windmill and drove his spear into its sail. But the wind caught it, smashed the spear, dragged horse and rider with it and threw them to the ground.

"My God, didn't I tell you?" Sancho said, helping Don Quixote to his feet. "Nobody could mistake them, unless he had windmills on the brain."

"Be quiet, Sancho," his master replied. "The giants were turned by magic into windmills, to cheat me of the glory of conquering them."

They rode on towards the Pass of Lápice and though it was soon dinner time Don Quixote, battered by his fall, had no appetite. Sancho ate as they went, helping himself from his saddlebags and drinking heavily from his wine bottle, deciding that these mad adventures were quite fun after all; and when they stopped at night under the trees he fell asleep. But Don Quixote tore off a branch for a makeshift spear and stayed awake all night, thinking of his impossible, unattainable, non-existent but totally believable Dulcinea: dreams that weren't so different from other men's, though his were excused by lunacy.

The windmills of La Mancha are not an ancient and immutable part of the landscape. The first ones had been introduced to Spain from the low countries in the 1570s, about twenty years before Cervantes began writing his book, and they represented a great leap forward for Spanish technology. When Don Quixote charged the windmills he was, therefore, doing battle with the menace of the machine.

Of the hundreds of windmills built in La Mancha during the 16th and 17th centuries, only a handful are still in existence, most near the town of Campo de Criptana, where Quixote's encounter is supposed to have taken place.

—Frederic V. Grunfeld,
Wild Spain: A Traveler's and Naturalist's Guide

In tonight's breeze, when I climb the hill above Campo de Criptana after supper, the windmills are motionless and silent as they have been for years, no longer grinding flour for bread but truly giants with a monstrous inhuman look. No wonder Sancho was frightened or that Don Quixote attacked. And Sancho was right: his master had windmills on the brain, grinding reality into his peculiar idea of truth.

May 19, Albacete. For a time in the Civil War this was headquarters of the International Brigade. Now old stone buildings round the cathedral, even ornate imperial offices in the commercial part, are being torn down in favour of angular blocks with no grace or humour, monuments to the peseta. It's all illusion and Don Quixote's style was less greedy, more humane.

The road southwest from Albacete runs dead straight for 30 kilometres, not a flicker of the bus driver's fingers on the wheel, to the first hills. It's like coming ashore at last, climbing up among poplars and small fields; no longer the far horizon and the infinite eye-strain.

We follow an abandoned railway: embankments and cuttings and tunnels that engineers of the last century sweated over, now holding their rusty rails like bloodless arteries; and derelict country stations, still tiled and whitewashed, once the pride of some local functionary, his whistle silenced like the hiss of steam and clank of buffers. The road takes over, ripping through the *sierra*, being widened and straightened and flattened, doing more damage than the railway ever did.

Spain often wears a wrinkled, unchanging face. But often too there is a new factory, a cement works, a mill. It was the noise of local industry, one dark night when they were lost, that Don Quixote and Sancho Panza heard. Riding near a stream, they were struck by sounds of thudding iron and rattling chains. Don Quixote brandished his spear, ready to charge and even die for the sake of Dulcinea, but his squire persuaded him to wait till dawn, though he had to tie up Rocinante's legs to stop him. Sancho was petrified, trembling all night till his bowels burst, then forgetting his terror in the morning and mocking Don Quixote when they found that the noise was only the machinery of a cloth mill.

"It's no joke," Don Quixote said, hitting Sancho with his spear. To him, the evidence of cold reality meant nothing. In the dark his courage had made no distinction between a factory and a dragon, and in the light of day his idealism was above ridicule.

Mercifully the giant billboards in the landscape of Franco's time—¡Todo por la Patria!—have gone. Even the sinister green-uniformed tricorn-hatted Civil Guards, in pairs to emphasize their menace, are rare now. Yet under a lingering whiff of violence there remains an element of surrender in the people's character. They give in, to the rich men's gain and the baffled disadvantage of the rest. The national fate, the agony, the submission, are still there. Sometimes Spain seems too terrible to live with. It has no benevolence or bounty, but only the hard bleached *sierras*, the dried rivers, the unremitting sun. No wonder men conquered America from here: it was impossible to stay at home.

> *Courage comes such a short distance; from the heart to the head; but when it goes no one knows how far away it goes.*
>
> —Ernest Hemingway, *Death in the Afternoon* (1932)

No wonder also that Cervantes's two travellers are still relevant. Things are not what they appear, in Spain as elsewhere. Unlike Sancho, who saw only what was visible, Don Quixote elevated it into a dream. He was the greatest conquistador of all, fixed on some inner vision—of the human soul, no less—blind to the facts of life around him. His story, though a picaresque adventure, is spiritual and universal—the revelation of oneself. Sometimes the facts may have proved him wrong but nobody, not even Sancho, was any better for the facts.

In the bus a copper-skinned Gypsy and her daughter, having slept till now across the Manchegan plain, wake up as we wind through the first olive groves of Andalusia and begin cracking melon seeds in their teeth.

May 22, Valdepeñas. In an old house round a covered courtyard, in a tall room with a tiled floor and a balcony over the narrow street, I read *Don Quixote*. Alone, I can think myself into the mad knight's adventures which, shared with someone else, would be difficult. "Unfortunate is he," Unamuno wrote in sympathy with his hero, "who is sound of mind in solitude as well as in public."

But I must go out into the town, defying my idleness, in search of experience or ideas. There are times when I have to keep telling myself I'm a writer, like a wavering believer who repeats the creed again and again for fear that somehow, unless he says the words, they will stop being true.

In the Plaza de España, surrounded on three sides by blue-and-white arcaded buildings and on the fourth by the stern and dominating and gravely splendid church of the Assumption, the liveliest bar is the "Penalty," a haunt of football fans. Among photos of teams it offers frogs' legs and English lessons and three-day trips to the shrine of Fátima for ten thousand pesetas, bus and hotel and meals included. A pretty girl comes to sit next to me, and rehearsing my opening sentence I begin by offering a smile. But she doesn't return it, I'm not worth her scorn.

Next door is a funeral parlour, "Our Lady of Consolation." Round the corner in John Lennon Street the Manchegan wind blows the last blast of winter, and on a wall is written, "We do not want more planes, we prefer the humming of the bees."

Don Quixote would agree. At supper once he surprised the company with a perfectly sane speech on warfare, swallowing not a mouthful while the others ate. "Have you considered, gentlemen, how far fewer people profit from war than perish in it?" Even to a knight in armour, ready to fight injustice anywhere, the greatest good that man could wish for in this world was peace. But it grieved him to have chosen a soldier's life in such a terrible age: "It was a blessed time before the invention of these hellish weapons...."

May 28, Toledo. The Plaza de Zocodover is where the poet Laurie Lee, busking in the cafés with his violin before the Civil War, met the poet Roy Campbell who was making a living horse-coping and trick-riding. Campbell claimed that humanity could be divided roughly into the Don Quixotes and the Sancho Panzas:

"I belong emphatically to the former," he wrote. "I live three-quarters of the time in my imagination." He invited Lee back to supper in his house where he read his poems aloud late into the night. "I was young, full of wine and in love with poetry," Lee wrote long afterwards, "and was hearing it now from the poet's mouth. What had I read till then?—carloads of Augustan whimsy. This, I felt, was the stuff for me."

For Roy Campbell, who was baptized, confirmed and remarried in the Catholic church, Toledo was the heart of Spain, the city of God that embodied the crusade for Christianity against Communism in the Civil War. During the siege, living on cucumbers picked at night in his garden, he gave shelter to Carmelite friars who brought the archives of St. John of the Cross to his house for safety. But though he was a friend of the governor, a tavern-keeper under whose rule a thousand unarmed

S pain's official and political capital is Madrid, but its artistic capital, and for almost 1,000 years the center of its cultural life, is Toledo, a mere 40 miles to the southwest.

The majestic, brooding grandeur of this fortress city, so high above the winding Tagus River it seems to be of the clouds, was described by Cervantes as "that rocky gravity, glory of Spain and light of her cities."

Its winding streets, its soaring towers and domes, its crests and coats-of-arms surmounting portals that have remained unchanged for centuries, invest Toledo with a regal splendor that is unmatched anywhere else in the country. The whole city has been declared a national monument, and indeed it is.

—John Wilcock and Elizabeth Pepper DaCosta, *Magical and Mystical Sites: Europe and the British Isles*

citizens were killed, his quixotry, a private brand of fascism, couldn't save the friars from being shot and he found their seventeen bodies under a tarpaulin. He was lucky to escape himself; and lived to translate the mystic poetry of St. John of the Cross, songs of the soul that yearn for God: "*¡Oh mi Dios!* When will it be, that I can truly say—I live at last because I shall not die?"

In the Plaza de Zocodover now there is a pavement artist, for ever touching up his enormous crayon version of St. Peter in tears,

A voyage in the footsteps of Don Quixote can only begin in the city of Toledo. It is the capital of the Castile-La Mancha region, and harbors a famous 16th-century painting in the chapel of Santa Tomé by Domencio Theocopulos, known as El Greco.

The painting, The Funeral of the Count of Orgaz, *contains the largest collection of Don Quixotes to be found in a single work of art. They feature long and severe faces, rendered even longer by beards that flow over starched collars, every one just like the image we have of both Cervantes and Don Quixote, transmitted to us from the first portraits of the writer to the 18th-century illustrations for his novel by French artist Gustave Doré, and the works of Spanish painter Salvador Dalí.*

—Mario Picchi,
"Don Quixote's Spain," *l'Espresso*

more El Greco than El Greco. He has a baby in a pram beside him and drops his crayons to give it a bottle. Behind him old men sit along the wall—the faces of Spain. Some are Don Quixotes, long and solemn, gravely courteous; others are Sanchos, round and wrinkled, good-humouredly patient; a few could have heard Laurie Lee fiddling for pesetas. They like to compare walking-sticks—there is great interest in a silver band or a carved head or candy striping. A party of teenagers, bored with culture and ice creams, start dancing in the plaza, stamping and clapping to defy the loudspeakers. A little old man, mad or drunk, trips in among them and they dance on, laughing at him.

Up the hill from the Plaza de Zocodover is the massive four-

Toledo

square *alcázar,* fortress, palace, barracks, a monument to nationalism and autocracy. In the Civil War the garrison held out against
the Republicans till they were relieved, though the building was
half destroyed. For the third time in its history it was rebuilt: a
huge, absurd castle—one day, perhaps, to become a *parador* for
tourists.

Across the city in the evening, under the cathedral walls, someone has parked a big Peugeot in a narrow cobbled street. Nobody
can pass and soon a line of cars forms, tailing back into a small
plaza. One driver shouts and sticks his tongue out, another slips
into a bar for coffee, the rest blow their horns, then settle down to
wait. Patience is part of the Spanish soul: *paciencia y barajar,* patience
and shuffle the cards—the maxim that Don Quixote learnt in the
cave of Montesinos. A better deal may turn up next time.
Optimism is the essence—meanwhile, patience. People look out of
their windows, pedestrians stop to watch.

Three policemen arrive with truncheons, pistols, radios. The
drivers blow their horns again, the police tell them to stop: "We'll
sort this out, don't worry." They peer through the Peugeot's windows, talk into their radios; and soon there are four policemen,
then five and at last a sixth turns up with a man in a breakdown
truck. Slowly he unshackles his chains, bars, hooks, and crawls
under the Peugeot, hoists its back wheels, drives away with it. One
of the policemen pulls out a ticket—"*vehículo retirado por la grúa,* vehicle removed by crane"—and sticks it to the cobbles, pressing it
down with his foot. By the time all the cars, kept waiting an hour
and blowing their horns for relief, have driven over it there is
nothing left.

In a bar the man beside me has a sack of fish the size of cod,
their gills gasping for breath, on offer to customers. I ask him what
they are.

"*Campo,*" he says.

I'm no wiser: "From Galicia?"

"From the Mediterranean."

Trying to imagine a man selling live fish in an English pub I go
upstairs to the little dining-room—six tables with one other man

enjoying his dinner alone and a woman with a cleft palate, in an apron, cooking behind a curtain: beans with bacon, pork fillet and salad, custard flan and half a litre of wine for six hundred pesetas.

Descending to the bar afterwards I catch sight of a half-familiar figure, a lean, harrowed man, no longer young, not yet decrepit, his eyes a little agonized by some misty private vision, blind to the facts of life around. He might be a crayon portrait of Don Quixote by that pavement artist in the Plaza de Zocodover, in the style of El Greco.

Of course, he is myself in a mirror.

Nicholas Wollaston also contributed "Quixote's Parable of Life" in Part One, "Quixotic Adventures" in Part Two, and "Where Quixote's Fortunes Fell" in Part Four. All of these stories were excerpted from Tilting at Don Quixote.

✳

Let us leave famous men for a moment and turn to places, particularly the magical city of Toledo, which I discovered in 1921 when I went there for a few days with the philologist Solalinda. My first memories are of a performance of *Don Juan Tenorio* and an evening at a brothel, where, since I had no desire to avail myself of her services, I hypnotized the girl and sent her to knock at Solalinda's door.

Toledo filled me with wonder, more because of its indefinable atmosphere than for its touristic attractions. I went back many times with friends from the Residencia until finally, in 1923, on Saint Joseph's Day, I founded the Order of Toledo. I was the grand master....

There were really only two rules: each member had to contribute ten pesetas to the communal pot (meaning, to me), and he had to go to Toledo as often as possible and place himself in a state of receptivity for whatever unforgettable experiences might happen along. We used to stay at an unusual inn called the Posada de la Sangre—the Inn of Blood—which hadn't changed very much since Cervantes situated *La Ilustre Fregona* in its courtyard. Donkeys still stood in the yard, along with carriage drivers, dirty sheets, and packs of students. Of course, there was no running water, but that was a matter of relatively minor importance, since the members of the Order were forbidden to wash during their sojourn in the Holy City....

Our adventures tended toward the bizarre, like the day we met a blind man who took us to his home and introduced us to his family, all of whom were also blind. There was no light in the house, no lamps or candles, but on the walls hung a group of pictures of cemeteries. The pictures were made entirely of hair, right down to the tombs and the cypresses.

On another occasion, late one snowy night, as Ugarte and I were walking through the narrow streets, we heard children's voices chanting the multiplication tables. Sometimes the voices would stop suddenly and we'd hear laughter, then the graver voice of the schoolmaster, then the chanting again. I managed to pull myself up to the window by standing on Ugarte's shoulders, but as I did so, the singing ceased abruptly. The room, like the night, was totally dark and silent.

—Luis Buñuel, *My Last Sigh,* translated by Abigail Israel

PART FOUR

IN THE SHADOWS

ALASTAIR BOYD

The Road to Arcadia

*The prospect of a new highway in Spain raises
questions about the nature of progress
in the Serranía de Ronda.*

NEWS OF THE MOTORWAY CAME TO ME SHORTLY AFTER HOLY
Week. Suddenly it was on everyone's lips.

Roque said, "It will be an *autovía*. They have already started at
the Algeciras end. It is due for completion in 1996."

An *autovía* means four lanes. He thought it would come on our
side of the river and that land values would double because we
should be able to get a link road over the railway track instead of
our unguarded crossing.

Rafael Alarcón seemed sceptical at first.

"The new road? Look, there was a plan 50 years ago when I was
a boy for one that would run over the hillside just above this farm,
and it still isn't there. Anyway, they say it will be on the other side
of the valley; it won't affect us."

I could not agree with him there; if it ran on the other side of
the valley, it would bring us nothing but disadvantage from increased traffic and noise without any improvement of access to
compensate.

"But on past experience you think it will come to nothing?" I
asked hopefully.

385

"Oh, they'll do it this time, all right," he said. "It is traced from Algeciras to Ecija where it will join the national route from Cádiz vía Córdoba to Madrid."

At the request of the kings of Spain and Morocco, engineers have drawn up a plan to link the two nations—and the two continents—by building a tunnel under the Strait of Gibraltar. No decision to start burrowing is imminent, but the plan's advocates have said the passage would open an alluring new route for trade and tourism.

Building such a passage is an old dream. Medieval Moslem traders talked of it and so did 19th-century engineers. Yet now that technical prowess makes this feat possible, there are new reasons to make approval by Spain and, inevitably, its European Community partners, difficult.

Spain says it will ask for help from the European Union. "It can never be only a Spain-Morocco project," said José Alberto Zaragoza, Spain's Deputy Minister of Public Works. "It will be done only if the European Union thinks it is strategically and economically important."

—Marlise Simons, "To Join Europe and Africa, Will a Tunnel Suffice?" *The New York Times*

"But why cut through some pretty rough country when there is already a perfectly good road from Algeciras to Ronda and so to Córdoba?"

"Ah," said Rafael importantly, "because it is required for military purposes."

I raised my eyebrows.

"Yes, with the European Common Market and all that, there will have to be joint manoeuvres with Britain and other countries and a fast road is needed down to the Strait."

"But there is no European *army*," I said, "only NATO. There is some overlap but the community has no army of its own; it has no joint high command...."

He shrugged.

"Well, logically, with the United States of Europe there will be one."

I left him, reflecting how far the valley was from the realities of European diplomacy, only to open a paper the same evening and read that a new NATO rapid strike force under British command would incorporate Spanish units with special responsibility for the "southern flank" including the Strait of Gibraltar.

Whatever sort of geopolitical sense this might make, it hardly seemed to require a four-lane highway. Why should flying columns of armoured cars need something the width of an airstrip? What about planes and helicopters? And where would the mules, beloved of Spanish generals, pass if not on the old bridle paths?

I went off to see other interested parties. For Paco Sánchez, who was to lose something over an acre, it was all a question of whether the compensation price was right. But was it really necessary at all, this motorway? Paco shrugged. He had heard it was connected with the tunnel that was to be dug under the Strait linking Spain to North Africa. I was slightly incredulous, and said so. Well, hadn't the British just done precisely that with France? Yes, but Spain linked to *Africa*? After all those centuries spent expelling Islam? Ah, he couldn't say. It was just a rumour. When I mentioned the tunnel to Paco el Bueno he smiled and dismissed it as childish talk; there was not the slightest likelihood of it. But as far as he was concerned anything that improved communications between one pueblo and another was good; besides, he sometimes needed to go to Algeciras and it would save him an hour each way.

Others were more dubious. An old *huerta* across the river has been split into three or four *fincas de recreo*. The cashier of the Banco Hispano Americano and his wife have an acre plot; the rough local grass has been painstakingly turned into a fine lawn pleasantly shaded by old fruit trees. The house is a three-bedroomed chalet where they planned to retire. The large garage is a den of do-it-yourself wizardry.

How would the *autovía* affect them? Well, they said bravely, it would be at least a hundred metres away from their door; it wouldn't touch their land. But the wife was clearly less than happy. The real threat was the noise. Their Ronda flat was very noisy and as soon as she got down here she could feel the relaxation seeping through her. But with the *autovía*...she did indeed wonder if it would be quite the same. Perhaps the speed of the traffic would produce no more than a faint swish, I suggested soothingly. That might be so if it were used mainly by *turismos*, said her husband, but he feared the main traffic would be heavy freight, in particular the great refrigerated lorries that thundered through the night to get fresh fish and seafood onto the Madrid fishmongers' slabs and into the restaurants early in the morning. The pair of them looked at one another with almost identical wistful smiles.

"Ah well," they sighed almost in unison, "if it is for the good of humanity…"

There was a hint of irony in the man's voice, but it was muted: the idea of some universal advance was, I suspected, what made the motorway just tolerable to them. Their sense of duty, a Spanish equivalent of the stiff upper lip, was touching. Sadly, Spanish sub-urban sensibility has not yet developed sufficient muscle or self-confidence to fight off such powerful interests as the Ministry of Public Works, the army and the automobile industry, whose combined might seems to possess some of the awesome inevitability of the great religious orthodoxies of the past to which all other views must bow or be crushed.

The last person I went to see was the retired restaurateur [in town]. Civilised and a little world-weary, he had been the pioneer of bourgeois penetration of the valley. He had a copy of the plans for the *autovía*. We sat under his old trees beside his not-too-shriekingly-blue swimming pool—he is a man of taste—and he showed me who would be shaved here and who would be spared by a whisker there and who would find himself caught between the two ribbons of the highway. He himself was on the fringe. Yes, it would be a great nuisance. Yes, he too had heard about the tunnel. Threat from the east? He smiled craftily. Had I not observed how Arabophile Spanish foreign policy had recently been, with no more than symbolic assistance in the Gulf War? I nodded. I had. But, nearer home, wouldn't a motorway go completely against the Junta's policy of promoting rural tourism? The railway was one thing: it followed the natural contours; it was obliged to work its way up to the head of the valley and describe a great hairpin bend before reaching the town; the landscape was its master, not vice-versa; furthermore, it had many little halts to let people on and off. The motorway would do none of this: it would slide slickly over the natural features; access to the locality would be limited to major sliproads every 20 or 30 kilometres and neither local farmers nor rural tourists would benefit one jot. How did any of this square with the Junta's attempt to attract people from the coasts into the interior? Not at all well, he agreed. But I had to realise that, apart from the additional layers of bureaucracy, the "autonomy" of Andalusia was largely a fiction. The interests of the national economy and the demands of "progress" overrode all that.

So there we were, back with progress—but *whose* progress was uncertain. The progress of refrigerated lorries to satisfy Madrid's penchant for fish? (How absurd to build a capital in the centre of arid Spain, without so much as a proper river, and expect gleaming fresh fish every morning!) The progress of British marine commandos rushing south on some make-believe exercise? The progress of migrant Moroccans flooding north with overloaded old cars and over-numerous families in search of scarce work in northern Europe? Or simply the march of Progress with a capital P in aid of the Good of Humanity, also with capitals? All of these perhaps. But not the progress of the Serranía, whose natural beauty was to be scarred by an impersonal conveyor belt taking people and goods to more important places. Not the progress of the valley, which required, if anything, better tracks to the farms and a piped domestic water supply to replace unreliable old wells. And certainly not my progress or that of my family and friends.

Where then did hope lie? With the geologists revising their assays of the soil and predicting landslides? With rival bureaucrats gaining acceptance for an alternative blueprint up someone else's valley? With the environment department of the Junta de Andalucía plucking up its courage and flexing its muscles against central government? Or with the Mother of God, no less, whose *tierras de María Santísima* were being disembowelled under her eyes? Might she not descend and admonish the planners and engineers and leave them dumbfounded? In such a way did my thoughts smoulder and splutter impotently.

More immediate concerns soon imposed themselves. Vicente

had sown a good crop of oats on our land. When cut and raked and baled there were over seven hundred bales to be collected by people to whom he had sold them verbally. A couple of hundred were removed by one buyer. On the eve of Corpus Christi—we are in June now—it rained suddenly and heavily. This was not good for the oats, but it did not last long and if no more came they would dry out.

The day of Corpus Christi dawned cloudy and damp, but the rain held off. The main street of Ronda was strewn with palm leaves. The procession came out of the Iglesia Mayor. All the bigwigs, the heads of *hermandades* and *cofradías* were there in suits and ties with silver staffs of office; and many other local worthies, to say nothing of plenty of solemn rascals, walked ahead of the floral float with its sacred monstrance containing the Host, which through transubstantiation becomes the body of Christ and is known therefore as "El Señor."

The Alameda had been prepared with the traditional carpet of yellow and coloured sands with thousands of decapitated carnations forming swirling baroque patterns; this stretched for two hundred metres or more to an open-air altar, where seven priests performed; nearby the municipal band (including my bandsman friend Juan, always glad to earn an additional small wage) struck up with drums and cymbals as the chief priest presented the golden monstrance with the Host to the people. The more devout citizens toed the edge of the sand carpet; others loitered more casually behind the front line. When the Host was raised, many sank to their knees and crossed themselves; even the most ribald inclined their heads. Then the procession with its long tail returned to the Iglesia Mayor, followed immediately, as if they formed an integral part of it, by bustling sweepers making much of their zeal and efficiency in removing the palm fronds that had been laid only an hour or so before. In Spain the minor parts are also important, and usually add a touch of comic relief—like the bullring servants, the *monosabios*, who help the *picador* up when he has been floored, haul up his capsized nag and scamper out with the bull when it is being dragged by the mule-team from the ring.

All this time it was fine. The Lord looks after his own. But when I got back to the *campo* the heavens opened again and the remaining five hundred or so of Vicente's bales were virtually ruined. If only he had got them off the ground a few days earlier and ploughed and sowed his maize, how divine this rain would have been. In the event it was an unmitigated disaster, to which Spanish stoicism was the only answer. Thoughts of the motorway receded. Fretting about a road some years off and with no absolute certainty of completion suddenly seemed an indulgence compared to this sharp and immediate blow to an individual's economy. On such occasions the shrug assumes heroic proportions.

Nonetheless, the motorway was there on the drawing board; it was a seed that threatened to grow into something rather monstrous on our horizon. Threats have a vibrant life of their own, even if they never come to fruition. My perception of the valley had altered slightly but irreversibly. It would never be quite the same again: whether as threat or as future reality, the motorway already existed. What does an old, frayed romantic do in such circumstances? My answer was to go and buy five straggling Spanish rose plants with thick stems and talon-like thorns, the toughest flowers in creation, and dig them in just below our terrace facing the projected route of the motorway, as a gesture of defiance.

Should you drive along the motorway from Algeciras to the north in a few years' time and look down on your left three or four kilometres short of Ronda, you will see a patch of a few acres cradled in an elbow-shaped bend of the river, whose course is clearly marked by willows and tall swaying poplars. That is the *campo*, more formally the Huerta del Rincón. If the game of life, in the parlance of the landlady of the little hotel in Arcos, is *buscar rincones*, to seek out quiet corners, this was once one of the quietest and most secluded, hard for newcomers to find at all. But now it will be exposed to your gaze like a toy farm, only more untidy, with the foursquare little house set back against the rising fold of the bigger hill farms and the cliff of the table-mountain.

If you have sharp eyes, you may see my wife Hilly hanging out the washing on the terrace or my son Jaime casually getting out of his Suzuki jeep or me bowed with my adze over an irrigation ditch. Or you may see Vicente and his son turning over bales of barley to expose them to the sun after a wetting. Or you may see none of these things, because the hard shoulders of a motorway do not invite stops except in emergencies and the next lay-by may be miles off. Or we may not be there at all. And the *huerta* in its present form may not be there either: Miguel de la Granja may have bought us out to extend his battery-farming empire, in which case all you will see (out of the corner of your eye as you whizz by) will be long gleaming aluminium-roofed sheds, punctuated by circular silver turrets whose function is to release the feedstock down to the unfortunate beasts penned in beneath.

If that is what meets your eye, we shall clearly have departed: whether to Alpandeire or Benalauría or Cortes de la Frontera or Alcalá de los Gazules or Setenil or El Burgo I cannot say. But I do not think we shall have thrown in our hand, whatever the aggravation. These days no country is an island. Air routes and motorways spread their universal culture around the world. But there are pockets where the island effect is partly preserved. They are not pockets of resistance in the conscious sense, because everyone accepts the main features of the mass culture, notably automobiles and television. Yet, intuitively, such places are still strongly attached to their old roots; in them the concept of the pueblo as Utopia remains deeply embedded and is likely to survive.

Thus, though the state has forcibly shifted the feast of Corpus Christi from the Thursday after Trinity Sunday to the Sunday itself to cut down on the number of religious holidays, the people (having protested vociferously) will still lay their palm leaves on the streets and bring out the Host in its golden vitrine. Thus, Cartajima will celebrate its strange little encounter between the Christ child and his mother with her wobbly crown. Thus, buxom lasses will come swinging down the slope from the *Ciudad* to the *Barrio,* chanting *¡guapa…guapa…guapa!* in praise of the gorgeous Astarte with her bulbous gilded crown and the mass of lilies at her feet, whom they bear aloft with such *élan.* Thus, the hill farmers will continue to kill their pigs for home consumption at their annual *matanzas*. Thus, civilisation will continue to take the form of the *paseo* in the town. Thus, Ronda's intellectuals will continue their *causeries* in the bookseller's tiny den. All these things will still be found for many a year to come in the sierras of the south.

Of course, they are "at risk" from such developments as the motorway and other aspects of the mass culture. Yet that is a condition which applies to deep-rooted practices and observances everywhere. The motorway is a metaphor for change, as is the valley for stability, and these are in constant tension. For me this brings an added sharpness and a fresh poignancy to the people and places I have encountered. One intelligent countrywoman refused to believe that a man had been landed on the moon; it was a TV trick. The ground is shifting under them, as it is under us all.

Finally, Arcadia has always been to a large extent a country of the mind. Those of us who thought we had glimpsed it here on earth and have tried to pin it down will always find ourselves in some conflict with the Arcadians themselves, who have their eyes on other horizons. But that is no reason why we should not follow our dream over the mountain and into the next valley, taking a chance that another motorway or another battery farm will not creep up behind us. Who knows, in time the Arcadians may change their minds about these aspects of progress. And even in the worst scenario the hard core of the region will remain inviolate: the people are stubbornly attached to their pueblos and their festivities; the mountains cannot be pulled down or the sunsets plucked out of the sky. Somewhere in the *sierras* there will always be a refuge for the likes of me and mine, and possibly of you and yours. But anyone wanting a soft option must look elsewhere.

Alastair Boyd lived for twenty years in Andalusia, where he founded a language school and attempted self-sufficiency on a small farm with his second wife, Hilly, and their son. His books on Spain include The Road from Ronda, The Companion Guide to Madrid and Central Spain, The Essence of Catalonia, *and* The Sierras of the South: Travels in the Mountains of Andalusia, *from which this piece was excerpted.*

✳

Spain is always conscious of her own symbolisms, and rightly so. "Spain *hurts* me," cried the essayist Miguel de Unamuno more than 50 years ago. "When I speak of Spain," wrote the poet Antonio Machado in the '30s, "I speak of Man." Time and again Spain has been a cockpit, where the conflicts of the world have had their first round, and sometimes even their last.

—Jan Morris, *Spain*

RICHARD SCHWEID

A Legacy of Intolerance

Bigotry and repression didn't end with
Isabella and Ferdinand.

SPAIN IS THE COUNTRY THAT MOST SYMBOLIZES THE "FORWARD progress" of a united Europe. The nation has achieved an incredible modernization in the years following Franco's death. Freedom of speech, democratic elections, and a free press are public reflections of the liberty with which people live their own private lives. Spain has become thoroughly contemporary.

There is another side to Spain's success, however, to the blossoming of Barcelona. Two anniversaries [in 1992] testify to the dark side of the Spanish character, to the long Iberian history of wars with their hatred and blind aggression; of a people willing to be governed by greed and savage righteousness, to obey strong authorities in the form of church or state, and to commit atrocities for those authorities, or stand by passively while they are being committed, with scarcely a whimper of protest.

One is the 500th anniversary of Columbus's first voyage to the New World, and the commencement, under Isabella and Ferdinand, of Spain's age of conquest. While Europeans generally regard it as a high point of modern history, Native Americans tend to note it more as an occasion for sackcloth and ashes.

The other quincentenary falling in 1992 marked Isabella and Ferdinand's edict of Expulsion, decreeing that all of Spain's approximately 200,000 Jews had four months to either convert to Catholicism or leave the country. The Iberian peninsula is thought by many historians to have been the westernmost point of Jewish immigration after the destruction of the Second Temple at Jerusalem in 70 A.D. In four months during 1492, a people and culture that had been on the peninsula for more than a millenium was systematically and totally wiped out. This was, furthermore, the final bitter end of the generally peaceful and fruitful coexistence of Islam, Judaism, and Catholicism that had produced so many wonders in both the arts and the sciences over six centuries. (Muslims outlasted the Jews only a little—in 1525 they were forced to convert or leave, and in 1609, the descendants of those who had accepted normal conversion were expelled from Spain.)

The coming together of Muslims and Jews in Al-Andalus, the southern half of Spain now known as Andalusia, seems particularly poignant given 20th-century political realities. In the medieval centuries of Al-Andalus there was an amalgam of the two great semitic traditions of knowledge. While they had their struggles, the two desert monotheisms generally worked together and exchanged their best. Many learned Jews spoke Arabic during those centuries, and there were Muslim scholars who read Hebrew. Most of the important literature in one language was translated into the other, and the Muslims brought the works of the Greeks to the Jews and the Catholics.

Gone. Finished, in 1492. What an infamous year! Isabella and Ferdinand acted to wipe out ancient cultures in the Old and the New Worlds. At the same time as they converted, exiled, or killed every Jew living in Spain, they launched a national policy of colonization that would exterminate the millenia-old civilizations of the New World, while bankrupting Spain economically and morally for centuries. In both worlds, people were made to bend the knee before the church. Catholic Spain would impose its morality and judgment on both subjects and citizens for hundreds of years to come. Almost without respite Spain would be under the dominion of the Church until the late 1970s.

The Plaza del Rey is where the Inquisition was headquartered in Barcelona, beginning in 1488. Its offices were, fittingly, around the corner from the cathedral. It was here that the Church's Inquisitors judged whether a person's faith was strong and real, or whether that person was guilty of being a Catholic only in name. The Inquisitors had the job of rooting out sinners and nonbelievers, whether they were among those born Catholic or those who had converted. Reports from anonymous sources and torture were among the tools they used to do the job. Accusations against a person's faith were made in secret. The accused were arrested, taken to a secret prison, and tried by the Inquisitors without the right to confront their accusers. Those who confessed their guilt had the chance to repent their sins in public, pay heavy fines, and perform penance. Those who refused to confess and were found guilty were "relaxed," which is what the Inquisitors called being burned at the stake, taking their inspiration from the New Testament admonition in John 15:6: "If a man abide not in me, he is cast forth as a branch and is withered: and men gather them and cast them into the fire, and they are burned."

The Sefarad, as the Spanish Jews called themselves, who continued to practice Judaism, were immune to the Inquisition. It only had jurisdiction over the *conversos* and their descendants, those Jews who had converted to Catholicism. The *conversos*, alone, were plentiful enough to keep the Inquisitors busy. For many Jews, conversion had been a way to escape the frequent outbreaks of

> *In Hebrew, Spain is called Sepharad. It is the name the Jews gave this country according to a certain exegesis by the Prophet Abdias, and it referred to the whole peninsula, without distinguishing one kingdom from another—Castile from Aragón, for example. For the Jews, there was only one Sepharad, and when they spoke this name, they were referring mainly to the Jewish communities established throughout the length and breadth of the Iberian Peninsula.*
>
> —José Luis Lacave, *Viaje por la España Judia: A Trip through Jewish Spain*

anti-Semitism that erupted on the Iberian peninsula during the Middle Ages. Jews converted to protect or save their lives, and numerous families continued to practice Judaism secretly.

Many of the Sefarad felt themselves to be more Catalán or Iberian than Jewish, and if the way to continue raising children and doing business here was to be washed in the Blood of the Lamb, then they chose to get sprinkled, and kept their fingers crossed. They simply could not imagine leaving Spain. Their families had been here too long to leave, many of them for more than twenty generations, partaking in one of the world's most vibrant centers of Jewish culture, where their forefathers had led total, fulfilled lives. They had lost any sense of the diaspora, of being outcast, wandering Jews.

Outbreaks of anti-Semitism in Christian Spain increased over the centuries, with a corresponding rise in the number of converts. Many Jewish communities suffered annually during Easter Week, when Catholic resentment of the Jews as Christ-killers was naturally at its highest. Mobs formed, and angry Christian warriors descended on the Jewish ghettos and raised hell, killing and burning. Worse, there were years in both Muslim and Christian Spain where attacks on Jews were more or less constant. In one town, then another, people were murdered, those who weren't murdered either converted or left town, expelled, driven from one place to another, from pillar to post. Conversion seemed one way of ending the exhausting and frightening cycle.

The mob attacks on the Jews were inspired by the idea of reward both in this world and the next. That the Jewish people were allowed to live, having killed Jesus, seemed blasphemous to many Christians and they saw merit in serving the Lord by ridding his flock of these pestilent unbelievers. In addition, many of them owed lots of money to particular Jews who they were glad to see get murdered, or run out of town.

Isabella and Ferdinand, or the Catholic Monarchs as they liked to call themselves, were the first to unite the various kingdoms of the Iberian peninsula into the Spain we know today. In order to do so, they spent the initial years of their rule engaged in a war with the Muslims for Al-Andalus and Granada. While this war was going on, they were disposed to continue providing their Jewish subjects with the traditional rights and protections. They were, no doubt, influenced by the fact that Jews bore a disproportionately heavy burden in providing the revenues to finance the campaign against the Moors. On July 9, 1477, Isabella wrote: "All the Jews in my kingdom are mine and under my protection, and belong to me to defend and shelter and maintain in justice."

However, once the reconquest was complete and Spain was brought under their rule, on January 2, 1492, Ferdinand and Isabella began to listen more closely to [the director of the Inquisition], Tomás de Torquemada's constant insistence that the Jews had to go, his claims that they represented a persistent threat to the spiritual well-being of Spain. On March 31 of that year, fifteen years after Isabella signed her commitment to protect the Jews, the Catholic Monarchs issued a proclamation giving every Jew in the country four months to convert, or get their affairs in order and leave.

Spain passed more than four hundred years with no Jewish communities inside its borders. A few Jews came to Madrid and Barcelona during the 1860s as representatives of the French-based Rothschild banking empire, but it was not until the early 20th century that communities reappeared. The first group of Jews to arrive came from Turkey, descended from Sefarad who fled to the Ottoman empire during the Middle Ages. Their families had been living there ever since. They were eventually joined by descendants of Sefarad who came from other European countries, as well as Jews displaced by one or another European upheaval who had no family ties to Spain.

During World War II, Franco, despite his fascist sympathies, provided refuge to a certain number of European Jews fleeing the Third Reich. There was always widespread apprehension among Spanish Jews during the war that Franco might open the country's borders to the Nazis, whom Spain supported. But he did not.

Franco never encouraged Jews to come to Spain, nor did he grant their religion official recognition, but they were allowed to live there in relative peace and, eventually, to organize congregations.

Though Franco protected many Jews fleeing the Nazis, he was not so protective of Republicans who had opposed him during the Civil War. The following was taken from Montserrat Roig's "Catalans in Nazi Death Camps," an essay included in Catalonia: A Self-Portrait, *edited by Josep Miquel Sobrer (1992):*

Teachers, draftsmen, farmers, barbers, waiters, young scouts, adolescents, immigrants from poorer areas of Spain, volunteers to the Spanish war. These are our deportees, our "reds," the "criminals" who crossed the border early in 1939. These are the ones who were locked up like cattle, treated like subhumans in the Nazi extermination camps. From provincial towns, rural areas, the city; from the working or the middle class; farmers, fugitive Catalans, defeated, twice the victims of the irrationality of fascism. They could not return home. Franco had stated so very clearly in his Law of Political Responsibilities of February 13, 1939. At home they would be welcomed by overcrowded prisons, the fear of execution at any dawn.

—LMc

After the Second World War, Jews continued to arrive in small numbers from all the pre-war points of origin. They were joined in the 1950s by thousands of Moroccan Jews, who chose to leave when that country gained independence from the French. There was another large wave of immigration during the late 1970s, when many Argentine Jews fled their repressive military dictatorship. Throughout those years, the Catholic Church controlled life. It was the state religion, and there was no warm welcome waiting for those Jews who chose to settle in Spain. They faced stereotypes built up by Spaniards during more than four hundred years of having no practicing Jews in their midst.

When Mònica Adrian went to elementary school in Barcelona, in 1966, her nine-year-old classmates asked her, in all seriousness, why she drank the blood of Christian children at Easter. That is what their priests and their parents had told them Jews did.

"They also wanted to know why I didn't have horns if I was

Jewish," said Adrian, the director of Barcelona's Baruch Spinoza Foundation, which was organized in the quincentennial year of the Expulsion to gather oral histories from the Jews who had come to Barcelona this century.

"It was all pure ignorance. They had never known a Jew and, to them, Jew was synonymous with bad. This was, of course, not the sort of thing that would make a nine-year-old girl very happy. What matters at that age is what the other kids think of you, and it was hard for me."

During the Franco years, religion was an obligatory class in school. In many classrooms, whenever Jews were mentioned during the lessons, the children were taught to spit on the floor. Textbooks of Spanish history during the Franco years portrayed the Jews as traitors to Catholic Spain, and as people who ritually tortured and murdered Christian children. What would never, ever be mentioned was the substantial amount of Jewish blood flowing in the veins of Spaniards, nor the role that medieval Jews played in making Spain what it is today.

As the quincentenary approached, there was a spate of television shows to mark the date. Most of them featured interviews with contemporary Spanish Jews, and for many viewers it was the first time that they had seen someone they knew was a Jew, according to Jaume Riera. "Even these days, many, many Catalans have never consciously seen an example of what a Jew might be. There is not one single thing to mark the Jews among them. When a Jew passes them on the street, or does business with them, they have no way of knowing that person is a Jew.

"When you talk to older people they all have the same idea of a Jew—old, greedy, counting his money at night, and with a beautiful daughter. This is the typical image of the centuries. Why they should all be thought to have beautiful daughters I don't know, but don't forget that the Blessed Mother, the Virgin, was herself a Jew, and is considered the most beautiful of all women."

Another explanation occurs to me while I am sitting in the Plaza del Rey, listening to some amazing flamenco/jazz work by guitarist Pedro Javier González and his two percussionists. As I look at the female occupants of the seats around me, I think that the Catalans applied that particular stereotype to Jews because it was so true of themselves. Catalans certainly have a reputation as the most enterprising, and thrifty of all Spaniards. And, their raven-haired daughters are exceptionally lovely, with Mediterranean, olive-dark skin that looks as soft as suede.

> "*Is there any anti-Semitism in Spain?*" *I asked him.*
>
> *He looked straight ahead and the fingers of his right hand wandered to his neatly knotted tie, making sure that the folds were straight, acceptable to the world.*
>
> "*No,*" *he said after a long hesitation.*
>
> *Was he willing to talk or unable to? He had lived through bloody pogroms and surely he knew what I was asking. Or did he feel that I, a Negro, had no right to invade that dark domain of his heart? His evasiveness nettled me and I opened up broadly.*
>
> "*Maybe it was all solved back in 1492 when Ferdinand and Isabel drove the Jews from Spain?*"
>
> "*Yes,*" *he breathed.*
>
> *My irritation vanished. It was not that he did not wish to talk; it was simply almost impossible for him to talk. All right. I would wait. He cleared his throat.*
>
> "*You see, there are only 2,500 of us here in Spain,*" *he said.*
>
> "*And since there are practically no Jews in Spain, there can't be a problem, can there?*" *I asked.*
>
> "*That's right.*" *He sounded as though he were forcing the words out of his throat.*
>
> —Richard Wright,
> *Pagan Spain* (1957)

Prudencio Mdomio is a Spanish citizen from the ex-Spanish territory of Equatorial Guinea on Africa's west coast. He spent his life's savings on a bar in Barcelona. At the age of 40, he wanted to establish his future. Mdomio's choice was a place for sale in a working-class *barrio,* away from the center of the city. Prudencio is an easygoing man, with a slow, laid-back, African rhythm behind the bar, serving up plenty of conversation and laughter while he works. One of the primary reasons he was attracted to the place was because, when he saw it, there was a feeling of peaceful sociability inside. He bought it from a white Catalán who wanted to retire.

He was puzzled when some of his customers advised him to keep a weapon behind the bar.

But it did not take him long to understand why. There was a bar just down the block where a lot of young Catalán men gathered in the evenings. Most of them wore combat boots and had shaved heads. They tended to stand around together outside the place and yell insults down the block at Mdomio's customers. Flyers began appearing under his door, waiting for him when he opened in the morning. They carried messages like, *Una Europa imperial, limpia de negros y judíos* (One imperial Europe, clean of blacks and Jews). He found similar messages scrawled on the wall outside.

"It came to a crisis on a Thursday night," he told me one morning, shortly thereafter, in his bar. "My wife was closing. I was already at home, and she called me to say I should come back quickly. She was terrified.

"The skinheads were shouting and swearing at her when she closed, then kicking the locked door and urinating on it. We called the police. They came and arrested one down the street, but the others got away. Since then, it has been quiet, but I keep a machete under the bar now. I'm ready for them if they want to cause more trouble."

Mdomio's experience is not an isolated incident. Although neo-Nazis are neither as numerous nor as well organized in Spain as in France and Germany—each of which has far greater numbers of immigrants—racism and xenophobia are present in Barcelona and seem to be growing. With Communism no longer the unifying threat that it was in Franco's time, the ultra-Right has returned its focus to its traditional enemies: non-whites, homosexuals, and Jews. They found an audience waiting for their message and a willing legion of shock troops in the gangs of skinheads, modeled after those that grew up in England a decade earlier around soccer clubs. Barcelona's skins started out as a bunch of bad boys who liked to get violent and rowdy after home games of the widely adored pro soccer team, the Football Club of Barcelona, better known as el Barça. From those early rampages of football hooliganism, they grew into something more hateful and focused.

Barcelona's police estimate that the city is home to about seven hundred skinheads, and, of these, a third was deeply committed to a violent, Nazi ideology. They acknowledge that the groups have spread over the past few years. Now there are skinheads in all of Spain's largest cities, including Madrid, Bilbao, Seville, and Valencia. Barcelona's skinheads have been photographed on a number of occasions at rallies as far away as Dresden, Germany. To what extent they are being funded by ultra-right groups like Blas Piñar's National Front—allied with the party of the same name in France, headed by Jean Le Pen—is a matter of debate.

"At the moment we have no actual evidence that the skinheads are being financed by political parties, but there are probably some common points of interest between these groups," Paco Castro, a spokesman for Barcelona's police department, told me. "If those parties were able to organize and use these groups of violent youths it would be dangerous, but right now we know who the skinheads are and we feel we have them under control."

Richard Schweid lives in Tennessee but has periodically lived in Spain's Balearic Islands, "when I needed some place very cheap to stay for months at a time." Though Spain is no longer cheap, he returned to spend time in Barcelona during its critical year of 1992 and wrote Barcelona: Jews, Tranvestites, and an Olympic Season, *from which this piece was excerpted. He has written on Spain for publications including the* Associated Press *and the* San Francisco Chronicle, *as well as writing two critically acclaimed novels,* Catfish and the Delta *and* Hot Peppers.

⋆

In 1572, at the height of a brilliant career as Spain's leading theologian and humanist, Fray Luis de León was attacked by jealous persons in the university, who whispered to the Inquisition, "We all know that Fray Luis is half Jewish, so he's suspect to begin with. But he has now translated King Solomon's Song of Songs into the vernacular. He invites even the most ordinary man in Salamanca to read it. And that is heresy." Especially serious was the additional charge that often, after studying the original Hebrew version of the Bible, he would question the accuracy of the Latin. Fray Luis was apprehended and for several months was under interrogation, after which he was thrown into jail at Valladolid, where he heard only silence.

On the morning of his reappearance notable persons came to the university to hear his reaction to his persecution. As he made his way from his rooms, his gown slightly askew in his usual careless manner, the university plaza was crowded with silent students. Fray Luis walked with eyes straight forward, not daring to acknowledge the furtive glances of approbation which greeted him. As he entered the cloisters and elbowed his way through the crowd he came at last to the room in which he had taught for so many years, and when he saw its familiar outlines, with his friends perched on the narrow benches, and when he knew that among them must be those whose rumors had caused his imprisonment and who would surrender him again to the Inquisition within a few years (he was to die in disgrace at Madrigal de las Altas Torres), he must have wanted to lash out against the injustice he had suffered and would continue to suffer as a Jew and a humanist. Instead he stepped to the rostrum, took his place behind the lectern, grasped the lapels of his robe and smiled at the crowd with the compassion that marked all he did, and said in a low, clear voice, "As we were saying yesterday..." And he resumed his lecture at the precise point of its interruption five years before.

—James A. Michener, *Iberia: Spanish Travels and Reflections*

MARGUERITE RIGOGLIOSO

Among Spanish Men

At what point does flattery become violation?

IT WAS EARLY ON IN MY COLLEGE SEMESTER IN SPAIN AND I HAD not yet learned about the *litera,* the bed cabin that one may purchase on overnight train rides for a few hundred more pesetas. So traveling the long journey from Madrid to Lisbon one September night, I remained bolt upright in a day car, wedged between snoozing passengers on a bench-like seat for hours. By three in the morning, I had had enough torture and tried to find a cabin where I might be able to stretch out.

As I traversed the aisles of the speeding train, I stumbled upon a car with plush, roomy, reclinable seats. This had to be first class. The entire car was dark and blissfully empty. I snuck into a cabin, slid the door closed, and sank into the comfort of the cushions.

No sooner had I begun to relax than a conductor snapped open the door with a flourish and stood there, hat askew, looking somewhat stern. "*Hola,*" I said, playing dumb. An American train attendant, I knew, would have ejected me immediately. But this was Spain, where rules were often bent or broken altogether. I smiled at him.

The man swiftly discarded the professional demeanor that fit him like a bad suit and gleefully plopped down next to me. The fact that he was middle-aged and portly—and that I was utterly exhausted—did not seem to cross his mind as he began to engage me in flirtatious banter with all of the brio of Don Juan.

I was used to this sort of thing by now. As a young American woman in Spain I had quickly learned that few Spanish men could resist a pretty face—or any face at all, as long as it was attached to a female body. Spaniards seemed to treat the wooing of women as a kind of sacred duty.

I could not fail to notice that the custom had been institutionalized as a national male pastime called *piropeando,* or "throwing compliments." I had already had a lifetime of *piropos*—by American standards—thrown at me just in my first two weeks in Spain. From street corners everywhere, men would burst into a chorus of whistles, hisses, odd clucking noises, and mysterious calls every time I'd pass by. Their aggressiveness and raw sexuality startled me at first, but I soon grew used to it.

Maybe that's because the one thing I did learn very quickly about Spanish men was that they were harmless. Any *piropo* perpetrator I'd approach would inevitably turn out to be a good-natured, somewhat ingenuous man who would break into a smile and invite me to a night of dancing. Though I hated to admit it, I was actually beginning to enjoy my new power as a woman—a power I had never felt in America, where I found male culture, for all of its growing sensitivity to sexism, to be much better at making women feel judged and vulnerable than making them feel honored and appreciated.

Sonia told me the story that after the birth of her son she suffered temporarily from Bell's palsy, which paralyzed the left half of her face and caused that eye to close. She had felt very self-conscious about this (Jorge had taken to calling her "the Pirate") until one day on her shopping rounds she received a few words of "piropo." She felt better for days.

—Thomas Swick, "Letter from Madrid: A View from the Street," *The American Scholar*

So sitting in the misty darkness as the train moved swiftly over the obscure Spanish countryside, I indulged the conductor, despite my fatigue, as he teased and flattered. I hoped that my charm would buy me first-class passage for the night. Eventually, however, he told me I'd have to return to the other car. Duty had won out over gallantry. I made a move to get up.

"*Pero primero, un beso,*" he said, pointing to his cheek in case I didn't understand.

I protested cheerfully, but he persisted. The thought flashed through my mind that if I complied, perhaps he would not make me leave after all. The man seemed harmless enough. I leaned over and gave him a quick peck on the cheek.

Before I could sit back up, he grabbed me and mashed his mouth against mine. He looked at me slyly. Chirping away in Spanish, I maneuvered around him to the door. "*Adiós,*" I finally said with a wave. He did not pursue me as I retraced my steps down the aisle, swaying unsteadily with the motion of the train.

When I returned to the States, from time to time I would cavalierly tell friends and acquaintances about the train conductor who tried to seduce me, about how I rebuffed him with a laugh and a smile. It was not until many years later, when I was no longer a naïve young woman, that I began to reflect about how differently the story might have ended. Only then did it occur to me that no one in the world had known where I was on that September evening. That no one would have been likely to pass through the dark and empty car to see the struggle or hear my cries for help over the roar of the train wheels.

Only then did it occur to me that I had come too close to accepting what, in any language, women are so often taught: to barter sex appeal as a commodity and mistake violation for flattery.

Marguerite Rigoglioso spent a college semester studying at Madrid's Instituto Internacional. She is now a freelance writer who lives in Cambridge, Massachusetts, and an associate editor of the Harvard Business School alumni magazine. She is currently writing a book about a women's spiritual pilgrimage she made to Crete.

★

We four girls eschewed the Spanish style of riding sideways in favor of riding astride behind our gallant hosts. Somehow it seemed safer, and, as it turned out, we needed all the safety we could muster. Each of us went riding off in different directions across a field, and I soon found myself alone with my *caballero*, fending off his amorous attentions. Santiago was particularly insistent that I put my hand on a part of his body that I really didn't want to become that familiar with. When I refused, he kicked our horse into a bone-wrenching gallop, hoping, I suppose, to frighten me into doing whatever he asked. I bailed out, luckily landing on my feet, and began walking towards where the others were gathered up ahead. I could see by the looks on my friends' faces that they had had similar experiences.

—Archer T. Gilliam, "*La Vida en Sevilla*"

MICHAEL JACOBS

Terrorism for Autonomy

*The ETA continues bombing in the name
of liberation for Basque people.*

ON THE EVENING COMMUTER TRAIN BETWEEN GUERNICA AND
Bilbao I took out a newspaper and caught a glimpse on the front
page of a smiling, slender-legged teenage girl, dressed in a miniskirt
for her school dance. The accompanying story involved another
terrorist atrocity, justified as part of the armed struggle for the liberation of the Basque people, and doomed ultimately to be a forgotten incident in the long history of blame and counter-blame
that trails away into the mists shrouding Guernica.

If blame has to be apportioned, one has to go back at least to
1876, when the outrage caused by the abolition of the Basque lib-
erties supplied a rallying cry to nascent Basque nationalism. The
passionate desire for an autonomous Euskadi [Basque Country]
soon became the dominant political conviction in the region, with
the result that the inherently conservative Basques of Guipúzcoa
and Vizcaya would side during the Civil War not with Franco, as
they would otherwise have done, but with the Republicans, who
had offered them in 1932 the choice of future autonomy, and had
kept to this promise by giving them at the outbreak of the war a
provisional statute of home rule. Basque allegiance to the
Republicans led to Franco's notorious bombing raid on Guernica

410

so famously depicted by Picasso. The extent of the devastation caused was probably exaggerated by the Basques, but the viciousness of Franco's retaliatory measures against them could hardly have been greater.

ETA (an acronym for Homeland and Freedom, as well as the Basque word for "and") was founded towards the end of the 1950s, but did not become an active terrorist group until a decade later. Thereafter it began gaining considerable popular support throughout Spain, particularly after 1973, when it brought off its most spectacular coup by assassinating Franco's prime minister and probable successor, Admiral Carrero Blanco, whose blown-up car is still one of the attractions of Madrid's Army Museum. With democracy, however, and the granting of semi-autonomous status to the Spanish regions in the late 1970s, ETA lost more and more of its followers within the Basque country, and those that remained became divided into splinter groups, which in turn were shattered into further splinters; acronyms flourished (LAIA, EIA, KAS, HASI, HB, etc.), as did qualified acronyms such as

More than 800 people have died in the ETA conflict since 1968.

Terrorist attacks by ETA have declined in recent years and the number of its hardcore militants is thought to have fallen from the hundreds of fifteen years ago to several score. Officials in Madrid assert that this is so because the organization is split between militants and moderates and is being undermined by a loss of popular support and by police counter-terrorist operations....

Only now are details emerging of links between the government security forces and a shadowy anti-ETA organization [called GAL] that killed 28 people, mostly suspected terrorists, between 1983 and 1987. The scandal over the death squads is reaching high into government, with a former top security official, Rafael Vera, who led the government's campaign against the Basques for nine years, awaiting trial on a variety of charges.

—John Darnton, "Basques Find Inspiration as I.R.A. Talks of Peace," *The New York Times*

ETA-*militar* and KAS-*alternativa*. The principal divisions revolved around the issues of violence and non-violence, support or rejection of Spain's democratic progress, and the extension or not of the Basque conflict into other struggles, such as international class conflict and battles against drug-running and pollution. "Mr Herri Batasuna," as a *Times* correspondent once mistakenly personified this party, is now the only Spanish party not to have denounced ETA, but it has nonetheless suffered over the last few years from growing internal rifts, some of its many factions being as appalled as the wider Spanish public by ETA's more recent terrorist tactics.

Politicians, the army, and above all the Guardia Civil may be "legitimate targets" for ETA, but in attacking them, innocent members of the public have suffered, especially children. In November 1990, a sixteen-year-old girl was killed by a bomb intended for her father, a member of the intelligence services; in May 1991, four children aged between seven and fourteen were among those killed by a car bomb directed against Guardia Civil families resident in Vic. Later in 1991, there were Spaniards I knew personally who were calling for the death of "all Basques" following a bomb attack perpetrated in the Madrid suburb of Carabanchel and shown afterwards on television in such graphic detail that many of those watching the report felt ill.

A collapsed middle-aged woman, wondering what had happened to her daughter, was seen struggling to try and stand up, unaware at first that she had lost her arms. The daughter lay a few feet away, alive, but without legs.

The legs were those of the teenage girl featured on the paper I was reading on the Bilbao train. "She loved dancing," read the caption.

Michael Jacobs first traveled to Spain at the age of sixteen and returned to write A Guide to Andalusia *and* Between Hopes and Memories: A Spanish Journey, *from which this was excerpted. He is also the author of* A Guide to Provence.

★

I knew straight away what it was. I'd heard that sound before, many years before in London, on one of those dying days which we've grown so used to in our city under sporadic attack. That time I had been out shopping when I heard the rumble, followed by the silence, followed by the sirens, been maybe half a mile away from the insanity. This time I was in Barcelona, and further away, but out again strolling and talking aimlessly with Inka, enjoying the cool of a Friday evening in early summer, when that same big, slow hollow sound rolled into the air. "That's a bomb," I said straight away.

"It can't be," said Inka looking puzzled, staring at the sky to search for some lightning which would prove me wrong.

That night everybody seemed personally battered and severely baffled too. Was this the work of ETA, the Basque terrorist group, who were still waging a bloody war against Spain? They were the most likely perpetrators, but why would they blow up working-class Catalans out shopping for the weekend? In the days when Franco represented the common enemy, the people of Barcelona had been the strongest allies of the Basques in the struggle against the generals of Castile. To kill these people didn't even seem to make twisted terrorist sense.

On Sunday afternoon, in a move unprecedented for the silent, violent men of ETA, an official apology was published which talked about a "serious error," but which went on predictably to blame the Spanish government. No one in Catalonia was blaming Spain this time though, and no one was willing to take this shoddy sorry.

—Robert Elms, *Spain: A Portrait after the General*

DAMIEN ELWOOD

No Day at the Beach

Beware the entertaining vagabond.

July in Barcelona is always warm but we had run into an oppressive hot spell. It would reach 100 degrees that day. Budget backpacking around Europe is a real mixed blessing on days like that. Air conditioning is a fantasy even at the nicer *pensiones* and we were twice our daily budget away from those. Showers are almost futile because you are no sooner stepping out into the narrow stone streets when a motorscooter speeds by dusting you in exhaust. Under those circumstances there is only one place to go.

There was no hiding how excited my girlfriend Tina and our friend Cheech were to see a European beach. This would be the first beach any of us had ever been to on a continent other than North America. Somehow this was important. The waters would be bluer and the sand whiter. The wind would carry fragrances we had never smelled before.

We took the subway to Estación de Sants where Tina went into action. She was our official translator by virtue of her two years of high school Spanish and her Italian heritage. I think the latter of the two qualifications got her furthest. She had a strong vocabulary of hand signals. Tina bought the tickets and handed them out. I took the time to put Tina's and my tickets in the zipped front pouch of

414

my backpack. Cheech had a large duffel bag with a shoulder strap in which she placed her ticket.

Descending beneath the station to the trains we discovered that we were not the only young travelers escaping to the beach. Our platform was packed, sweaty body to sweaty body. It looked as if everyone in Barcelona under the age of 25 had decided to take this train. A powerful collection of smells hung in the stale air and though there was stiff competition from an inversion layer of exhaust, the smell of body odor was the dominant fragrance. It was hot and humid despite being underground.

It was not long before I developed a dryness in the back of my throat. I took out a bottle of water I had purchased at the open-air market on Las Ramblas and took a drink. Tina and Cheech had decided to wait until we got to the beach to buy their bottles, probably because they knew they could get a sip out of mine if needed. Understanding this, I passed the bottle around. As I was returning it to my backpack a particularly dirty and rather smelly young Spanish man approached with a friend. He motioned for the bottle and asked for a drink. A momentary feeling of panic ran up my spine. There were a lot of untidy people surrounding us but this guy took the cake. I would not want to touch the bottle after he drank from it, much less drink from it again. A quick glance at Tina and Cheech confirmed the disgust I felt as it was mirrored in their faces. But something took hold of me. I wanted to be the compassionate youth, not the ugly American. So I gave him the bottle.

I looked away, feigning indifference as he prepared to drink. My brief moment of indecision had been long enough for us to become the center of attention at our end of the platform. It amused me to see that the look of disgust so brazenly displayed on Tina's and Cheech's faces was appearing on the faces of Spaniards and tourists all around us. But no sooner had I noticed this when the expressions changed to amazement. I turned around to see a footlong, unbroken stream of water delicately leaving the top of the bottle and disappearing down the Spaniard's sweat-streaked throat. And with a tilt of his wrist the stream of water stopped and the bottle was returned to me. Amazingly, not a drop spilled. And, more importantly, the bottle did not touch his lips.

The author is describing a particularly awe-inspiring method of drinking wine or water in Spain. Most easily accomplished using a bota—those jugs with long spouts that you see throughout the country—the drinker holds the bottle in the air and directs a lengthy stream into the mouth and throat without touching the spout, and without swallowing until tipping the bottle upright again. People truly practiced in the art can send a stream arcing across a table into friends' mouths— without a dribble.

—LMc

A wave of mixed feelings washed over me. Certainly I was glad he had been courteous enough to preserve the cleanliness of our bottle but there was a part of me which felt bad about feeling disgusted in the first place. As I was digesting what had just happened I looked for his friend who, I was certain, would want the bottle next. He, however, had circled around the back of Tina and Cheech and proceeded to leave the platform. Our talented water drinker followed him up the stairs. The crowd turned away and a low multilingual murmur could be heard. Tina for her part was delighted at the unexpected courtesy displayed by the now less-disgusting Spaniard. But she was quick to scold me for endangering the water supply that way. After all, not all young, smelly Spaniards would be so skillful.

We returned to our waiting and I pondered what had just happened. Yes, next time I would refuse and just be an unfeeling bastard. But what were the chances of this occurring again? How many people will ever be approached in the same way under similar circumstances, much less do the approaching? The whole thing was just strange. I began to feel uneasy.

An antiquated train finally rolled up and we joined the crush to get on. Not knowing for sure when we would be asked for our tickets I retrieved them from my pack, but Cheech couldn't find hers. She dug around quickly, finding it had slipped down inside her bag. As we boarded I reminded Cheech to zip up her bag because crowded trains offer ample opportunity to be pick-pocketed. We pressed far into the car and stood in a corner. The number of passengers grew to the point where I could not see the door through which we had just entered. A few long minutes passed before the train lurched forward. Finally we were on our way.

Upon reaching Vilanova i la Geltrú we pushed our way off the train and took a deep breath of saltwater air. My mood was improving. The Mediterranean rose in the distance and I started walking towards it, but my friends were insistent on making a detour towards a stand selling water. Tina did not trust my assurances I would not risk tainting our water supply again. She insisted on having her own bottle. Cheech as well wanted a bottle of water and one of those Italian ice-cream cones. But when Cheech started looking for the fanny pack containing her wallet, she could not find it. She had placed it on top of the towel in her duffel bag, or at least she thought, but it was not to be found in the duffel bag at all. Tina and Cheech then discussed whether or not she had left it on the bed in the *pensión*. Cheech was certain she had brought it. Tina did not remember seeing her bring it.

I listened to the two of them retrace our steps that morning, and when they got to the scene on the platform at Estación de Sants, the sense of panic returned. The oddities of the water bottle incident at once became clear, creating a lump in my throat like peanut butter and Wonder bread. We had been scammed. Our two dirty friends had orchestrated the picture-perfect pick-pocketing. They had worked as a team. One distracted while the other lifted Cheech's fanny pack out of her *open* duffel bag. Cheech had not zipped it back up after she put her ticket in it. I had noticed her oversight but had not said anything to her, thinking we would be safe until we got on the train. How naïve. How stupid. We were so easily fooled. Hell, everyone standing at that end of the platform had probably been fooled. What he did was pretty amazing. But had he spilled water all over his face he still would have succeeded. We had been sitting ducks.

Damien Elwood is a native of Los Angeles who has lived in Florence, eaten couscous in Marrakech, and witnessed the last Communist May Day in

Moscow. He now sings, writes, and makes art on L.A.'s west side, along with his partner and wife, the sculptor Lauren Evans. Much of Elwood's work is posted on the World Wide Web at: http://glyfix.com/damo/.

✳

I'm still not sure which was greater: our naïveté or the cabbie's audacity. Kevan and I had just arrived at the Seville airport, and were still in the never-never land the mind occupies when first arriving on foreign soil. Well-meaning if green travelers, we were determined to like and trust all our Spanish hosts. So we didn't raise an eyebrow when our cabbie, without looking at the clock on his dashboard, told us the last evening train to Córdoba, our ultimate destination, was just departing. We didn't think to question his knowledge that *all* the *pensiones* in Seville were full, owing to the upcoming grand prix car race. And naturally, when he offered to *drive* us to Córdoba—some 140 kilometers away—we agreed. After all, it would cost, by our exchange-rate reckoning, only US$40. As the cabbie turned off the meter, we leaned forward and enthusiastically asked about his family.

Eventually we exhausted our crash-course Spanish. The silence must have had a sobering effect, for I asked again: The ride would cost *cinco mil pesetas,* yes? "Tch, no," he responded, in that peculiarly Spanish way. "*Cincuenta mil pesetas.*" The ride would cost $400, not $40. I didn't bother to translate "Are you crazy? Let us out immediately!" Our driver seemed to understand. Within minutes we were standing outside a gas station in the middle of nowhere, and our driver was heading back to Seville, $50 richer. Inside the station, fluorescent lights cast a surreal glare as Kevan and the gas station attendant took turns talking on the phone to our friend in Córdoba, who acted as translator in our quest to figure out where we were.

To our delight, we discovered we were near an old Roman town called Carmona, and only a couple kilometers up the road we'd find a *pensión.* Gone were fast-talking cab drivers; here among the whitewashed buildings, the clock tower that stood like an omniscient sentry, and the magical parador built in the remains of an old *alcázar*, we felt a little safer. By day we discovered a bustling town, where men in cafés beckoned us in and winked at us and women in black dresses waddled by and smiled at us. We winked and smiled back; but our looks were knowing.

We did learn later that there were vacant *pensiones* in Seville and we hadn't missed the last train, although I'll never know if the fare increase was a result of our miscalculation or the driver's dishonesty. In retrospect, I think we knew subconsciously we were being taken for a ride—not just literally. But perhaps we were unwilling to surrender our illusions—about the universal honesty of people, the simplicity of travel—so soon. For as long as we could, we remained innocents abroad.

—Catherine Olofson, "Two for the Road"

Where Quixote's Fortunes Fell

Of what befell the Knight of Sad Countenance in Barcelona,
and other tales of mayhem in the city.

JUNE 10, BARCELONA. FOLLOWING UNFREQUENTED ROADS DON Quixote and Sancho Panza found signs that they were reaching the end of their journey. At night, passing through a wood, Sancho felt something brush the top of his head. He put up his hand and touched a pair of human feet, in socks and shoes. Under the next tree it was the same—the trees were full of feet and legs. Sancho shook with terror and shouted for Don Quixote, who calmed him: "There's nothing to be afraid of. These are bandits who have been hanged where they were caught. It means we are approaching Barcelona."

The dead still give warning to a traveller that he is coming into Barcelona. In an immense cemetery at the edge of the city they are filed away in hillside tombs for safe-keeping.

It was the only town Don Quixote visited on his travels, and he wasn't happy there. Recognized at once, he was greeted with drums and music, and paraded through the streets with a placard on his back, "This is Don Quixote of La Mancha," for extra mockery. Boys tied bundles of prickles under the tails of Rocinante and Sancho's donkey, which spurred them into bucking their riders off. After being exhibited like a monkey on a balcony while the citizens passed by and stared, the famous hero was entertained at night with a ball, tempted by grand ladies, tormented into dancing till he could only gasp an oath of loyalty to Dulcinea and sit down exhausted on the floor. He didn't fit into this sophisticated urban society, he belonged on the empty Manchegan plain. Only the sea, which he and Sancho had never seen before, could please him here: it was so wide and spacious, far bigger than the lagoons of Ruidera.

Barcelona is a modern place, hardly Spanish at all. The language is a version of Provençal, the flavour is of Marseille or Genoa or Naples, yet with a character of its own—energetic, ambitious, successful. The factories are working, the dockyard cranes are loading and unloading. Tension, action, profit are in the air, with a whiff of violence. Barcelona faces Europe, turning its back on the bleached old heartland of Spain, the land of Don Quixote.

I try to picture the two-day revolution in July 1936 at the beginning of the Civil War, when the city was seized by Anarchists and more than five hundred people were killed, some of them army officers shot by their own men. All 58 churches except the cathedral were burned or demolished. Hotels, shops, cafés, banks, factories were taken over or closed. Shoeshine boys were collectivized and middle-class habits—giving a tip, wearing a tie, calling a man *señor* instead of *camarada*—were banned at peril of arrest. But the new order didn't last. It was the only occasion in history, Hugh Thomas wrote, when Anarchists have controlled a great city and it was remarkable what little use they made of their opportunity.

Dimly I can see George Orwell in militia uniform marching up the Ramblas, the famous leafy boulevard, on his way to the station and the war front. He had trouble with his equipment and had to be shown how to put on his leather cartridge cases by a gentle-eyed Spanish girl, who gave him a bottle of wine and a length of *chorizo* sausage—"who looked as though her life-work was to rock a cradle, but who as a matter of fact had fought bravely in the street battles." Back on leave a few months later, he got caught up in the war-within-a-war between rival revolutionary parties, with the

Ramblas a battlefield raked by machine-guns on the roofs and at least another four hundred dead. A thousand or so more were killed when Barcelona was raided by Italian bombers.

In a crowded street a girl coming towards me wraps her fingers briefly round my waist as she passes, but doesn't look back. Outside the cathedral the young people playing flutes and jiggling puppets for money aren't Spanish, or even Gypsies, but foreigners on the great drop-out trail round the world, the pilgrim route to some misty shrine evoked by dope. The flock of white Roman geese in the cloister, with their private pool, look sleeker and more satisfied.

At midday I sit with a beer at a café in the Plaza Real. Moroccans kick a football among the palms, a pop singer belts out the chorus of Beethoven's Ninth Symphony. Four times in half an hour I'm offered drugs for sale: *estupefacientes*, stupefiers is the vivid word. This morning, across the plaza in his hotel room, a man of 23 died of heroin. The shock is greater for being in Spain. They have gone from authoritarianism, the dictatorship of Franco and the Church, to a novel kind of democracy—from the Falange to AIDS—in double quick time. They are catching up on the '60s and '70s, the decades they never had. I feel sorry rather than envious: to go through all that permissiveness, swinging and rocking and drugging—like going through my early life again.

I move into a restaurant for lunch. A lean grizzled military man, with medal ribbons on his chest and a forage cap clipped under his shoulder strap, sits reading a German newspaper at another table. Could he be a veteran of the Condor Legion sent by Hitler to help Franco in the Civil War? Could he have bombed Guernica? He marches to the bar, brings back a glass of brandy and pours it into his coffee, at which the waiter fetches the

> *By the end of 1994 the total number of AIDS cases reported for all of Spain was 27,584, or 69 cases per each 100,000 people, according to the World Health Organization. The comparable figure for the United States was 401,789, or 158 cases per each 100,000 people.*
>
> —LMc

brandy bottle and fills his glass again. The TV on the wall is show-ing a lunchtime medical programme—huge coloured diagrams of human genitals. The German barks at the waiter who switches the channel, and we get close-ups of [government officials] instead. People staring at the first programme go on staring: penises, vagi-nas, presidents, prime ministers—they have their passing interest, their moments of curiosity in a crowded Barcelona restaurant.

"The place is dead," a young woman tells me in the travel agency where I book a seat on this evening's express train to Madrid and tomorrow's flight to London.

Dead?—it's what Benito, the bar owner, said about El Toboso three weeks ago. Outside in the street the traffic is as noisy as any-where in the world.

"Nobody shouts anymore," she complains. "And today is elec-tion day!" In the Franco days she was a university student and re-members their demonstrations, their involvement in a wider game. Now the graffiti stick to local politics, the tiff between Catalán and Catalán over independence for Catalonia. "Our writers and painters have gone to Madrid. It's too comfortable here—there's no enemy anymore."

Certainly all is peaceful though not quiet in the Ramblas, where Orwell marched to the front. Blue carnations and green parakeets are for sale, and lottery tickets and the London papers. In the evening *paseo*, the daily promenade when everyone comes out to display themselves, to walk and talk with everyone else, the avenue becomes a stream of life. Revolution isn't conspicuous and down near the port the trees, which once gave cover for snipers, are heavily outnumbered by prostitutes. They were shamed off the streets by the Anarchists of 1936 and during Franco's long dicta-torship were said not to exist at all. Few of them are beautiful. Some of the most startling—a dark red-lipped panther lounging on the bonnet of a parked car or an immensely tall, lusciously feminine blonde mincing down the pavement—are men.

Others are more tragic. A pretty girl, no more than a child, tot-ters against a shop window, then lurches blindly round the corner to lean against another shop. She isn't doing much trade. She is someone's daughter, knocked out by drugs.

My companion pointed at the tall, elegant woman behind the bar and whispered that she was a man; not exactly a man, but a travesti *(transvestite or transsexual). "She" heard us talking about her, and smiled. I studied her face and realised it was true. I wasn't long out of Ireland, and this came as a bit of a shock. Soon I noticed* travestis *all around the city center, but mainly on the Ramblas and Barri Xinès. All of them had long thin legs and bodies like models. They moved in twos and threes, walking with great pride and nonchalance down the Ramblas. Some of them, I was told, did great business, better than the male and female prostitutes who also hung around the Ramblas.*

—Colm Tóibín,
Homage to Barcelona

Barcelona was Don Quixote's furthest point from home. Riding along the beach one morning he was challenged by another knight, a stranger who claimed that his own mistress was incomparably more beautiful than Dulcinea of El Toboso. They charged in mortal combat but Don Quixote was easily unhorsed and the conqueror stood over him, pinning him to the ground with his spear.

"Finish me off," the shattered old man begged in a voice that seemed to come already from the tomb. Ignominy was piled on dishonour and only the virtue of his faith was left: "Dulcinea is the loveliest woman in the world and I'm the unhappiest knight."

Whatever else, love was unconquerable: the love, or truth, that he had created and by which he lived.

In fact the stranger was an old friend in disguise who only wanted to force Don Quixote to forsake this crazy life and go home. Sancho Panza agreed and when his master lay in bed, melancholy and brooding, he tried to cheer him up: "Thank God that though you were knocked to the ground you got off without one broken bone. Stuff the doctor!—there's nothing he can do for you. Let's give up wandering about, looking for adventure in places we don't know."

Sorrowfully they set off home. "This is where my deeds were wiped out," Don Quixote lamented as they left the city, "and my fortunes fell, never to rise again." When Sancho blamed it all on luck Don Quixote replied that there was no such thing: "Every man is architect of his own destiny. I have been so of mine, though not always with the necessary prudence. But I did what I could."

In his old age, turning back to his own village which he knew he would never leave again, the Knight of the Sad Countenance was beginning to show the faintest recognition of his fallibility.

Nicholas Wollaston also contributed "Quixote's Parable of Life" in Part One, "Quixotic Adventures" in Part Two, and "The Way of Quixote" in Part Three. All of these pieces were excerpted from his book Tilting at Don Quixote.

＊

When the day began to break, they raised their eyes and saw the fruit of the trees, which were the bodies of bandits....

If the knight and his squire were unnerved by these dead bandits, how much more did they quake when they suddenly found themselves surrounded by more than 40 living bandits who ordered them in the Catalán tongue to halt and not to move till their captain arrived? Don Quixote happened to be on foot, his horse unbridled, his lance leaning against a tree some distance away; in short, being defenseless, he thought it best to cross his hands, bow his head, and reserve himself for a better opportunity.

—Miguel de Cervantes Saavedra, *Don Quixote of La Mancha*
(1605/1615)

PART FIVE

THE LAST WORD

LAWRENCE O'TOOLE

A Journey's End

The author searches the landscape
of Galicia for home.

IT WAS A FUNNY YET FEARSOME SIGHT THAT FLITTED ACROSS MY
peripheral vision on my first day in Galicia's greenery, which was
now blushing its way into autumn. The image—fleeting, bizarre,
still floating in my head—made me turn back to make sure it was
not a temporary aberrance of my imagination. But there it was: a
twin-engine plane suspended—hanging, it seemed—in the trees
by the side of the road. Closer investigation revealed that the plane
had been mounted on granite pillars, with makeshift steps up to
the cockpit for the curious to explore. Pasted across the side of the
plane's nose was a banner. It read: "LA FORTUNA." Fate, indeed. Was
this the Galician sense of humor—a cocktail of pessimism spiked
with black humor?

I had come to Galicia knowing it would be different from the
rest of Spain. In Galicia, the northern tip above Portugal, I knew
not to expect any flamenco, *toreadores, mantillas, paella* or even
sunny skies. Claiming the heaviest rainfall in all of Europe, isolated
Galicia was once known as "The End of the World." Prior to the
discovery of the Americas, it *was* the end of the known world—
as far as you could go before dropping off its edge beyond the unsure horizon.

Its original inhabitants were Celts, my people, and to this day Galicians mostly speak *Gallego,* not Spanish, and play *bagpipes,* for God's sake. One reason for going there was to discover my faraway origins (black Irish, mix of Celtic and Hispanic); another was to further feed my fascination with people who live in relative isolation; and yet another was longing to be somewhere other than where I am. The north and northwest coasts of Galicia, with their craggy cliffs and sheltered coves, bear more than a passing resemblance to my own home of Newfoundland. And its mauzy ol' weather—drizzly, with a chill to the bone sometimes on otherwise halcyon days, was all too familiar.

But there was another reason for going to Galicia, one that has drawn travellers there for centuries: the cathedral of Santiago de Compostela, where the bones of Santiago, or Saint James, are supposedly buried. (History is very unclear about this fact.) During the Middle Ages it was to this site, close to the end of the world, that pilgrims brought their greatest troubles and deepest wishes from all over Europe, in effect creating the Western world's first tourist town. All kinds of people, religiously inclined and otherwise, still journey to Santiago de Compostela, which over the years has built up a legend as a place of magic. Or spiritual solace at the very least.

The early pilgrims made the journey across the Pyrenees in France and the wide top of Spain, carrying no more than a rucksack and a walking staff. Not ten minutes from Santiago's airport, I spotted my first pilgrim, staff in hand, slightly bent under his pack, on the last leg of his travels—an ancient sight in a modern world. But I wanted to savor Santiago last, so I headed south, which was where I encountered the airplane in the trees. Santiago would be the last stop on my own little pilgrimage. I had, however, no idea how much of a pilgrimage it would turn out to be.

It was on the road from the city of Vigo to the border town of Túy that it happened. A loud bang and everything was instantly out of control—quickly almost off the highway into the deep gutter—a reflexive wrench of the steering and back onto the road—then the ungodly tear of metal and the dry, surprising shattering of glass…. When I woke up, my car was moving slowly, bumpily, down the road. Another car had stopped, its driver inquiring anxiously, "*Tranquilo?*" I looked at myself. A little blood, a lot of glass, but I seemed to be okay. Yes, *tranquilo.*

I walked away from the car and up the road to discover that the driver of the other car was, like me, only slightly bruised, had a few cuts, was shaken up, but essentially fine. Given the facts, I ought to have been just another statistic, taken The Big Siesta; at least been maimed in some way. Galicia may or may not be a place of magic, but I know that it's one of miracles. I also know that proximity to death is a great whetstone for sharpening the senses. It's surely a cliché, but afterwards food tasted better, scents were more seductive, images more intense, touch was like music to the skin and I was more engaged by my own feelings than I'd ever been. I had become a walking raw nerve; it was not unpleasant.

Accidents do happen to tourists and most find themselves asking, What do I do now? My answer is: you start the trip over. With, of course, very new and different baggage. The next night, having picked up a new car and driven back over the same route, then further down the province's southernmost coast, which serves as a holiday spot for the sunbaked rest of Spain, I treated my battered self to a night at the Grand Hotel La Toja: grand, indeed, in the old *fin-de-siècle* style. La Toja is an islet that's actually a mineral spring, and it produces a beautiful black soap, headily scented, called Magno. The place was a paradise pit stop.

The next morning I awoke and sat on the balcony of my room in my grand hotel wrapped like royalty in my immense, snowy-white Grand Hotel La Toja bathrobe, and saw, through a pearly-white impressionistic haze, several fishermen in dories tending their nets, calling across the untouched membrane of the water to one another as they caught *mejillones* (mussels) for someone's dinner.

Make no mistake about it: Galicia is gorgeous and it can be as active a playground as other European sandboxes. Its beaches, even along the perilous northern coast, where the roads wind bewitchingly and the Atlantic keeps lashing the land with spray and gale, are among the best on the continent. Nearly every little town and village is travel-brochure perfection: old men in berets berating cows homeward with canes; old women in widow's weeds carrying huge bundles atop their heads; porticoed and cobbled streets; small cemeteries with elaborate monuments; Visigoth, Romanesque and baroque churches in every hamlet; serene monasteries; coiffed haystacks Van Gogh might have envied; wild horses, in the south, grazing at the side of the road; and, of course, *hórreos* (granaries) resting on stilts with crosses atop them, giving them the appearance of graves above ground.

In the evenings the streets are filled with the sound of discreet human merriment from the *tapas* bars and *whiskerías* competing with TV and the clip-clop of feet on cobblestones. For the Galicians *are* subdued. Like their neighbors, the Portuguese, they are a very formal people, pleasant but never forward. Galicians are an inward people. They're very Celtic.

In the north, the climate, landscape and the tenor of life change. Villages such as Malpica and Camariñas have the smell of gutted fish, no different from any Newfoundland outport, where salted cod hangs out to cure and old men stare out to sea remembering either better or bitter days—it's hard to tell with old men gazing out at the ocean. In Muxía, they built a church on a promontory where a lighthouse would normally be. It stands, surreal and impervious to the howling winds and ocean spray, on an open expanse of eroded rock. The waves sometimes come up to the door.

The sea in Galicia is an inextricable part of life, taking as much as it gives. Those who climb down steep cliff faces to wrench the toothsome barnacles that cling to them sometimes lose their lives; others, working on the furious seashores, are surprised and carried away by what the Galicians call "the seventh wave." A substantial portion of the Atlantic coast, twisting through an extremely jagged landscape, has been christened the Costa de la Muerte, or Coast of Death, having claimed a large number of shipwrecks and auto accidents. Death, in Galicia, almost seems an *ordinary* thing. Or was I especially inclined to think so?

As a Celt, that's my natural inclination: to look towards the shadows rather than the sunlight. Surely the stubborn crowd of Celts who came to Galicia more than 3,000 years ago must have had some kind of death wish to settle at "The End of the World." But for many the area of Galicia, and Santiago de Compostela in particular, was often a new beginning. It used to be that travel was either a means of getting from one place to another or else a spiritual undertaking. People didn't travel to see as much as to feel, and this is what can happen if you take the pilgrim's route in Galicia, which begins in the mountainous east just before Cebreiro.

When the pilgrims got to Cebreiro they were greeted by the monks who lived there. There was a church (built in the 9th century, still standing) and a hospital for sick travellers. Perhaps Spanish tourism has been just a little too diligent in replicating the Celtic thatched huts here: the place is dangerously close to being a spiritual theme park. The highway people were also working on the snaky roads, which is a bit like landscaping around Vesuvius. But once past Cebreiro, the pilgrim's route becomes tinged with the otherworldly. If Finisterre still seems the end of the world, then this seems the top of it. An endless vista of overlapping mountains spreads in every direction, the afternoon haze an aura burnished by the slipping sun.

The pilgrim's route counts among the profound moments travel can offer; and it is the only drive that makes you want to get out and walk—or at least constantly stop and listen to the near silence. For 80 kilometers or so the traveller passes through a place that onward rushing time has given only a passing glance and then continued without affecting anything. This includes the village of Piornedo, cradled along the side of a deep valley, its thatched Celtic houses huddled into an image that's close to being a mirage from the past. Or the imposing Monastery of Samos from 700 A.D., built in an idyllic river setting where peace and quiet seem to acquire fresh meaning.

Something took hold of me on that drive. At first I thought it might be something as simple as the late afternoon light hitting an old woman's face as she rested under a tree; or maybe a lone, modern pilgrim on the road and the poignancy of his intent. But it was more than that. I began weeping, a soft weeping that would not cease. I would stop the car every once in a while and dry my eyes, but the weeping would continue. Tears just flowed, naturally, as if this was what happened to me during every waking hour. I began to think of all the pilgrims who had trod this road, and I felt overwhelmed by their proximity to me, as if a microscopically thin film separated us right here, right now, on this road, and I had to weep some more. I was extremely close to something I had never touched during my lifetime. Perhaps it was my own proximity to death that made me open, raw, receptive. All these people, these souls, filling every available space of the landscape and beyond it. I could feel them all around me, those I knew and loved and who were gone—people who were going to die and be in that same place soon, people I'd never heard of, yet to whom somehow I was now firmly connected.

It may sound strange or stupid or unbearably mystical, but that's how it was. And it was during this sort of weeping trance that two things occurred to me. One was that I should, in my dealings with all people, behave towards them as if I knew they would no longer be here the next day. The second was the possibility that home is not here at all, not on this earth, not on this place; and that the end of expectation—of longing—is the beginning of peace. Then the weeping stopped. As casually and unexpectedly as it began. I drove onward to Santiago de Compostela.

When each band of pilgrims approached Santiago de Compostela, the first among them to spot the spires of the cathedral shouted "*Mon joie!*" and was made king among them. That hill is now known as Mount Joy. In the crypt of the cathedral where the saint's bones are supposedly buried there is a written explanation of two angels at the apex of a pillar. The angels seem to hold up the ceiling all by themselves. The writing says the image is "expressing man's relationship with the unforgiving minute."

But, for me, the minute forgave.

Santiago de Compostela itself (the name means Saint James of the Field of Stars) is, at its core, a medieval city, built for the sole purpose of worship, and remains so. It was bitterly cold my last night there and I hadn't dressed for it. I wanted to go some place simple, a place a pilgrim might have sought out centuries ago, and I did manage to find Santiago's only hole in the wall. An old woman (I seemed to be the only patron under 70) served me consommé, chicken, bread and fruit. I felt immensely warmed by it and immensely satisfied. I thought of this trip to Galicia, this latest search for home now ending, and how I was in a place and among people who had been around a long time, and I felt the incalculable comfort of knowing that I was here, alive, still among them.

This is what the pilgrim soul in me had sought all along: merely to be here and stay for a while.

Here. Home.

Lawrence O'Toole is a Canadian writer who lives in New York. This was adapted from his book, Heart's Longing.

WHAT YOU NEED TO KNOW

𝒲EATHER AND WHEN TO GO

Late spring to early summer, as well as early autumn, are ideal times for traveling throughout Spain. July and August can get unbearably hot in southern and central areas, while in the north, midsummer may afford the only opportunity to visit without an umbrella. Try to avoid big cities and resort areas in August when Spaniards take their annual holiday, and crowds and accommodation rates soar.

Spanish winters, though usually fair, can be brisk and damp, with coldest temperatures in the central plains and higher elevations. If you're a skier, head for the slopes of the Pyrénées, Sierra Nevada or Guadarrama mountains. The Canary and Balearic Islands enjoy pleasant weather virtually all year round.

𝒞USTOMS AND ARRIVAL

Citizens of most countries, including New Zealand, Canada, and the United States, need only a valid passport for a visit of up to 90 days. Australian and South African nationals must obtain a visa. If you intend to stay longer than three months, contact a Spanish embassy, consulate, or tourist office for advice.

Customs usually are not a problem, unless you are arriving from North Africa, in which case you and your luggage may be subjected to a more rigorous search. Once inside the country, you are required to carry your passport or national identification card with you at all times.

𝒢ETTING INTO THE CITY

All direct flights to Spain, go through Madrid and Barcelona. From these central cities you can transfer to planes, trains, and buses to get to outlying towns. In both cities, the airport is about twenty minutes from downtown

THE NEXT STEP

in normal traffic. Typical rush hours, when people are commuting to and from work, can lengthen the trip.

In Madrid, it is cheapest to take the airport *autobús* downtown to Colón Plaza, where you can catch a taxi, public transportation, or rare and expensive direct shuttle to your hotel. Here, you can also find a way to get to another destination in Spain.

In Barcelona, take the *tren* to the Sants train station downtown. Here, like Madrid's Colón Plaza, you can connect to your hotel or other Spanish destinations.

HEALTH

Overexposure to the sun and "Spanish tummy" are the most common health problems encountered by travelers. With a little moderation and good judgment, you should be able to enjoy the sunshine, food, and water with no adverse effects.

Bring all prescription and non-prescription medications you will need for your trip; products familiar to you may differ from those used by pharmacies in Spain. Although Spanish pharmacists do not accept foreign prescriptions, they will advise, and even prescribe, drugs for minor complaints.

At least one pharmacy in every town remains open all night, on Sundays and on holidays. To find the nearest *farmacia de guardia* (emergency pharmacy), look for postings in Spanish newspapers, or on the door or windows of your local pharmacy. *Farmacias* are signposted with a red or green illuminated cross.

If you need medical attention in a hurry, inquire at any hotel, call the *Cruz Roja* (Red Cross) or make your way to the nearest *Urgencias* (hospital emergency ward). Local emergency numbers and ambulances are listed under *servicios de urgencia* and *ambulancias* in local newspapers or in the phone book.

No special vaccinations are required for entry to Spain, unless you are traveling to or from a country where cholera or yellow fever are found. For further information, contact the London Travel Clinic's medical advisory service (0171 388 9600), or the Centers for Disease Control International Traveler's Hot Line in the United States (404-332-4559).

SAFETY

In Spain, as in most countries, big cities and tourist areas are subject to petty crime. Foreigners are easy to spot and, consequently, make tempting targets for pickpockets and bag snatchers. Be on your guard and never leave your belongings unattended, even in your car. If you do suffer a loss or theft, report it to the police immediately.

TIME

Clocks in Spain are one hour ahead of Greenwich Mean Time in the winter, while clocks in the Canary Islands coincide with GMT. Therefore, when it is noon in Madrid, it is also noon in Paris; 11 a.m. in London and the Canary Islands; 6 a.m. in New York; 1 p.m. in Johannesburg; and 9 p.m. in Sydney.

During daylight-saving time from late March until the end of October, clocks move forward one hour (Spanish time is then two hours ahead of GMT), and the sun may shine until as late as ten.

MONEY

The Spanish unit of currency is the peseta, abbreviated as pta. Denominations come in coins of 1, 5, 10, 25, 50, 100, 200 and 500, and bank notes of 1,000, 2,000, 5,000 and 10,000 pesetas. You may hear Spaniards talking about prices in duros, a duro being the colloquial word for five pesetas.

The best exchange rates for foreign currency and travelers' checks can be obtained at banks. Look for the foreign exchange desk marked *cambio de moneda extranjera,* or withdraw your pesetas at the automatic teller machine. You can also change money at your hotel, currency exchange shops (*Oficinas de Cambio*), and stores which cater to tourists. Credit cards are widely accepted throughout Spain.

Non-EU residents who spend more than 15,000 pesetas on a single item may be entitled to a tax refund off the purchase price. If your purchase qualifies, present the unused goods, receipt and refund form (provided by a shopkeeper) to the VAT airport officer when you depart. You usually receive the refund by mail or on your credit card account.

𝓑USINESS HOURS

Traditionally, shopping begins at 9:30 or 10 a.m and comes to a halt around 1:30 or 2 p.m. for a long Spanish lunch and siesta. Doors re-open from 5 to 8 p.m., with the exception of banks, post offices, and some museums that close in the afternoon. Supermarkets and department stores remain open all day, while open-air markets get going in the early morning and wrap up in time for the midday meal.

Most shops are shuttered on Saturday afternoons and Sundays, apart from museums which generally close on Mondays instead. In smaller towns, churches and castles may be locked around the clock. Ask if you can borrow the key at the nearest house, town hall, or neighborhood bar.

𝓔LECTRICITY

Electrical current is 220 volts AC, although the 110-volt system occasionally operates in older buildings. In both cases, plugs have two round pins. Ask when hotel sockets do not indicate which voltage applies.

𝓜EDIA (NEWSPAPERS, RADIO, TV)

El País, El Mundo, and *ABC* are Spain's biggest and best national newspapers, providing coverage of international events, as well as regional information on festivals, all-night pharmacies, television, theater, and cinema.

International publications are available at news stands in major cities and tourist areas. Some go on sale on the day of publication; others arrive a day or two late.

In addition to the state-run Radio Nacional de España, several hundred FM stations can be picked up around the country. The BBC World Service broadcasts on short-wave frequencies during the better portion of the day.

Spanish television offers a mix of news, soap operas, and sports, as well as English-language exports dubbed into Spanish. Satellite channels, such as Eurosport, CNN and Sky News, are popular in bars, private homes, and luxury hotels.

TOUCHING BASE (PHONE CALLS, FAXES, EMAIL)

To make an international call, dial 07, wait for the tone, and follow with the country code, the area code and the number. Country codes include 61 for Australia, 353 for Ireland, 64 for New Zealand, 27 for South Africa, 44 for the United Kingdom, and 1 for the United States and Canada.

For internal calls from one province to another, first dial the provincial code prefixed by the number 9, and then the number itself. Within a province, dial the number directly. Domestic calls are relatively inexpensive, whereas international ones rank among the most unreasonable in Europe, particularly if you phone from your hotel.

Ask the bartender at any café if you may use the coin-operated or metered telephone on the counter. Street pay phones accept coins and newer models accept telephone cards (*tarjeta telefónica*). Phone cards can be purchased at post offices (*correos*) and tobacco shops (*estanqueros*), and are especially convenient for long-distance dialing.

Unless you need to send a package, don't waste your time in long post office queues. Tobacco shops sell stamps (*sellos*) as well, and usually will know the correct postage for your letters. Mail boxes (*buzones*) are wall-mounted or in pillar form. The slot labeled *extranjero* is for overseas mail.

Fax facilities exist in most hotels and post offices, although private shops with telefax signs tend to offer better rates. If you are traveling with your computer, you can access e-mail and the Internet in one of Spain's increasingly popular Internet cafés. Otherwise, check with your Internet service provider to see if they have international coverage. Compuserve and America Online provide international coverage, but getting through can still be challenging.

CULTURAL CONSIDERATIONS

ℒOCAL CUSTOMS

Should you be invited to a meal in a Spanish home, take along a small token of your appreciation, perhaps flowers, chocolates, or a bottle of wine. Bear in mind that it is considered bad manners not to keep both hands on the dinner table at all times.

Meal times in Spain begin considerably later than in most countries. Unless you want to eat with foreigners, have lunch at 2 p.m. and never go to dinner before 9:30 or 10.

Spanish bar and restaurant bills customarily include service, *servicio incluido,* although an additional gratuity is always appreciated, usually five to ten percent. Taxi drivers, theater ushers, and gas station attendants also expect a small tip.

Courteous as they are, Spaniards often lack patience, and are loath to form or keep to a line. Wherever there are queues, you usually will find a queue-jumper.

If you want to spend time with the locals, choose your wardrobe with care. Spaniard like to look their best and take every opportunity to dress smartly. Skimpy tops and shorts, though common in resort areas, will make you feel conspicuous elsewhere.

Spaniards speak Castilian Spanish or Castellano, officially the national language of Spain. However, many regions prefer to use additional languages of their own, including Catalán in Cataluña, Gallego in Galicia and Euskera in the Basque regions. As in any country, every attempt to speak the language will be genuinely appreciated by all.

It is not uncommon for strangers to greet each other when entering waiting rooms, elevators, and shops.

When being introduced, shaking hands is never a mistake. Subsequent greetings and farewells are sealed with kisses on both cheeks. If in doubt, stick to the handshake.

According to law, Spaniards have two last names. The first, is their father's surname. The second is their mother's first surname. So Antonio, the son of José Romero Rojas and Isabel García López, is Antonio Romero García. Spanish women do not change their names when they marry, but may add their husband's surnames (preceded by "*de*") on to their own. To ascertain whether someone is married, look for the ring on the fourth finger of the right hand.

Most Spaniards bear the name of their patron saint, each of whom has a nominated day. It is customary to call up friends on their saint's day to wish them a happy day.

*F*ESTIVALS

Spain is justifiably renowned for its festivals, the most famous of which are "Carnival" in Cádiz (February or March), "Las Fallas" in Valencia (March), "San Fermines" in Pamplona (July), the "Feria" in Sevilla (March or April) and "Semana Santa" or Holy Week, which is celebrated throughout the country.

Festivities, however, are by no means limited to those mounted on a massive scale. There is no village in Spain too small to honor its patron saint, hero or annual harvest with a *fiesta popular*. And whether it takes the form of a mock Moorish battle, the carpeting of local streets with flowers, or dancing perched on stilts, Spaniards know how to throw a party.

🌀HE NEXT STEP

For details of places, dates, and times of these and other events, get hold of the current *Festivals of Special Interest to Tourists* booklet from the Tourist Office of Spain. In addition, don't forget to consult local *oficinas de turismo* for information on smaller, and as yet undiscovered *fiestas populares.*

𝓗 OLIDAYS

Spaniards enjoy a number of public holidays throughout the year, frequently taking advantage of what are known as *puentes* (bridges). This means that when a holiday falls close to a weekend, people like to take the intervening day off work, thus creating a longer break.

It is generally safe to assume that everything will close down on: New Year's Day, January 6 (Epiphany), Holy Thursday, Good Friday, Easter Sunday, May Day, Corpus Christi (May or June), July 25 (St. James' Day), August 15 (Assumption), October 12 (Columbus Day), November 1 (All Saints Day), December 6 (Constitution Day), December 8 (Immaculate Conception) and, of course, Dec. 25 (Christmas).

IMPORTANT CONTACTS

𝓞FICINAS DE TURISMO

Tourist Information Offices are invaluable resources of information while traveling in Spain. Stop by the Oficina de Turismo in each city and/or region you visit for free leaflets, maps, and listings of local accommodations, entertainment, and festival dates. The Michelin *Red Guide España–Portugal* lists the addresses and phone numbers of many *oficinas de turismo,* the smallest of which may be found in rural town halls or *ayuntamientos.*

𝓣OURIST OFFICES

8383 Wilshire Boulevard, Suite 956
Beverly Hills, CA 90211
Tel (213) 658–7188; Fax (213) 658–1061

666 Fifth Avenue, 35th Floor
New York, NY 10103
Tel (212) 265–8822; Fax (212) 265–8864

Water Tower Place
845 North Michigan Avenue, Suite 915 East
Chicago, IL 60611
Tel (312) 642–1992; Fax (312) 642–9817

1221 Brickell Avenue, Suite 1850
Miami, FL 33131
Tel (305) 358–1992; Fax (305) 358–8223

2 Bloor Street West, Suite 3402
Toronto, Ontario M4W 3E2
Tel (416) 961–3131; Fax (416) 961–1992

United Kingdom
57–58 St. James' Street
London SW1A 1LD
Tel (0171) 499 0901; Fax (0171) 629 4257

*E*MBASSIES

All embassies are located in Madrid, while consulates are spread throughout
the country. Be sure to call first to find out where to go for information.

Australia (91) 579 04 28
Austria (91) 556 53 15
Belgium (91) 577 63 00
Canada (91) 431 43 00
Denmark (91) 431 84 45
France (91) 435 55 60
Germany (91) 319 91 00
Ireland (91) 576 35 00
Italy (91) 577 65 29
Morocco (91) 563 10 90
Netherlands (91) 359 09 14
New Zealand (91) 523 02 26

Norway (91) 310 311
Portugal (91) 561 78 00
South Africa (91) 576 53 69
Sweden (91) 308 153
Switzerland (91) 431 35 17
Tunisia (91) 447 35 08
United States (91) 587 22 00

FIFTEEN FUN THINGS TO DO

- Do a summer tour of the *fiestas populares* in the villages, drinking the local red wine, dancing the *paso doble* music and sampling the array of *tapas.*
- In July, take to the streets with the bulls of Pamplona during the festival of San Fermín.
- Walk, bike, or drive the 500-mile-long pilgrim's path to Santiago de Compostela, home of Hostal de los Reyes Catolicos, one of the most magnificent *paradors* in Spain.
- A trip to Granada is not complete without a stroll through the *barrio* of Albaicín on a summer evening. For unparalleled views of the Alhambra and Sierra Nevada, take your sweetheart to the terrace of the Church of Saint Nicholas at sunset.
- Visit Cordoba in May for the traditional Patios competition that lasts about a week and is followed by the Feria (traditional horse fair). Private homes in the Barrio Judio (Jewish Quarter) open their interior patios to the public, decorated with geraniums, bougainvilla, and jasmine. Sevillanas can usually be heard, and some hosts set up a wooden *tablao* for dancing. Fino sherry is offered, and the hosts often dress in *mantillas.* A prize is awarded annually to the most attractive patio. Some of the best are found in the neighborhood of San Basilio, not far from the Mezquita but off the beaten track.
- From June to September, take the luxury train El Transcantabrico on a week-long journey along the northern coast, from Galicia to the

Basque Country (or the reverse), stopping at fishing villages and cities along the way for guided historical and architectural tours and some of the best seafood in Spain.

- On May 11 in Barcelona, attend the Festival of St. Ponce on L'Hospital Street (off the Ramblas) for an unusual exhibition by herbalists and beekeepers from all over Spain selling their wares, including hundreds of kinds of honey.
- In the Alpujarras near Granada, drive through picturesque Moorish towns such as Capileira and Pampaneira that stand high along the steep terraced hillsides.
- In Barcelona, visit Gaudí's whimsical creation La Pedrera (Casa Mila). It's a private apartment building, but tourists can enter and go to the multiterraced roof for a view of the Mediterranean, the mountains, and Gaudí's Sagrada Familia cathedral. There's also an exhibition about Gaudí's work on the attic level.
- At noon on Sundays in Barcelona, watch Catalans young and old step to the folkdance, the Sardana, accompanied by a band in the plaza before the Cathedral de Barcelona in Barri Gothic.
- In Madrid, take in the nightlife scene at the Palacio Gaviria, a palace that now houses a nightclub where dancers move to a different kind of music in every room, from waltz to disco.
- After staying out all night eating tapas and dancing in nightclubs, in most Spanish cities you can get churros y chocolate (donut-like sticks to dip in thick hot chocolate) at cafes that begin getting crowded around 3 a.m.
- If you're on the Costa del Sol, visit La Axarquia, a group of villages east of the city of Malaga that includes Torrox, Torre del Mar, and Sayalonga, in which you can taste the villages' own wines and visit Roman and Moorish ruins.
- Before or after dinner, join the locals for the evening paseo around any city's main plaza or along the main road through town.
- During Christmas week, visit the Plaza Mayor in Madrid for a display of practical joke gifts (fake vomit and the like), celebrating the Day of the Innocents (Dec. 28), the Spanish equivalent of April Fool's Day.

THE NEXT STEP

SPAIN ONLINE

Search the World Wide Web under "Spain, Travel," or point your browser to the following sites:

"Discover Spain" with the Tourist Office of Spain: http://www.spain-tour.com

Tourist Office of Spain in the United States of America: http://www.ok-spain.org/

Lonely Planet Spain:
http://www.lonelyplanet.com.au/dest/eur/spa.htm/

All About Spain: http://www.red2000.com/index3.shtml

Traveling In Spain:
http://www.internationalist.com/TRAVEL/spain.html

Principal Festivals in Spain: http://www.spaintour.com/festiv2.htm

Madrid's Great Museums: http://www.spaintour.com/museomad.htm

Relais & Châteaux: Welcome: http://www.integra.fr/relaischateaux

RECOMMENDED READING

Armstrong, Mark, Susan Forsyth, John Noble, Corinne Simcock, and Damien Simonis. *Lonely Planet Spain.* Oakland, California: Lonely Planet Publications, 1997.

Ballard, Sam & Jane. *Paradores of Spain.* Boston, Massachusetts: The Harvard Common Press, 1986.

Brenan, Gerald. *The Face of Spain.* Hopewell, New Jersey: The Ecco Press, 1996.

Brown, Clare, Ralph Kite and Cynthia Sauvage. *Karen Brown's Spain: Charming Inns & Itineraries.* San Mateo, California: Travel Press, 1997.

Cela, Camilo José. *The Family of Pascual Duarte.* New York: Little, Brown & Co., 1990.

Crow, John A. *Spain: The Root and the Flower.* Berkeley, California: University of California Press, 1985.

Debelius, Harry. *Independent Traveler's Guide Spain.* Ashbourne, England: Moorland Publishing Co Ltd, 1994.

España–Portugal Red Guide. Greenville, South Carolina: Michelin Travel Publications, 1997.

Eyewitness Travel Guide Spain. London: Dorling Kindersley Limited, 1996.

Facaros, Dana and Michael Pauls. *Cadogan Guide Spain.* London: Cadogan Books, 1996.

Hotels of Character & Charm in Spain. New York: Fodor's Travel Publications, Inc., 1996.

Insight Guide Spain. Boston, Massachusetts: Houghton Mifflin, 1997.

Relais & Chateaux. New York: European Publications Inc., 1997.

Spain Green Guide. New York: Michelin Travel Publications, 1996.

Thomas, Hugh. *The Spanish Civil War.* New York: Simon & Schuster, Inc., 1994.

Walker, Ann & Larry. *To the Heart of Spain: Food and Wine Adventures Beyond the Pyrénées.* Berkeley, California: Berkeley Hills Books, 1997.

"The Next Step" was prepared by Joan Crete and the staff of Travelers' Tales, Inc.

Glossary

aceituna	olive
aguardiente	grain alcohol
alcázar	castle, fortress
alimentación	provisions, food; grocer's shop
alternativa	investiture of a *novillero* (apprentice matador) as a full matador, in which the apprentice is given the right by the matador to kill the first bull of the fight
ambiente	atmosphere
ambiente familiar	family-like atmosphere
apisonadora	steam roller
arriero	member of a famous fraternity of the road; usually used to refer to cork harvesters
artesonado	intricate, inlaid-wood patterns
autopista	highway
autovía	highway
ayuntamiento	city government; city hall
bailadora	dancer
banderilla	sharp-pointed dowel wrapped in colored paper, placed in pairs high into a bull's back
banderillero	bullfighter who reports to the matador and helps run the bull with the cape and places the *banderillas*
barranco	gully or ravine
barrera	the wooden fence around the actual bull ring; also, the first row of seats directly behind the fence

450

barrio	neighborhood, city quarter
bocadillos	sandwiches usually made with thick crusty bread
buhardilla	small attic apartment
caballero	gentleman
café con leche	coffee with milk
café sólo	black coffee
camarada	comrade
caminos	paths, walkways
campo	country, countryside, field
cante jondo	"deep song"—flamenco singing
capea	informal bullfight in a village square
capote	cape used in bullfighting
caudillo	leader
chabolas	shanty towns around big city areas
chocolatera	old-fashioned tar-throwing machine
chorizo	thick, spicy pork sausage
churros	deep-fried doughnut-like sticks or rings
cigarrera	vendor of cigarettes and cigars
cocedero de mariscos	seafood dish
coche	car
cofradía	brotherhood devoted to a particular virgin or saint
compás	rhythm or beat of the music; a measure of music
coñac	cognac
converso	person who has converted; usually refers to Jews who were forced to convert to Christianity or be expelled during the Inquisition
copa	glass of wine or brandy
corchero	harvester of cork (cork-stripper)

coro	choir or area in a church designated for the choir
correos	post office
corrida	bullfight
corriente	ordinary (*vino corriente*—table wine)
costa	coast
costumbrismo	a genre of literature born from the European Romantic movement that extols local life and customs
cuadrilla	the troupe of bullfighters under the orders of a matador
cursi	flashy, affected, or kitsch
de luto	in mourning
duende	a mysterious kind of a charm or presence that infuses a performance or place or moment in time
duro	a "nickel"—worth about five pesetas
encierro	the driving or running of bulls from a corral to the corral of the bullring in which they will be fought
espía	spy
falseta	an improvised, original flamenco melody
feria	town fair; period of celebration when the fair takes place
fiestero	one who sings, plays, or dances at a fiesta
finca	estate or property that could be a farm or ranch
fino	type of dry, chilled sherry
fonda	humble lodging house with a tavern
franctireurs	French for "sniper" or "combatant"
freidura	dish made in a frying pan
ganadería	estate on which bulls are raised
gitano	Gypsy

guapa	beautiful, elegant, handsome
Guardia Civil	Spanish civil guard regiment
hidalgo	of the nobility (literally, "*hijo de algo*"—son of something or someone)
huerta	plot of irrigatable land; vegetable garden
infante	prince
jamón serrano	cured ham
jerez	sherry
lengua de toro	a dish made from bull's tongue
litera	sleeping cabin on a train
macho	male
madrugada	dawn or very early morning
majestad	majesty
majo	gallant and elegant person
marisma	lake formed by an overflow of a tide
matanza	killing of an animal for food; usually the two to three day event of killing a pig and preparing the hams for unrefrigerated storage
mikveh	Jewish steambath
mirador	place from which to see a view
mudéjar	Moorish brick, ceramic, and stucco architectural work
novillero	apprentice matador
panadería	bread shop or bakery
papel	paper
parador	State-owned inn, often located in renovated castles and monasteries
paseo	public promenade, usually in early evening and especially on Sunday
paso	religious float; also, a dance step
peña	a "fan club" (for a particular bullfighter or singer or soccer team) headquartered at a bar

pensión	rooming house
peregrino	pilgrim
picador	man under orders of a matador who pokes bulls from horseback with a long, steel-pointed pole
pija	rich, spoiled young woman (also called *niña de papá* for "daddy's girl")
piropo	"flattery" or compliment called out to women passing by on the street
plaza mayor	main city square
polvo	dust
privado	private
puente	bridge
quejigo	type of tree
quiosco	kiosk
romería	local pilgrimage to a country shrine on a feast day
saeta	a religious outcry or ecstatic song poured forth by a crowd member during a procession (literally, an "arrow")
santuario	sanctuary
sardana	traditional Catalán dance
Sefarad	Hebrew for Spain and for the Jewish communities established throughout the Iberian Peninsula
sevillanas	type of flamenco danced to tunes from Sevilla and containing four parts
sierra	mountain range
silbo	whistled language originating with the ancient Guanche people of the Canary Islands
sol	sun
soleares	the flamenco "song of loneliness"
sombra	shade

sopa de cocido	slow-cooked soup
taberna	tavern
tapa	small plate of food
ternera	veal
terraza	outdoor terrace café
tertulia	social gathering
tinto	red wine (*vino tinto*)
típico	typical; representative of the place (refers to restaurants, shops, etc.)
toque	touch; the playing of an instrument
toreo	the art of bullfighting
torero	bullfighter, matador
tormenta	storm, tempest
toro bravo	fierce fighting bull
tortilla	omelette
tranquilo	calm, contented, in peace
travesti	transvestite
tricornio	three-cornered hat traditionally worn by the Guardia Civil
tuna	group of wandering minstrels
tuno	member of a group of wandering minstrels
txacoli	type of Basque wine
viento	wind
vino	wine
zarzuela	Spanish opera that is light and brief

Index

Index of Contributors

Acknowledgements

My sincerest thanks to the series editors, Larry Habegger and James O'Reilly, who so graciously invited me along on this book adventure and whose collaboration, faith, and humor made the journey such a pleasure. Many thanks to Tim O'Reilly, to the amazing Raj Khadka, and to others who blessed this project with their talent and input: Ruth Aguilera, Judy Anderson, Cindy Collins, Hanna Dyer, Edie Freedman, Dana Furby, Deborah Greco, Cynthia Lamb, Jennifer Niederst, Sean O'Reilly, Deborah Perugi, Nancy Priest, Trisha Schwartz, Linda Sirola, and David White. Moreover, this book would not have been possible without the dedication and superb abilities of Susan Brady, production coordinator and *paella*-maker extraordinaire.

I'm grateful to my family and friends who encouraged me. A blessed cohort of those people also contributed directly to the making of this book at various stages, and, impossible as it is to adequately honor them, I thank in particular Alan Andres, Laura Critchfield, Anne Friedman, Rob Fulop, Susan Jampel, Suzanne LaVoie, Mike Lewitt, Tehila Lieberman, Ricardo Maldonado, Bilal Mughal, Dan Ochsner, Cathy Olofson, Marguerite Rigoglioso, Lynn Shirey, David Todd, my agent Carolyn Jenks, and my parents Liz and Ray McCauley. Thanks also to my sister Beth McCauley, my brothers Steve and Cley, and to my extraordinary niece and nephew, Nikki and Shane. And thanks to everyone from the Pensión María, with whom this book really began.

"Crossing into Spain" by Ann and Larry Walker excerpted from *A Season in Spain* by Ann & Larry Walker. Reprinted by permission of Simon & Schuster, Inc. and the authors. Copyright © 1992 by Larry Walker and Ann Walker.

"Watching the Rain" by Gabriel García Márquez, translated from Spanish by Margaret Costa excerpted from *Granta*. Reprinted by permission of Agencia Literaria Carmen Balcells, S.A. Copyright © 1983 by Gabriel García Márquez.

"A Night of *Duende*" and "Agreeing to Forget" by Robert Elms excerpted from *Spain: A Portrait after the General* by Robert Elms. Reprinted by permission of Reed Consumer Books, Ltd. Copyright © 1992 by Robert Elms.

"One Pilgrim's Progress" by Jack Hitt excerpted from *Off the Road: A Modern-Day Walk Down the Pilgrim's Route into Spain* by Jack Hitt, published in 1994 by Aurum Press. Reprinted by permission of Aurum Press and Simon & Schuster, Inc. Copyright © 1994 by Jack Hitt.

"Life in Cuenca" by Ted Walker excerpted from *In Spain* by Ted Walker, published by Secker & Warburg Ltd. Reprinted by permssion of David Higham Associates. Copyright © 1987 by Ted Walker.

"Yesterday's Paper" by Joel Simon published with permission from the author. Copyright © 1995 by Joel Simon.

"Where the Map Stopped" by Barbara Kingsolver reprinted from the May 17, 1992 issue of *The New York Times Magazine (Sophisticated Traveler)*. Copyright © 1992 by The New York Times Company. Reprinted by permission.

"The Legacy of War" and "Demons and Dragons" by Colm Tóibín excerpted from *Homage to Barcelona* by Colm Tóibín. Reprinted by permission of Simon & Schuster Ltd. Copyright © 1990, 1992 by Colm Tóibín.

"A Noble Apology" by Terry Richard Bazes reprinted from the June 19, 1994 issue of *Newsday*. Reprinted by permission of the author. Copyright © 1994 by Terry Richard Bazes.

"The King Who Saved His Country" by T. D. Allman reprinted from the August 1992 issue of *Vanity Fair*. Reprinted by permission of the author. Copyright © 1992 by T. D. Allman.

"Man and Beast" by Bruce Schoenfeld excerpted from *The Last Serious Thing: A Season at the Bullfights* by Bruce Schoenfeld. Reprinted by permission of Simon & Schuster, Inc. Copyright © 1992 by Bruce Schoenfeld.

"How to Get There" by Ricardo Maldonado published with permission from the author. Copyright © 1995 by Ricardo Maldonado.

"A Sacramental Return" by Peter Feibleman originally appeared in the November 1990 issue of *Travel & Leisure* as "Seduced by Seville." Reprinted by permission of the author. Copyright © 1990 by Peter Feibleman.

"Quixote's Parable of Life," "Quixotic Adventures," "The Way of Quixote," and "Where Quixote's Fortunes Fell" by Nicholas Wollaston excerpted from *Tilting at Don Quixote* by Nicholas Wollaston. Reprinted by permission of Andre Deutsch Ltd. Copyright © 1990 by Nicholas Wollaston.

"Bulls Before Breakfast" by Kevin Gordon reprinted from the May 1990 issue of *Travel & Leisure*. Reprinted by permission of the author. Copyright © 1990 by Kevin Gordon.

"Lost and Found in Segovia" by Jared Lubarsky reprinted from the March 15, 1987 issue of *Great Escapes*. Copyright © 1987 by Jared Lubarsky.

"Package Tour Blues" by Harry Ritchie excerpted from pages 14–31 of *Here We Go: A Summer on the Costa del Sol* by Harry Ritchie, published by Hamish Hamilton Ltd. (London). Reprinted by permission of Hamish Hamilton Ltd. Copyright © 1993 by Harry Ritchie.

"To the Alhambra" by Penelope Casas excerpted from *Discovering Spain: An Uncommon Guide* by Penelope Casas. Copyright © 1992 by Penelope Casas. Reprinted by permission of Alfred A. Knopf, Inc.

"In a Majorcan Garden" by Jill Burberry reprinted from the July 1989 issue of *Contemporary Review.* Reprinted by permission of The Contemporary Review Company Ltd. Copyright © 1989 by The Contemporary Review Company Ltd.

"Biking Cataluña" by Barbara Savage, copyright © 1983 Barbara Savage. Adapted with permission from the publisher from *Miles From Nowhere: A Round-the-World Bicycle Adventure* by Barbara Savage, The Mountaineers, Seattle.

"Leaving Madrid" by Pier Roberts published with permission from the author. Copyright © 1995 by Pier Roberts.

"The Road to Arcadia" and "The Gibraltar Question" by Alastair Boyd excerpted from *The Sierras of the South: Travels in the Mountains of Andalusia* by Alastair Boyd. Copyright © 1992 by Alastair Boyd. Reprinted by permission of HarperCollins Publishers, Ltd. and Aitken, Stone & Wylie, Ltd.

"A Legacy of Intolerance" by Richard Schweid excerpted from *Barcelona: Jews, Tranvestites, and an Olympic Season* by Richard Schweid. Reprinted by permission of Ten Speed Press (POB 7123, Berkeley, CA). Copyright © 1994 by Richard Schweid.

"Among Spanish Men" by Marguerite Rigoglioso published with permission from the author. Copyright ©1995 by Marguerite Rigoglioso.

"Terrorism for Autonomy" by Michael Jacobs excerpted from *Between Hopes and Memories: A Spanish Journey* by Michael Jacobs. Reprinted by permission of Pan Macmillan Publishers Ltd. Copyright © 1994 by Michael Jacobs.

"No Day at the Beach" by Damien Elwood published with permission from the author. Copyright © 1995 by Damien Elwood.

"A Journey's End" by Lawrence O'Toole reprinted from the December 1993 issue of *Discovery.* Reprinted by permission of Harold Ober Associates. Copyright © 1993 by Lawrence O'Toole.

Additional Credits (arranged alphabetically by title)

Selection from "Alhambra" by Jorge Luis Borges excerpted from *Historia de la Noche* by Jorge Luis Borges. Copyright © 1977 by Emecé Editores, copyright © 1989 by Maria Kodama y Emecé Editores. Reprinted by permission.

Selections from *As I Walked Out One Midsummer Morning* by Laure Lee reprinted by permission of Andre Deutsch Ltd. Copyright © 1969 by Laurie Lee.

Selection from *Barcelona* by Robert Hughes first published in Great Britain in 1992 by Harvill. Copyright © 1992 by Robert Hughes. Reproduced by permission of The Harvill Press (London), and Janklow and Nesbit Agency.

Selection from *Barcelona: Jews, Tranvestites, and an Olympic Season* by Richard Schweid reprinted by permission of Ten Speed Press (POB 7123, Berkeley, CA). Copyright © 1994 by Richard Schweid.

Selection from "Barcelona Dreaming" by Jed Perl reprinted from the January 1992 issue of *Vogue.* Reprinted by permission of the author. Copyright © 1992 by Jed Perl.

Selection from "Basques Find Inspiration as I.R.A. Talks of Peace" by John Darnton reprinted from the April 16, 1995 issue of *The New York Times.*

Selection from *Farewell Spain* by Kate O'Brien reprinted by permission of Beacon Press. Copyright © 1937 by Mary O'Neill.

Selection from "Federico García Lorca" by William Carlos Williams reprinted from *The Kenyon Review.* Reprinted by permission of *The Kenyon Review.* Copyright © 1939 by *The Kenyon Review.*

Selections from *Federico García Lorca: The Selected Poems* edited by Francisco García Lorca and Donald M. Allen reprinted by permission of New Directions Publishing Corp. Copyright © 1955 by New Directions Publishing Corp.

Selection from *For Whom the Bell Tolls* by Ernest Hemingway excerpted with permission of Scribner, a division of Simon & Schuster, Inc. and the Ernest Hemingway Foreign Rights Trust. Copyright © Ernest Hemingway Foreign Rights Trust. All rights outside U.S., Hemingway Foreign Rights Trust, by a Deed of Trust of Mary Hemingway, 16 March 1962, as Widow and Sole Legatee of the Author. Copyright © 1940 Ernest Hemingway; copyright renewed © 1968 by Mary Hemingway.

Selection from "Getting Down in Pamplona" by Doug Lansky published with permission from the author. Copyright © 1995 by Doug Lansky.

Selection from *A Guide to Andalusia* by Michael Jacobs copyright © 1990 by Michael Jacobs. Reprinted by permission of the author.

Selection from "Hanging Houses of Cuenca" by Isabel Soto reprinted from the October 21, 1990 issue of *The New York Times.* Copyright © 1990 by The New York Times Company. Reprinted by permission.

Selection from "High-Speed Snooze" by Marshall Fisher published with permission from the author. Copyright © 1995 by Marshall Fisher.

Selections from *Homage to Barcelona* by Colm Tóibín reprinted by permission of Simon & Schuster Ltd. Copyright © 1990, 1992 by Colm Tóibín.

Selections from *Homage to Catalonia* by George Orwell. Copyright © 1952, 1980 by the estate of the late Sonia Brownell Orwell and Martin, Seckler & Warburg. Reprinted by permission of Harcourt Brace & Company and A. M. Heath and Company, Ltd.

Selection from "How Tweet It Is: Great Bird Watching in—Where Else?—The Canary Islands" by Richard Homan reprinted from the March 29, 1994 issue of *The Washington Post.* Reprinted by permission of *The Washington Post.* Copyright © 1994 by *The Washington Post.*

Selections from *Iberia: Spanish Travels and Reflections* by James A. Michener copyright © 1968 by Random House, Inc. Reprinted by permission of Random House, Inc.

Selection from "In Pamplona" by Barnaby Conrad III published with permission from the author. Copyright © 1995 by Barnaby Conrad III.

Selections from "In Salamanca" by James O'Reilly published with permission from the author. Copyright © 1995 by James O'Reilly.

Selection from *Jogging Round Majorca* by Gordon West published by Transworld Publishers Ltd. Copyright © 1994 edition by Transworld Publishers Ltd.

Selections from *Journey to the Alcarria: Travels through the Spanish Countryside* by Camilo José Cela, translated by Frances M. Lopez-Morillas, reprinted by per-

Selections from "Morning in Madrid" by Gordon Cotler reprinted from the March 1993 issue of *Travel Holiday*. Reprinted by permission of the author. Copyright © 1993 by Gordon Cotler.

Selections from *My Last Sigh* by Luis Buñuel, translated by Abigail Israel. Translation copyright © 1983 by Alfred A. Knopf, Inc. Reprinted by permission of the publisher.

Selection from "The New World of Spain" by Bill Bryson reprinted from the Aprill 1992 issue of *National Geographic*. Reprinted by permission of the National Geographic Society. Copyright © 1992 by the National Geographic Society.

Selection from *!No Pasarán! The 50th Anniversary of the Abraham Lincoln Brigade* by John Sayles, edited by Abe Osheroff & Bill Susman, reprinted by permission of The Abraham Lincoln Brigade and John Sayles.

Selection from *Not Part of the Package: A Year in Ibiza* by Paul Richardson reprinted by permission of Macmillan London Ltd. Copyright © 1993 by Paul Richardson.

Selection from *Off the Road: A Modern-Day Walk Down the Pilgrim's Route into Spain* by Jack Hitt, published in 1994 by Aurum Press. Reprinted by permission of Aurum Press and Simon & Schuster, Inc. Copyright © 1994 by Jack Hitt.

Selection from "One Sketch of Spain" by Jan Haag reprinted by permission of the author. Copyright © 1995 by Jan Haag.

Selections from "Our Far-Flung Correspondent: Catalonia" by William Finnegan reprinted by permission. Copyright © 1992 by William Finnegan. Originally in *The New Yorker*. All rights reserved.

Selections from *Pagan Spain* by Richard Wright copyright © 1957 by Richard Wright. Reprinted by permission of John Hawkins & Associates, Inc.

Selection from "The *Pensión María*" by Lucy McCauley published with permission from the author. Copyright © 1995 by Lucy McCauley.

Selections from *The Pilgrimage: A Contemporary Quest for Ancient Wisdom* by Paul Coelho, translated by Alan R. Clarke, reprinted by permission of HarperCollins Publishers, Inc. Copyright © 1992 by Paulo Coelho and Alan R. Clarke.

Selection from *Pilgrim's Road: A Journey to Santiago de Compostela* by Bettina Selby reprinted by permission of Little Brown & Company. Copyright © 1994 by Bettina Selby.

Selection from *The Prime of Life* by Simone de Beauvoir, translated by Peter Green, reprinted by permission of Les Editions Gallimard, Marlowe & Company (USA), and Allen Lane, The Penguin Press (U.K.).

Selection from "Raging Bull" by Charles Leocha reprinted from the May 1990 issue of *Travel & Leisure*. Reprinted by permission of the author. Copyright © 1990 by Charles Leocha.

Selections from *A Rose for Winter: Travels in Andalusia* by Laurie Lee reprinted by permission of Chatto & Windus. Copyright © 1955 by Laurie Lee.

Selection from *The Tragic Sense of Life in Men and Nations* by Miguel de Unamuno reprinted by permission of Princeton University Press. Copyright © 1972 by Princeton University Press.

Selection from "Two for the Road" by Catherine Olofson published with permission from the author. Copyright © 1995 by Catherine Olofson.

Selection from *Viaje por la España Judia: A Trip through Jewish Spain* by Jose Luis Lacave published by the Spanish Ministry of Industry, Commerce and Tourism. Reprinted by permission of the Spanish Ministry of Industry, Commerce and Tourism.

Selection from "Walking after Midnight" by Marshall Fisher published with permission from the author. Copyright © 1995 by Marshall Fisher.

Selections from *Whereabouts: Notes on Being a Foreigner* by Alastair Reid published by North Point Press reprinted by permission of the author. Copyright ©1963, 1975, 1976, 1978, 1980, 1981, 1982, 1985, 1987 by Alastair Reid.

Selections from *White Wall of Spain: The Mysteries of Andalusian Culture* by Allen Josephs reprinted by permission of Iowa State University Press. Copyright © 1983 by Allen Josephs.

Selection from "Wild Fiesta Brings out Basic Animal Instincts" by Tracey Ober reprinted from the July 24, 1994 issue of *The Seattle Times*. Reprinted by permission of Reuters. Copyright © 1994 by Tracey Ober.

Selections from *Wild Spain: A Traveler's and Naturalist's Guide* by Frederic V. Grunfeld reprinted by permission of Prentice Hall and Sheldrake Press Ltd. Copyright © 1988 Sheldrake Publishing Ltd. Main text copyright © 1988 by Frederic V. Grunfeld.

Selection from *The Wind in My Wheels: Travel Tales from the Saddle* by Josie Dew reprinted by permission of Little, Brown & Comapny (UK). Copyright © 1992 by Josie Dew.

Selection from "Who Won the Spanish Civil War? The Barricades and Beyond" by Octavio Paz reprinted from the November 9, 1987 issue of *The New Republic*. Reprinted by permission of *The New Republic*. Copyright © 1987 by *The New Republic*.

About the Editor

Lucy McCauley first went to live and study in Spain in 1982. She has also lived and journeyed in places such as Central and South America, North Africa, and Eastern Europe, part of a nomadic lifestyle begun in childhood as the daughter of an Air Force test pilot. A freelance writer and editor based in Cambridge, Massachusetts, her writing on travel, the arts, and business has appeared in national and international publications, and she has worked in Latin America, writing about its government and judicial systems for Harvard University. She is now compiling an anthology of historic writing on Spain and is writing a travel memoir about Bolivia.

TRAVELERS' TALES
GUIDES

LOOK FOR THESE TITLES IN THE SERIES

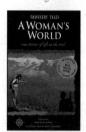

LOVE & ROMANCE

Edited by Judith Babcock Wylie
ISBN 1-885211-18-X, 294 pages, $17.95

"...a passion-filled tribute to the undeniable, inescapable romance of the road."
—Debra Birnbaum, Feature Editor, *New Woman*

A DOG'S WORLD

Edited by Christine Hunsicker
ISBN 1-885211-23-6, 232 pages, $12.95

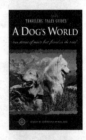

"The stories are extraordinary, original, often surprising and sometimes haunting. A very good book."
—Elizabeth Marshall Thomas, author of *The Hidden Life of Dogs*

THE ROAD WITHIN

Edited by Sean O'Reilly,
James O'Reilly & Tim O'Reilly
ISBN 1-885211-19-8, 443 pages, $17.95

"A revolutionary new style of travel guidebook."
— *New York Times News Service*

NEPAL

Edited by Rajendra S. Khadka
ISBN 1-885211-14-7, 423 pages, $17.95

"Always refreshingly honest, here is a collection that explains why Western travelers fall in love with Nepal and return again and again."
—Barbara Crossette, *New York Times* correspondent and author of *So Close to Heaven: The Vanishing Buddhist Kingdoms of the Himalayas*

PARIS

Edited by James O'Reilly, Larry Habegger & Sean O'Reilly
ISBN 1-885211-10-4, 424 pages, $17.95

"If Paris is the main dish, here is a rich and fascinating assortment of hors d'oeuvres. *Bon appetit et bon voyage!*"
—Peter Mayle

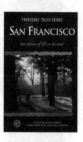

SAN FRANCISCO
Edited by James O'Reilly,
Larry Habegger & Sean O'Reilly
ISBN 1-885211-08-2, 432 pages, $17.95

"As glimpsed here through the eyes of beatniks, hippies, surfers, 'lavender cowboys' and talented writers from all walks, San Francisco comes to vivid, complex life."
—*Publishers Weekly*

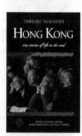

HONG KONG
Edited by James O'Reilly,
Larry Habegger & Sean O'Reilly
ISBN 1-885211-03-1, 438 pages, $17.95

"*Travelers' Tales Hong Kong* will order and delight the senses, and heighten the sensibilities, whether you are an armchair traveler or an old China hand."
—Gladys Montgomery Jones
Profiles Magazine, Continental Airlines

BRAZIL
Edited by Annette Haddad & Scott Doggett
ISBN 1-885211-11-2, 433 pages, $17.95

"Only the lowest wattage dimbulb would visit Brazil without reading this book."
—Tim Cahill, author of *Jaguars Ripped My Flesh* and *Pecked to Death by Ducks*

FOOD
Edited by Richard Sterling
ISBN 1-885211-09-0, 444 pages, $17.95

"Sterling's themes are nothing less than human universality, passion and necessity, all told in stories straight from the gut."
—Maxine Hong Kingston, author of *The Woman Warrior* and *China Men*

VISIT **TRAVELERS' TALES** ON THE WORLD WIDE WEB

http://www.oreilly.com/ttales

You'll discover which books we're working on, how to submit your own story, the latest writing contests you can enter, and the location of the next author event. We offer sample chapters from all of our books, as well as the occasional trip report and photo essay from our hard-working editors. Be sure to take one of our web tours, an exhaustive list of Internet resources for each of our titles, and begin planning your own journey.

SUBMIT YOUR OWN TRAVEL TALE

Do you have a tale of your own that you would like to submit to Travelers' Tales? We highly recommend that you first read one or more of our books to get a feel for the kind of story we're looking for. For submission guidelines and a list of titles in the works, send a SASE to:

Travelers' Tales Submission Guidelines
P.O. Box 610160, Redwood City, CA 94061

or send email to ***ttguidelines@online.oreilly.com***
or check out our web site at **www.oreilly.com/ttales**

You can send your story to the address above or via email to ***ttsubmit@oreilly.com***. On the outside of the envelope, ***please indicate what country/topic your story is about***. If your story is selected for one of our titles, we will contact you about rights and payment.

We hope to hear from you. In the meantime, enjoy the stories!